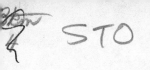

# LEFTOVERS

*Coralie Castle*
*With Sharon Silva*

*101 Productions*
*San Francisco*

*OTHER BOOKS BY CORALIE CASTLE*

*Soup*
*Hors d'Oeuvre, Etc.*
*The Art of Cooking for Two*
*Real Bread*
*Country Inns Cookery*

*Cover photograph: Rik Olson*

*Some of the recipes in this book appeared in previous books
by Coralie Castle.*

*Printed and bound in the United States of America.*

*Distributed to the book trade in the United States
by The Scribner Book Companies, Inc., New York.*

*Published by 101 Productions
834 Mission Street
San Francisco, California 94103*

*1  3  5  7  9  11  13  15  17  19  KP  20  18  16  14  12  8  6  4  2*

*Library of Congress Cataloging in Publication Data*

*Castle, Coralie.
  Leftovers.*

  *Includes index.
  1. Cookery (Leftovers)   I. Title.*
*TX652.C385  1983      641.6        83-17203*
*ISBN 0-89286-218-1*

# CONTENTS

# Introduction

A leftover can be many things. The first image that comes to mind is of bowls of cooked foods on the refrigerator shelf—a few green beans, some gravied meat, a portion of rice. Then, too, there are the small amounts of raw vegetables in the crisper, and the half-used packages and containers of cream cheese, pimientos, yoghurt, sour cream and half-and-half cream. And something must be done with the hard-cooked eggs from the Easter weekend or the stuffed eggs from today's picnic.

But the definition of leftover encompasses more. There are the doggy bags brought home from an evening out, foods that can be more than simply reheated. Those Mexican-restaurant leftovers of half an enchilada, some beans, rice and shredded lettuce, and a couple of tortillas can all be broken up into a rich stock and served as a delicious soup, garnished with freshly shredded cheese and chopped coriander. The leftovers from a dinner at a prime-rib or steak house can just as easily be transformed: cut the meat into strips and marinate for a salad, and brown the skin from the baked potato in butter to eat with fried eggs for the next morning's breakfast.

Leftovers are also the surplus from a bountiful garden: berries and persimmons slipped into the freezer for future desserts, tomatoes frozen whole and then used to make sauces in the winter months, and summer or winter squash cooked and puréed, frozen and then made into soups any time of the year.

There are even "planned" leftovers, when one deliberately cooks a larger portion than is needed for a single meal. The "extra" measure then becomes the basis for a dinner on another evening. Planned leftovers save cooking fuel, conserve the time and energy of the cook (who much prefers washing one rice pot to washing two), and makes dinner a more relaxed affair. Before the meal, there's time to play a set of tennis, spend time with the children, sit down to talk with family or guests, or simply relax after a long workday. Develop a planned-leftovers schedule that works for you and you won't feel so "tied" to the kitchen.

Though some talk of leftovers as being unwelcome intruders on a household's menu, I find them an interesting and fun challenge. Unnecessarily fearing that there would not be enough food at a company or even a family dinner, I have always prepared too much.

That tendency to excess combined with testing recipes for a number of cookbooks over the years has presented me with more than my fair share of leftovers. The challenge comes with using one's imagination to create complementary combinations with what is on hand and never to throw out food. My one failure on this front is the dressed tossed salad, which is one leftover without a future. That long-held belief that you can whirl it in the blender for a delicious gazpacho will never be proven by me.

Imagination and a willingness to engage in a little risk-taking with combinations and seasonings are the most important elements that go into creating a successful dish from leftovers. For example, I recently made a main meal soup with what seemed an almost unimaginable variety of leftovers: cooked lentils, split peas and wheat berries, a small amount of lamb in gravy, yellow squash that had been cooked with red onion, and cream sauce and stock from the freezer. This true potpourri of ingredients, enhanced with carefully selected seasonings and a colorful garnish, garnered raves from my dinner guests.

Working on this book has presented me with yet a new challenge, the "leftover leftover": having tested a recipe made with leftovers, I ended up with that dish half-finished on the refrigerator shelf. But even these leftovers can appear in an interesting new form: Grain Pilaf becomes Grain Pilaf Casserole; a noodle or rice casserole becomes the filling for a frittata; and broccoli purée with slivered almonds made from leftover steamed broccoli becomes an addition to a ground-meat mixture for meatloaf. Oh yes, there is also the "leftover" leftover leftover, which I most often relegate to the compost pile.

There are many, many ideas in the pages of this book, far too many for you ever again to question what to do with leftovers, whether they are the foods that accumulate from daily meals or the ones you are trying to clean out of your refrigerator before a summer vacation. This book is organized with the ease of the reader in mind. Following this introduction, there is a section of general information on cooking and freezing methods particularly suited to working with leftovers, a glossary of terms and commercial food products used in the book, and, under the heading Cooking Guidelines, preparations for basic ingredients called for throughout the book. The next major section is A Guide to Ingredients, a general survey of the ingredients that most often appear as leftovers. This includes dairy products, grains and grain products, vegetables and fruits, and meats, fish and poultry. There are literally dozens and dozens of ideas here, plus some Cooking Guidelines for preparing foods that will result in the best-tasting and most versatile leftovers, and indexes to the major recipes in the book using the specific foods discussed. Finally, there is a large, multichaptered section of recipes and recipe ideas.

With this book in hand, you will never again be discouraged by the sight of leftovers. Many of the meals you create with these foods will be as delicious and as interesting as when these same foods first appeared on your table. Many will taste even better.

—Coralie Castle

# 1
# A GUIDE
# TO TECHNIQUES

## Steaming Foods

Steaming is a practical way to cook a large variety of foods, as it keeps flavors and colors intact, allows only a minimal loss of the water-soluble vitamins and minerals, does not require the use of fats, and reduces the need for salt and other seasonings because natural flavors are retained. Almost any food can be steamed, from eggs and vegetables, to poultry, meats and seafood. Steaming is also an excellent way to reheat leftovers.

A collapsible perforated steaming rack that expands to fit any size saucepan is ideal for steaming vegetables. (A colander, strainer or perforated tray may be substituted.) Place the steaming rack in a saucepan with water to a depth of one inch. Place the vegetables directly on the rack, cover the saucepan tightly and bring the water to a rapid boil. The water must never touch the vegetables as they cook. Lower the heat and, keeping the water at a gentle, steady boil, cook until the vegetables are just tender. If cooking some of the vegetables as planned leftovers, remove them when they are not quite tender if they are to be used for salads or for reheating as they are, rather than puréed. Save the steaming water for adding to soups and stocks.

Other foods should be steamed in a serving dish (or wrapped in foil) set on a rack over simmering water. If you do not have stacking bamboo steamers or a single- or multileveled aluminum steamer, use any metal rack about 1-1/2 inches tall (or a tuna fish can with the ends removed) set in the bottom of a saucepan with a tight-fitting lid. Pour water into the pan to a depth of about 1 inch, which should be sufficient for thirty minutes of steaming. (With a steamer, you may be able to add more water than this if it will take longer than thirty minutes to cook the foods.) Bring the water to a rapid boil; be sure it does not touch the dish. Place the dish in the steamer, covered, if possible, so that water that condenses on the steamer lid will not collect in the steaming vessel. Reduce the heat to a simmer and begin timing. If you are steaming for an extended period, check the water level from time to time and add more water if the level drops.

COPPER RIM

## The Microwave Oven

The microwave oven is a handy kitchen tool when working with leftovers. It can be used to quickly defrost a variety of foods—cream sauces, soups, casseroles, uncooked meats and poultry, planned leftovers of every type—or to reheat leftovers from the refrigerator.

There are many microwave units on the market, so follow the manufacturer's directions for your particular oven. General hints on using them can, however, be given here. To defrost foods, place them frozen in microwaveproof dishes in the oven and set at 50 percent; stir the contents occasionally to evenly distribute it from the center to the sides of the dish and rotate the dish a quarter turn several times as the food defrosts. To defrost sauces, soups or foods in liquid packed in jars or other upright containers, remove the lids, place the microwaveproof containers in the oven, set at 50 percent and stir the contents as before.

Leftovers from the refrigerator can be reheated in just a matter of minutes. Be sure they are in a microwaveproof dish and stir the contents and rotate the dish to ensure even warming. Dishes that

# Freezing Foods

Freezing foods is a money saver. You can cook a large amount and freeze a portion of it for future use, thus saving cooking fuel and time, and a well-stocked freezer means less trips to the market and a lower gasoline bill. Unexpected bounty—specials at the market, a bumper crop in the garden, fresh fish from a successful day's outing—can be packed into the freezer and enjoyed at times when the costs for these same foods are higher. Plus, you can pop leftovers into the freezer to prevent them from spoiling and having to be discarded.

Throughout this book there is information on freezing specific foods, both cooked and uncooked, but here some general rules can be given. First, packaging must always be airtight to ensure a minimal loss of quality and nutrients. The choices of packaging are many: plastic or styrofoam containers with snap-on lids and wide-mouthed jars with spin-on tops (all good for liquids and foods in liquid), aluminum foil (for breads, uncooked meats), polyethylene bags with ziplock tops or sturdy plastic bags that can be "spun" closed and the top taped shut (best for small portions of cooked foods without liquid), plastic wrap or bags secured closed with a heat sealer (such as

a Dazey brand sealer), coffee tins with plastic lids (ideal for cookies, small meringues), even milk cartons taped tightly closed (see freezing instructions in fish section). Foods may also be tightly wrapped in ordinary plastic wrap, but must never be frozen more than two weeks.

Sheet freezing is suitable for a variety of foods, from crêpes, dolmas, pastries, hamburgers and berries to green onion tops. Arrange the food to be frozen in a single layer on a baking sheet and freeze until solid. You may now pack the foods close together in plastic bags or other containers in sizes appropriate for a serving or a meal.

If freezing liquids or foods in liquid, always leave a space equal to one-tenth the volume of the contents, or about one inch in a quart container. This space, called head space, is necessary to accommodate the expansion of the liquid as it freezes. Also, never bang glass jars together in the freezer, as they crack easily.

Always choose your containers wisely, but especially if you have limited freezer space. Straight-

*Always leave sufficient head space—the space between the contents and the lid—when freezing liquids.*

cannot be stirred, such as lasagne or turkey divan, may be defrosted in the microwave, but should be reheated to serving temperature in a conventional oven, for the food will overcook and dry out at the edges before it is heated through to the center.

The microwave oven is also good for readying ingredients for a recipe. Use it for softening cream cheese or butter, heating liqueur for a flambé dish or defrosting lemon juice, stock or egg whites. You must watch the foods *carefully,* though, for it is very easy to overheat them. Save time on cleanup by reheating cooked foods on individual serving plates that go directly from the oven to the table. You can even dry garden-fresh herbs in the microwave: wash the herbs, pat dry, place in a single layer on a paper plate or napkin in the oven and dry on Hi for three to four minutes.

sided containers that can be easily stacked are best; a variety of shapes and sizes will take up precious freezer space unnecessarily. If you are rich in freezer space and cookware, freeze a prepared entrée in the same casserole you will use to reheat it (bring to room temperature before putting it in the oven). For dishes served in individual ramekins, line each ramekin with foil, fill the ramekin, fold over and seal the foil and then freeze ramekin and all. When the packet is frozen solid, remove it from the ramekin and place the packet in the freezer. Now the ramekin is free to use for other things. When it's time to reheat the packet's contents, remove the packet from the freezer, unwrap it, place in the same ramekin, defrost on the refrigerator shelf, bring to room temperature and bake—a perfect fit.

Whichever wrapper or container you use, always label it carefully, including a complete description of the contents, its size (in pounds, cups, servings, etc.) and the date. This will help you keep good track of what is in the freezer. Don't merely put "mashed sweet potatoes," if they are "seasoned mashed sweet potatoes." No matter how good your memory, you may not recall the "seasoned" two months later.

Chest-type freezers are best for long-term storage, since the interior temperature remains lower and more constant than in upright or top-of-the-refrigerator freezers. A freezer should always be at zero degrees or lower, so keep a thermometer inside to monitor the temperature. A fuller freezer keeps foods better, though you must never *overload* it because overloading causes the temperature to rise. When introducing new packages or containers into the freezer, set them near the edges so that they freeze solid more quickly. The exception to this is baked goods, as they will take on too much moisture if in contact with the freezer walls.

If your freezer stops because of a power failure or mechanical malfunction, all is not lost. Do not open the freezer door, and if power is restored or the freezer is repaired within twelve hours, the frozen foods will be fine. If, however, there is a prolonged loss of power, pack the freezer with dry ice (look to the yellow pages or call a local ice cream manufacturer for a source). First, lay a sheet of heavy-duty cardboard over the foods, then, with gloved hands to prevent "burns," set the dry ice on top. Close the freezer immediately, and replenish the dry ice every twenty-four to thirty-six hours until the power is restored. Never try to break up the dry ice and do not open the freezer door unless it is absolutely necessary.

If the foods in your freezer begin to thaw, follow these rules for using them: Fruits suffer less from partial thawing than other foods. You may taste them without danger of harmful effects and they can be refrozen if ice crystals remain on them, or, if completely thawed, transform them into jams, jellies or other preserves. If ice crystals remain on vegetables, they may also safely be refrozen, or if they have thawed and are *still cold,* they may be eaten. Vegetables that have become the least bit warm  should  be discarded. Fruits and vegetables with ice crystals that are refrozen, however, should be puréed when they are finally used, for they soften and lose texture in the refreezing. Uncooked fish that has begun to thaw even the slightest amount must be fully cooked before refreezing. Though some authorities suggest that meats with ice crystals can be refrozen, it is not recommended. You can, however, marinate thawed poultry or meats (for no less than twelve hours) in the refrigerator and then refreeze with the marinade for no more than two weeks. If not marinating, the poultry and meats must be fully cooked before refreezing.

Thawed leftover cooked foods, such as soups, stocks, beef stew and other gravied dishes, may be brought to the boil, cooled, put into containers and refrozen, but there will be a noticeable loss of texture and flavor in the solid portions of these foods. Cooked fish in sauce is best if eaten as soon as possible after thawing, for its texture will be lost if reheated and refrozen. Grated cheeses, whole or ground nutmeats, unsauced cooked legumes and grains and egg whites may be slipped directly back into the freezer if they have been defrosted no more than two hours. Breads and cookies may also be refrozen, but they will take on considerable moisture and be quite soggy when thawed again.

Frozen foods should be thawed in their original containers, preferably in the refrigerator. If thawing at room temperature, cook or reheat promptly, as the warm environment will cause bacteria to grow. In general, though, it is advisable to cook any food as soon as possible after thawing to prevent loss of nutrients and flavor.

Remember, your freezer must be managed. Don't continue to add new items without thinking of all those foods that may be failing in quality because of being frozen too long. The freezer should hold a continually changing array of both uncooked foods and leftovers.

# Dehydrating Vegetables & Fruits

There are a number of home dehydrating units on the market that are ideal for drying any vine-ripened vegetables and fruits. These units are particularly attractive to those with limited freezer space, since the dried produce can be stored in airtight containers in any cool place. (If you are unsure the food has been *thoroughly* dried, pack it in tightly closed plastic bags, slip the bags into tins with lids and store in the refrigerator.)

Complete directions come with any unit you purchase. It is important that you select unblemished ripe vegetables and fruits for drying, and that you slice or cut them uniformly. Dehydrated vegetables, such as tomatoes, onions, celery, bell peppers and mushrooms, are excellent for making vegetable and meat soups and stocks and for adding to skillet dishes and stews.

To reconstitute dried vegetables and fruits, place them in a bowl and add boiling water to cover. Let them stand in the water for from five to fifteen minutes to soften completely. Stir occasionally with a fork, and add more boiling water if all the water has been

absorbed. Drain, reserving the water for adding to soup or stock pots, gravies or sauces. Use the vegetable or fruit as is or cut as needed for a specific recipe.

You may reconstitute any number of vegetables or fruits together if they are to be added to a dish at the same time. Also, measures need not be exact, but do be aware of how lightweight dehydrated foods are. For example, one ounce of dehydrated tomato slices numbers sixteen, or approximately three fresh whole tomatoes.

Dried vegetables may also be pulverized in a blender or processor and added to dishes for a very concentrated flavoring. These vegetable powders should be stored in airtight containers in the refrigerator for no more than three weeks.

The dehydrator can be used for drying garden-fresh herbs. Simply dry the sprigs, remove the leaves, crumble them and store in airtight containers, preferably dark glass ones, in a cool, dry place. The flavor of these dried herbs will be much stronger than commercially

dried ones, so use caution when adding to dishes. You may also leave the dried sprigs intact to make a bouquet garni when your herb garden has waned.

An alternate method of drying herbs is to tie the stems of several sprigs together and hang the bunch upside down in a dark place with good air circulation. If you fear the herbs will become dusty before they dry completely, slip a brown paper bag over the bunch and poke holes in the bag so the air reaches the herbs. Crumble and store the herbs in the same way as those dried in a dehydrator.

Sun drying requires less elaborate equipment than a home dehydrator. You can either build or purchase a simple, inexpensive set of screened shelves that rest on tracks in a box, much like the drawers in a dresser. Arrange cut-up vegetables or fruits on the shelves and set in the sun (cover sweet fruits with cheesecloth to protect against insect invasion) until the foods are free of moisture, bringing the shelves in at night if the weather cools or is damp. Pack and store as for vegetables and fruits dried in a dehydrator. An even simpler drying setup is a baking sheet with a cake rack to hold the produce. The amount of time it will take to dry any vegetable or fruit depends upon the intensity of the sun and the sugar content of the produce.

# Cooking Guidelines

The basic recipes and methods given here are used throughout the book to enhance dishes made with leftovers.

**BEER BATTER** For approximately 1-1/2 cups batter, beat 2 eggs lightly with 1/2 cup beer. Combine 1 cup unbleached flour, 1 teaspoon baking powder and 1/4 teaspoon salt. Gradually add eggs and beer mixture, stirring until smooth. Cover and refrigerate at least 2 hours. Adjust beer or flour measure as desired. A thinner batter will result in a light coating. A thicker batter will result in a puffier coating. Use to coat vegetables for deep frying.

**BROWN BUTTER** Slowly melt clarified butter over medium-low heat until a rich brown color. The nutty flavor is enhanced by the addition of fresh lemon juice. Serve on freshly cooked vegetables such as cauliflower, broccoli, green beans and asparagus.

---

*To measure lard (or butter or shortening), fill a 1-cup measure with amount of water that is the difference between 1 cup and the amount of lard called for. Add lard until water level reaches the 1 cup mark.*

---

**CHIFFONADE** Sauté 1/2 cup chopped fresh sorrel, spinach, lettuce or other leafy vegetable or combination in 2 tablespoons butter until soft. Season according to suggested seasonings for specific vegetable. Use as a garnish for meats or soups.

**CLARIFIED (DRAWN) BUTTER** To clarify butter, cut butter into small pieces and melt in a saucepan over low heat. Remove from heat and let stand until the white milk solids sink to the bottom of the saucepan. Skim the clear liquid (the clarified butter) from the top and discard the white milk solids. Strain liquid through a sieve lined with cheesecloth. Cool, jar, cover and refrigerate up to 1 month. One pound of butter will yield approximately 3/4 cup clarified butter.

**CURRY POWDER** To make approximately 2 tablespoons curry powder, combine 2 teaspoons ground coriander, 1 teaspoon *each* ground cumin, cardamom and cloves, 1/8 teaspoon ground mace and 1/16 teaspoon cayenne pepper. Store in a covered jar in a cool, dark place.

**GARLIC OLIVE OIL** Lightly mash 2 or 3 garlic cloves and place in a jar. Add olive oil and let steep 2 days or up to 1 week. Discard garlic cloves; store in a covered jar.

*Solve your sticking problems by keeping Lecithin Oil and Lecithin Butter on hand. Cleanup will also be easier.*

**LECITHIN BUTTER** Combine 4 tablespoons softened butter and 2 teaspoons liquid lecithin. Store in a covered jar in refrigerator up to 3 weeks.

**LECITHIN OIL** Combine 2 parts safflower oil and 1 part liquid lecithin. Store at room temperature in squeeze bottle for easy application. Shake well before using. Keeps up to 4 months.

**MIREPOIX** For approximately 3/4 cup, heat 2 tablespoons butter in skillet. Add 1/2 cup *each* very finely diced carrot and onion, 1/4 cup very finely diced celery, 1 to 2 thyme sprigs and 1 bay leaf, broken. Cover and cook very slowly until vegetables are soft and lightly browned. Discard thyme sprigs and bay leaf. Use as a flavorful bed for roasting or braising meats.

**RENDERED FAT** Cut chicken, ham, pork or beef fat into tiny bits and cook slowly in a heavy skillet over low heat until melted. Strain and cool slightly. Pour into small containers, cover and refrigerate up to 1 week or freeze up to 3 months. Alternately, for a clearer rendered fat, cook bits of fat in water until melted, skimming off any scum that rises to the surface and adding water as needed. Pour into a jar and cool. Fat will rise to the top. Remove fat and wrap or jar; refrigerate up to 1 week or freeze up to 3 months.

**SEAFOOD SEASONING** For approximately 1 tablespoon seasoning, combine 1/2 tablespoon sea salt, 1/2 teaspoon dry mustard, 1/4 teaspoon *each* celery salt, ground ginger, freshly ground white pepper and freshly ground black pepper, 1/8 teaspoon *each* ground allspice and ground thyme and a dash of cayenne pepper. Store in a small covered jar in a cool, dark place.

**TERIYAKI MARINADE** For approximately 1/3 cup marinade, combine 3 tablespoons soy sauce, 2 tablespoons sake or dry sherry, 1 slice ginger root, 1 garlic clove, lightly mashed, 1/2 teaspoon five spices powder (optional) and 3 to 4 drops Oriental sesame oil (optional). If not using at once, jar, cover and refrigerate up to 3 days.

# Glossary

**BELL'S SEASONING** A commercial blend of dried rosemary, oregano, sage, ginger, marjoram, thyme and pepper. Primarily used as seasoning for poultry, but also good for egg salad, ham salad and other meats and vegetables.

**BIND** To hold together a mixture with mayonnaise or other sauce or to thicken a mixture with cornstarch, flour, arrowroot, eggs or other thickening agent. Mix cornstarch, flour or other dry thickener with cold water or other cold liquid before adding.

**BLANCH** To dip quickly into boiling water. Fruits and nuts are kept in water just until skins loosen; plunge fruit immediately into cold water. Salt pork and some vegetables are blanched to precook slightly and/or remove strong flavors. Some vegetables may also be blanched and frozen (see introduction to vegetable section).

**BOUQUET GARNI** A bouquet of herbs and/or spices or other seasonings tied together with string or tied in a cheesecloth bag, immersed in a sauce, soup or stew, and then removed before serving.

**BRAISE** To cook meat or vegetables by first browning in a little fat and then cooking covered with a small amount of liquid. This may be done on top of the stove or in the oven.

**BROWN BEAN SAUCE** Also known as yellow bean sauce and ground bean sauce. Brown or yellowish thick, salted bean sauce made of ground or partially mashed small brown beans, flour and salt. Available in cans and jars in Oriental markets. Store in a jar with a tight-fitting lid in the refrigerator.

**DEEP FRY** Also known as French fry. To cook food by submerging it in hot oil, fat or clarified butter (or oil and butter mixture). Temperature of oil should be approximately 375°F or cause a 1-inch cube of bread dropped into hot oil to turn golden in about 50 seconds. Peanut oil is preferred for deep frying, as it absorbs less flavors and does not become rancid as quickly as other oils. Keep oil in which seafood has been fried in separate container. To recycle cooking oil, drop several chunks of raw potato into the hot oil immediately after removing deep-fried foods and deep fry potato until golden, then cool oil, strain and refrigerate.

**DEGLAZE** After cooking meats or poultry, remove fat from pan (see Gravy), add water or specified liquid and bring to boil, scraping bottom and sides of pan.

**HOISIN SAUCE** Thick, smooth, dark reddish-brown sauce made from soybeans, spices, sugar, chili and garlic. Mildly sweet in flavor, it is used in Oriental cooking or as a condiment at the table. Available in cans; after opening, store in the refrigerator in a glass jar with a tight-fitting lid.

**JULIENNE** To cut vegetables or meat into match-size pieces.

**LECITHIN** A natural product that is used medically to lower cholesterol and is used commercially in the manufacture of nonstick spray coatings for cookware. Sold in liquid and granular forms at natural-foods or health-food stores.

**MASK** To evenly coat foods with a sauce or mayonnaise-type dressing, covering surface completely. Coating should be no more than 1/4 to 3/8 inch thick.

**MISO** Japanese fermented paste of malt, salt and soybeans. Sold in Oriental markets as akamiso (red) and shirumiso (white).

**ORIENTAL SESAME OIL** Golden brown oil made from toasted sesame seeds. Used mainly as a flavoring for its distinctive pungent aroma and nutty taste. Use sparingly. Available in bottles in Oriental markets.

**OYSTER SAUCE** A thick, brown sauce made of oysters, soy and brine. Often used as an alternative seasoning to soy sauce or as a table condiment. Sold in bottles or cans in Oriental markets and some supermarkets. Store refrigerated.

**PLUMP** To soften raisins or other dried foods in hot water or other liquid.

**SCALD** To heat liquid to just below the boiling point; in the case of milk or cream until edges start to bubble and a *light* film just begins to form on top.

**TOFU** Fresh bean curd cake made of puréed soybeans pressed into cakes. Most often available in squares approximately 2 inches square and 1/2 inch thick. Sold in Oriental markets and some supermarkets. Firmer cakes are preferred for stir-fry dishes, softer cakes for soups and cold dishes. Place in fresh cold water after opening, changing water daily and storing in refrigerator. Use within pull date. Rinse under cold water before using. (See additional information on tofu in grains and legumes section.)

# 9
# A GUIDE
# TO INGREDIENTS

# EGGS, CHEESES & OTHER DAIRY PRODUCTS

## *Eggs*

Buy the best-quality eggs available, preferably directly from the farm or from a market where they are frequently restocked, and only as many as you will use in a two- to three-week period. Look for dates indicating shelf life on the cartons. Large grade A eggs (two ounce) are the size most commonly called for in recipes; it makes no difference whether the eggs are brown or white, or have light or dark yolks.

Store eggs in the refrigerator pointed end down, either in the carton or in the refrigerator's egg compartment. Never wash the shells, as you will remove the natural protective coating, and never store eggs close to strong-smelling foods, as they may pick up odors. Refrigerate whites in a tightly covered container up to three days, or freeze up to two months. Cover unbroken egg yolks with a thin layer of water and refrigerate in a well-sealed container up to two days (the water prevents a skin from forming on the yolks), or freeze up to one month. Though some authorities recommend the freezing of beaten fresh yolks and whole eggs, stabilized with sugar or water, the end products are quite unsatisfactory. Refrigerate hard-cooked eggs in the shell up to four or five days, but once peeled, keep no more than twenty-four hours.

Very fresh eggs should be used for poaching and soft boiling. Do not use eggs that are less than three days old for hard cooking or for making baked goods. They produce a hard-cooked egg that is difficult to peel and with a greenish rather than a yellow yolk; when beaten, they do not increase in volume sufficiently for successful baking. Older eggs, in general, should be reserved for hard cooking and for making any dish that requires them to be beaten, such as an omelet.

To check if an egg is spoiled, immerse it in a bowl of water. If it sinks, it is still good, but if it floats, discard it. Also, discard any egg that has an unpleasant odor, is discolored or has a break in its shell. A fresh egg, when cracked onto a plate, will have a translucent white and a yolk that mounds.

Even the most organized person in the kitchen sometimes confuses fresh eggs with hard-cooked ones. Here is an easy test: Lay the egg on its side on a flat surface and rotate it so it will spin. If it spins quickly and evenly it is hard cooked; if it spins slowly and begins to wobble, it is fresh.

The Index to Recipes that follows covers hard-cooked eggs and egg yolks and raw yolks and whites, the ways in which eggs most often appear as leftovers. The index does not include recipes in which hard-cooked eggs and yolks are used only as a garnish, nor does it include the many recipe ideas that are scattered throughout the book. The numerous ideas in the chapter on salads are particularly useful for using hard-cooked eggs.

# COOKING GUIDELINES

**HARD-COOKED EGGS** With a needle, put a hole in center of blunt end of unshelled eggs. Put eggs in a saucepan with cold water to cover and bring slowly to boil. Simmer gently 2 minutes, remove from the heat, cover and let stand 15 to 18 minutes. Plunge into cold water and refrigerate when cool; do not peel until ready to use.

**HARD-COOKED EGG YOLKS** Bring water to simmer in a small saucepan. Carefully pour water off egg yolk if it has been stored, then slip the yolk into the simmering water. Cook gently 4 to 6 minutes.

**POACHED EGGS** Fill a saucepan with enough water to cover eggs, adding 1 teaspoon distilled white vinegar for each 2 cups water. Bring water to boil and lower heat to a gentle simmer. Carefully break eggs into simmering water and cook until set as desired. (Alternately, break each egg into a small shallow dish and then slip the egg into the simmering water. This method makes it easier to avoid breaking the yolk.) Lift eggs out with a slotted utensil and serve

immediately, or immerse in cold water and refrigerate 2 to 3 days. To reheat, dip briefly into simmering water.

**SCRAMBLED EGGS** Beat eggs until lemon colored, adding 1 teaspoon cold liquid (water, milk, cream, stock) for each 2 eggs used. Add seasonings and small bits of fresh or firm cheeses as desired. Heat butter in a skillet until foamy (or until a nutty brown for added flavor). Add eggs and cook, stirring frequently for dry scrambled eggs, or letting edges set slightly and then turning loosely and slowly for moist eggs.

**EGG GARNISH** Combine 4 eggs, lightly beaten, 1/4 teaspoon Oriental sesame oil, 2 teaspoons water and dash salt. In a crêpe pan or small skillet, heat 1 teaspoon corn oil. Pour in 3 tablespoons of the egg mixture, quickly tip pan to coat bottom and cook egg until just set and lightly browned. Flip onto wire rack and repeat with remaining egg mixture, adding corn oil to pan as needed. When cool, roll each pancake loosely, slice thinly then unroll to use. Use as garnish on Oriental soups and other dishes.

**EGG YOLK BINDER** Beat egg yolk with a little of whatever hot mixture you wish to bind, then whisk into

mixture; do not allow to boil. One egg yolk will thicken about 2 cups sauce or 3 to 4 cups soup.

**EGG WASH** Beat together 1 egg white and 2 teaspoons water until well mixed. Refrigerate in a tightly covered container up to 3 days, or freeze up to 2 months. Thaw, use as desired, then return to freezer if defrosted less than 2 hours; repeat defrosting and refreezing up to 3 or 4 times, then discard. Brush wash on breads and rolls before baking to provide a shiny appearance or to help sesame seeds, poppy seeds, etc. adhere to bread; also brush on baked and unbaked pie shells to keep pastry from becoming soggy after filling.

## IDEAS FOR EGGS

● Beat egg whites until frothy. Dip flowers, such as violets, or seedless grapes into whites, then dip in superfine granulated sugar. Dry on wire rack and use as garnish for desserts.

● Add 1 extra egg white for every 2 or 3 eggs used in soufflés.

● Add 1 extra egg white to Basic Crêpe Batter.

● Use egg whites and egg shells to clarify stock (see Stocks from Leftover Cooked Bones).

• For a soup garnish, beat 1 egg white until stiff but not dry, fold in 2 tablespoons finely grated Parmesan cheese and poach mixture in large pot of boiling water, stirring constantly. Separate gently and, with slotted spoon, transfer onto hot rich stock or vegetable cream soup.

• Use 1 extra egg white or yolk in scrambled eggs and frittatas.

• Use egg yolks to enrich cream soups and cream sauces.

• When making open-pot coffee, add crushed egg shells at the finish so grounds will sink.

• Crumble egg shells into a jar, fill jar with water and keep adding shells for several days. Use the water for fertilizing house plants.

• When breaking eggs, break so that one-half of shell is a bit larger than the other. Pierce bottom of larger halves with an ice pick and place in an egg carton. Fill shells with good soil and plant seeds. When transplanting, gently break bottom of shell and place shell with seedling in soil in pot or garden.

## IDEAS FOR HARD–COOKED EGGS

• Encase whole hard-cooked eggs in sausage meat, dip in beaten egg and then in fine dry bread crumbs. Dry on wire rack several hours. Deep fry, a few at a time, in peanut oil until golden brown. Drain on paper toweling and serve immediately.

• Tuck stuffed hard-cooked egg halves into a bed of cooked rice, spinach or Swiss chard in a buttered casserole. Pour Light or Medium Cream Sauce over, sprinkle with grated Gruyère or Cheddar cheese and bake in a preheated 350°F oven until bubbly.

• Heat halved hard-cooked eggs in Cheese Sauce seasoned with Worcestershire sauce. Spoon on toasted halved English muffins, rolls or biscuits, sprinkle with grated cheese and paprika and broil until cheese melts.

• Heat halved hard-cooked eggs gently in Mushroom or Quick Mushroom Sauce. Serve on toast.

• Float halved hard-cooked eggs sprinkled with paprika on hot or cold cream soups.

• Chop hard-cooked eggs and add to Basic Vinaigrette or Basic Mayonnaise.

• Chop hard-cooked eggs and sprinkle on cooked spinach, broccoli, asparagus, or cream or cheese soups just before serving.

• Combine chopped hard-cooked eggs with Mustard Mayonnaise, olive oil, Worcestershire sauce, finely minced onion, minced fresh chives and dash Tabasco sauce. Use as topping for freshly cooked green vegetables.

• Gently stir chopped hard-cooked eggs into Light or Medium Cream Sauce seasoned with freshly grated nutmeg and chopped fresh chives and parsley. Serve on toast, toasted halved English muffins or biscuits or toasted cornbread.

• Combine chopped hard-cooked eggs with a little softened butter, Lemon Mayonnaise, minced green onions and tops, salt and freshly ground white pepper. Spread in a shallow dish and chill. Cover with sour cream and lumpfish caviar, sprinkle with freshly grated lemon rind and serve with crackers or Melba Toast.

*To add egg yolks to hot mixtures, first beat a little of the hot mixture into the yolks, then whisk into the mixture.*

• Combine chopped hard-cooked eggs and chopped black olives with Mustard or Curry Mayonnaise to bind. Stuff hollowed-out cherry tomatoes and serve as an hors d'oeuvre or salad accompaniment.

• Combine sieved hard-cooked eggs with a little softened butter and finely grated or shredded Cheddar cheese to spreading consistency. Spread on toast, sprinkle with paprika and broil until bubbly.

• Combine equal parts sieved hard-cooked eggs and ground cooked ham. Season to taste with salt, freshly ground white pepper and dry mustard. Bind with Basic Mayonnaise and chill. Form chilled mixture into small balls, flatten balls slightly and press 1 or 2 drained capers into each ball. Chill and serve as an hors d'oeuvre.

---

*Sprinkle a little corn germ on fried eggs just before serving.*

## INDEX TO RECIPES

# Cheeses

Fresh, soft, uncured cheeses cover a whole range of products: uncreamed, partially creamed and creamed cottage cheese; cream and neufchâtel cheese; farmer's, baker's and hoop cheese; and ricotta cheese. Most of these cheeses are sold in tubs, usually stamped with a date indicating shelf life. To maximize the lives of these cheeses, invert the tubs on the refrigerator shelf, always use a clean utensil for removing the contents, and never return to the container cheese that has been spooned out of it. Though some advise the freezing of uncreamed cottage cheese, much of its characteristic texture is lost; the others are not recommended for freezing.

Brie and camembert, perishable soft, ripened cheeses, should not be kept in the refrigerator more than seven days. Use caution when buying them on sale, for a merchant may be trying to clear the shelves of overripened cheeses. Both may be wrapped airtight and frozen up to two months.

Semisoft cheeses, such as Muenster, Monterey Jack, fontina, bel paese, mozzarella, Samsoe and teleme, will keep ten to fourteen days in the refrigerator. Wrap well in plastic wrap, then in a cloth that has been lightly dampened with cider vinegar and finally again in plastic wrap. Store in the cheese compartment or in the lower part of the refrigerator, in a covered jar or crock if possible. These semisoft cheeses should be frozen only if they have been shredded first, and then kept no more than one month. It is best to freeze the cheese in small portions that would be suitable for a single recipe, always remembering to wrap them airtight.

Romano, Parmesan, dry Monterey Jack, pecorino and Asiago are firm, grating-type cheeses. They should be wrapped for refrigeration in the same way as the semisoft varieties, but may be kept up to two months. Grate these cheeses before freezing and keep no more than three months.

Other firm cheeses, such as Cheddar, provolone, Gouda, Gruyère, Edam, Emmenthaler, Swiss and Havarti, will keep refrigerated up to three weeks if the vinegared-cloth method of wrapping is used. Small portions, either diced or grated, may be wrapped airtight and frozen up to two months.

The blue-veined cheeses, Roquefort, Stilton, gorgonzola and Maytag, will keep up to three weeks in the

refrigerator and four months in the freezer. Roquefort, gorgonzola or Maytag should be used for recipes in this book calling for blue cheese; Stilton is better eaten strictly as an after-dinner cheese. All of the blue cheeses should be wrapped in a vinegared cloth for refrigerating, and in airtight packaging for freezing. When thawed, use only for crumbling into spreads, salads, sauces or dressings.

Feta cheese, made with sheep or goat's milk, is a type of "pickled" cheese that is cured by salting. Usually brought from the market with some of its whey, feta should remain stored in this liquid in the refrigerator, adding a small amount of water if necessary to keep the cheese moist. Feta will keep in a covered container in the refrigerator about one week, but it does not freeze well.

If mold forms on any piece of non-blue-veined cheese, cut the moldy area off with a knife blade that has been dipped in vinegar, rewrap and refrigerate or freeze the cheese. If the mold has not worked its way deep into the piece, the flavor will not be ruined.

Freeze any cheese for as short a time as possible, for freezing adversely affects the texture. Thaw frozen cheese in the refrigerator, and then use it primarily for cooking where the loss of texture will be the least noticeable.

## IDEAS FOR COTTAGE CHEESE

**ENTREE ACCOMPANIMENTS** Prepare an entrée accompaniment by mixing one of the following suggestions with cottage cheese.

- Sliced radishes and cucumbers.
- Chopped salted peanuts, minced bell pepper and onion.
- Onion juice, chopped fresh chives and parsley.
- Prepared horseradish, Basic Mayonnaise, minced radishes and green onions, minced fresh parsley, chopped toasted walnuts or filberts.
- Chopped apples, pears or peaches sprinkled with fresh lemon juice, raisins, chopped toasted walnuts, honey.
- Chopped black or pimiento-stuffed olives, grated raw carrot, toasted sesame seeds, chopped hard-cooked egg, alfalfa sprouts.
- Fresh lemon juice, chopped pimientos, salt, freshly ground black pepper.

**SALAD DRESSING** With a fork, stir cottage cheese into Basic Vinaigrette before tossing with salad greens.

**SCRAMBLED EGGS** With a fork, stir cottage cheese into eggs before scrambling.

**MASHED OR BAKED POTATOES** Mix cottage cheese into mashed potatoes or use as an accompaniment to baked potatoes in place of butter.

## IDEAS FOR CREAM CHEESE

- Roll softened cream cheese into small balls, coat balls with finely chopped walnuts and serve with fruit salad.

- Combine softened cream cheese with date nuggets and serve as a cracker spread.

- Cover a block of cream cheese with soy sauce, Worcestershire sauce or chutney. Refrigerate several hours, bring to room temperature and serve as a cracker spread.

- Combine softened cream cheese with cooked spinach, chopped cooked artichoke hearts or bottoms, minced fresh jalapeño peppers, minced raw mushrooms, minced celery and/or sweet red or white onions. Serve as a cracker spread or raw-vegetable dip.

- Combine softened cream cheese with Basic Mayonnaise, chopped pecans, chopped black olives, and cayenne pepper, olive juice to make a rather runny mixture. Refrigerate to harden and serve as a spread with toasted Bread Rounds or Melba Toast.

- Combine softened cream cheese with chopped ripe tomatoes; chopped fresh or crumbled dried sage; mashed ripe bananas and chopped peanuts; chopped walnuts; or mashed avocado and minced fresh chives. Serve as sandwich spreads.

- Soften cream cheese with a little Basic Mayonnaise. Spread evenly in shallow crystal bowl. Spread lumpfish caviar over, sprinkle with chopped green onions and tops, make a pattern with separately sieved hard cooked egg whites and yolks, sprinkle with paprika and freshly grated lemon rind and serve as a spread with crackers or Melba Toast.

- Combine 3 parts softened cream cheese and 1 part crumbled blue cheese; add minced celery and onion, salt, freshly ground white pepper and cayenne pepper, Basic Mayonnaise if too stiff. Chill, form into small balls and roll in finely chopped pecans or walnuts. Chill and serve as an hors d'oeuvre.

● Combine 1 part softened cream cheese, 3 parts grated Cheddar cheese and pressed garlic to taste. Chill and form into small balls. Roll balls in chili powder, chill and serve as an hors d'oeuvre.

● Rub raw mushroom caps with fresh lemon juice. Fill just to rim with mixture of softened cream cheese, sour cream, fresh lemon juice and freshly ground white pepper. Top with red caviar and tiny sliver of lemon rind.

● Rub raw mushroom caps with fresh lemon juice. Fill with mixture of softened cream cheese, softened butter, chopped ripe tomatoes and minced cooked or smoked salmon. Sprinkle with paprika.

● Rub raw mushroom caps with fresh lemon juice. Fill with mixture of equal parts softened cream cheese and crumbled blue cheese, minced fresh chives, sour cream and brandy to soften. Sprinkle with paprika and chill.

● Heat cooked brussels sprouts or green beans with softened cream

cheese. Sprinkle with chopped fresh savory.

● Sauté chicken breasts or veal scallops in butter and oil. Remove and deglaze skillet with dry white wine, add small bits of cream cheese and cook, stirring, until melted. Spoon over chicken or veal and sprinkle with minced fresh parsley and chives.

● Fill hollows of apples to be baked with softened cream cheese.

● Add bits of cream cheese to beaten eggs before scrambling.

## IDEAS FOR RICOTTA CHEESE

● Spread ricotta cheese on bread, drizzle with honey, sprinkle with ground cinnamon or allspice, top with banana slice rubbed with fresh lemon juice. Broil or bake until heated.

● Season ricotta cheese with salt and freshly ground white pepper,

roll into small balls, roll in finely chopped fresh chives and/or parsley. Serve as a salad garnish.

● Rub raw mushroom caps with fresh lemon juice. Fill with mixture of ricotta cheese, curry powder, salt, grated onion and minced fresh chives. Sprinkle with minced fresh dill and paprika.

● For dessert, season ricotta cheese with pure vanilla, rum or almond extract. Spoon onto fresh melon halves or sliced fresh fruits. Top with crushed strawberries.

## IDEAS FOR BRIE AND CAMEMBERT

● Dip wedges of brie or camembert in flour, then beaten egg, then finely chopped almonds. Chill and deep fry in hot oil until golden. Drain on paper toweling and serve immediately.

● Brown sliced almonds in butter. Pour over wedge of brie or camembert and bake in a preheated 375°F oven 5 minutes, or just until cheese softens. Do not overbake.

● Fill cooked jumbo pasta shells with brie or camembert and arrange in a buttered shallow baking dish. Heat in a preheated 350°F oven just until cheese starts to melt. Garnish with parsley sprigs.

• Place a dab of brie or camembert on a small round of pastry, top with another round and seal. Bake in a preheated 375°F oven 15 to 20 minutes, or until golden.

• Place a dab of brie or camembert on a small round of pastry, bring dough up and around to encase cheese, forming a ball, and seal. Bake in a preheated 375°F oven 10 to 15 minutes, or until golden.

• Use brie or camembert as a filling for Chicken or Turkey Rolls.

## IDEAS FOR SEMISOFT AND FIRM CHEESES

• Finely grate cheese and add to biscuit, yeast bread and pastry doughs.

• Finely grate cheese and sprinkle on top of oven dishes, such as scalloped potatoes, duchess potatoes and rice casseroles.

• Coarsely grate cheese or cut it into small bits and add to eggs before scrambling.

• Coarsely grate cheese and toss into green salads.

• Combine grated or shredded cheese with minced fresh dill as a filling for pastry tarts.

*For* shredded *cheese, use large or medium holes on grater; for* grated *cheese, use the tiny ones.*

• Grate cheese into chicken soup with heavy cream and chopped fresh parsley, then crumble in a little blue cheese.

• Toss together torn lettuce, chopped apples sprinkled with fresh lemon juice, orange sections, cubed Gouda or Edam cheese and Sour Cream Dressing. Garnish with chopped fresh parsley and pass bowl of croutons.

• Sprinkle filled apple pie shell with favorite grated cheese, then add top crust and bake.

## IDEAS FOR BLUE CHEESE (Gorgonzola or Roquefort Cheese)

• Combine crumbled blue cheese with mashed garlic cloves and sour cream. Spoon over chicken parts before baking.

• Crumble blue cheese onto cream-sauce dishes and return to oven just to melt. Or crumble onto freshly broiled filet mignon or baked fish fillets.

• Quickly sauté fresh prawns in butter, add a little dry vermouth and sprinkle with crumbled blue cheese and lots of minced fresh chives.

• Soften crumbled blue cheese with a little half-and-half cream, spoon over freshly poached eggs and broil to melt.

• Toss crumbled blue cheese into freshly cooked fettuccine with heavy cream, unsalted butter, freshly grated Parmesan cheese, minced garlic, minced fresh parsley and freshly ground black pepper.

• Crumble blue cheese into turkey or chicken salad and toss with toasted blanched almonds.

• Crumble blue cheese into freshly mashed potatoes.

- Toss crumbled blue cheese and chopped walnuts into Waldorf salad.

- Combine crumbled blue cheese with chopped fresh chives and parsley and freshly ground white pepper. Roll into balls, roll balls in chopped nuts and paprika. Serve as a salad garnish.

- Rub raw or lightly blanched mushroom caps with fresh lemon juice. Fill with mixture of equal amounts crumbled blue cheese and softened cream cheese, one-fourth as much softened butter, and grated onion, salt and Worcestershire sauce. Top with finely minced bell pepper.

- Cream crumbled blue cheese with softened butter and minced fresh dill. Serve as a sandwich spread.

- Combine equal parts sour cream, crumbled blue cheese, Basic Mayonnaise and chopped watercress and/or spinach, fresh lemon juice, and minced fresh dill, fresh tarragon and garlic. Serve as a cracker spread or raw-vegetable dip.

- Mash crumbled blue cheese with Worcestershire sauce, Tabasco sauce, salt and Basic Mayonnaise to bind. Spread on toast rounds, sprinkle with toasted sesame seeds and serve as an hors d'oeuvre.

- Roll out Puff Pastry and cut into small rounds. Combine crumbled blue cheese, minced green onion and fresh parsley, Worcestershire sauce, Tabasco sauce, salt and freshly ground white pepper. Place a dab on round, top with another round, seal, brush with Egg Wash and bake in a preheated 375°F oven 15 minutes, or until golden.

## IDEAS FOR FETA CHEESE

- Crumble feta cheese onto chicken fricassee, cover and continue cooking 10 minutes or until melted.

- Crumble feta cheese onto sliced ripe tomatoes, drizzle with Basic Vinaigrette, and sprinkle with chopped fresh basil and parsley, salt and freshly ground black pepper.

- Mix crumbled feta cheese with softened cream cheese and chopped cooked spinach or Swiss chard. Use as a filling for savory phyllo pastries.

- Combine equal parts crumbled feta cheese and softened cream cheese, milk or fresh lemon juice to spreading consistency, minced fresh chives and parsley, salt and freshly ground white pepper. Serve as sandwich spread or vegetable dip.

# Other Dairy Products

## MILKS

Milk is available in many forms: homogenized, raw or pasteurized, low fat, nonfat and whole, evaporated, condensed and powdered. Shelf life varies for each of these, but the products to be most concerned about are those that require refrigeration. (The exception to this statement is noninstant nonfat powdered milk, which should be refrigerated because it cakes badly when stored at room temperature.) Fresh milk that has some or all of the butterfat removed has a shorter shelf life than whole milk; in all cases, however, it is best to use fresh milk within four to five days of purchase. Most containers are dated by law, so look for these "pull" dates when buying. Do not freeze milk, as freezing will diminish the flavor and alter the texture.

## CREAMS

The choices of fresh creams are as varied as those of milk. There is half-and-half cream, also called single or cereal cream, whipping or heavy cream, and simply cream, known variously as light, coffee or table cream. The terms heavy and whipping are often used interchangeably by American dairies, thus confusing the buyer. The one-time distinction of heavy cream containing considerably more butterfat than whipping cream no longer holds. If possible, find out the butterfat content of the cream you purchase; 40 percent butterfat is preferred for any recipe in this book calling for heavy cream. Additionally, some heavy and whipping creams are marked ultrapasteurized and will not whip into stiff peaks, so look for this labeling before purchase. As with fresh milk, check for pull dates on all cream containers.

Whipping-type creams may be beaten until stiff (with a little sugar if to be used for desserts) and then frozen. Form the stiffly beaten cream on a baking sheet in the size mounds desired. Freeze at once until firm, then wrap the mounds individually and keep frozen up to three weeks. Remove the mounds from the freezer as needed and place on a piece of cake or pie, where they will quickly soften, float on hot soups or melt into cream sauces.

*If the pull date on your half-and-half cream carton is quickly approaching, make Light or Medium Cream Sauce, cool, jar and freeze up to 2 months.*

## BUTTERMILK

At one time, buttermilk was the residue that remained in the churn after making butter. Today it is most often skim milk to which a culture has been added to produce a thick consistency and sharp flavor. Buttermilk is most often available in quart containers and less frequently in pints and half-pints. You may also buy powdered buttermilk (keep refrigerated) and mix up only as much as you need for a specific recipe, or use this substitute: for each cup of buttermilk, add two tablespoons cider vinegar or one tablespoon fresh lemon juice to one cup fresh milk. (This same substitute can be used in recipes calling for sour milk.)

## SOUR CREAM AND YOGHURT

Tubs of sour cream or yoghurt should be stored upside down on the refrigerator shelf. Always use a clean utensil when removing these products from their containers and never return any of the spooned-out portion to the tubs. These three procedures will lengthen the shelf life of these dairy products considerably. Before adding either of them to other ingredients, beat well with a fork to create a free-flowing consistency. Sour cream should never be frozen; fruit-flavored yoghurt may be frozen and served as a frozen dessert but not thawed for other use.

## CREME FRAICHE

Crème fraîche is a cultured cream of French origin with a rich, slightly tangy flavor and smooth consistency. It can be substituted

*Yoghurt is a good accompaniment to soups, curries and legume dishes.*

for heavy cream in sauces (use a little less), is delicious spooned over fresh fruit or as a dressing for fruit salads, and can replace sour cream in most recipes. Crème fraîche is sold in tubs (usually imported from France, though there is now some small-scale production in the United States) and should be stored in the same way as sour cream. A credible substitute for crème fraîche can be made at home using one of three basic methods. All three methods require heavy cream with a butterfat content

of at least 40 percent, a sterilized jar and a period of time when the mixture must stand, loosely covered, at room temperature. All three can then be refrigerated in a tightly covered container up to two weeks. Try each method and select the crème fraîche that best suits your taste: 1). Combine two tablespoons buttermilk and one cup heavy cream. Let stand twelve to fourteen hours, stir well and refrigerate. 2). Combine one tablespoon buttermilk and one cup heavy cream. Let stand twenty-four hours, stir well and refrigerate. 3). Combine equal parts sour cream and heavy cream. Let stand overnight, stir well and refrigerate.

## INDEX TO RECIPES

# BREADS, PASTAS
# GRAINS & LEGUMES

## *Breads*

The best bread is homemade, hot from the oven. Grind the grains yourself for better flavor and to retain the natural vitamins and nutrients, and add honey, cooked cereal or potato, a generous measure of oil or butter, freshly ground seeds or some soy flour for a loaf that will stay moist longer. If bread making is not part of your household's routine, buy good-quality loaves, preferably whole grain and without additives.

Store any white, whole-wheat, whole-grain or rye bread loosely wrapped at room temperature for two to three days, then transfer to the refrigerator for an additional two days. Refrigerating bread dries it out, so reserve your freshest bread for sandwiches or at-table accompaniment. Crusty breads, such as French and Italian, should be eaten within two days of baking. If they begin to harden, revive them in one of the following ways: spray mist the loaf with water and heat in a moderate oven, or place the loaf in a brown-paper bag, sprinkle the bag with water and heat in the oven.

To freeze bread with a thin crust, wrap in airtight freezer bags or heavy foil and place in the freezer for up to two months. Crusty breads should be wrapped airtight and frozen no more than one week, as the crust will begin to disintegrate. Freshly baked bread must be allowed to cool completely before bagging and freezing. For a household of only two or three, wrap and freeze a half loaf at a time, or slice the loaf and remove only as many slices as needed.

All breads are best defrosted at room temperature in their wrappings; if wrapped in foil, they can also be thawed in a slow oven. Frozen sliced bread may go directly from the freezer to the toaster. If freezing bread for sandwiches, store no more than three to four weeks.

Unbaked bread dough may be frozen, but this should be done only in an emergency. Oil the dough well, secure in an airtight bag and freeze up to two months. Defrost at room temperature six to eight hours, or in the refrigerator overnight. Remove wrapping, place in an oiled bowl in a warm place, cover with a tea towel and let rise, then shape and let rise again. If you are deliberately making the dough to freeze, increase the yeast measure by 50 percent, as freezing inhibits the yeast's growth.

Bread, especially in the form of crumbs, croutons and coatings, is important to the success of many of the recipes in this book. All of the "bread basics" included in the Cooking Guidelines are easy to make ahead and store well until needed. Most of them can be put in airtight containers and refriger-ated up to one week or frozen up to three months. Any bread that has been served warm at table one day can be turned into these recipes and ideas a day or two later.

The Index to Recipes included in this section covers only those recipes where bread in all its various forms is an integral part of the dish. Because the dried bread forms, such as crumbs and coatings, store well, those instances where they are merely used as a topping or garnish are not included.

## COOKING GUIDELINES

**DRY BREAD CRUMBS** For coarse crumbs, break bread into bits, place on shallow baking sheet and dry in 325°F oven. With fingers, crumble into coarse crumbs. For fine crumbs, whirl in food processor or blender.

**FRESH BREAD CRUMBS** For coarse crumbs, break fresh bread up into bits with fingers and roll in palms of hands. For fine crumbs, whirl in food processor or blender.

**TOASTED BREAD CRUMBS** Place fresh bread crumbs on shallow baking sheet and toast in a 325°F oven until golden.

*Put some crunch and extra nutrition in crumbs: mix 1 to 2 tablespoons corn germ into Buttered Bread Crumbs.*

**BUTTERED BREAD CRUMBS** Toss 2 cups fresh or dry bread crumbs in 3 tablespoons melted butter, stirring until evenly moist. Toss in dried herbs, such as basil, thyme, and/or oregano, if desired.

**SEASONED BREAD CRUMBS** Combine 1 cup fresh or dry bread crumbs with 1/2 teaspoon *each* salt and paprika and 1/4 teaspoon *each* freshly ground black or white pepper and ground oregano, basil, thyme and/or sage.

**PARMESAN CRUMB TOPPING** Toss 2 cups fresh bread crumbs with 3 tablespoons melted butter to coat evenly. Toss in 1/4 cup freshly grated Parmesan cheese.

**CORNBREAD CRUMB TOPPING** Crumble cornbread and toss with melted butter. Season as for Seasoned Bread Crumbs.

**SESAME BREAD CRUMB COATING** Toss 1/2 cup fine dry bread crumbs with 1/4 cup sesame seeds, 1 teaspoon lemon pepper, 1/2 teaspoon curry powder and salt to taste.

**BREAD CRUMB MIXTURE FOR ROAST MEATS** Combine dry bread crumbs with finely minced garlic, finely minced fresh herbs to complement the meat, salt and freshly ground black or white pepper.

Moisten with a little safflower or olive oil and pat onto top of roasting meat 30 to 45 minutes before roast is done.

**WHEAT GERM TOPPING** Combine 3 parts dry bread crumbs and 1 part wheat germ. Season as for Seasoned Bread Crumbs.

**BREAD FINGERS, ROUNDS, SQUARES, TRIANGLES, RINGS** Thinly slice whole-wheat, white, rye, French, Italian or pumpernickel bread, remove crusts and cut into desired shapes. Let dry 1 day, then top with one of the following suggestions. Bake in a 200°F oven one hour or until crisp and dry. Serve as an accompaniment to soups and salads.

● Combine melted butter and curry powder to taste.
● Combine melted butter with freshly grated Parmesan cheese and paprika to taste.
● Melt butter with minced fresh chives and/or parsley and minced fresh oregano, basil or tarragon.
● Melt butter slowly with mashed garlic cloves. Remove garlic and add Worcestershire sauce and salt to taste.
● Melt butter with fresh lemon juice and freshly grated lemon rind. Sprinkle with paprika.

**CROUTONS** Cut white, whole-wheat, whole grain, pumpernickel, rye, French or Italian bread into 1/2-inch cubes. Bake in a 200°F oven 1 hour, stirring occasionally, until completely dry. For each 3 cups of cubed bread, melt 4 to 5 tablespoons butter. Mix with any one of the following suggestions and toss bread cubes into mixture to coat evenly. Transfer to shallow baking pan and, tossing often, brown lightly in a preheated 350°F oven. Use croutons on tossed salads or in cream soups, omelets or dumplings.

● Add to butter 1/4 cup freshly grated Parmesan cheese, 1/2 teaspoon paprika, dash cayenne pepper and salt to taste.
● Add to butter 1-1/2 tablespoons fresh lemon juice, 1 tablespoon freshly grated lemon rind and 1/2 teaspoon paprika.
● Add to butter 2 to 3 garlic cloves, grated or mashed, 1/2 teaspoon ground oregano and freshly ground white pepper to taste.

**MELBA TOAST** Freeze day-old white bread (homemade, if possible) several hours until firm but not frozen through. Cut into paper-thin slices and place, not touching, on baking sheet. Bake in a 250°F oven, turning occasionally, 15 minutes or until curled and golden brown. Serve with soups or salads,

as a base for dishes such as Welsh Rabbit, or in place of crackers with spreads.

**FRIED BREAD** Slice slightly stale French or Italian bread 1/3 inch thick. Fry in skillet in butter with mashed garlic. Serve on French onion soup, with sautéed mushrooms, or as a base for creamed dishes.

**FRENCH TOAST** For 6 to 8 slices of 1- to 2-day-old bread. Lightly beat 1 egg with 1/2 tablespoon light corn syrup or honey, 1/8 teaspoon salt, 1/4 teaspoon ground cinnamon (optional), 1/8 teaspoon freshly grated nutmeg and 1/2 teaspoon freshly grated orange rind (optional). Beat in 3/4 to 1 cup milk or evaporated milk. One at a time, dip bread slices into batter so batter penetrates almost halfway through from each side, turning over to soak second side. If bread is very hard and dry, let soak until fork will barely penetrate with light pressure. Pan fry in half butter and half safflower oil to a golden color, turning only once. Serve with honey, maple syrup, fresh fruit heated in butter and brown sugar, or creamed meats or vegetables.

*Combine toasted wheat germ and toasted sesame seeds. Sprinkle over cereal topped with sliced bananas.*

## IDEAS FOR BREADS

**HOT APPETIZERS** Toast thinly sliced 2-day-old-bread rounds (whole-wheat, rye, French, Italian, pumpernickel) on one side, flip over and cool. Spread or layer untoasted side with the following, then broil just until bubbly.

● Mixture of crumbled blue cheese, softened butter and chopped pecans seasoned with celery salt; sprinkle with paprika.
● Butter, water chestnut slice, Cheddar cheese slice, minced fresh parsley.
● Butter, mixture of grated Cheddar cheese and minced cooked ham, chopped black olives, minced chutney; sprinkle with freshly grated Parmesan cheese.
● Mixture of softened butter, pressed garlic, finely minced mild canned green chili peppers; top with mixture of equal parts finely grated Cheddar cheese and Basic Mayonnaise.
● Homemade Mustard, thin slice of cooked ham or corned beef, thin slice of Gruyère cheese.
● Mixture of chopped black olives, minced green onion and tops, minced garlic, grated sharp Cheddar cheese, Curry Mayonnaise to bind. Best on rye bread. After broiling, top with leaf of parsley or watercress.

**TOMATO–BREAD APPETIZER**
Sauté minced white of leeks and minced garlic in olive oil until soft. Add chopped peeled ripe tomatoes. Cook, stirring occasionally, until thickened. Soak stale coarse crusty bread in water until soft, squeeze dry and gradually add to tomato mixture, mixing in well. Season with salt and freshly ground black pepper and serve at room temperature. Pass a bowl of olive oil.

**VEGETABLE–TORTILLA SOUP** Add to any vegetable soup, chopped ripe tomatoes, cooked white rice, minced garlic and ground cumin. Add shredded Monterey Jack cheese, heat to melt and just before serving, toss in stale tortillas, torn into pieces.

**PITA BREAD SALAD** Toss broken stale pita bread with torn Romaine lettuce, tomato wedges, minced fresh parsley, bell pepper and green onion tops and sliced radishes. Dress with Mexican Dressing.

## IDEAS FOR CORNBREAD AND BISCUITS

● Split day-old cornbread squares, muffins or biscuits. Butter lightly and brown under broiler until butter is bubbly. Serve plain or with honey, or top with creamed meats or vegetables.

---

*No dried currants on hand? Use coarsely chopped raisins.*

---

● Top split day-old cornbread squares, muffins or biscuits with a slice of Cheddar or Monterey Jack cheese. Broil to melt cheese.

● Crumble cornbread or biscuits into yeast breads, adding 1/4 cup for each cup of unbleached flour used in recipe.

● Crumble cornbread or biscuits, moisten with melted butter and mix with freshly grated Parmesan cheese. Use as a topping for oven dishes.

● Crumble cornbread or biscuits and use in ground-meat mixtures (for hamburgers and meatloafs) in place of bread crumbs.

## IDEAS FOR BREAD CRUMBS

● Use fine dry bread crumbs for thickening gravies made with the pan juices of roasted meats.

● Dip thinly pounded veal scallops or boned pork steaks or chicken breasts in beaten egg and then coat with Seasoned Bread Crumbs, mixed with freshly grated Parmesan cheese if desired. Fry in butter until golden.

---

● Sprinkle fresh Buttered Bread Crumbs over fish steaks or fillets that have been blanketed with cream sauce.

● Coat the sides and bottom of a buttered shallow baking dish with dry bread crumbs before spooning in any vegetable or vegetable and cheese casserole.

● Add plain or Seasoned Bread Crumbs to frittata mixtures.

● Mix Seasoned Bread Crumbs with melted butter to moisten. Use as a topping for cooked cauliflower, broccoli or asparagus. Toss chopped hard-cooked eggs into crumb mixture, if desired.

## INDEX TO RECIPES

# Pastas

The term pasta is a generic one, used here to identify the multitude of noodle-dough creations. Pasta is the spaghetti of Italy, the somen of Japan, the mein of China. For the most part, this book concentrates on the Italian pastas, the ribbon noodles such as fettuccine and tagliarini, the rod types—linguine, vermicelli, spaghetti—and the fanciful "shaped" ones: the corkscrewlike fusilli; the "quills" called penne; creste di gallo, or cockscomb pasta; and the tiny kernel form, orzo. For stuffing, there are jumbo shells, large, cylindrical manicotti and cannelloni squares.

Wrap fresh pasta, well dusted with flour, in waxed paper, then in a tea towel and finally in a plastic bag and refrigerate up to two days. Fresh pasta may also be wrapped airtight in aluminum foil and frozen up to two months; defrost in the refrigerator before cooking. Commercial dried pastas should be kept in well-sealed canisters and stored no longer than six months. Fresh pasta can, of course, also be dried and stored in this same manner, but it loses its fine texture and flavor in the drying process.

Pasta is an ideal planned leftover. Prepare an extra portion when making a pasta dinner, then turn that portion into a meal a day or so later. Cook pasta in a generous amount of boiling salted water to which a little oil has been added (the oil helps to prevent the noodles from sticking together) until *just* tender (al dente). Cooking times vary depending on whether the pasta is fresh or dried; fresh should take no more than one to three minutes, while dried may take as long as ten minutes. Check pasta for doneness frequently once it begins to soften. Drain the pasta well, rinse in cold water and then store immersed in water in the refrigerator up to three days; if reheating, drop into boiling water for thirty seconds, or warm in a sauce. Alternately, toss the rinsed pasta with olive oil, or peanut oil if cooking an Oriental noodle, cover and refrigerate up to two days; if reheating, moisten with a little stock and warm in a Teflon-type skillet, or in a sauce.

## IDEAS FOR PASTAS

● Toss warmed cooked pasta with plain yoghurt, finely minced garlic and finely chopped walnuts or toasted slivered almonds.

*Store shelled nuts in the freezer in airtight containers. No need to defrost before using.*

● Toss medium or wide cooked noodles with Quick Tomato Sauce, transfer to a shallow baking dish, sprinkle with grated sharp Cheddar or Gruyère cheese, or shredded mozzarella or bel paese cheese. Bake in a preheated 350°F oven 20 minutes, or until bubbly and cheese is melted.

● Add to above suggestion chopped cooked broccoli, cooked peas and/or diced cooked meat.

● Add any cooked pasta to heated rich stock, with cooked vegetables and/or meats if desired. Serve with freshly grated Parmesan cheese.

● Sauté minced onion and garlic in butter and safflower oil, sprinkle with curry powder, cook several minutes, add chicken or beef stock to moisten, toss in cooked pasta and reheat. Sprinkle with chopped fresh chives and parsley and pass freshly grated Parmesan or Romano cheese.

● Toss medium or wide cooked noodles with Mushroom Sauce. Transfer to a buttered shallow baking dish, sprinkle with Buttered Bread Crumbs and bake in a preheated 350°F oven 20 minutes, or until heated through.

● Sauté minced bell peppers and sliced mushrooms in butter and olive oil until mushrooms are golden. Add half-and-half cream and cooked pasta. Heat gently and toss in crumbled gorgonzola or Roquefort cheese. Garnish with chopped fresh parsley and chives.

● Heat together cooked broccoli flowerets, peas and asparagus spears, finely minced garlic, chopped ripe tomatoes, minced fresh basil and parsley and half-and-half cream. Toss in cooked pasta, reheat and sprinkle with freshly grated Parmesan or Romano cheese.

● Break an egg into bottom of soup bowl. Ladle in cooked udon or somen noodles reheated in dashi or rich stock. Sprinkle with chopped green onions.

● Toss cooked pasta with chopped cooked spinach, crumbled feta cheese and freshly ground black pepper. Place in a buttered shallow baking dish and sprinkle with Buttered Bread Crumbs. Bake in a preheated 350°F oven 15 minutes, or until heated through.

● Pan fry thin cooked pasta in butter and safflower oil until crispy. Serve as a bed for Stir Fry Meats and Vegetables.

● Toss warmed cooked pasta with hot Fresh Tomato Sauce; Quick Tomato Sauce; Creamy Quick Tomato Sauce with chopped fresh parsley; Tomato Cheese Sauce; Shallot Cream Sauce with low-fat cottage cheese, cooked peas, chopped fresh parsley and chives; or Quick Mushroom Sauce. Serve with freshly grated Parmesan or Romano cheese.

## INDEX TO RECIPES

# Grains & Legumes

Grains cover a whole range of healthful, flavorful foods, including some seven thousand known varieties of rice. This book deals with only the most common grains: white and brown rice, wild rice, barley, bulghur (cracked wheat), millet, wheat and triticale berries (both whole grains), and wheat germ (the "live" part of the wheat berry).

Most uncooked grains should be stored in a cool, dry place in an airtight container. Some grains, like triticale and rye berries, are perishable and can be refrigerated or frozen to extend their shelf lives. Wheat germ, however, must be refrigerated or frozen, for it becomes rancid quite easily. If you feel you will be unable to use up any grain in six months, refrigerate or freeze it.

As with grains, there are a great number of legume varieties, but all fall within the three basic categories of beans, peas and lentils. These staples of many of the world's cuisines were among the first cultivated plants in the history of agriculture. Only the best-known legumes are covered here: the peas, garbanzo beans (chick-peas) and split peas; the beans, soybeans and red, kidney, pinto, lima and small white beans; and lentils.

The soybean deserves special attention, for it is extremely high in protein and has been a part of the diet of the peoples of the Orient for centuries. It is the base of the popular condiment soy sauce, is combined with malt and salt to make the Japanese fermented paste called miso, and is used to make tofu, or bean curd.

Tofu can be mashed, puréed or cubed, and can be eaten raw, sautéed, steamed, fried or boiled. It has a bland taste, thus mixes well with other ingredients to bring out their flavors. There are two basic types of tofu, firm and soft, though it can also be purchased pressed, dried and deep fried. Both types come in plastic containers, usually stamped with a date indicating shelf life. Once the tofu has been opened, remove it, rinse with fresh water, place in a bowl, cover with water and refrigerate. Change the water daily.

If you do not like the custardy texture of tofu, or you need to store it beyond the pull date, drain the tofu well, pat dry, wrap in aluminum foil and freeze up to three weeks. Defrost in a sieve, press out any moisture, shred with your fingers and season with a little soy sauce, if desired. The tofu will now have a texture reminiscent of ground meat and can be added to a variety of dishes, such as meatloaf or scrambled eggs.

Once thawed, it can be kept in the refrigerator in a covered container up to three days.

Many grains and legumes, including triticale berries, wheat berries, garbanzo beans, soybeans, lentils, whole peas and mung beans, may be sprouted and the sprouts used in salads, stir fries, omelets and other dishes. Sprouting kits are available in health food and department stores, often with an organic mineral-food solution to add to the sprouting water for increased vitamin and mineral content.

Cooking Guidelines for the most commonly used grains and legumes follow, or you may prepare the grains as described in Grain Pilaf. Grains and legumes are excellent planned leftovers for using in casseroles, quick skillet dishes and soups. They may also be combined; complementary pairings include split peas and rice, red beans and millet or rice and garbanzo beans and rice. Store cooked grains and legumes in a covered container in the refrigerator up to three days, or freeze up to three months. Bring to room temperature before mixing with other ingredients or reheating. In many recipes, one grain or legume may be substituted for another, but keep in mind what texture and flavor are most suitable for a dish.

## COOKING GUIDELINES FOR GRAINS

**WASHING RICE** To wash raw rice, place in a saucepan, cover with water, rub briskly with fingertips and pour off water. With white rice, repeat until water is clear.

**STEAMED WHITE RICE** For approximately 3 cups cooked rice, level 1 cup washed raw rice in a saucepan. (The saucepan should have a capacity at least double the measure of cooked rice.) Add water to cover 1/2 inch above level of rice. Let stand at least 30 minutes, or longer if time allows. Over high heat, uncovered, bring water to a rapid boil. Lower heat slightly and cook until *all* the water has evaporated and bubbles have disappeared from the surface. Cover tightly, reduce heat immediately to lowest point and cook 20 minutes. Do not stir while cooking. Turn off heat and let pot stand 5 minutes, then fluff rice with a fork before serving. If cooking a large quantity of rice, increase water measure slightly.

*Cooked wild rice and white rice are a good combination.*

**BOILED BROWN RICE** For approximately 3 cups cooked rice, bring 2-1/2 cups rich stock to a boil. Slowly pour in 1 cup washed brown rice, stirring constantly. Bring stock back to boil, turn heat to lowest point, cover and cook until all liquid is absorbed, about 40 minutes. Do not stir while cooking. Turn off heat and let pot stand 5 minutes, then fluff rice with a fork before serving.

**BOILED WILD RICE** For approximately 4 cups wild rice, soak 1 cup washed raw rice in water to cover 1 hour. Drain. Bring 3 cups rich stock to a rapid boil and slowly pour in rice, stirring constantly. Bring stock back to a boil, turn heat to low, cover and cook until all liquid is absorbed, about 45 minutes.

**MILLET** For approximately 2 cups cooked millet, wash 1/2 cup millet. Bring 1-1/2 cups rich stock to a rapid boil and slowly add millet, stirring constantly. Bring stock back to a boil, turn heat to low, cover and cook until all liquid is absorbed, about 45 minutes.

**BARLEY** For approximately 3 cups cooked barley, wash 1 cup barley. Bring 3 cups stock to a rapid boil and slowly pour in barley, stirring constantly. Bring stock back to a boil, turn heat to low, cover and cook until all liquid is absorbed, about 1 hour and 10 minutes. Check liquid level and add more stock, if needed.

**WHEAT OR TRITICALE BERRIES** For approximately 3 cups cooked berries, wash 1 cup wheat or triticale berries. Pour 2 cups boiling water over the berries, bring to a boil, cover, lower heat slightly and boil 3 minutes. Remove from heat and let stand, covered, 1 to 2 hours. Add 3 cups rich stock, bring to a rapid boil, cover with slightly tilted lid, lower heat and cook at a slow boil 2 hours, or until berries are done to taste. If berries are still too crunchy, add more stock and continue cooking. Remove lid and cook until all moisture is absorbed.

**BULGHUR (CRACKED WHEAT)** Bulghur lends itself best to the pilaf method of cooking (see Grain Pilaf). To prepare plain, cook as for millet, using 1 part bulghur to 2 parts stock and reducing cooking time to 15 to 20 minutes. Uncooked bulghur doubles its measure when cooked.

## IDEAS FOR
## WHITE OR BROWN RICE

● Sauté minced green bell pepper, onion and garlic in peanut oil until starting to soften. Add diced cooked chicken, pork or lamb and brown slightly. Moisten with soy sauce and toss in cooked rice. Heat mixture and toss in freshly scrambled eggs or Egg Garnish and chopped roasted peanuts. Garnish with chopped green onions and tops.

● Toss cooked rice with minced pimientos, minced fresh parsley and green onions, crumbled dried basil, salt, paprika and freshly ground white pepper. Moisten with sour cream thinned with a little milk, transfer to a buttered shallow baking dish, cover with aluminum foil and bake in a preheated 350°F oven 25 to 30 minutes until heated through.

● Soak chopped pitted dates 20 minutes in fresh lemon juice. Toss into cooked rice with sliced almonds browned in butter, salt and freshly ground black pepper. Heat with a little stock.

● Heat cooked rice with chopped ripe tomatoes, slivered black olives, minced fresh basil, salt and freshly ground black pepper.

● Toss cooked rice with cubed cooked turkey or chicken, sautéed sliced mushrooms, minced garlic, salt and freshly ground black pepper. Moisten with a little Tomato Sauce and heat. Just before serving toss in chopped hard-cooked eggs. Sprinkle with minced fresh parsley.

● Toss cooked rice with chopped green onions and tops, minced water chestnuts, julienned cooked ham, diced softened dried mushrooms and freshly ground black pepper. Heat with a little stock.

● Line the bottom and sides of a buttered shallow baking dish with cooked rice to make a shell 3/4 inch thick, pressing in firmly. Fill with any creamed or gravied meat, stew or curry dish. Bake in a preheated 400°F oven 20 minutes.

● Moisten cooked rice with rich stock and heat in a skillet. Make hollows in the heated rice and break an egg into each hollow. Cover and cook until eggs are set

to taste. If desired, sprinkle with grated cheese, re-cover and cook just until cheese is melted.

● Sauté sliced mushrooms, minced onions and minced garlic in butter until soft. Toss in cooked brown rice, plumped raisins, chopped cashews, ground oregano, salt and freshly ground black pepper. Heat with a little stock and sprinkle with minced fresh chives.

## IDEAS FOR WILD RICE

● Toss cooked wild rice with chopped cooked chicken livers, minced green onions and tops, minced garlic, minced green bell pepper, salt and cayenne pepper. Moisten with Light Cream Sauce made with chicken stock. Heat, adding more chicken stock if needed to moisten.

● Toss cooked wild rice with cooked peas, sliced almonds browned in butter and freshly grated orange rind. Cover and heat, adding a little chicken stock and/or dry vermouth if needed to moisten.

---

*Substitute fresh lime or lemon juice for small amounts of wine in recipes.*

● Toss cooked wild rice with minced leeks and fresh parsley, finely chopped Swiss chard, chopped walnuts, salt and freshly ground black pepper. Bind with beaten egg and transfer to a buttered shallow baking dish. Bake in a preheated 350°F oven 30 minutes, or until eggs are set.

● Sauté minced onion in butter. Sprinkle with curry powder and cook, stirring, 2 minutes. Add chopped apples, cover and cook, stirring several times, 5 minutes, or until apples are almost tender. Toss in cooked wild rice and rich stock to moisten. Heat and garnish with chopped fresh chives.

● Toss cooked wild rice with sautéed mushrooms, fresh lemon juice, diced green bell pepper and diced cooked chicken, turkey or duck. Heat with a little stock and serve with Garlic Mayonnaise.

## IDEAS FOR WHEAT GERM

● Combine toasted wheat germ and toasted sesame seeds. Sprinkle over cereal topped with sliced bananas.

● Stir toasted wheat germ into beaten eggs before scrambling.

● Substitute 1/4 cup toasted wheat germ for 1/4 cup of the flour in pancake, waffle or muffin batter recipes.

● Add 1 tablespoon toasted wheat germ to Parmesan Crumb Topping.

● Add toasted wheat germ to oatmeal or cornbread batter recipes, ground-meat mixtures or yeast bread dough.

## IDEAS FOR OTHER GRAINS

**MILLET** Sauté minced onion and garlic in butter until soft. Toss in diced cooked zucchini, chopped cooked greens, cooked millet, cooked wheat or triticale berries and grated or shredded firm or semifirm cheese. Moisten with Tomato Sauce or add chopped ripe tomatoes. Season to taste, transfer to a buttered shallow baking dish and sprinkle with Wheat Germ Topping or Parmesan Crumb Topping. Bake in a preheated 350°F oven 20 minutes, or until heated through and lightly browned.

**MILLET** Toss together cooked millet and cooked brown rice. Reheat and transfer to heated platter. Pour any curry dish over grains and sprinkle with minced fresh parsley and chives.

**MILLET** Toss cooked millet with minced garlic and fresh basil and chopped cooked spinach, Swiss chard or other greens. Moisten with Tomato or Quick Tomato Sauce, or chopped ripe tomatoes, and heat through. Season and sprinkle with shredded bel paese, Gouda or Edam cheese. Cover and cook until cheese is melted. Sprinkle with minced fresh parsley and chives.

**MILLET** Sauté minced onion and celery in butter until soft. Toss with cooked millet, fresh lemon juice, chopped walnuts, dried currants, freshly grated Parmesan cheese, salt and freshly ground black pepper. Moisten with stock and transfer to a buttered shallow baking dish. Sprinkle with freshly grated Parmesan cheese and paprika and bake in a preheated 350°F oven 20 minutes, or until heated through.

---

*Fresh lemon juice brings out the flavors of a number of foods, from fish and chicken to apple pie.*

**BULGHUR** Sauté minced onion in butter with a sprinkling of ground cumin. Toss into cooked bulghur with toasted slivered blanched almonds, dried apricots soaked to soften and chopped, plumped raisins, ground cinnamon, ground cloves, salt and freshly ground black pepper. Heat with a little stock and sprinkle with minced fresh parsley.

**BARLEY** Combine cooked barley, cooked peas, chopped green onions and tops, minced fresh parsley, toasted pine nuts or sliced almonds, salt and freshly ground black pepper.

Moisten with rich stock, tomato juice or a combination. Transfer to a buttered shallow baking dish and top with ripe tomato slices. Sprinkle Buttered Bread Crumbs over and bake in a preheated 350°F oven 20 minutes, or until heated through and browned.

**BARLEY** Toss cooked barley with cooked peas, cubed cooked lamb roast and chopped ripe tomatoes. Heat and season with minced fresh oregano, salt and freshly ground black pepper, moistening with tomato juice if needed. Sprinkle with grated Gruyère cheese, cover and cook until cheese is melted.

**WHEAT BERRIES** Heat cooked berries in a covered skillet with a little stock to moisten. Top with shredded or sliced Monterey Jack cheese, re-cover and cook until cheese is melted.

**WHEAT OR TRITICALE BERRIES** Heat cooked berries in gravied chicken or turkey, thinning with chicken or turkey stock, if needed. Toss in minced green onions and tops, slivered black olives and minced fresh parsley. Sprinkle with freshly grated Parmesan cheese.

## INDEX TO RECIPES

## COOKING GUIDELINES FOR LEGUMES

Legumes should be well washed and rinsed and any imperfect ones discarded. Some legumes, such as garbanzo beans, kidney beans and soybeans, should be soaked overnight in water (see following chart for amount of soaking water). Additional cooking liquid, preferably stock, is then added to the pot and the legumes are cooked. An alternate method of soaking is to pour boiling water (same amount as for overnight soaking) over the legumes, bring the water to a boil, lower the heat, cover and simmer five minutes. Let stand off the heat, covered, two hours, and then proceed with further cooking, adding stock or additional water.

Cook legumes at a gentle boil with the pot lid slightly tilted, as rapid boiling will break the skins. Cook them only until *just* tender if preparing some of the legumes as planned leftovers for a salad or for a dish in which they will be reheated whole. Lift out these "extras" with a slotted spoon and then continue cooking the remaining legumes until tender. If the planned leftovers are to be puréed, cook them until they are quite soft.

If you are using only water to cook the legumes, add vegetables and seasonings to enhance their flavor: chopped onion, green bell pepper, carrot and celery, mashed garlic cloves, bay leaf, parsley sprigs, oregano sprigs, dill feathers, chili powder or crumbled dried chili pepper, celery seeds or leaves, ground cumin, lightly crushed peppercorns, chopped tomatoes and diced salt pork or slab bacon, in any combination. Once the legumes are cooked, season with salt, soy sauce, cider vinegar or red wine vinegar (especially good with lentils) and/or safflower or olive oil.

Cooking times will vary depending upon the age of the legume, where it was grown, how it was processed and how full the cooking pot is. The chart that follows is only *a guide*. Once legumes begin to soften, check frequently so that they do

## LEGUME COOKING CHART

| LEGUME (1 cup dry measure) | SOAKING WATER | ADDITIONAL LIQUID | CHECKING TIME | APPROXIMATE YIELD |
|---|---|---|---|---|
| Garbanzo beans (chick-peas) | 2 cups | 1½ cups | 45 min. | 2⅔ cups |
| Kidney beans | 1½ cups | 2 cups | 30 min. | 2⅔ cups |
| Lentils | | 2½ cups | 20 min. | 2¾ cups |
| Limas, baby | 1 cup | 2 cups | 30 min. | 3 cups |
| Pinto beans | 1½ cups | 1½ cups | 45 min. | 2½ cups |
| Red beans | 1½ cups | 1½ cups | 45 min. | 2½ cups |
| Soybeans | 2 cups* | 1½ cups | 1 hr., 15 min. | 3 cups |
| Split peas | | 2½ cups | 20 min. | 2¾ cups |
| White beans, small | 2 cups | 2 cups | 1 hr. | 2⅔ cups |

*If soaking overnight, refrigerate.*

not overcook. Checking time rather than cooking time is indicated on the chart. If you will need bean cooking liquid for a recipe, add some additional stock or water when the initial checking time is reached, so the liquid will absorb the flavor of the legumes.

## IDEAS FOR LENTILS AND SPLIT PEAS

• Sauté minced onion and garlic in butter until soft. Add cooked lentils and heat. Stir in cubed fresh pineapple and season with salt and freshly ground black pepper. Serve as an accompaniment to a meat or poultry entrée.

• Heat cooked lentils in a little stock or cooking liquid. Toss with minced onion and garlic sautéed in bacon drippings and with sliced cooked Italian sausage. Garnish with minced fresh Italian parsley.

• Combine cooked lentils with Quick Tomato Sauce made with the optional onions and bell peppers, halved black olives, minced fresh oregano, ground cumin, chili powder, salt and freshly ground black pepper. Spoon into a shallow baking dish and cover with Cornbread Crumb Topping mixed with grated Cheddar cheese. Bake in a preheated 350°F oven 30 minutes, or until heated through.

• Add chopped ripe tomatoes, minced garlic and cooked lentils to vegetable soup. Heat and just before serving add dry sherry and sprinkle with freshly grated Parmesan cheese.

• Sauté sliced onion, minced ginger root and minced garlic in butter or olive oil until onion is soft. Sprinkle with curry powder and cook, stirring, 2 minutes. Add cooked lentils and stock to moisten. Heat and serve over rice with a sprinkling of minced fresh chives.

• Combine cooked lentils with Lemon Vinaigrette and let stand 2 to 3 hours. Toss lentils with chopped walnuts, minced shallots, freshly grated lemon rind and minced fresh parsley. Serve in lettuce cups garnished with lemon wedges.

• Heat cooked lentils in rich chicken stock. Add shredded spinach or Swiss chard, bring just to boil and serve as a soup course with garnish of chopped hard-cooked eggs.

• Combine cooked lentils with equal amounts cooked brown rice, curry powder, fresh lemon juice and chopped cooked spinach or Swiss chard. Heat with a little rich stock to moisten and toss in lots of minced fresh parsley.

• Combine cooked split peas and cooked fine noodles with minced fresh parsley, chopped tomato and sour cream. Reheat and season with salt and freshly ground white pepper. Thin with a little rich beef or chicken stock, if needed. Serve as an accompaniment to a meat or poultry entrée.

• Mash cooked split peas with softened butter, thin with rich stock or cooking liquid and season with freshly grated nutmeg, salt and freshly ground white pepper. Serve as an accompaniment to a meat or poultry entrée.

• Heat cooked split peas and cooked white rice in a skillet with chicken stock to moisten. Toss in minced water chestnuts and chopped roasted peanuts. Serve with Steamed Chicken with a garnish of chopped fresh coriander.

*Dehydrate your sprouts for more concentrated vitamin content. Grind in blender and add to yeast bread dough, 1 tablespoon per cup of flour.*

# IDEAS FOR OTHER LEGUMES

**SMALL WHITE BEANS** Combine cooked small white beans with cubed cooked chicken in a light gravy thinned with dry white wine. Cook, stirring often, 10 minutes to blend flavors. Add sliced pimiento-stuffed olives and heat. Garnish with orange sections and serve as a main meal.

**SMALL WHITE OR GARBANZO BEANS** Marinate cooked garbanzo or small white beans in Mustard Vinaigrette and minced garlic. Just before serving, toss with vegetables of choice: sliced sweet red or white onion, radishes, mushrooms, green or red bell pepper, green onions and tops, or celery; sliced cooked artichoke hearts or bottoms; or cooked corn kernels, cut-up green beans or small broccoli flowerets. Mound on lettuce leaves and garnish with minced fresh parsley, chives, basil or dill, crumbled crisply cooked bacon, croutons, slivered black olives, tomato wedges and/or chopped hard-cooked eggs.

**SMALL WHITE OR GARBANZO BEANS** Heat cooked small white or garbanzo beans in lamb or beef stew with cooked broccoli flowerets. Sprinkle with grated Gruyère cheese, cover and cook until cheese is melted.

**SMALL WHITE OR PINTO BEANS** Sauté sliced onion and minced garlic in olive oil until soft. Layer half in a shallow baking dish. Top with slices of whole-grain bread soaked in bean cooking liquid, then layer with cooked small white or pinto beans, finely shredded cabbage, chopped ripe tomatoes and minced fresh basil. Sprinkle with salt and freshly ground black pepper. Repeat layers, pour in a little bean cooking liquid and bake in a preheated 350°F oven 35 minutes, adding more liquid if mixture appears too dry. Top with shredded bel paese cheese and sprinkle with paprika. Continue baking 15 minutes until cheese is melted.

**SMALL WHITE OR LIMA BEANS** Purée cooked small white or lima beans in a blender or food processor with fresh lemon juice and olive oil. Add finely minced garlic, salt and freshly ground white pepper. Moisten with stock or bean cooking liquid, if needed. Serve with a sprinkling of minced fresh parsley as a raw-vegetable dip or a spread for Melba Toast.

**KIDNEY, PINTO OR RED BEANS** Sauté minced onion, garlic and green bell pepper in butter until soft. Add chopped apple and sprinkle with curry powder. Cook, stirring, 2 minutes. Toss in well-seasoned cooked kidney, pinto or red beans and chopped ripe tomatoes. Season with a little granulated sugar and cider vinegar. Cover and cook, stirring occasionally, until flavors are blended and mixture is thick. Just before serving, sprinkle with freshly grated Parmesan cheese.

**KIDNEY, PINTO OR RED BEANS** Combine well-seasoned mashed cooked kidney, pinto or red beans, shredded Cheddar cheese, minced green bell pepper, Worcestershire sauce, Tabasco sauce and bean cooking liquid or stock, if needed. Heat until cheese is melted and serve over Fried Bread or as a spread for French or Italian bread.

**KIDNEY, PINTO OR RED BEANS**
Purée cooked kidney, pinto or red beans with cooking liquid to spreading consistency. Stir in grated onion, finely minced cooked ham or tongue and seasonings to taste. Mound on a serving plate and garnish with sour cream, finely minced sweet red or white onion and minced fresh parsley. Serve as an hors d'oeuvre with tortilla chips.

**KIDNEY, PINTO OR RED BEANS**
Moisten mashed cooked kidney, pinto or red beans with a little Quick Tomato Sauce. Heat and transfer to a shallow baking dish or ovenproof plate. Sprinkle generously with grated Monterey Jack cheese and bake in a preheated 400°F oven 5 minutes, or until cheese is melted. Garnish with slivers of black olive, sliced radishes and minced sweet red or white onion. Serve with tortilla chips.

**LIMA BEANS** Sauté minced onion and garlic in butter until soft. Combine with cooked lima beans, chopped walnuts, minced fresh chives or green onion tops, salt and freshly ground black pepper. Moisten with rich stock, transfer to a buttered shallow baking dish and sprinkle with grated or shredded firm or semifirm cheese and paprika. Bake in a preheated 350°F oven 20 minutes, or until heated through and cheese is melted.

**ANY BEANS** Add any cooked beans to enough rich lamb stock to make a soup and reheat with slivered cooked lamb roast (or shanks or blocks) and chopped cooked vegetables. Sprinkle with minced fresh oregano and serve with crusty bread as a main meal soup.

**ANY BEANS** Add to any pot of beans the last 30 minutes of cooking time chopped raw vegetables such as carrots, potatoes, turnips or rutabagas.

**ANY BEANS** Add to any pot of beans the last 15 minutes of cooking time vegetables such as chopped green or red bell pepper, Swiss chard or spinach and/or tomatoes, grated winter squash or carrots, or coarsely shredded potatoes.

*To save fuel, bring foods to room temperature before cooking.*

## IDEAS FOR TOFU

● Mash soft tofu with peanut butter, ripe bananas, fresh lemon juice and honey for a sandwich spread.

● Mash firm or soft tofu with olive oil, fresh lemon juice, Dijon-style mustard, minced garlic, salt, freshly ground white pepper and cayenne pepper. Serve as a dip for raw vegetables or crackers.

● Toss cubed firm tofu into green salads with chopped roasted peanuts.

● Substitute 2 to 4 tablespoons mashed soft tofu for 2 to 4 tablespoons of the milk in waffle or muffin batter.

● Add mashed firm or soft tofu to yeast breads for extra moisture and nutrients.

● Cut firm tofu into squares and heat in rich stock. Serve as a soup course garnished with minced fresh coriander or chives.

● Purée firm or soft tofu and add to tomato soup. Serve icy cold or reheat; sprinkle with minced fresh chives.

● Toss cubed firm tofu into Creole Sauce, heat and serve over rice.

• Mash firm or soft tofu, or crumble home-frozen tofu, and mix with soy sauce and minced green onions and tops (optional). Add to beaten eggs, mix well and scramble.

• Crumble home-frozen tofu into sautéed minced onions and garlic and add to cooked legumes for added protein.

• Add firm or soft tofu, lightly mashed, or home-frozen tofu, shredded, to meatloaf, hash or meat or fish casseroles.

• Stir fry cubed firm tofu and remove; then add to finished stir fry dish.

• Cut firm tofu into lengthwise slices 3/8 inch thick. Dip in egg beaten with a little soy sauce, then in a little flour or fine dry bread crumbs. Quickly brown on both sides in peanut oil and sprinkle with slivered green onions and tops.

• Arrange 1-inch squares of firm tofu and softened and slivered dried mushrooms in a ceramic or glass serving dish with sloping sides. Strew over the top minced bamboo shoots, water chestnuts, green onions and tops, garlic and ginger root and crushed seeded dried hot chili peppers. Drizzle soy sauce and a little Oriental sesame oil over. Steam over simmering water 10 minutes and serve over steamed rice.

## INDEX TO RECIPES

# VEGETABLES & FRUITS

The number of cultivated vegetables is so great, this section requires selective categories. Only the following vegetables are included: ones that often result in cooked leftovers, such as broccoli and green beans; those, like tomatoes and zucchini, of which there may be a garden surplus; the good candidates for planned leftovers, such as potatoes; leafy greens, mushrooms and others with a particularly short shelf life; and those that, when purchased, are of a size not always easily eaten in one meal, such as an eggplant or head of celery.

The vegetables are presented in alphabetical order, each with general information on selection. For those not used principally as seasonings, there are complementary seasoning and combination suggestions and a number of ideas for using the vegetable. Some entries also include Cooking Guidelines, methods of preparation that will result in leftover cooked vegetables that lend themselves to being combined with other ingredients in new dishes.

An Index to Recipes is included with those vegetables that frequently turn up as cooked leftovers and those that are particularly perishable, such as raw mushrooms and jarred or canned pimientos. Do not be limited by these indexes, for they contain only the *major* recipes and not the substantial number of recipe and ingredient substitution ideas that appear throughout the book. There are also a number of recipes for which a variety of vegetables, alone or in combination, are suitable: Vegetable Stock from Leftovers, Rich-Stock Suggestions, Grain and Root Vegetable Soup, Cream Soups from Cooked Vegetables, Stir Fry Meats and Vegetables, Creamed Vegetables, Croquettes, Cooked-Vegetable Purées and Vegetable Curry, to name a few. And don't forget that leftover cooked vegetables are good fillings for omelets, frittatas and savory pastries, can be made into

*Purée cooked vegetables and use as part of liquid measure in yeast bread doughs.*

a soufflé or dressed as a salad.

All vegetables are best when they are at their freshest. They should be picked or bought at the peak of their maturity and treated with care when storing, cooking and serving. Unless otherwise specified, store all vegetables, unwashed, in a plastic bag in the vegetable crisper of your refrigerator and use as soon as possible after purchase or harvest. Once cooked, most vegetables may be stored in a covered container in the refrigerator for no more than three days.

Most vegetables should be cooked until just tender. This preserves vitamins, minerals, flavor and texture. In general, steaming is the preferred method of cooking, though the obvious exceptions would be many of the root vegetables, such as beets, rutabagas, turnips and parsnips, which are most often boiled. Vegetables can be prepared as planned leftovers by simply removing a portion from the steaming basket or boiling water while they are still very firm. They are then perfect for adding to salads or to dishes in which they will be reheated.

You can freeze vegetables that have already been cooked, as well as those that are uncooked but are beginning to wilt in the refrigerator. To freeze cooked vegetables, store them as they are and then purée them once they are thawed, or, preferably, purée them before freezing. For uncooked vegetables, such as onions, mushrooms, lettuces and zucchini, chop them and sauté in butter and/or oil until barely tender; cool, pack in containers and freeze. Then, except for mushrooms, which can be defrosted and simply added as is, purée before using. Some uncooked vegetables— asparagus, corn, green beans, peas, snow peas, broccoli—may be blanched and then frozen. Slice or leave whole, immerse in boiling water one to two minutes, drain quickly and then immerse in ice water. Pat the vegetable dry before packing into freezer containers. For directions on how to freeze leafy greens, see the spinach entry.

All vegetables must be packed airtight before freezing, or they will crystallize and be ruined. Label and date them clearly and do not freeze too long, for most will quickly diminish in flavor and texture. See specific vegetables for suggested freezing methods and times.

# *Artichokes*

The sign of a fresh artichoke is a compact green head with tightly cupped leaves. When the artichoke is still on the stalk, a cold snap will sometimes cause the outer leaves to blacken and curl. Remove these leaves and the artichoke will still be quite good. If, however, the artichoke has turned a brownish or grayish color, do not buy it for it is past its prime. Although they appear hardy, artichokes quickly lose their moisture and the heads open if stored too long.

Artichoke hearts and bottoms are available in jars packed in oil or water, in cans and frozen. If you are fortunate enough to have a garden or to find very young artichokes (weighing less than one ounce) in your market, they can be trimmed, cooked and the whole heart eaten. The recipes in this book use hearts and bottoms packed in water or home cooked.

The best way to freeze cooked artichokes is to scrape the pulp from the leaves and mash it with the bottom. Store in an airtight container up to one month. The mashed pulp may then be puréed with stock and used as a base for soups or as the liquid for a cream sauce.

## COOKING GUIDELINES

**COMPLEMENTARY SEASONINGS AND COMBINATIONS** Oregano, bay, dill, chives, parsley, lemon, cream, blue and Parmesan cheese, garlic, shallots, onion, mushrooms, celery root, tomatoes, fish and seafood, chicken, lamb, veal.

**ARTICHOKES COOKED IN STOCK** For 4 good-size artichokes. Cut tough stems evenly off bottom of artichokes, then cut about 1 inch off of the tops. Pull off any unsightly outer leaves; with scissors, snip off 1/2 inch of the remaining leaf tips. As you work, place the artichokes in cold water to which lemon juice or vinegar has been added. (This acidulated water will prevent the artichokes from discoloring and chase out any bugs that may be trapped between the leaves.) Place the artichokes in their soaking water in the refrigerator 30 minutes to 1 hour.

Select a saucepan (never aluminum or iron) with a tight-fitting lid. The pan should be just large enough to hold the artichokes close together standing upright. In the saucepan, sauté 1/3 cup minced onion, 2 to 3 garlic cloves, minced, and 2 teaspoons minced fresh oregano in 2 tablespoons olive oil 5 minutes. Stand the trimmed artichokes in pan and add 2 teaspoons fresh lemon juice and stock (select one that will complement your entrée) to a depth of 2 inches. Spoon stock over artichokes and top each artichoke with a slice of lemon. Cover pan, bring stock to a boil, lower heat and cook gently, adding more stock as needed, 30 to 45 minutes. Artichokes are ready when leaves can easily be pulled off. Remove artichokes from saucepan and invert 3 minutes to allow excess moisture to drain off, then set upright on a serving plate. Strain the cooking liquid and reserve for poaching eggs, or for adding to soups, gravies or sauces.

## IDEAS FOR ARTICHOKES

● Spread cooked artichoke bottoms with Lemon Mayonnaise and top with a room-temperature poached egg; garnish with a dab of Lemon Mayonnaise and grind white pepper over. Serve as a luncheon dish.

● Stuff cooked artichoke bottoms with crab or shrimp salad, any Sandwich Salad Spread or Chicken Liver Pâté. Garnish with minced fresh parsley or freshly grated lemon rind.

*Cook your artichokes, topped with lemon slices, in the same pot as lamb or veal stew. The flavors blend beautifully and cooking fuel is saved.*

● Scrape pulp off cooked artichoke leaves and mash with the bottoms. Mix with softened cream cheese, fresh lemon juice, salt and freshly ground white pepper. Use as a sandwich filling, add to Light or Medium Cream Sauce for a soufflé, or add to cream soups.

● Cook minced shallots and garlic in olive oil 3 minutes. Stir in cooked artichoke hearts and heat. Add fresh lemon juice and toss in crumbled blue cheese. Heat just to melt cheese and sprinkle with minced fresh chives. Serve on Bread Fingers.

● Slice cooked artichoke bottoms and marinate with shredded raw or blanched celery root in Mustard Vinaigrette. Serve on lettuce leaves and garnish with wedges of ripe tomato.

● Make a frittata with diced cooked artichoke hearts or bottoms, grated Gruyère cheese and minced fresh basil. Sprinkle with minced fresh chives.

● Dice cooked artichoke bottoms and reheat in Light or Medium Cream Sauce made with fish stock, minced fresh chives, flaked cooked firm white fish and Seafood Seasoning. Serve in patty shells or on toasted English muffin halves.

● Surround lamb roast with cooked artichoke bottoms the last 15 minutes of roasting. Baste artichokes frequently with pan juices and serve as a garnish.

● Dice or slice cooked artichoke bottoms and heat in Mushroom or Quick Mushroom Sauce. Serve on toasted biscuit halves or cornbread slices with a garnish of lemon wedges and parsley sprigs.

## INDEX TO RECIPES

# *Asparagus*

Select asparagus spears that are straight, round, firm and with closely formed tips that show no sign of flowering. The spears should be evenly green almost to the end, and the cut stem should have a moist appearance. Asparagus should be eaten the same day they are purchased, but if this isn't possible, wrap the stem ends in a dampened terry towel before slipping the spears into a plastic bag for refrigeration.

When ready to cook, snap the ends from the asparagus where they break easily and lightly but thoroughly scrub the stalks with a vegetable brush and clear water to release any dirt trapped under the scales or in the tips. With a vegetable peeler or paring knife, remove the large scales and then lightly peel the lower portion of the stalk so that it will be tender when cooked. Now cook the asparagus, either steaming them whole or cutting into two-inch lengths on the diagonal and stir frying. Store cooked asparagus whole or puréed in an airtight container in the freezer no more than one month, then use as a purée in soups and sauces. Raw asparagus may be blanched and frozen up to one month.

COMPLEMENTARY SEASONINGS AND COMBINATIONS Marjoram, thyme, dill, tarragon, chervil, caraway seeds, sesame seeds, sunflower seeds, Brown Butter, lemon, cheese, hard-cooked eggs, mushrooms, tomatoes, sweetbreads, veal, ham, chicken, turkey.

## IDEAS FOR ASPARAGUS

● Arrange cooked asparagus spears on a bed of lettuce. Dress with Lemon Mayonnaise thinned with a little sour cream. Garnish with pimiento strips and chopped hard-cooked eggs.

● Toss cooked asparagus tips, sliced raw mushrooms rubbed with fresh lemon juice and low-fat cottage cheese into a green salad.

● Toss cooked asparagus tips in Mustard Vinaigrette made with fresh lemon juice and minced shallots. Serve on a bed of lettuce with carrot curls and minced fresh parsley.

● Purée cooked asparagus ends with chopped ripe tomatoes. Combine with enough rich chicken stock for a soup and season with minced fresh basil and freshly ground white pepper. Chill thoroughly, thin with half-and-half cream, if desired, and adjust seasonings with salt. Serve in chilled bowls with a sprinkling of minced fresh parsley and chives. Pass a bowl of Parmesan Croutons.

● Make a quiche with diagonally sliced cooked asparagus and julienned cooked veal sprinkled with fresh lemon juice, seasonings as desired and grated Gouda cheese. Follow directions for layered method in Basic Method for Quiches.

● Use whole cooked asparagus spears as crêpe filling. Prepare crêpes, wrapping around the asparagus spears. Line and blanket with Egg Cream Sauce and top with grated Gruyère cheese. (See Basic Method for Crêpes.)

• Arrange cooked asparagus spears in a buttered shallow baking dish. Cover with Cheese Sauce and sprinkle with shredded Havarti cheese and paprika. Bake in a preheated 375°F oven 15 minutes, or until bubbly and cheese is melted.

• Arrange cooked asparagus spears on toast or toasted English muffins. Top with a poached egg and sprinkle with shredded fontina cheese. Broil until cheese is melted.

• Sauté minced shallots in butter until soft. Toss in cooked asparagus tips, freshly grated Parmesan cheese and minced fresh parsley. Use as a filling for omelets. Top with sour cream.

## INDEX TO RECIPES

# Beets

Do not be attracted to the large beets at the market, for they can be quite woody. Select the smallest beets possible, with fresh-looking, evenly colored greens, if they are sold with the tops intact. The beet root itself should be firm and without wrinkles. Store in the refrigerator in a plastic bag up to seven days.

It is important never to cut into the flesh of the beet until it is cooked, for the beet will "bleed" as it is boiled and lose much of its distinctive coloring and flavor. Trim off all but one inch of the stem and boil the beets whole, then peel and trim before serving. The greens may be prepared in the same way as spinach. It is not recommended that you freeze cooked beets.

Seasonings and foods that combine well with beets are more limited than for most vegetables. The ideas included here cover the most popular flavorings and combinations.

## IDEAS FOR BEETS

• Hollow out tiny cooked beets, fill with any Sandwich Salad Spread and serve as an hors d'oeuvre or as a salad accompaniment.

• Julienne or dice cooked beets and dress with fresh lemon or lime juice, prepared horseradish, granulated sugar and salt.

• Julienne or slice cooked beets and use as a salad garnish with chopped hard-cooked eggs.

• Dice cooked beets and add to grain soups.

• Shred cooked beets, combine with shredded onion and apple and heat together gently.

• Julienne or slice cooked beets, heat gently in butter and sprinkle with poppy seeds, salt and freshly ground black pepper.

• Julienne or slice cooked beets, heat gently in butter and season with red wine or red wine vinegar, honey, ground allspice, freshly grated orange rind, salt and freshly ground black pepper.

• Julienne or slice cooked beets, heat gently in olive oil and season with ground cardamom, fresh lemon juice and minced fresh parsley.

## INDEX TO RECIPES

# *Broccoli*

Broccoli is high in selenium, a trace mineral important to proper diet, as well as vitamins A and C. Most of the broccoli available at the market is bluish green in color, though there are also strains of a purpler hue. Look for deep, rich color without any evidence of yellowing, tightly packed heads, and firm, green stalks with moist, solid stem ends. If harvesting from the garden, check for aphid colonies.

Cut off and discard only the tough ends of the stalks, then lightly peel away any coarse skin with a vegetable peeler or a paring knife. To assure even cooking, slit thick stalks from the bottom up to the top, or break the heads into flowerets and cut the stems into thin strips or slices. Broccoli can then be steamed or stir fried, but be sure to cook only until *barely* tender for the most flavorful result. If the leaves are small and tender, they may be cooked along with the stalks.

Cooked flowerets in a cream sauce may be frozen very briefly, or plain flowerets may be puréed and frozen up to one month. Raw broccoli may be blanched and frozen up to one month.

**COMPLEMENTARY SEASONINGS AND COMBINATIONS** Oregano, dill, garlic, ginger root, onion, Brown Butter, lemon, cheese, olive oil, sesame seeds, walnuts, almonds, hard-cooked eggs, cauliflower, water chestnuts, anchovy, salmon, firm white fish, chicken, turkey, veal, lamb, liver.

## IDEAS FOR BROCCOLI

● Sauté minced garlic in butter. Toss in chopped cooked broccoli, then add crumbled blue cheese, freshly grated Parmesan cheese and a little Crème Fraîche. Heat, tossing with a fork, until cheeses are melted. Quickly toss into freshly cooked pasta.

● Arrange cooked broccoli in a buttered shallow baking dish. Pour Light Cream Sauce or Cheese Sauce over, sprinkle with grated Gruyère cheese and bake in a preheated 375°F oven 15 minutes, or until bubbly.

● Toss chopped cooked broccoli with cooked pasta. Moisten with low-fat cottage cheese and transfer to a buttered shallow baking dish. Sprinkle with Parmesan Crumb Topping or Buttered Bread Crumbs, sprinkle with paprika and bake in a preheated 350°F oven 20 minutes, or until heated through.

● Make a quiche with small cooked broccoli flowerets and flaked cooked salmon, seasonings as desired and freshly grated Parmesan cheese. Follow directions for layered method in Basic Method for Quiches.

● Chop cooked broccoli or use tiny flowerets. Combine with slivered cooked ham as a filling for omelets. Top with Crème Fraîche or Basic Hollandaise.

● Substitute finely chopped cooked broccoli for the asparagus in Asparagus Timbales.

● Purée cooked broccoli and substitute for pumpkin in Pumpkin Crêpes.

● Substitute chopped cooked broccoli for the Swiss chard in Stuffed Egg Casserole.

## INDEX TO RECIPES

# *Cabbage*

Cabbages range in color from green to red to white, and in shape from round to cylindrical. The important things to remember when selecting any cabbage are that the head has a fresh and crisp look, a solid feel when pressed and is heavy in relation to its size. Do not buy very large heads for they may be too mature and have begun to go to seed. Also, check the stem end before purchase for signs of repeated trimming, the way some merchandisers try to save their produce.

There are many occasions when you will not use up a whole head of cabbage for a meal, and fortunately this vegetable is one of the sturdier ones. It will keep well for about a week if stored in plastic in the vegetable crisper. If the outer leaves have begun to wilt and discolor, discard them; the center of the head will probably remain good.

Chopped cooked cabbage can be frozen briefly, then added to vegetable soups. Be careful not to overcook when reheating.

---

*A little coarsely chopped celery added to brussels sprouts or cabbage water will reduce cooking odors.*

---

**COMPLEMENTARY SEASONINGS AND COMBINATIONS** Dill, basil, poppy seeds, onion, carrots, tomatoes, potatoes, sour cream, mayonnaise, vinaigrette, sugar and vinegar (sweet-sour), ham, bacon, sausage, corned beef.

## IDEAS FOR CABBAGE

- Finely shred raw white cabbage and use as a bed for serving deep-fried foods.

- Add chopped apples to your favorite cole slaw. Season with caraway or poppy seeds and minced fresh dill.

- Toss together 2 parts shredded raw white cabbage and 1 part shredded raw carrots. Dress with Sour Cream Dressing and toss in raisins. Serve on a bed of lettuce.

- Toss together equal parts shredded raw white cabbage and cut-up mixed fresh fruits. Dress with 2 parts plain yoghurt, 1 part fresh lemon or lime juice and honey to taste.

- Sauté sliced red onion in butter until soft. Toss in shredded raw white cabbage and sauté briefly. Add enough rich stock to make a soup, chopped ripe tomatoes and minced fresh basil. Bring to boil and cook just until cabbage is tender. Float Fried Bread on top and sprinkle with minced fresh chives.

- Cook shredded raw white cabbage, covered, in butter until just tender. Toss in cooked peas and sliced water chestnuts and reheat. Season with salt and freshly ground white pepper.

- Braise wedges of raw Napa cabbage and softened dried shiitake mushrooms in rich chicken stock. Arrange on platter and drizzle with oyster sauce.

- Sauté minced onions in butter. Add equal parts shredded cooked white cabbage and seasoned mashed potatoes and heat through; if mixture is too stiff, add sour cream or plain yoghurt to soften slightly. Transfer to a buttered shallow baking dish, cover with shredded Cheddar cheese and bake in a preheated 350°F oven 20 minutes, or until browned and cheese is melted.

---

## INDEX TO RECIPES

# Carrots

Among the most healthful of vegetables, carrots should be well shaped, firm and without cracks. In general, small carrots have better flavor and texture than large ones, so look for these at the market. If the carrots have been topped, look for a light-colored stem end; if the tops remain, they should have a fresh appearance. Carrots, like all root vegetables, keep well, but for optimal nutritional value they should be eaten as soon as possible after harvest or purchase.

Very young carrots need only be washed before cooking. More mature ones should also be scraped, but only very lightly or valuable vitamins will be lost. Puréed cooked carrots can be frozen up to six weeks, then made into a soup or added to cream sauces.

An Index to Recipes is not included here, as raw carrots keep well. If you have a good-size portion of leftover cooked carrots, make Carrot Puffs or creamed carrots (see Creamed Vegetables), or prepare the ideas that follow.

**COMPLEMENTARY SEASONINGS AND COMBINATIONS** Mint, thyme, rosemary, dill, tarragon, marjoram, bay, parsley, chives, cloves, cardamom, ginger, nutmeg, anise, mustard, celery salt, lemon, orange, white wine, poppy seeds, sesame seeds, raisins, celery root, potatoes, peas, cauliflower, meat stews and roasts.

## IDEAS FOR CARROTS

● Purée cooked carrots and add enough rich chicken stock to make a soup. Add fresh orange juice, ground ginger and cardamom, and freshly grated nutmeg and heat just to a boil. Season with salt and freshly ground white pepper and garnish with mint sprigs.

● Purée cooked carrots and cooked celery root and add enough rich chicken stock to make a soup. Add half-and-half cream to desired richness and season with minced fresh thyme. Heat just to a boil and garnish with chopped fresh parsley.

● Heat cooked carrots in Madeira wine mixed with beef extract.

● Mix carrot purée (see Cooked-Vegetable Purées) into mashed potatoes; season with prepared mustard.

● Combine julienned cooked carrots and cooked peas. Heat in butter and sprinkle with minced fresh dill.

● Heat julienned cooked carrots in butter and dry sherry until liquid evaporates. Season with salt and freshly ground white pepper and sprinkle with chopped fresh chives or chervil.

● Substitute puréed cooked carrots for Swiss chard in Swiss Chard Soufflé.

● Shred raw carrots into hot cooked rice or into mixture for meatloaf.

● Dice raw carrots and add to soups and stews.

● Parboil raw carrots and add to meats the last 30 minutes of roasting.

---

*When steaming a whole cauliflower, place a few lemon slices on top. Sprinkle fresh lemon juice over cauliflowerets as they steam.*

# *Cauliflower*

Creamy-colored, tightly packed heads of cauliflower are to be prized. Pass up heads with dark, smudgy-looking patches on the ivory "curds" and a feathery feel. Occasionally, you will come upon bright-colored varieties in purples and greens; try them for a pleasant change.

To cook cauliflower, remove the leaves and break the head into flowerets; if preparing whole, simply cut out the core. (The core may be cut in julienne and eaten raw, used as a substitute for water chestnuts, or prepared in the same way as celery root and sunchokes.) If you find you do not like the smell of whole cauliflower as it cooks, slip a few chunks of raw potato, several pieces of celery or slices of stale bread into the steaming water. This should reduce the odor. Cooked cauliflower may be puréed and frozen up to one month.

**COMPLEMENTARY SEASONINGS AND COMBINATIONS** Rosemary, tarragon, marjoram, savory, thyme, dill, parsley, chives, celery salt, nutmeg, curry powder, mustard, lemon, cheese, onion, garlic, mushrooms, bell peppers, shallots, tomatoes, peas, carrots, broccoli, hard-cooked eggs, ham, beef, liver, lamb, sausage, meatloaf, anchovy.

## IDEAS FOR CAULIFLOWER

● Heat cooked cauliflowerets in Light or Medium Cream Sauce with cooked peas and/or carrots. Sprinkle with minced fresh chives.

● Heat cooked cauliflowerets in a little rich stock and toss with crumbled blue cheese and minced fresh dill and parsley.

● Heat cooked cauliflowerets in butter and fresh lemon juice. Sprinkle with freshly grated nutmeg.

● Arrange cooked cauliflowerets in a buttered shallow baking dish. Strew with thin slices of cooked ham and sautéed sliced mushrooms. Pour a little rich stock over and top generously with Buttered Bread Crumbs. Bake in a preheated 350°F oven 15 minutes, or until heated through.

● Arrange cooked cauliflowerets in a buttered shallow baking dish and mask with Cheese Sauce or shredded fontina cheese. Sprinkle with paprika and bake in a preheated 350°F oven 15 minutes, or until heated through.

● Toss cooked cauliflowerets with cooked peas, minced fresh parsley and sliced almonds browned in butter. Cover and just heat through.

● Mash cooked cauliflower and add to gravies as a thickener, to Twice-baked Potatoes or to Potato Cakes.

● Heat sliced cooked sausages and cooked cauliflowerets in Creole Sauce. Garnish with finely minced green bell pepper and pass freshly grated Parmesan cheese.

● Marinate cooked cauliflowerets in Mustard Vinaigrette made with fresh lemon juice. Toss with slivered black olives, sliced pimientos and finely shredded sorrel. Mound on lettuce leaves and garnish with thin slices of green bell pepper.

● Sauté sliced onions and minced garlic in butter until soft. Add curry powder and cook, stirring, 2 minutes. Toss in cooked cauliflowerets, cover and heat through. Mix in chopped ripe tomato and fresh lemon juice and let stand, covered, 2 to 3 minutes before serving. Sprinkle with chopped roasted cashews.

## INDEX TO RECIPES

# Celery

Celery is principally a seasoning, but it is also good served raw, braised as a vegetable side dish, or added to mixed-vegetable stir fries. High in fiber and low in calories, it needs cool temperatures to stay fresh; buy it at the market only if it has been kept in a refrigerator case.

As large stems are generally woody and stringy, look for well-formed medium-size bunches with firm, evenly green stalks. If possible, buy bunches with the leaves intact. The leaves are good additions, either fresh or dehydrated, to soups, legumes and stews.

Puréed cooked celery may be frozen, but no more than three weeks, as it becomes quite watery. Because cooked celery is seldom a leftover, an Index to Recipes is not provided here. You will, however, find uncooked celery frequently sautéed as a seasoning in the recipes in this book. If you have a large quantity of raw celery in your refrigerator that has started to wilt, make Celery Broth, Cream of Celery Soup, Split Pea Soup, Turkey Soup with Oysters, or Basic Bread Stuffing, or chop the celery and boil it in rich stock thirty minutes, then strain, discard celery and use stock as you would

any stock. A few additional ideas for using celery follow.

## IDEAS FOR CELERY

● Stuff raw celery sticks with a mixture of crumbled blue cheese and softened butter. Sprinkle with minced fresh parsley and paprika.

● Slice raw celery on the diagonal and toss with crumbled feta or blue cheese, slivered black olives and flaked cooked salmon. Dress with Basic Vinaigrette made with fresh lemon juice.

● Blanch raw celery sticks and stuff with a mixture of sautéed minced onion and garlic, sliced mushrooms and slivered cooked ham combined with Seasoned Bread Crumbs. Place in a shallow baking dish, sprinkle with shredded Gouda cheese and paprika and bake in a preheated 350°F oven 15 minutes, or until heated through and cheese is melted.

● Slice raw celery on the diagonal and sauté with chopped onion and minced garlic. Place in a shallow baking dish, pour Tomato Sauce over, sprinkle with grated Cheddar cheese and bake in a preheated 350°F oven 15 minutes, or until heated through and cheese is melted.

# Corn

The fine, sweet flavor of garden-fresh corn begins to slip away the moment the ear is picked. The freshest corn will have very green husks, free-flowing silks and a moist stem end. Pull back a little of the husk and check the kernels. They should have a plump appearance, a nice clear yellow or white color and none of the cob visible between the rows.

The recipes in this book call for cooked corn in two forms, corn kernels and scraped corn. For corn kernels, stand the cooked ear of corn on a plate or shallow bowl, stem end down. With a sharp knife, cut three or four rows of kernels at a time from the ear, working from the top to the bottom and being careful not to cut too deeply. Separate kernels before using or freezing. For scraped corn, lay the cooked ear on a plate and, with a sharp knife, slit each row down the center, cutting about halfway through the kernels. Then stand the ear on a plate or shallow bowl stem end down and, with the back of a knife, scrape down the rows to remove any flesh and "milk." Corn kernels and scraped corn may be frozen up to three months. Uncooked corn on the cob may be blanched and frozen up to two months.

Coarsely ground dried corn is called hominy; when medium ground, it is grits and when finely ground, cornmeal. In many cases, the corn germ, source of many vitamins and minerals, is removed from dried corn products during processing. Look for packaging that specifies "nondegerminated" for products in which the corn germ is retained. You can buy just the corn germ in natural-foods stores. Its crunchy texture is a nice addition to breakfast cereals or the germ can be soaked overnight in milk and served alone as a cereal. Corn germ is also good mixed into pilafs, ground beef mixtures and baked bean dishes.

## COOKING GUIDELINES

**COMPLEMENTARY SEASONINGS AND COMBINATIONS** Sage, oregano, parsley, chives, nutmeg, curry powder, granulated sugar, mustard, Worcestershire sauce, capers, cheese, hard-cooked eggs, onion, garlic, tomatoes, pimientos, lima beans, bell peppers, black olives, pimiento-stuffed olives, ham, ground beef, liver, pork, lamb, barbecued chicken.

**BARBECUED CORN** If corn is very fresh, soak unhusked ears of corn in water several hours. Turning often, cook on barbecue grill over medium hot coals 20 to 30 minutes until just tender. The resulting flavor precludes the use of butter.

**STEAMED CORN** Shuck ears of corn and place stem end down in large steamer. Bring water in steamer to a boil and start timing at this point. Check after 3 minutes and continue steaming until barely tender. Line a serving platter with a towel, remove ears of corn to towel and bring towel up and around corn. Corn will continue to cook until cool enough to eat, so do not overcook.

**BOILED CORN** If corn is old, bring 1/2 teaspoon granulated sugar and equal parts milk and water to a rapid boil. (Watch carefully; if pot is covered the mixture will boil over when you turn your back.) Add shucked corn ears, bring back to boil and cook 3 minutes, or until tender. Alternately, add corn, bring back to boil, cover and remove from heat. Let stand until corn is tender.

## IDEAS FOR CORN

● Simmer cooked scraped corn and grated onion in milk until very soft. Combine with Light Cream Sauce made with rich chicken stock and thin to soup consistency with half-and-half cream. Season with crumbled dried sage or freshly grated nutmeg, salt and freshly ground white pepper. Serve with a sprinkling of minced fresh parsley and chives.

● Heat cooked scraped corn in half-and-half cream until cream has thickened. Toss in chopped pimientos, reheat and toss in slivered black olives.

● Heat cooked scraped corn with cooked lima beans or cut-up green beans in butter. Sprinkle with finely minced red bell pepper and minced fresh oregano.

● Sauté minced onions and garlic in butter until soft. Sprinkle with curry powder and cook, stirring, 2 minutes. Toss in cooked scraped corn and reheat. Add beaten eggs, scramble and garnish with finely chopped ripe tomato.

---

*Older corn has fewer natural sugars; add a little sugar to the cooking water.*

● Heat cooked corn kernels in Creole Sauce and serve over hot rice with freshly grated Parmesan cheese.

● Sauté minced onion and garlic in butter until soft. Toss in cooked corn kernels, add Worcestershire sauce and half-and-half cream and reheat. Garnish with halved cherry tomatoes.

● Layer sliced ripe tomatoes, cooked corn kernels and sautéed minced onion and garlic in a buttered shallow baking dish, sprinkling each layer with salt, freshly ground black pepper and a little granulated sugar. Top with Buttered Bread Crumbs and bake in a preheated 350°F oven 25 minutes, or until heated through.

● Mix into 1 cup cheese grits 1 egg, lightly beaten, 1 cup shredded sharp Cheddar cheese and cayenne pepper. Lightly press into a shallow dish and refrigerate overnight. Cut into bite-size squares and coat lightly with flour. Deep fry in hot peanut oil until golden. Drain on crumpled paper toweling and serve at once as an hors d'oeuvre.

● Sauté minced onion and garlic in butter until soft and combine with cooked corn kernels, crumbled meatloaf, finely minced fresh oregano and Tomato Sauce to bind. Use as a filling for cannelloni or crêpes. Fill as directed in Basic Method for Crêpes, lining and blanketing with Cheddar Cheese Sauce. Top with ripe tomato slices and shredded Monterey Jack cheese.

● Combine cooked scraped corn or corn kernels with cooked wheat or triticale berries, chopped ripe tomato and rich stock to moisten. Heat, sprinkle with shredded bel paese cheese, cover and cook until cheese is melted. Sprinkle with minced fresh chives.

● Substitute scraped corn (drained if very milky) for the asparagus in Asparagus Timbales.

● Combine cooked corn kernels with finely minced celery, green onion and tops, green bell pepper and fresh parsley. Toss in chopped hard-cooked eggs and Mustard Mayonnaise. Season with Worcestershire sauce, salt and freshly ground black pepper. Chill, mound into lettuce cups and garnish with drained capers.

## INDEX TO RECIPES

# Eggplant

The two varieties of eggplant most commonly sold in the market are the globe and the long, slender Japanese type, both with shiny, purple skin. There are many other varieties—large and small, snow-white, variegated green-and-white, and lavender—but they are usually only found in areas with large Asian populations.

Eggplants should be firm and without blemishes. Once bruised, they will spoil rapidly, so select carefully and store well protected for as short a time as possible. Do not attempt to freeze cooked eggplant, as it becomes watery and loses flavor.

## COOKING GUIDELINES

**COMPLEMENTARY SEASONINGS AND COMBINATIONS** Thyme, marjoram, oregano, basil, bay, chervil, turmeric, pine nuts, Greek olives, red wine vinegar, mozzarella, Parmesan and Romano cheeses, garlic, onion, spinach, zucchini, tomatoes, pork, lamb, ground beef or lamb.

If not steaming eggplant for a specific recipe, prepare by one of the following suggestions for best use as a leftover. You may salt the slices before cooking to draw out some of the moisture so that the eggplant will not absorb as much cooking oil. Sprinkle paper toweling with salt, place eggplant slices on salt, sprinkle salt over and top with paper toweling. Let stand 30 minutes, patting the toweling so it will absorb the moisture. Brush and pat as much salt as possible off the slices and decrease the salt in the recipe in which you use the eggplant.

**BROILED EGGPLANT** Slice peeled or unpeeled eggplant 3/8 inch thick and salt, if desired. Place slices on a baking sheet liberally brushed with Garlic Olive Oil. Brush slices with more oil and sprinkle with seasonings as desired. Broil 5 inches from heat until just tender. Alternately, brush slices with oil and spread each slice with commercial or Basic Mayonnaise. Sprinkle with freshly grated Parmesan cheese and paprika, seasonings and Buttered Bread Crumbs or with Parmesan Crumb Topping. Broil 5 inches from heat, or until eggplant slices are just tender.

**SAUTEED EGGPLANT** Slice eggplant as for broiling, and salt, if desired. Dip slices into egg beaten with a little fresh lemon juice, then in fine Seasoned Bread Crumbs that have been mixed with freshly grated Parmesan cheese, if desired. Sauté quickly in butter and olive

oil, turning once to brown both sides. (For a luncheon or entrée dish you may sandwich thin slices of provolone cheese and proscuitto or mortadella between 2 eggplant slices and then treat the "sand-wiches" as for sautéed eggplant.)

## IDEAS FOR EGGPLANT

● Heat broiled eggplant slices in Creole Sauce. Top with grated Cheddar cheese and broil to melt cheese.

● Arrange broiled eggplant slices in a shallow flameproof dish. Top with hot spinach purée (see Cooked-Vegetable Purées), sprinkle with freshly grated Parmesan cheese and paprika and broil briefly until cheese is melted.

● Moisten cooked brown rice with Tomato Sauce and heat. Toss in julienned cooked pork and plain broiled eggplant slices, cut into strips. Sprinkle with grated mozzarella cheese, cover and cook until heated through and cheese is melted. Sprinkle with minced fresh parsley.

• Chop broiled eggplant and heat in a little olive oil with minced garlic, chopped ripe tomato, chopped fresh basil and pine nuts. Toss into freshly cooked pasta and serve with freshly grated Parmesan cheese.

• Combine chopped cooked eggplant with other chopped cooked vegetables of choice, chopped ripe tomatoes, minced onion and garlic and seasonings. In a shallow baking dish, make a thin layer of vegetable mixture, top with a layer of cooked millet and sprinkle with grated mozzarella cheese. Repeat layers several times, ending with a cheese layer. Bake in a preheated 350°F oven 20 minutes, or until heated through and cheese is melted.

• Layer cooked eggplant slices in a shallow baking dish brushed with Garlic Olive Oil. Cover with Light or Medium Cream Sauce made with chicken stock and sea-

soned with freshly grated nutmeg. Sprinkle with Parmesan Crumb Topping and bake in a preheated 350°F oven 20 minutes, or until bubbly.

• Cook minced onion, garlic and fresh rosemary and oregano, covered, in olive oil until onion is soft. Sprinkle with curry powder and enough unbleached flour to absorb most of the oil. Cook, stirring, 2 to 3 minutes. Gradually stir in equal parts milk and chicken stock to make a smooth, slightly thickened soup liquid. Add chopped cooked eggplant and simmer 15 minutes. Purée mixture in blender or food processor. (If eggplant is unpeeled, force through a sieve and discard skins.) Add heavy cream, if desired, and reheat. Adjust seasonings with salt and freshly ground black pepper and sprinkle with minced fresh parsley.

## INDEX TO RECIPES

# Green Beans

The flat Kentucky Wonder and the round Blue Lake are both green snap beans, more commonly called simply green beans. The older term, string beans, is less frequently encountered, as most green beans have been hybridized to the point that they no longer have strings that must be removed. Green beans are best when about five to six inches in length and are usually cooked whole. More mature green beans should be cut in half lengthwise, snapped or cut into pieces, or cut thinly on the diagonal for cooking.

The Italian or Romano bean is a wide, flat relative, best when about five inches long. The Chinese long bean, in contrast, reaches about a foot in length. These long beans are round like the Blue Lake, but thinner, and have a unique texture and flavor. Try them cut in lengths and stir fried.

All green beans should be crisp, pliable and have good color. If very fresh when purchased, they can be stored in the refrigerator up to five days. To freeze uncooked beans, blanch and store up to one month. Purée cooked beans and freeze no more than one month, then defrost and use in soups.

*Never salt green beans until after they are cooked or they will toughen. Top with a sprig of savory (or sprinkle with a dash of ground savory) before steaming.*

**COMPLEMENTARY SEASONINGS AND COMBINATIONS** Rosemary, thyme, dill, tarragon, fennel, sorrel, parsley, oregano, savory, lemon, cayenne pepper, walnuts, almonds, sesame and sunflower seeds, onion, garlic, cheese, mushrooms, water chestnuts, bamboo shoots, hard-cooked eggs, any meats or poultry.

## IDEAS FOR GREEN BEANS

● Heat cooked green beans in butter and toss with toasted sesame seeds and a few drops of Oriental sesame oil.

● Heat cooked green beans in butter with minced fresh rosemary. Top with freshly grated Parmesan cheese.

● Toss cooked green beans with chopped hard-cooked eggs and chopped walnuts. Heat briefly in olive oil with mashed garlic, crushed fresh rosemary, salt and freshly ground white pepper.

● Heat cooked green beans in Basic Vinaigrette, letting the dressing boil away. Sprinkle with minced fresh parsley.

● Sauté minced onion and garlic in butter until soft. Toss in cooked green beans, freshly grated Parmesan or Romano cheese, minced fresh dill and parsley, sour cream, salt, freshly ground white pepper and cayenne pepper. Heat briefly and serve with extra grated cheese.

● Add sliced cooked beans to mashed potato for Potato Cakes.

● Toss cooked green beans and chopped raw fennel and tops into melted butter. Heat, sprinkle with shredded fontina cheese, cover and cook until cheese is melted. Sprinkle with minced fresh parsley.

● Reheat cooked green beans in Tomato Cheese Sauce or Mushroom Sauce. Serve on cooked flat noodles.

● Sauté chopped onion, white of leek and minced garlic in rendered chicken fat and/or butter until soft. Add cut-up cooked Italian (Romano) green beans and a sprinkling of fennel seeds. Cook, stirring, several minutes, then add enough rich chicken stock to make a soup. Cover and simmer 15 minutes. Purée and reheat with equal parts milk and half-and-half cream, sour cream, salt and freshly ground white pepper. Serve garnished with minced fennel feathers or parsley and chives.

● Simmer cooked green beans in enough rich lamb stock to make a soup 20 minutes. Purée and cool. Add sour cream thinned with a little half-and-half cream to bean purée. Season with fresh lemon juice, ground savory and freshly ground white pepper. Chill thoroughly, adjust seasonings and garnish with lemon slices and tiny parsley leaves.

● Toss cooked green beans in Mustard Vinaigrette and refrigerate several hours. Just before serving, toss with toasted sesame seeds, chopped hard-cooked eggs and chopped ripe tomato. Mound on lettuce leaves and garnish with strips of pimiento.

## INDEX TO RECIPES

# *Greens*

There are a number of leafy green vegetables, all very nutritious, that can be handled in much the same way as spinach. These include collard, mustard, turnip, dandelion and beet greens, as well as the more delicate watercress and sorrel. Look for evenly colored, small, tender-looking leaves and freshly cut stems.

Remove the central rib from large-leaved greens, as they will not become tender when cooked. Fold the leaf in half and, with a single lengthwise cut, slice away the rib. Old greens and the larger varieties benefit from cooking in rich stock, as the stock will improve their sometimes bitter flavor. Young, tender greens may be coarsely cut or left whole and sautéed, cooked as for spinach, or steamed. Never cook any green in aluminum or cast iron and never overcook them; they easily lose their distinctive flavor and texture. Some sharp-flavored greens, like mustard, are enhanced by the addition of bacon drippings or salt pork to the cooking pot.

In general, these leafy green vegetables should be stored in the same way as spinach, both uncooked and cooked and frozen. Watercress, however, should be kept in the refrigerator with the stems sub-merged in water and the "bouquet" loosely covered with damp paper toweling.

Sorrel has a wonderful lemony flavor, and though many people consider it only an herb, its leaves can be used in soups, salads, egg dishes, fish dishes and sauces. Rarely found in the market, sorrel will flourish in the home garden in frost-free climates.

Since many of these greens can be prepared in the same manner as spinach, see that entry for ideas and for specific recipes in this book using cooked greens. Ideas for sorrel and watercress, the least widely used of the greens discussed here, follow.

## IDEAS FOR SORREL

● Finely chop raw sorrel leaves and drop into boiling rich chicken stock. Cook until tender, then bind with Egg Yolk Binder with or without half-and-half cream.

● Chop or shred small raw sorrel leaves, steep in cider vinegar, drain and add to melted butter. Use for cooking fish, scrambling eggs or in hot potato salad.

● Finely mince raw sorrel leaves and sauté with finely minced onions in butter. Use to fill Rolled Omelets.

● Add raw sorrel leaves to Bread Stuffing for Fish.

● Add whole raw sorrel leaves to spinach or other greens while they are cooking.

● Add small or shredded raw sorrel leaves to tossed salad.

● Chop raw sorrel leaves, add to seasoned Light Cream Sauce and bind with Egg Yolk Binder. Spoon on poached eggs.

## IDEAS FOR WATERCRESS

● Mince raw watercress, add to Potato Cream Soup (see Cream Soups from Cooked Vegetables) and heat slowly until flavors blend and watercress is tender. Garnish with tender leaves.

● Heat rich chicken stock with watercress sprigs and diced tofu (bean curd) until watercress is tender. Season with salt and white pepper.

● Mince raw watercress leaves and mix into beaten eggs for omelet.

● Mince raw watercress leaves and mix into fruit salads.

● Add chopped raw watercress leaves to Waldorf salad.

# *Lettuces*

The wide variety of lettuces can be divided into four basic types: the tightly wrapped, round, crisp head known as iceberg, the elongated head of narrow leaves called Romaine or cos, the loosely packed, small, round butter types—Boston, Bibb and limestone—and the loose leaf, nonhead types, such as red and salad bowl.

Buy lettuce that is very fresh looking. Iceberg should be quite firm, well shaped and with crisp outer leaves. The butter heads are best when they have a puffy, waxy look and firm leaves, while Romaine should be tightly bunched. Never buy lettuce that shows any sign of wilting or is the least bit slimy to the touch.

If the lettuce from the market is quite damp, stuff a few paper towels into the plastic bag it came in before storing in the refrigerator. Ideally, wash lettuce a few hours before serving, especially if it is to be used in a salad. Rinse the leaves with tepid water, dry by shaking off as much of the water as possible, wrap in a terry towel and put in a plastic bag. (Iceberg lettuce need have only the exterior leaves well washed, since the tightly packed head does not trap dirt.)

If lettuce has begun to wilt in the refrigerator, chop it coarsely, sauté in a little butter and then freeze up to one month. Once thawed, it can be puréed and used in soups or combined with another vegetable purée and served as a side dish.

Lettuce is generally seasoned in accordance with what it accompanies. Most of the lettuce varieties are mild flavored and take well to almost any seasoning and combine favorably with almost any food, so Complementary Seasonings and Combinations have not been included here. Lettuce is used throughout the book, principally as a base for other foods, so an Index to Recipes does not appear.

## IDEAS FOR LETTUCES

● Finely shred iceberg lettuce and use as a bed for deep-fried foods or as a garnish for clear or cream soups.

● Cook raw lettuce in rich stock, purée and combine with puréed cooked peas; season with salt and freshly ground black pepper and serve as a side dish with dollops of Crème Fraîche.

● Shred raw firm lettuce and add to peas as they cook.

● Use firm lettuce leaves, lightly blanched, for the cabbage leaves in Dolmas.

● Sauté very finely minced raw lettuce in butter, then whip into mashed potatoes.

● Make a Chiffonade of lettuce, or lettuce and sorrel and/or spinach.

● Cut raw iceberg lettuce into 2-inch pieces and stir fry in peanut oil just until wilted. Transfer to a serving plate and drizzle with oyster sauce.

● Sauté minced garlic and celery thinly sliced on the diagonal in rendered chicken fat and/or butter, covered, until celery is almost tender. Add shredded raw red leaf or other leaf lettuce and shredded sorrel. Cook, stirring, several minutes and add enough rich chicken or veal stock to make a soup. Cover, bring to gentle boil and cook 2 to 3 minutes. Season with fresh lemon juice, salt and freshly ground white pepper. Bring back to boil and, with a fork, beat in 1 egg beaten with 1 egg yolk and a little fresh lemon juice. Stirring constantly, cook until egg is set. Garnish with tiny celery leaves and dollops of sour cream.

# *Mushrooms*

Ideally, standard commercial mushrooms, whether light brown, white or golden, have close-fitting caps protecting the segmented underside, or gills, of the fungus. The cap holds in the moisture, resulting in a firmer, more flavorful mushroom. Never soak fresh mushrooms in water to clean them. Simply whisk with a soft-bristled brush or wipe with a dampened towel.

Exotic varieties of mushrooms, such as the shiitake of the Orient, can now be found fresh in some markets. Treat them gently, as you would any mushroom, and use them as soon as possible after purchase, for moisture will be lost in storage.

Mushroom stems are packed with flavor. If a recipe calls for only the caps, save the stems for adding to soups, stocks and sauces. To freeze mushrooms for adding to a sauce, slice them and then sauté with a little chopped green onion in butter until barely tender, adding some white wine or Brown Sauce for moisture. Freeze no more than six weeks.

Because sometimes a few mushrooms remain in the vegetable crisper, the ideas and index that follow will help you use up both raw and cooked mushrooms.

**COMPLEMENTARY SEASONINGS AND COMBINATIONS** Oregano, dill, bay, ginger, nutmeg, savory, paprika, marjoram, thyme, parsley, chives, saffron, cayenne pepper, lemon, vermouth, dry white wine, caraway seeds, shallots, sorrel, garlic, onion, peas, broccoli, spinach, tomatoes, celery, hard-cooked eggs, cheese, sour cream, sweetbreads, ham, poultry, meatloaf, ground beef, steak, veal, clams.

## IDEAS FOR MUSHROOMS

● Sauté sliced raw mushrooms with minced shallots in olive oil. Squeeze fresh lemon juice over and sprinkle with freshly ground black pepper. Toss into cooked pasta and sprinkle with minced fresh parsley.

● Top Fried Bread with minced sautéed mushrooms mixed with spinach purée (see Cooked-Vegetable Purées), then with a poached egg. Mask with Light Cream Sauce made with chicken stock and sprinkle with a little freshly grated nutmeg. Serve as a luncheon dish.

● Cook quartered raw mushrooms, covered, in butter with minced shallots until starting to soften, then until moisture has boiled away. Stir in a pinch of saffron mixed with dry white wine and heavy cream, cook until blended and season with salt and freshly ground white pepper to taste.

● Dip halved raw mushrooms in Beer Batter, deep fry until golden, drain on crumpled paper toweling and serve immediately on a bed of shredded lettuce or daikon.

● Combine chopped raw mushroom stems and minced shallots sautéed in butter with chopped cooked sorrel and Light Cream Sauce made with chicken stock. Mound mixture into raw mushroom caps brushed with fresh lemon juice, top with Buttered Bread Crumbs and bake in a preheated 400°F oven 10 to 15 minutes until mushrooms are just tender and top is browned. Serve as an hors d'oeuvre or a luncheon dish.

*To soften dried mushrooms, soak in warm water 10 minutes, drain and use as directed, discarding tough stems. Save water for adding to soups and stews.*

• Make a quiche with cooked sliced mushrooms, sautéed minced onion and garlic, chopped cooked broccoli, seasonings as desired and grated Gruyère cheese. Follow directions for layered method in Basic Method for Quiches.

• Combine minced or chopped cooked mushrooms, minced shallots sautéed in butter, cooked peas and freshly grated Parmesan cheese as a filling for omelets. Top with sour cream and minced fresh chives.

• Rub sliced raw mushrooms with fresh lemon juice and toss into spinach or tossed salad just before serving.

• Marinate blanched mushrooms in Mustard Vinaigrette at least 2 hours. Mound in lettuce cups and top with sliced hard-cooked eggs and pimiento strips.

## INDEX TO RECIPES

# *The Onion Family*

Onions may be red, white or yellow, mild, hot or sweet, globe or elongated. Before you buy, ask your produce man to describe the various onions available, for color and shape are not consistent indicators of flavor or pungency. Select only those onions that are firm, dry and without soft spots or dark patches. Beware of sale onions packaged in plastic or mesh bags; they are likely to spoil rapidly. Store onions in a cool, dry place, away from your potatoes, or they will take on moisture and spoil. If you have a cut onion, store in a plastic bag on the refrigerator shelf rather than in the too-moist environment of the vegetable crisper. Chop extra onions, sauté in a little butter and freeze up to two months; add them to soups and stews. Onions may also be chopped and dehydrated to make onion flakes (see Dehydrating Vegetables and Fruits).

Leeks should have very white bulbs and bright green tops. Buy medium-size ones, as they are more tender than the large ones. Usually one cooks only the white bulb, and occasionally a little of the tender green. Do not, however, cut off all of the greens or the root ends until you are ready to cook the leeks, for they will not keep as well once they are trimmed. Leeks may be stored in plastic in the refrigerator up to one week, or frozen in the same way as onions.

Also called scallions and bunching onions, green onions are young onion plants that are harvested while the tops are still green and the bulbs about a half-inch in diameter. The green tops are quite tender and are frequently used cooked and raw. Store green onions in plastic in the refrigerator up to one week; if the greens begin to spoil, strip them off and discard. The white bulbs may be frozen as for onions, while fresh green tops may be left whole, sheet frozen raw and then transferred to an airtight container and frozen up to one month. Chop the greens and add to any cooked dishes for seasoning. Green onions may also be dehydrated.

Chives are an unusual member of the onion family because they are grown only for their green tops. The common variety is a very thin rod, while the Chinese chive has a flat leaf and a hint of garlic flavor. Chives are perishable and should be used as soon as possible after picking, or they may be sheet frozen as for green onion tops. They can be easily grown in the home garden.

Shallots come in pink, gray and golden-brown varieties. They are delicate and sweet and enhance the flavor of other ingredients. Stored in a cool, dry place, they will keep several months. Shallots are especially good in sauces, but be careful when cooking, for if they brown too much they become bitter. If you are growing your own shallots, use the green tops as you would green onion tops. Clip off only the top third of the greens, or the underground shallot cluster will not mature properly.

Garlic imparts a distinctive flavor and aroma that are irresistible to those who like this versatile relative of the onion. Select good-size heads with large cloves and papery skins. To facilitate peeling, firmly hit the clove with the flat side of a knife blade to "pop open" the skin. Garlic will keep in a cool, dry place up to three months, or freeze unpeeled cloves (separated) in an airtight container two to three weeks.

Since all of the members of the onion family are used principally as seasonings and all store well, they are seldom in the ranks of leftovers. They are, however, important to the task of enhancing leftovers.

*Long cooking rids garlic of its odor and sharp taste.*

# *Peas*

Choose fresh peas in small, slender, vibrant-green pods. Pods that appear full to the point of bursting are too mature and the peas will not have the best flavor or the desirable crisp texture. Always store peas unshelled and never for too long a time.

Fresh peas are irresistible, raw and cooked. They can add texture, color and flavor to a variety of dishes. On occasion, however, you may find yourself buying frozen peas because of ease of preparation or the absence of fresh ones in the market. Frozen peas are superior to most other frozen vegetables and are good for making soups, purées and vegetable side dishes, and for adding to salads. Buy frozen peas in heavy-duty plastic bags rather than the paper-wrapped packages, as the peas often crystallize in the latter. To avoid having half a package deteriorate on the freezer shelf, look to the ideas that follow for interesting ways to use them.

Never put frozen peas in boiling water to cook them. Just heat them with a little butter in a shallow skillet until they are barely tender. Thawed peas can be added without cooking to most of the recipes in this book, especially if they are petite peas.

To freeze cooked peas, put them in a covered container whole or puréed and store up to two months. To freeze raw peas, blanch briefly and freeze up to one month.

A second type of pea is eaten pod and all. The two most common varieties are the Chinese pea pod or snow pea and the sugar pea. Snow peas are very flat and the seeds quite small, while sugar peas are much rounder. Purchase both varieties only when they are very crisp and bright green.

**COMPLEMENTARY SEASONINGS AND COMBINATIONS** Basil, marjoram, rosemary, savory, tarragon, thyme, mint, chives, celery salt, garlic, onion, mushrooms, tomatoes, almonds, rice, ham, chicken, turkey, lamb, pork, liver.

*Pack frozen peas into a jar. Good snack for preschoolers on car trips.*

## IDEAS FOR PEAS

Use cooked fresh peas or uncooked (defrosted) frozen peas to prepare the following ideas.

● Add peas to potato salad; season with chopped fresh mint.

● Cook shredded lettuce in butter, covered, until barely tender. Toss in peas and minced cooked carrots (optional). Heat briefly and sprinkle with minced fresh chives.

● Heat peas, slivered cooked ham and softened and slivered dried mushrooms in a little rich stock. Toss into cooked millet, bulghur or rice pilaf (see Grain Pilaf).

● Add peas to Fresh Tomato Sauce, heat and toss into cooked pasta. Serve with freshly grated Parmesan cheese.

● Add peas to scalloped or creamed potatoes when reheating.

● Heat together Light Cream Sauce made with chicken or turkey stock, cooked small thin-skinned potatoes, cooked pearl onions and peas. Stir in minced fresh parsley and chives.

● Stir fry peas with diced tofu (bean curd), or add to Tofu in Brown Bean Sauce and heat briefly.

● Add peas to a chopped or sliced cucumber and sour cream side dish; season with minced fresh dill.

● Toss peas with minced celery, chopped black olives, fresh lemon juice, minced fresh thyme and freshly grated Parmesan cheese. Serve in lettuce cups.

● Toss peas into rice, pasta or green salads.

● Toss peas with chopped green onions and tops and moisten with Lemon Mayonnaise. Serve in lettuce cups with halved cherry tomatoes and a sprinkling of fresh basil.

## INDEX TO RECIPES

# *Peppers*

Bell peppers are green when young and turn red as they mature. The red ones are prized for their sweeter flavor and greater concentration of vitamins A and C. Select firm, deep-colored peppers; never buy ones without full color, and always check that the stem end has not begun to soften. In general, bell peppers are used for adding color and flavor to dishes or for stuffing, though they may also be sliced, sautéed in olive oil, seasoned with lemon juice and served as a side dish. You need not be fussy about the shape of peppers that you cut up for a recipe, but you will need broad-bowled, well-formed ones for stuffing.

Chili peppers come in a whole range of shapes, sizes, colors and degrees of hotness. Use caution when working with them, as they can burn your skin, and always wash your hands immediately after handling them. If using canned chili peppers, store the unused peppers in a covered container in the refrigerator up to one week. Look for the same qualities in fresh chili peppers as in bell peppers. They may be minced or chopped for seasoning, or blistered over an open flame, peeled and stuffed.

Fresh pimiento peppers are nearly impossible to find in the market, so you will need to rely on pimientos available in jars or cans. Once opened, store no more than one week in the refrigerator, discarding at once if any sign of mold appears.

Because peppers, like onion and celery, are used principally as seasonings, no ideas or Index to Recipes follows for fresh peppers. An Index to Recipes for pimientos is included, however, because a half can or jar often remains in the refrigerator. If you have only a *very small* amount of pimientos, use them as a salad garnish. They add color and a tart flavor.

## INDEX TO RECIPES

# *Potatoes*

Potatoes are usually categorized as being either thick skinned or mature, or thin skinned or immature (the latter are often referred to as "new potatoes" as well). The mature potato is generally used for baking and frying and is usually peeled, while the immature ones are ideal for boiling and steaming, though they make excellent scalloped potatoes as well. Buy thin-skinned potatoes that are firm and well formed. They will have a slightly waxy consistency and moist flesh and should never be peeled. Thick-skinned potatoes are drier. They should be evenly shaped and without any flaking skin, breaks in the flesh or sprouts beginning to form. Never purchase a potato that has green patches on the skin, for it will have a sharp, unpleasant taste and may be poisonous. Also, avoid buying potatoes that have been sprayed with water to keep them fresh looking; the dampness shortens their shelf life.

Always store potatoes in a cool, dark, dry place; the thick-skinned ones will keep well up to one month, while thin-skinned potatoes are best cooked within ten days. Never store potatoes in a closed plastic bag or in the refrigerator, and never wash them until you are ready to cook them. Mashed potatoes, if they are to be used in a casserole, may be frozen up to two weeks; defrost and then beat the potatoes to return them to a smooth consistency. Do not freeze other cooked potatoes, as they become watery.

Cooking Guidelines follow, but seasonings and foods that complement potatoes are not included. Almost any seasoning enhances potatoes and, because they combine well with almost any food, use seasonings that complement the entrée or other foods the potatoes will accompany.

## COOKING GUIDELINES FOR MASHED POTATOES

Thick-skinned potatoes are best for mashing. To retain as many nutrients as possible, do not peel until after they are cooked. For 4 servings, slice 6 medium thick-skinned potatoes into thick slices and place in a large saucepan. Add water to barely cover and add for flavor a chunk of onion, a piece of celery and some leaves, a lightly mashed garlic clove, a bay leaf and/or herb sprigs such as oregano. (Alternately, these flavorings may be heated with the milk or cream

that will be stirred into the mashed potatoes.) Cover saucepan and bring water to a boil, lower heat slightly and cook until potatoes are soft. Drain, reserving the cooking water for yeast breads, cream sauces or soups.

Ricing the potatoes will result in fluffier and lighter mashed potatoes and the skins will remain in the ricer or food mill, saving the task of peeling. If mashing with a potato masher, quickly peel the potatoes before mashing. (Do not use a blender or food processor to mash the potatoes as they will become sticky and gummy.) With a fork, beat about 3 tablespoons softened butter into the riced or mashed potatoes, and then beat in about 1/2 cup heated milk or half-and-half cream, or half rich stock and half milk or cream. Season with salt, freshly ground white pepper and ground herbs. At this point grated vegetables such as raw carrots, cooked shredded cabbage or zucchini, or other bits of cooked foods may be added. If not serving at once, keep warm 10 to 15 minutes over a pan of hot water.

## IDEAS FOR MASHED POTATOES

Mashed potatoes stiffen upon refrigeration, so they need to be softened before they can be used. With a fork, fluff them and beat in sour cream, buttermilk, half-and-half cream or stock as needed for good consistency. One egg yolk for each 1-1/2 to 2 cups mashed potatoes will bind them, keeping them firm when they are reheated. If, however, you are reheating them in a double boiler, adding them to yeast bread doughs, ground-meat mixtures for meatloaf or vegetable purées, or using them as a base for soups, egg yolks need not be added. Two egg yolks will be needed for this same amount of potatoes if the potatoes are to be used as a piping.

Always consider the way in which the potatoes were seasoned when you initially mashed them before deciding to transform them into another dish. Those seasonings must complement the ingredients of the new dish.

• Pipe mashed potatoes beaten with egg yolk around a roast on an ovenproof platter. Return to a 375°F oven until the potatoes are golden.

• Mix mashed potatoes with sour cream, egg yolk, minced green onions and tops and celery salt. Spread over freshly cooked meatloaf and return to the oven until potatoes are browned.

• Beat mashed potatoes with egg yolk and pat into a well-buttered shallow baking dish. Top with grated or shredded firm or semifirm cheese (freeze, if desired, up to 2 weeks, then defrost in the refrigerator before baking) and bake in a preheated 350°F oven 20 minutes, or until heated through and cheese is melted.

• Reheat mashed potatoes in a double boiler. Mound in a buttered shallow baking dish and mask with whipped cream mixed with celery salt, freshly ground white pepper and a dash of cayenne pepper and grated firm cheese. Bake in a preheated 375°F oven 10 minutes, or until lightly browned.

## INDEX TO RECIPES

## COOKING GUIDELINES FOR SCALLOPED POTATOES

### OVEN SCALLOPED POTATOES

Unpeeled thin-skinned potatoes are best for scalloped potatoes, although peeled thick-skinned potatoes may be used. For 4 servings, slice enough potatoes to measure approximately 3 cups. Layer half of the potatoes in a well-buttered shallow baking dish. Sprinkle with a little unbleached flour, salt and freshly ground black or white pepper. Dot with butter and cover with a layer of very thinly sliced onion (optional). Repeat layers. Heat 1/2 to 2/3 cup each half-and-half cream and rich stock seasoned, if desired, with dry mustard. Pour over potatoes, sprinkle with paprika and bake in a preheated 350°F oven 40 minutes, or until potatoes are tender and have absorbed most of the liquid.

### QUICK SKILLET SCALLOPED PO-TATOES

In a heavy or Teflon-type skillet, layer sliced thin-skinned potatoes and thinly sliced onions (optional). Add rich chicken or beef stock to halfway cover the potatoes, sprinkle with seasonings, cover and bring to a gentle boil. Cook, adding more stock as needed, until potatoes are almost tender. Turning the potatoes several times, cook until almost all the stock has boiled away. Sprinkle with chopped fresh chives or parsley.

## IDEAS FOR SCALLOPED POTATOES

● Heat scalloped potatoes, covered, in a skillet, adding a little stock if needed. Break 1 or 2 eggs per serving over the potatoes, cover and cook until eggs are set. Serve for breakfast, or for a light supper with a sprinkling of minced fresh parsley.

● Make a single layer of scalloped potatoes in a buttered shallow baking dish. Sprinkle with grated semifirm or firm cheese and bake in a preheated 350°F oven, or until heated through and cheese is melted.

● Make Scalloped Potato Soufflé.

## COOKING GUIDELINES FOR CREAMED POTATOES

Prepare potatoes as directed in Creamed Vegetables, using diced cooked thick-skinned or thin-skinned potatoes and Light Cream Sauce made with chicken stock. Add grated onion, Worcestershire sauce, dry mustard and/or other seasonings of choice.

## IDEAS FOR CREAMED POTATOES

● Heat creamed potatoes in a skillet, top with grated cheese, cover and cook until cheese is melted.

● Hollow out ripe tomatoes, fill with creamed potatoes, top with Buttered Bread Crumbs, sprinkle with paprika and bake in a preheated 350°F oven 15 minutes, or until heated through and browned.

● Add diced cooked vegetables and/or meats or poultry when reheating creamed potatoes.

● Place creamed potatoes in a buttered shallow baking dish. Top with shredded fontina or Monterey Jack cheese and sprinkle with Buttered Bread Crumbs. Bake in a preheated 350°F oven 20 minutes, or until bubbly and cheese is melted.

## IDEAS FOR COOKED POTATOES

Bake or boil thick-skinned potatoes; steam or boil new potatoes. If boiling, be sure to drain well, returning the potatoes in the pot to the heat briefly to make sure all moisture is gone. Use potatoes cooked in any of these ways in the following.

● Slice cooked potatoes and layer in a well-buttered shallow baking dish. Spread a mixture of sour cream and minced garlic cloves over and sprinkle with grated Gruyère cheese and minced fresh parsley. Repeat layers 3 times, sprinkling last layer with paprika. Bake in a preheated 350°F oven 20 minutes, or until heated through and cheese is melted.

● Slice cooked potatoes and brown with minced onion in butter and bacon drippings, seasoning with celery salt or other seasonings of choice. Sprinkle with minced fresh chives.

● Dice cooked potatoes and toss with minced bell pepper and onion, grated or shredded firm or semifirm

cheese, seasonings of choice and unbleached flour to coat lightly. Transfer to a buttered shallow baking dish, pour hot milk over to come about halfway up potatoes, sprinkle with coarse dry bread crumbs, dot with butter and bake in a preheated 350°F oven 30 minutes.

● Slice cooked potatoes and reheat in butter. Sprinkle with freshly grated Parmesan or Romano cheese.

● Dice cooked potatoes and heat with sautéed minced onion and garlic. Use as a filling for omelets or in scrambled eggs. Garnish with sour cream and minced fresh chives.

● Coarsely grate cooked thick-skinned potatoes and lightly pat into melted butter in a heavy skillet. Brown underside lightly, drizzle melted butter over top and flip over in 1 piece. Brown other side and serve with Crème Fraîche.

● Slice cooked thin-skinned potatoes and dress with Dijon-style mustard, prepared horseradish and a sprinkling of Basic Vinaigrette.

● Slice cooked thin-skinned potatoes and coat with plain yoghurt and chopped fresh parsley and chives.

● Dice cooked thin-skinned potatoes and toss into a green salad.

● Dice cooked thin-skinned potatoes and toss with slivered black olives, flaked cooked firm white fish or chopped shellfish, chopped hard-cooked eggs and Curry Vinaigrette.

● Serve cooked tiny thin-skinned potatoes cold with a dab of black caviar and sour cream.

● Dice cooked thin-skinned potatoes and toss with low-fat cottage cheese, plain yoghurt, minced green onions and tops, minced fresh parsley and finely minced garlic. Transfer to a well-buttered shallow baking dish and sprinkle with grated firm cheese. Bake in a preheated 350°F oven 15 minutes, or until heated through and cheese is melted.

## IDEAS FOR POTATO SKINS

● Leaving 1/4-inch shells, remove pulp from freshly baked potatoes and mash the potato for another use. Brush shells with butter melted with finely minced garlic, salt, freshly ground white pepper and cayenne pepper. Broil, or bake in a preheated 475°F oven until crisp and browned.

● Peel potatoes* and toss skins into heated butter and/or oil or bacon drippings. Cook, stirring often, until browned and crispy. Drain on crumpled paper toweling and sprinkle with salt and freshly ground black pepper. Serve with guacamole and sour cream. Skins may also be deep fried.

● Brown the potato skins as above. Sprinkle with grated sharp Cheddar cheese and broil to melt cheese.

*Immediately put the potatoes in cold water to cover to prevent discoloration. To retain vitamins and minerals, cook as soon as possible.

## INDEX TO RECIPES

# Spinach

Buy only the freshest spinach—bunches of crisp, dark green leaves with no yellow patches or damp tips. Remove any strings or twistems securing the bunch, then store in plastic for only a short time. If the bunch is very wet from being sprayed at the market, stuff a few paper towels into the bag to absorb some of the moisture.

To cook, cut off and discard any tough stems, rinse leaves under tepid water and place in pot with only the washing water that clings to the leaves. (If desired, put a bruised garlic clove or two in the bottom of the pot and drizzle the leaves with a little olive oil for flavor.) To use the cooked spinach in recipes calling for chopped spinach, press out all of the moisture and finely chop. To freeze cooked spinach, again press out the moisture, then form the spinach into a ball and store in an airtight container up to two months; defrost in a sieve at room temperature, press out any water and finely chop.

The quality of spinach does not diminish as much when frozen as that of other vegetables, so if your garden produces a bumper crop, freeze some of it as just described. Commercial frozen spinach can also be a good buy, as fresh spinach can be quite costly.

New Zealand spinach is a hardier variety, with smaller, sword-shaped leaves that have a lightly textured finish. It is easily grown in the garden and can be quite prolific if unchecked. Cook as you would regular spinach; it will not cook down as much, however. Most people find New Zealand spinach much less appealing raw than cooked.

**COMPLEMENTARY SEASONINGS AND COMBINATIONS** Rosemary, chervil, marjoram, mace, parsley, nutmeg, lemon, Worcestershire sauce, Tabasco sauce, sesame seeds, vinegar, soy sauce, sherry, cheese, sour cream, garlic, onion, tomatoes, hard-cooked eggs, sorrel, eggplant, zucchini, mushrooms, any meats, bacon, firm white fish, salmon, clams.

## IDEAS FOR SPINACH

● Mix finely chopped cooked spinach with sour cream, sautéed sliced mushrooms, grated onion, minced garlic, salt, freshly ground white pepper and freshly grated nutmeg. Put in a buttered shallow baking dish, sprinkle with Buttered Bread Crumbs, chopped hard-cooked eggs and paprika. Bake in a preheated 350°F oven 15 minutes, or until heated through.

• Mix finely chopped cooked spinach with freshly grated Parmesan cheese, then thin with half-and-half cream. Put in a buttered shallow baking dish, sprinkle with more grated cheese and some paprika and bake in a preheated 350°F oven 15 minutes, or until heated through.

• Use Cooked-Vegetable Purée made with spinach as filling for omelets, crêpes or cannelloni.

• Combine coarsely chopped cooked spinach, minced sautéed onion and garlic, sautéed sliced mushrooms and shredded fontina or Monterey Jack cheese as a filling for omelets. Top with sour cream or Crème Fraîche.

• Combine finely chopped cooked spinach with Heavy Cream Sauce or sour cream, soy sauce and grated onion. Put in a buttered shallow baking dish, sprinkle with crushed croutons and freshly grated Parmesan cheese and place in a preheated 350°F oven until heated through.

• Prepare Cooked-Vegetable Purée with spinach and use to fill cooked artichoke bottoms. Sprinkle with grated Gruyère cheese and paprika and place in a preheated 375°F oven until heated through and cheese is melted.

• Sauté minced garlic and onion in butter, add a little tomato paste and then mix in chopped cooked spinach. Heat to serving temperature and garnish with hard-cooked egg slices.

• Combine finely chopped cooked spinach with Light Cream Sauce. Heat to serving temperature and season with minced fresh parsley, Worcestershire sauce and Tabasco sauce. Spoon over poached eggs on toasted English muffins.

• Spoon heated chopped cooked spinach on ham when making eggs Benedict.

• Cook minced onion, garlic and diced mushrooms (optional), covered, in butter until soft. Raise heat and crumble in ground beef or lamb, cooking and stirring with a fork until meat is cooked. With the fork, toss in chopped cooked spinach, a little Tomato Sauce or catsup, seasonings of choice and freshly grated Parmesan cheese. Heat and with a fork gradually stir in eggs beaten with a little fresh lemon juice. Cook, stirring, until eggs have coated the meat-spinach mixture and are set. Serve with extra freshly grated Parmesan cheese.

• Add finely chopped cooked spinach to Meatloaf, Ham Loaf and Rice and Salmon Loaf mixtures, Three Noodle Casseroles and Ricotta or Pasta Frittata.

• Add finely chopped cooked spinach to fresh pasta dough.

• Dress chilled cooked chopped spinach with Oriental Dressing; sprinkle with additional toasted sesame seeds.

• Make a Chiffonade of spinach or spinach, sorrel and/or lettuce.

• Braise raw spinach in rich beef stock, sprinkle with freshly grated nutmeg and garnish with sliced hard-cooked eggs.

- Toss raw tender spinach leaves into green salad with crisply cooked crumbled bacon and chopped hard-cooked eggs.

- Substitute coarsely chopped (very well drained) cooked spinach for the asparagus in Asparagus Timbales.

- Substitute chopped cooked spinach for the sorrel in stuffed hard-cooked eggs (see Stuffed Egg Filling Suggestions).

- Substitute chopped cooked spinach for the Swiss chard in Swiss Chard Fritters or Swiss Chard Soufflé.

## INDEX TO RECIPES

# Squash, Summer

Summer squash—zucchini, scallop (also known as cymling and patty-pan), and yellow crookneck and straight-neck—pose two problems: they frequently turn up as cooked leftovers in the refrigerator and, because they are so prolific, they are often garden surplus.

These squash are perishable, so they must be chosen with care at the market. Check that they are firm and without bruises or breaks in the skin. Touch the stem end to be sure that it is not soft.

Zucchini are probably the most popular of the summer squash. When small, no more than six or seven inches long, they are ideal for cutting raw into salads or for stuffing and baking. Medium-size ones are perfect for shredding, while the large zucchini are best sliced or cut in strips and quickly sautéed. There are two methods for preparing zucchini in the Cooking Guidelines that follow. The shredded version reheats well for omelet or frittata fillings; baked zucchini remains firmer and is better suited to being cut up and reheated in a wider range of dishes.

A bonus for the home gardener is the blossom that forms on zucchini and yellow squash plants. These should be picked when full and colorful and used for stuffing,

or they may be dipped in batter and deep fried.

Cooked summer squash may be puréed and frozen up to two months, but it will become quite watery. If you want to freeze some of your garden surplus, chop and sauté with onion, garlic and seasonings in butter, freeze up to two months, then purée for use in soups.

## COOKING GUIDELINES

**COMPLEMENTARY SEASONINGS AND COMBINATIONS** Oregano, thyme, marjoram, chervil, parsley, dill, sage, bay, tarragon, cheese, garlic, onion, mushrooms, tomato, bell pepper, eggplant, grains, pork, lamb, ham, ground beef.

**SHREDDED ZUCCHINI** Cut and discard blossom and stem ends of zucchini, but do not peel. Just before sautéing, grate on a Rösti grater (3/8-inch openings). In a large skillet, heat 1 to 2 tablespoons butter for each 2 cups shredded zucchini. Add zucchini to skillet

*For a hint of garlic, lightly mash cloves and warm in butter (or oil) until just starting to turn golden; discard garlic and use butter for cooking meats and vegetables.*

and sprinkle with ground oregano or other seasoning, salt and freshly ground pepper to taste. Cook over medium-high heat, stirring, 3 minutes, or until zucchini is just tender. Do not cook too long or zucchini will draw water. Drain leftover shredded zucchini, if necessary, before adding to recipes; the fresher the zucchini when it is cooked, the more moisture it will release. Straight-neck and crookneck yellow squash may be prepared in this same manner, but since these squashes are not as flavorful as zucchini, sauté them with a little minced red onion.

**BAKED ZUCCHINI** Cut off and discard blossom and stem ends of zucchini, but do not peel. Cut in half lengthwise and steam 2 to 3 minutes until *barely* fork tender. Spread each half with softened butter and sprinkle with salt, ground oregano or other seasoning and freshly ground black pepper. Place zucchini halves close together in a buttered shallow baking dish, cover evenly with freshly grated Parmesan cheese or Parmesan Crumb Topping and sprinkle with paprika. Bake in a preheated 350°F oven 15 to 20 minutes, or until zucchini is just fork tender. If making extra to be used as a leftover, remove from oven while still firm.

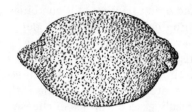

## IDEAS FOR ZUCCHINI AND YELLOW SQUASH

● Combine 1 egg, beaten, and 1/4 cup freshly grated Parmesan cheese for each 2 cups cooked shredded zucchini. Transfer to a buttered shallow baking dish, sprinkle with paprika and bake in a preheated 350°F oven 20 minutes, or until eggs are set.

● Make a frittata with cooked shredded zucchini, adding freshly grated Parmesan cheese if desired. Sprinkle with minced fresh parsley.

● Substitute sliced Baked Zucchini for the green tomatoes in Green Tomato Quiche.

● Cook minced onion, garlic and fresh oregano in olive oil, covered, until soft. Add enough rich lamb or beef stock to make a soup. Bring to a boil and add diced raw thin-skinned potatoes. Cook 3 to 4 minutes until *just* beginning to soften. Add cooked corn kernels and cooked shredded zucchini.

Bring back to a boil, remove from heat and add minced fresh parsley. Cool and chill. Add heavy cream, adjust seasonings with salt and freshly ground white pepper and chill until very cold. Serve in chilled soup bowls with a sprinkling of chopped hard-cooked eggs and minced fresh chives.

● Cook minced onion, garlic and fresh oregano, covered, in butter until soft. Sprinkle with enough unbleached flour to absorb most of the butter and cook, stirring, 2 minutes. Gradually stir in equal parts milk or half-and-half cream and rich chicken stock to make a smooth, slightly thickened soup liquid. Purée cooked shredded zucchini with a little of the liquid and add to soup. Stir in heavy cream, if desired, and reheat. Adjust seasonings with salt and freshly ground white pepper and serve topped with lemon slices and minced fresh chervil.

● Grate raw zucchini and add to meatloaf mixture.

• Toss thinly sliced raw zucchini into green salads.

• Slice large zucchini 3/8 inch thick. Dip in egg beaten with a little fresh lemon juice, coat with fine dry Seasoned Bread Crumbs and brown on both sides in half butter and half Garlic Olive Oil. Use any leftovers as you would Baked Zucchini.

• Dip zucchini blossoms in Beer Batter and deep fry until golden. Drain on crumpled paper toweling and serve at once on a bed of shredded lettuce.

• Chop zucchini blossoms and sauté with minced onion to use as a filling for enchiladas.

• Cut raw zucchini or yellow squash into strips, dip into Beer Batter seasoned with ground oregano and deep fry in peanut oil until golden. Drain on crumpled paper toweling and sprinkle lightly with sea salt. Serve immediately.

• Slice raw yellow squash and sauté quickly in butter and olive oil with thinly sliced red onions and minced garlic just until squash is tender. Toss with seasonings and minced fresh parsley.

• Drain sautéed yellow squash and onion mixture and combine with finely minced red bell pepper. Layer half in a shallow baking dish. Sprinkle with seasonings as desired and cover with shredded mozzarella cheese. Sprinkle with freshly grated Parmesan cheese and repeat layers. Top with Buttered Bread Crumbs and bake in a pre-heated 350°F oven 20 minutes, or until heated through and browned.

• Combine sautéed yellow squash and onion mixture with chopped ripe tomatoes, crumbled meatloaf or Ham Loaf, seasonings as desired and grated semifirm cheese. Transfer to a shallow baking dish and top with Parmesan Crumb Topping. Bake in a preheated 350°F oven 20 minutes, or until heated through and browned.

## INDEX TO RECIPES

# Squash, Winter

Acorn, banana, Hubbard, butternut, spaghetti and pumpkin are the most popular winter squash. Those bought at the market store well uncut in the refrigerator up to one week. Sometimes, some of the larger varieties are sold by the piece, making leftovers a less-frequent problem.

Look for good coloration of the hard shell and an absence of any cracks. If you are buying a piece of squash, the flesh should be bright colored and without bruises. Mashed or puréed cooked squash freezes well up to two months.

## COOKING GUIDELINES

**COMPLEMENTARY SEASONINGS AND COMBINATIONS** Basil, nutmeg, ginger, cinnamon, allspice, cloves, cardamom, thyme, honey, brown sugar, pecans, walnuts, dried fruits, cheese, sour cream, apples, pineapple, cranberries, garlic, onion, sorrel, carrots, spinach, ham, pork, lamb, beef.

**PUMPKIN PUREE** To make approximately 3 cups of pumpkin purée, cut 5 to 6 pounds pumpkin (seeds removed) into large pieces. Place

*Remove any fibrous strings attached to pumpkin seeds. Rinse, dry with paper toweling and place in a single layer on a baking sheet. Sprinkle lightly with salt and bake in 325°F oven 30 to 45 minutes, or until lightly toasted, stirring often.*

in a buttered shallow baking pan skin side up. Bake in a preheated 325°F oven 1 hour and 15 minutes, or until flesh is tender. Remove and discard any stringy pulp and scoop out flesh. Put flesh through a sieve, food mill, blender or food processor. At this point, cool and freeze, if desired, up to 2 months. Purée may be thinned with a little heavy cream or evaporated milk. Depending upon how purée is to be used, season with a choice of brown sugar, ground cinnamon, ginger and/or cloves, salt and freshly ground white pepper. Freshly grated orange or lemon rind, slivered blanched almonds browned in butter, plumped raisins or chopped pecans are also good additions. Hubbard and butternut squash may be cooked and puréed in this same manner, and used in recipes calling for pumpkin purée.

## IDEAS FOR WINTER SQUASH

Banana, butternut, pumpkin and Hubbard squash lend themselves best to the following suggestions.

● Layer sliced steamed winter squash in a buttered shallow baking dish with cooked noodles or rice, shredded fontina cheese and sliced tomatoes, ending with a cheese layer. Bake in a preheated 350°F oven 20 minutes, or until heated through and cheese is melted.

● Layer sliced steamed winter squash and *thinly* sliced unpared tart apples in a buttered shallow baking dish, sprinkling each layer with freshly grated orange rind, brown sugar, ground cardamom or allspice, salt and freshly ground white pepper. Moisten with fresh orange juice and top with chopped pecans. Bake in a preheated 350°F oven 20 minutes, or until apples are tender and top is lightly browned.

● Sauté minced onion, mushrooms and garlic (optional) in butter until soft, sprinkling with ground thyme, salt and freshly ground black pepper as they cook. Mix in cubed steamed winter squash and Cheese Sauce made with rich chicken stock. Transfer half the mixture to a buttered shallow baking dish, sprinkle with toasted slivered blanched almonds and spread remaining squash mixture over. Cover evenly with Parmesan Crumb Topping and bake in a preheated 350°F oven 20 minutes, or until heated through and lightly browned.

● Cook minced onion, celery and fresh basil in butter, covered, until soft. Add cubed steamed banana or butternut squash and cubed cooked carrots. Sprinkle with a little granulated sugar and ground cloves and cook, stirring, 3 minutes. Add enough rich chicken stock to make a soup, cover and cook until vegetables are very soft. Purée in blender or food processor and

*Cook diced winter squash in stews; cook a little extra to mash into the stew liquid at end of cooking to thicken.*

return to saucepan. Add half-and-half cream and season with salt and freshly ground white pepper. Cool, chill and add heavy cream, if desired. Adjust seasonings, chill thoroughly and serve in chilled bowls with a sprinkling of minced fresh chives and paprika. To serve hot, omit heavy cream, if desired. Serve with a Chiffonade of lettuce, spinach and sorrel.

● Mash steamed winter squash and heat in a heavy saucepan with butter, brown sugar or honey, ground ginger, ground cloves, freshly grated nutmeg, salt and freshly ground white pepper to taste. Thin, if desired, with sour cream, half-and-half cream, fresh orange juice and/or pineapple juice. Reheat and serve with a sprinkling of plumped raisins and chopped pecans sautéed in butter.

● Substitute mashed well-seasoned winter squash for the carrots in Carrot Puffs.

## INDEX TO RECIPES

# Sweet Potatoes & Yams

High in vitamin A and in calories, sweet potatoes and yams are members of the same botanical family. The yam commonly seen in the United States is a variety of sweet potato, and is not related to the "true" yam, a plant native to the tropics. Certain physical characteristics distinguish the sweet potato from its relative, the yam. Sweet potatoes are yellowish beige in color, with yellow to pale orange flesh. Yams, in contrast, have brownish skin and deep-rust-orange flesh.

When selecting sweet potatoes and yams, look for ones with smooth skin free of cracks and with nicely tapered ends. Both should be stored in a cool, dark place and will keep well up to two weeks. Always cook them (preferably baked) unpeeled for the best flavor and texture, and to conserve nutrients. Cooked sweet potatoes and yams may be frozen, mashed or puréed, up to two months.

The Centennial is a particularly flavorful variety of yam, quite similar in appearance to the sweet potato. It has a naturally sweet taste, but takes longer to bake than some other varieties.

Leftover cooked sweet potatoes and yams do not easily lend themselves to being combined with other foods, so there is no Index to Recipes included here. You can, however, make Sweet Potato Timbales, Sweet Potato Soup or Croquettes or prepare one of the following ideas with cooked leftovers you have on hand.

**COMPLEMENTARY SEASONINGS AND COMBINATIONS** Nutmeg, cloves, cinnamon, allspice, mace, ginger, cardamom, walnuts, pecans, almonds, raisins, orange, lemon, pineapple, apples, pears, cranberries, plain yoghurt, sour cream, honey, brown sugar, turkey, ham, lamb.

## IDEAS FOR MASHED COOKED SWEET POTATOES OR YAMS

● Combine mashed cooked sweet potatoes or yams with freshly grated orange rind, mashed ripe bananas or drained crushed pineapple, honey, spices and fresh orange juice. Transfer to a buttered shallow baking dish, dot with butter and bake in a preheated 350°F oven 15 to 20 minutes, or until heated through. Mixture may also be mounded into hollowed-out orange shells and then heated.

• Combine mashed cooked sweet potatoes or yams with crumbled meatloaf or Ham Loaf, sautéed minced onion and celery, dry bread crumbs, chopped fresh parsley and spices. Use to stuff chicken or turkey before roasting.

• Combine mashed cooked sweet potatoes with chopped cooked cranberries, plumped raisins, chopped pecans or walnuts, and spices. Transfer to a buttered shallow baking dish and bake in a preheated 350°F oven 15 to 20 minutes, or until heated through.

• Heat mashed cooked sweet potatoes or yams in butter, half-and-half cream, dry sherry and spices.

• Combine mashed cooked sweet potatoes or yams with butter, sour cream, chopped green onion tops and beaten egg. Transfer to a buttered shallow baking dish and heat in a preheated 350°F oven 20 minutes, or until lightly browned.

• Substitute mashed cooked sweet potatoes or yams (well seasoned) for the pumpkin in Pumpkin Crêpes or the carrots in Carrot Puffs.

## IDEAS FOR COOKED SWEET POTATOES OR YAMS

• Slice or dice cooked sweet potatoes or yams and heat in a skillet with butter, fresh orange juice, freshly grated orange rind, spices and brown sugar. Just before serving sprinkle with minced fresh parsley and/or chives.

• In a heavy skillet, melt butter, brown sugar, fresh lemon juice and thinly sliced lemon. Cook mixture until syrupy and add sliced cooked sweet potatoes or yams, turning to coat well. Heat and garnish with toasted slivered blanched almonds.

• Slice cooked sweet potatoes or yams and season with spices. Brown in butter, turning once.

• Slice cooked sweet potatoes and arrange in a buttered shallow baking dish. Heat sliced peeled oranges in brown sugar, butter, fresh orange juice and spices.

Pour over sweet potatoes and sprinkle with chopped pecans. Dot with butter and bake in a preheated 350°F oven 30 minutes, basting often with pan juices.

• Cook minced onion and celery, covered, in bacon drippings until soft. Add sliced cooked sweet potatoes or yams and cook, stirring, 2 to 3 minutes. Add enough rich chicken stock to make a soup, cover and simmer 15 minutes. Purée and return to saucepan. Reheat, adding half-and-half cream, if desired, and season with freshly grated nutmeg, salt and freshly ground black pepper. Pass a bowl of sour cream.

• Arrange sliced cooked sweet potatoes and sliced unpared tart apples or pears in a buttered shallow baking dish. Sprinkle with seasonings as desired and freshly grated orange rind and drizzle maple syrup over. Make a second layer and pour in fresh orange juice to moisten slightly. Dot with butter and bake in a preheated 325°F oven 30 minutes, or until heated through and apples are tender. (If desired, before dotting with butter, sprinkle with Wheat Germ Topping.)

# *Swiss Chard*

Treat Swiss chard in essentially the same way as you do spinach. The leaves should look fresh and crisp and be a deep, rich green or green tinged with red when purchased, and the stems should be firm and without breaks. Swiss chard, like spinach, is best when cooked with only the washing water that clings to the leaves, but remove the large stem sections, chop and place in the cooking pot for a short time before adding the quicker-cooking leaves.

See spinach for complementary seasonings and combinations and for ideas on how to use chard leftover in the refrigerator, as most uses for spinach are interchangeable with those for Swiss chard. The stems of chard can be prepared in special ways, however, and two ideas for cooking them follow.

## IDEAS FOR SWISS CHARD STEMS

● Dice and steam Swiss chard stems in chicken stock until tender. Dress with Brown Butter and fresh lemon juice and season with salt and freshly ground black pepper.

● Dip whole chard stems in Beer Batter and deep fry in peanut oil until golden. Drain on crumpled paper toweling and serve at once on a bed of finely shredded iceberg lettuce.

---

*When draining deep-fried foods on paper toweling, crumple the toweling rather than lay it flat. It will absorb more oil and you'll use less toweling, meaning money saved.*

---

## INDEX TO RECIPES

# *Tomatoes*

Full-flavored ripe tomatoes are seasonal, and whether you have them in your garden or they become available at the market, take advantage of the bounty. Transform them into sauces (the Italian-style plum tomatoes make very full-bodied sauces) and freeze the sauces for future use, or freeze the tomatoes straight from the market or garden. Put them whole in plastic bags, seal and then place in the freezer. Remove the tomatoes from the freezer, place in a single layer and defrost just until the skins peel off easily, or let them stand five minutes, hold them under cold running water and "rub" the peels off. Chop the tomatoes and use immediately before any of the juices are lost. These frozen tomatoes are suitable only for recipes in which they are cooked and they must always be peeled before using.

Tomatoes should have a rich, red color, be relatively firm to the touch, well formed and without bruises. You can buy tomatoes that are still pink and ripen them at home, but the flavor will never be as full as it is in those picked ripe from the vine. Take care

---

*Mix corn germ with crumb topping for broiled tomatoes.*

---

when storing tomatoes that they are not subjected to rough handling.

If tomatoes lack flavor and you wish to serve a tomato salad, slice them, sprinkle with ground oregano and marinate overnight in a vinaigrette-type dressing in the refrigerator.

Sun-dried tomatoes packed in olive oil in jars are available at specialty markets and some supermarkets, or you can dehydrate surplus tomatoes at home (see Dehydrating Vegetables and Fruits). Tomato paste from a can does not freeze well; store it in the freezer no more than two weeks and then use it only in cooked dishes. Once defrosted, it will keep in the refrigerator up to five days. If available, buy tomato paste in a tube, as it has a much longer shelf life.

Tomatoes are seldom a cooked leftover, but you may on occasion have a tomato or two beginning to overripen in the refrigerator. A few ideas on ways to prepare them follow. There is no listing of those seasonings and foods that combine well with tomatoes, since this particular vegetable is so versatile that the list would be almost

endless. You will, however, find an Index to Recipes to help solve the problem of that hard-to-finish can of tomato paste.

## IDEAS FOR TOMATOES

● Halve ripe tomatoes crosswise and drain cut side down on wire rack 10 to 15 minutes. Place close together, cut side up, in a broiler pan. Sprinkle lightly with salt, freshly ground black pepper and a minced fresh herb such as basil or oregano. Sprinkle lightly with fine dry bread crumbs and/or freshly grated Parmesan cheese and dot with butter. Broil about 5 inches from heat until heated through and lightly browned.

● Slice firm ripe tomatoes 3/8 inch thick, or green tomatoes 1/4 inch thick. Dip in egg beaten with a little fresh lemon juice, then in fine Seasoned Bread Crumbs with or without freshly grated Parmesan cheese. Let dry on wire rack 40 minutes. Brown quickly on both sides in butter and Garlic Olive Oil, turning only once.

● Slice firm ripe tomatoes and arrange on a broiler pan brushed with olive oil. Brush tomato slices with olive oil and sprinkle evenly with salt, freshly ground black pepper and finely minced garlic. Broil just until heated through.

● Cook minced white of leek, onion and garlic in butter, covered, until soft. Add sliced cooked thin-skinned potato, chopped tomatoes, chopped fresh parsley and watercress and enough rich chicken stock to make a soup. Cover and cook until potatoes are very soft. Purée in blender or food processor, or pass through a food mill. Return mixture to saucepan and add heavy cream. Reheat, season with salt and freshly ground white pepper and garnish with finely diced ripe tomato and watercress leaves. This soup may also be served icy cold.

● Halve ripe tomatoes crosswise and drain cut side down on wire rack 10 to 15 minutes. Place close together, cut side up, in a broiler pan. Cover with a mixture of grated Gruyère or sharp Cheddar cheese, minced green bell pepper, Worcestershire sauce, Dijon-style mustard, salt and freshly ground white pepper. Sprinkle with Buttered Bread Crumbs and broil about 8 inches from heat until heated through and lightly browned.

## INDEX TO RECIPES

# *Water Chestnuts & Bamboo Shoots*

The Chinese water chestnut, a tuber, and the bamboo shoot, a shoot vegetable, are generally available only in cans in North America, except in those areas with a large Asian population. These two foods are included here because a whole can is seldom needed for preparing a single meal.

Quality varies in these canned products, so shop until you find good ones. Also, it is always best to buy bamboo shoots that are whole or in large pieces, as the sliced ones often have poor texture. If you haven't a can of water chestnuts on the shelf, substitute raw jicama, celery root or the core of a cauliflower; all of these satisfactorily simulate the water chestnut's "crunch."

Once a can of water chestnuts or bamboo shoots has been opened, drain off the liquid and transfer them to jars. Add water to cover and top with a tight-fitting lid. Change the water daily and store in the refrigerator no more than five days.

## INDEX TO RECIPES

# *Fruits*

Fruits are not an important consideration when talking of leftovers, as they are seldom found cooked on the refrigerator shelf. Surplus—too much fruit ripening in the garden at one time—can be seen as a type of leftover, but this bounty is most commonly dealt with by putting up jams, jellies, chutneys, conserves and the like.

This is not to say fruits are totally ignored in these pages. The dessert chapter, for instance, features apples, strawberries, bananas and plums. You can use fruit to make a flavorful sherbet or a creamy icing for your favorite cake. Fruits can be used alone or combined with other ingredients in salads, made into hors d'oeuvres, even combined with rice and meats in skillet dishes.

In general, selecting good fresh fruits means choosing those that are firm, free of blemishes and with good color. Because most fruits are perishable, never buy more than you can eat in a reasonable amount of time. Also, never wash any fruit until you are ready to use it. Some fruits, like berries, should be stored in the refrigerator, while others, including peaches, apricots and nectarines, can be successfully ripened at room temperature and then refrigerated if needed to be kept longer.

Long-term storage of most fruits, either canned or frozen, is a complex subject that is best dealt with in volumes devoted to those forms of preservation. Berries can be simply sheet frozen and stored up to two months. Bananas may be treated in the same way, frozen with the peels intact, then the peel cut away with a knife and the bananas defrosted and mashed for use in breads, icings and puddings. Some fruits—pears, apricots, apples and peaches—are good candidates for dehydrating at home (see Dehydrating Vegetables and Fruits).

The general index at the back of the book includes specific fruits with recipes and the recipes with assorted fruits under the general fruit entry. Some preparations can be easily adapted to whatever fruit you have on hand, so review the fruit recipes carefully.

# FISH, SHELLFISH POULTRY & MEATS

## *Fish & Shellfish*

Fish are among the most perishable of foods, so they must be purchased from a reputable dealer and stored with care. To judge the freshness of fish, look for clear, protruding eyes, gills with a reddish tinge, firm flesh that springs back when depressed, and the absence of a strong "fishy" odor. At the market, fish are generally available three ways: whole, in 1/4- to 1/2-inch-thick slices called steaks, and in boneless lengthwise slices termed fillets.

Return home with any fish as soon as possible after purchase; one to two hours is the maximum time a fresh fish should remain unrefrigerated if the outdoor temperature exceeds 65°F. If there is a chance of delay, take along a cooler to put the fish in until you reach home. Fish that has been purchased frozen must be transferred to the home freezer promptly; if it

begins to thaw at all, it will spoil when put in the freezer.

Once home, remove the fish from the store packaging, rinse under cold, running water, pat dry and place in a nonmetallic container. Cover loosely and refrigerate in the coldest area of the refrigerator. Use the fish within twenty-four hours, if possible, and never keep it longer than forty-eight hours.

Occasionally, a market sale or a big catch will require you to freeze fresh fish. Divide into portions suitable for one meal and then freeze using either of these methods: Pack the fish in well-washed milk cartons and fill with water to completely surround the fish. Alternately, rinse the fish and pat dry and, if desired, rub with fresh lemon juice, then wrap airtight in aluminum foil. With either method, the fish may be frozen up to two months if it has a relatively high fat content, such as albacore, mackerel and butterfish, or up to three months if it is lean, like sea bass, halibut and red snapper. Thaw frozen fish on the refrigerator

shelf and cook immediately if you have rubbed it with lemon juice or within twelve hours if you have not. If you are in a hurry, cook the fish fillets or steaks while they are still frozen, increasing the usual cooking time slightly. Cooked fish may also be frozen, but never longer than two weeks.

The recipes in this book call for "firm white fish," a designation that includes many varieties: haddock, ling cod, sea bass, halibut, red snapper, swordfish, shad, sturgeon, white bait, etc. All of these are lean fish and flake more easily than oilier ones, making them more suitable for using as leftovers.

Shellfish are usually so expensive that there is seldom a need to store them or to create ways in which to use them up. For most people, they are a special-occasion purchase and are eaten on the same day. If by chance shrimp that was shelled and then boiled is leftover, store them in salted water to cover in the refrigerator up to three days, changing the water daily. Uncooked shellfish, such as crab and shrimp, that have not been previously frozen should be stored in the freezer for as brief a time as possible. Always check with your fish dealer to be sure that the shellfish you intend to freeze did not come into the market frozen. Cooked crab meat can be frozen, but again for only a short period of time; shrimp loses its distinctive texture when frozen. In general it can be said that shellfish suffers from freezing to the point that you should always try to use it fresh.

Canned fish—tuna, sardines, anchovies and lumpfish caviar—must be refrigerated once they are opened. They keep well, but often you find you want to use up that remaining pair of anchovy fillets or a few sardines. Look to the ideas and Index to Recipes that follow.

## COOKING GUIDELINES

**COMPLEMENTARY SEASONINGS AND COMBINATIONS** Tarragon, thyme, fennel, rosemary, bay, dill, basil, savory, chives, parsley, Seafood Seasoning, mustard, saffron, turmeric, garlic, onion, lemon, capers, black olives, tomatoes, spinach, asparagus, broccoli, green beans, mushrooms, rice, potatoes.

The following methods can be used to cook a piece of fish, a fillet or steak or a whole fish. Firm white fish or salmon cooked in these ways make the best leftovers. Wipe flesh with dampened paper toweling before cooking. Or, to freshen and bring out flavor, marinate the fish in fresh lemon juice no longer than ten minutes, then drain and pat dry. Cooking time will depend upon thickness and/or weight of fish. The timings given for each method are guides; start checking the fish early for doneness. It is done when the flesh flakes easily with a fork. The cooking liquid or juices should be strained and reserved to make cream sauces, fish soups or used in the place of fish stock. Garnish freshly cooked fish with lemon slices and parsley sprigs and/or watercress sprigs, or as desired, before serving.

**BAKED FISH** Place fish in a buttered shallow baking dish just large enough to hold fish. Pour in dry white wine to a depth of 1/4 inch. Sprinkle fish with Seafood Seasoning, paprika, salt and freshly ground white pepper. Strew sliced onions, minced fresh herbs and lightly mashed garlic cloves over and bake in a preheated 350°F oven 10 to 25 minutes, or until fish tests done. Remove to heated platter.

**STEAMED FISH** Rub fish with dry sherry and soy sauce. Place in a shallow dish with sloping sides and strew slivered green onions and slivered ginger root over. Drizzle with a little peanut oil and steam over gently simmering water 5 to 15 minutes, or until fish tests done. Serve from the dish.

**POACHED FISH** Lean fish is especially good poached, but oilier fish, such as albacore and black cod, are also good prepared in this manner. Wrap fish in cheesecloth

*Brush fish fillets with egg white or Egg Wash, sprinkle with salt and pepper, roll in unbleached flour or potato flour and deep fry until golden.*

and place in a skillet just large enough to hold fish. To measure the amount of poaching liquid needed to just cover the fish, pour water over, then remove fish. Pour water from skillet into a large measuring cup, pour off half of water and replace with an equal amount of dry white wine. Pour water and wine into a saucepan. For each 2 cups liquid, add 1/2 bay leaf, 2 parsley sprigs, 4 onion slices, 2 lemon slices, 2 allspice berries, lightly crushed, 4 black peppercorns, lightly crushed, and 1/2 teaspoon salt. Bring to a boil and boil gently, uncovered, 5 minutes. Return fish to skillet and pour water-wine mixture over. Cover skillet, bring *just* to boil, lower heat and simmer gently (do not allow to boil) 6 to 20 minutes, or until fish tests done. Be sure to check after 6 minutes. Lift out, unwrap and place on heated platter.

**BARBECUED FISH** Whole salmon lends itself especially well to barbecuing, but other fish and other cuts may be prepared in this manner. Place fish on double layer of heavy-duty foil. Strew onion and lemon slices, fresh parsley and tarragon or dill sprigs and bits of butter over fish. Sprinkle with salt, freshly ground white pepper and paprika. Bring sides of foil up around fish and pour in dry white wine to a depth of about 1/8 inch. Bring foil the rest of the way up and around fish, sealing top completely. Place on grill over moderately hot coals and cook 20 to 45 minutes, or until fish tests done. Unwrap and remove to heated serving platter.

## IDEAS FOR FISH

● Rub raw or lightly blanched mushroom caps with fresh lemon juice. Fill with mixture of equal parts softened cream cheese and flaked cooked salmon, grated lemon rind, minced fresh dill, salt and freshly ground white pepper. Sprinkle with paprika and chill. Serve as an hors d'oeuvre.

● Spread bread rounds with a mixture of flaked cooked firm white fish, grated Gruyère cheese, finely minced green onions and tops and Basic Mayonnaise to bind. Sprinkle with paprika and broil until bubbly. Serve as an hors d'oeuvre.

● Mash cooked firm white fish with softened cream cheese. Add finely minced celery, prepared horseradish, Worcestershire sauce, Tabasco sauce and Herb Mayonnaise to bind. Serve as a dip for raw vegetables or as a cracker spread.

● Toss flaked cooked firm white fish gently with chopped hard-cooked egg, finely minced celery, drained capers, fresh lemon or lime juice, seasonings and Lemon Mayonnaise to bind. Serve as a salad or as a stuffing for ripe tomatoes or halved avocados.

● Heat cubed cooked firm white fish gently in rich chicken stock with diced cooked vegetables such as carrots and potatoes. Season to taste and sprinkle with chopped fresh parsley and/or chives.

● Combine equal parts flaked cooked firm white fish or salmon and Light or Medium Cream Sauce made with fish stock. Transfer to buttered ramekins or large scallop shells, sprinkle with Buttered Bread Crumbs and paprika and bake in a preheated 350°F oven 15 minutes, or until bubbly.

● Flake cooked firm white fish or salmon and add to Rice or Pasta Frittata, to a spinach quiche, or to Egg Curry.

• Coarsely grind cooked firm white fish or salmon and add to Swiss Chard Soufflé or Scalloped Potato Soufflé.

• Grind cooked firm white fish or salmon and substitute for the turkey in Turkey Mousse. Use fish stock for the cream sauce.

## IDEAS FOR CANNED FISH

**ANCHOVY FILLETS** Chop anchovy fillets and add with capers to butter when making veal piccata.

**ANCHOVY FILLETS** Combine softened cream cheese, softened butter and mashed anchovy fillets. Stuff raw celery sticks and sprinkle with finely minced fresh parsley.

**ANCHOVY FILLETS** Mash anchovy fillets with unsalted butter, fresh lemon juice, Dijon-style mustard and freshly ground white pepper. Use as a filling for pastry squares. (See Filling Suggestions for Hors d'oeuvre Pastries.)

**ANCHOVY FILLETS** Mash anchovy fillets with some of their oil and combine with softened cream cheese and Dijon-style mustard. Use as a spread for crackers or Melba Toast.

**ANCHOVY FILLETS** Dress sliced ripe tomatoes with Basic Vinaigrette. Garnish with anchovy fillets and sprinkle with minced fresh parsley.

**ANCHOVY FILLETS** Mix together chopped anchovy fillets, minced garlic and olive oil. Toss into freshly cooked pasta and sprinkle with minced fresh parsley and chives. Pass the peppermill.

**ANCHOVY FILLETS OR SARDINES** Combine mashed anchovy fillets or sardines with chopped hard-cooked egg, minced capers and gherkins and Basic Mayonnaise to bind. Use as a stuffing for hollowed-out cherry tomatoes or tiny cooked beets. Garnish with a parsley leaf and serve as an hors d'oeuvre or as a salad garnish.

**SARDINES** Mash sardines with minced fresh parsley, minced shallots, fresh lemon juice and freshly ground black pepper. Use as a spread for crackers or Melba Toast.

**SARDINES** Bind mashed sardines with Basic Mayonnaise and add minced onion and dill pickle, fresh lemon juice and Worcestershire sauce. Use as a spread for crackers or Melba Toast.

**SARDINES** Chop sardines and toss with chopped hard-cooked eggs, minced fresh chives, fresh lemon juice and Lemon Mayonnaise to bind. Use as a spread or as a raw-vegetable dip.

**TUNA FISH AND ANCHOVY FILLETS** Combine ground cooked veal roast, flaked tuna fish, mashed anchovy fillets and cooked white rice. Bind with lightly beaten egg and season with freshly ground black pepper. Form into cakes and brown on both sides in olive oil and butter.

**TUNA FISH** Mound potato salad in a serving bowl lined with lettuce leaves. Garnish with chunks of tuna fish, hard-cooked egg halves, black olives, cooked green beans and anchovy fillets. Dress with Basic Vinaigrette and sprinkle with minced fresh parsley.

**TUNA FISH** Toss chunks of tuna fish with sliced cooked thin-skinned potatoes, green bell pepper cut into thin julienne, broken lettuce leaves and Lemon Vinaigrette. Garnish with ripe tomato wedges and parsley sprigs.

**TUNA FISH** Combine 2 parts grated sharp Cheddar cheese and 1 part flaked tuna fish. Moisten with dry white wine and season with freshly ground black pepper. Spread on toast rounds and broil until bubbly.

**TUNA FISH** Substitute flaked tuna fish for the salmon in Salmon Salad or in Rice and Salmon Loaf, for the meat in the Three Noodle Casseroles, or for the poultry in Hot Chicken or Turkey Salad.

**TUNA FISH** Gently heat flaked tuna fish in Fresh Tomato Sauce. Mix in coarsely cut black olives. Toss into freshly cooked pasta and sprinkle with minced fresh parsley.

**CAVIAR** Mash the yolk of hard-cooked egg and mix with lumpfish caviar, dry mustard, Worcestershire sauce and freshly ground white pepper. Bind with Basic Mayonnaise, fill hard-cooked egg whites and top with a sliver of lemon rind.

# *Poultry*

Chicken is an economical buy, especially when the birds are purchased whole and cut up at home. Young chickens—poussins, broilers, roasters, capons—can be pan fried, sautéed, stir fried, roasted or barbecued. Older chickens, usually labeled stewing hens or fowl, must be cooked in liquid.

Select a chicken that is plump and without patches of discolored skin. The color of a chicken's skin is determined by the bird's diet; it is only important that the skin have an even tone and a moist, fresh appearance. Check for the chicken's point of origin and buy only those that have been processed locally, for they will have superior flavor. Also, avoid purchasing chickens that have been fed food laced with additives or ones that have been processed with chemicals. If buying chicken parts, be sure they are well formed and fleshy.

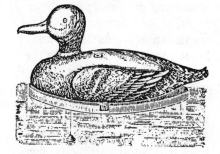

Remove the chicken from the store packaging, put in a plastic bag and refrigerate no more than twenty-four hours before cooking, or wrap airtight and freeze up to four months. Chicken parts are more perishable than a whole bird and should be cooked the same day they are purchased, but may be frozen up to four months. Cooked chicken may be frozen up to two months and should be used only in dishes that are heated or in salads where the meat is marinated, but never in sandwiches.

Keep two containers in your freezer, one for the livers and one for the giblets that come with whole chickens. For pâtés, the livers may be frozen up to two months; for sautés and other dishes, two weeks is the maximum. Raw or parboiled giblets may be frozen up to two months.

If you have bought a whole chicken, cut it into serving pieces and plan to cook only part of it, wrap, label, date and freeze the remaining pieces separately or together for a future meal. Chicken wings can be treated like livers; keep a separate container in the freezer and add the wings to it until there are enough for a recipe. The neck, wing tips, tail and other scraps can be frozen together for adding to the stock pot. If you have purchased a frozen chicken,

cook these parts with the chicken, then let cool and freeze.

The rules for refrigerating and freezing whole chickens and chicken parts apply to turkey and turkey parts as well, including the economy measure of cutting up the whole bird at home. Ducks and geese are usually bought for special meals because of their higher cost and only the refrigeration rules need be followed. Cornish game hens are generally available frozen and should be transferred to the home freezer as quickly as possible, unless they are to be cooked within twenty-four hours of purchase. All poultry should be defrosted in the refrigerator.

## COOKING GUIDELINES FOR CHICKEN

**COMPLEMENTARY SEASONINGS AND COMBINATIONS** Sage, oregano, bay, thyme, savory, tarragon, rosemary, basil, chives, turmeric, Bell's Seasoning or other poultry seasoning, curry powder, ginger, nutmeg, saffron, garlic, onion, lemon, cranberries, apricots, prunes, grapes, chutney, broccoli, spinach, mushrooms, artichokes, asparagus, sweet potatoes, sweetbreads, ham.

**ROAST CHICKEN** For a 3-pound chicken. Rinse chicken and pat dry with paper toweling. Sprinkle cavity with Bell's Seasoning and fill with 1 lemon, sliced, 2 oregano sprigs, 3 or 4 garlic cloves, lightly mashed, and 4 parsley sprigs. Place chicken on side on rack in shallow baking dish and spread with softened butter. Sprinkle with Bell's Seasoning and roast in a preheated 350°F oven 30 minutes. Turn chicken to other side, spread with butter and sprinkle with Bell's Seasoning. Continue cooking 30 minutes, or until juices run clear when thick portion of thigh is pierced with a fork. Remove from oven and pour 1/4 to 1/2 cup fresh lemon juice over. Let stand 10 minutes before carving.

*Allow about 3/4 pound chicken with bone in for each person; a 3- to 3-1/2-pound chicken will serve three or four.*

**STEAMED CHICKEN** For a 2-1/2- to 3-pound chicken or chicken parts. Rinse chicken and pat dry with paper toweling. Cut into serving pieces and place in a shallow dish with sloping sides. Pour in a mixture of 2 tablespoons soy sauce and 3 tablespoons dry sherry. Strew 8 to 10 garlic cloves, lightly mashed, 3 or 4 green onions and tops, cut up, and 4 to 5 slices ginger root over the chicken pieces. Drizzle with a little Oriental sesame oil and steam 35 to 40 minutes, or until juices run clear when thick portion of thigh is pierced.

**POACHED CHICKEN** Rinse chicken parts, wipe dry with paper toweling and place in skillet. Mix chicken stock with a little dry white wine (1/2 cup wine to 2 cups stock) and add to skillet to just cover the chicken pieces. Strew sliced onion, lightly mashed garlic cloves, tarragon or oregano sprigs and parsley sprigs over. Cover, bring to slow boil, lower heat and simmer gently 20 minutes, or until chicken is tender. Strain cooking liquid and reserve for Rich-Stock Suggestions (or thicken a portion with corn-starch dissolved in a little water to serve over chicken).

*Baste barbecuing meats and poultry with fennel, basil or rosemary sprigs dipped into marinade.*

## IDEAS FOR CHICKEN

● Heat cubed cooked chicken in Creole Sauce. Serve over cooked bulghur and sprinkle with minced fresh chives and parsley.

● Combine cubed cooked chicken with Light Cream Sauce made with chicken stock and heavy cream. Toss in chopped cooked artichoke hearts or bottoms, toasted slivered blanched almonds, diced pimiento, minced fresh parsley, salt and freshly ground white pepper. Heat gently and serve in patty shells or over toasted English muffin halves.

● Heat cooked chicken breast slices in Quick Mushroom or Shallot–Red Wine Sauce. Serve over cooked noodles with a sprinkling of chopped green onion tops.

● Heat diced cooked chicken, chopped cooked chicken livers and sautéed sliced mushrooms in Curry Cream Sauce made with chicken stock. Spoon on toasted halved biscuits and sprinkle with minced fresh chives or chervil and paprika.

● Heat julienned cooked chicken in Brown Bean Sauce with cubed firm tofu (bean curd). Toss into cooked somen noodles, heat briefly and sprinkle with chopped fresh coriander.

● Heat cubed cooked chicken with chopped ripe tomatoes, minced fresh basil, salt and freshly ground black pepper. Toss into cooked wheat or triticale berries, heat briefly and sprinkle with chopped fresh parsley.

● Mask cooked chicken breasts with Remoulade Sauce and arrange on a bed of lettuce. Surround with halved cherry tomatoes and garnish with halved black olives.

● Arrange cooked broccoli flowerets, pieces of cooked chicken and slices of pimiento artistically on a bed of lettuce. Dress with Herb Sauce and garnish with parsley sprigs and lemon wedges.

• Arrange julienned cooked chicken, cooked green beans or asparagus and quartered hard-cooked eggs on a bed of lettuce. Spoon Miso or Tofu Dressing over and garnish with parsley sprigs.

• Arrange julienned cooked chicken, orange sections, strips of banana and halved seedless grapes on a bed of lettuce. Spoon Cream Cheese or Blue Cheese Dressing over and sprinkle with chopped walnuts.

• Combine cubed cooked chicken, chopped apples or pears sprinkled with fresh lemon juice, raisins and chopped pecans. Toss with Sour Cream Dressing and mound into hollowed-out ripe tomatoes or into avocado halves. Sprinkle with minced fresh chives.

## IDEAS FOR
## CHICKEN LIVERS

The suggestions that follow are best when prepared with fresh livers or with ones that have been frozen no longer than two weeks. Dust the livers with flour before cooking, if desired; they are done when they have stiffened but are still pink in the center. Refer to the complementary seasonings for poultry for seasoning ideas.

• Sauté halved livers with the mushrooms in Quick Mushroom Sauce, substituting crumbled dried sage for the oregano.

• Sauté halved livers with sliced mushrooms and minced shallots in butter, add heavy cream, heat and toss into freshly cooked pasta. Sprinkle generously with freshly grated Parmesan cheese.

• Chop sautéed livers coarsely and combine with sautéed minced onions and shredded Gruyère cheese. Use as filling for Beef, Chicken or Turkey Rolls.

• Heat sautéed livers in sour cream and dry sherry and serve over freshly cooked pasta.

• Chop sautéed livers coarsely and combine with sautéed sliced mushrooms and minced garlic in Light Cream Sauce. Season to taste, serve on toast and top with poached eggs.

• Heat sautéed livers in Mushroom Sauce and serve over steamed rice.

• Dip halved livers in melted butter, coat with dry bread crumbs, thread on skewers and broil 3 to 4 minutes per side. Serve as an hors d'oeuvre with Teriyaki Marinade for dipping.

• Marinate halved chicken livers and sliced water chestnuts in Teriyaki Marinade. Wrap in blanched bacon, secure with toothpick and broil until bacon is crisp. Serve as an hors d'oeuvre.

• Wrap halved chicken livers around small pieces of sweet gherkin. Wrap in blanched bacon, secure with toothpick and broil until bacon is crisp. Serve as an hors d'oeuvre.

## IDEAS FOR
## CHICKEN GIBLETS

• Finely chop gizzards and hearts. Brown in butter with minced onion and garlic. Add Quick Tomato Sauce, cover and simmer until giblets are tender, adding dry white wine if sauce thickens. Add chopped fresh parsley and serve over cooked pasta with freshly grated Parmesan cheese.

• Marinate thinly sliced gizzards and hearts in Teriyaki Marinade. Sauté gizzards slowly in butter and oil until crunchy tender, sprinkling with Bell's Seasoning as they cook; add hearts last 3 minutes of cooking. Serve as an hors d'oeuvre with cocktail picks.

• Boil gizzards in salted water with thyme, bay leaf, onion slices and parsley sprigs 15 to 25 minutes or until tender. Drain (save cooking water for stock), trim and cut into bite-size pieces. Wrap in blanched bacon, secure with toothpick and broil until bacon is crisp. Serve as an hors d'oeuvre.

## IDEAS FOR CHICKEN WINGS

Cut tips from wings and cut wings into two pieces at joints, removing any excess fat and loose skin. (Reserve tips, fat and skin for soup stock.)

• Prepare as for fricasseed chicken and serve with dumplings.

• Cook in Quick Tomato Sauce until tender.

• Marinate in Teriyaki Marinade and barbecue over medium-hot coals.

---

*Rub salt or lemon juice into chicken or other poultry before cooking to bring out the bird's natural flavors.*

---

---

*For better flavor, marinate defrosted chicken in fresh lemon juice for 1 hour before cooking.*

---

## INDEX TO RECIPES

## COOKING GUIDELINES FOR TURKEY

**COMPLEMENTARY SEASONINGS AND COMBINATIONS** See Complementary Seasonings and Combinations for chicken.

**ROAST TURKEY** Cooking time depends upon age and fat content of turkey; minutes per pound decrease the larger the bird. A 6- to 8-pound bird, stuffed, will need 20 to 35 minutes per pound; a 10- to 12-pound bird, 18 to 20 minutes; and an 18- to 25-pound bird, 15 to 18 minutes. (If the bird is not stuffed, decrease cooking time 5 minutes per pound.) When using a meat thermometer, insert between thigh and body, being careful thermometer doesn't touch a bone. The thermometer should register 180°F when the turkey is done. Put the giblets (if not used in stuffing) and neck in a saucepan with water or chicken stock. Add

*For easy cleaning of your roasting pan, brush pan and rack with Lecithin Oil before roasting meat.*

sliced onion, carrot, celery leaves, lightly crushed black peppercorns, parsley sprigs and green onion tops. Bring to boil, lower heat and simmer as the turkey cooks; use for basting the bird and for making gravy.

The turkey should be at room temperature before roasting. Rub the bird with softened butter and sprinkle with salt, freshly ground white pepper and Bell's Seasoning or other ground seasonings to taste. Place the bird on its side on a rack in a shallow baking pan. Dip a piece of cheesecloth in melted lard or olive oil and drape cloth around bird. Roast in a preheated 325°F oven for half the total cooking time calculated with above minutes-per-pound figures. Baste with a mixture of half giblet stock and half dry white wine, sherry or vermouth, with a little butter added, or with other complementary stock. Turn bird over and re-cover with cheesecloth. Roast for balance of cooking time, basting often. Remove turkey from oven and place breast side up on a platter. Let stand 15 minutes before carving.

**ROAST TURKEY BREAST** For a 3-1/2- to 4-1/2-pound half turkey breast. Marinate turkey in fresh lemon or lime juice several hours. Drain and pat dry. Sprinkle underside of breast with salt and freshly ground black pepper. Place on a rack in a shallow baking pan. Combine 1 tablespoon peanut oil, 1 teaspoon soy sauce, 1 teaspoon *each* minced garlic and ginger root and 1 tablespoon fresh lemon juice. Rub this mixture over skin side of breast. Roast in preheated 325°F oven 30 minutes. Pour 3 tablespoons dry white wine or sherry over turkey and, basting often with pan juices and adding more wine or turkey stock if needed, cook 45 minutes or until meat thermometer registers 180°F. If breast is browning too rapidly, cover loosely with foil. The last 10 or 15 minutes of cooking, brush on 1 to 2 teaspoons honey when basting. Remove from oven, drizzle with 1 tablespoon fresh lemon juice and let stand 5 minutes before carving.

## IDEAS FOR TURKEY

● Cook minced onion and garlic in butter, covered, until soft. Add julienned cooked carrots or zucchini, or chopped cooked broccoli, and shredded cooked turkey. Toss to coat well and add heavy cream, freshly grated Parmesan cheese, salt and freshly ground white pepper. Toss into freshly cooked pasta. Sprinkle with chopped fresh parsley and serve with extra Parmesan cheese.

● Cook minced green bell pepper and onions in butter until soft. Mix with cubed cooked turkey, chopped fresh chives, salt and freshly ground white pepper. Moisten with turkey gravy and use as filling for Turnovers.

● Prepare stuffing crust (see Turkey Pie with Stuffing Crust) and fill with turkey in gravy. Sprinkle with freshly grated Parmesan cheese and bake in preheated 350°F oven 20 minutes, or until heated through and bubbly.

● Prepare Corned Beef Hash, using shredded cooked turkey for corned beef, and toss in chopped pecans that have been lightly browned in butter.

● Combine and heat turkey in gravy with chopped cooked vegetables of choice. Top with mashed potatoes (see Shepherd's Pie), sprinkle with freshly grated Parmesan cheese and bake in a preheated 350°F oven 15 to 20 minutes, or until heated and bubbly.

● Arrange cooked broccoli flowerets on bottom of buttered shallow baking dish. Sprinkle with freshly grated Parmesan cheese and strew cubed cooked turkey over. Fold a little whipped cream into Light or Medium Cream Sauce made with turkey stock and pour over broccoli and turkey, letting sauce flow down into dish. Sprinkle with extra Parmesan cheese and paprika and bake in 400°F oven 15 minutes, or until bubbly.

## INDEX TO RECIPES

# Meats

Commercial beef, veal, pork and lamb are available in six basic grades that are based on tenderness, juiciness and flavor. The home consumer, however, need only be concerned with two of these grades, choice and good, as the other four are usually only sold outside the home market. All of these meats are divided into basically the same cuts, with the differences between the cuts of each animal distinguished by flesh to bone ratio. The tender cuts, principally steaks, are generally cooked by dry-heat methods, such as broiling, pan frying, stir frying and sautéing, while the tougher cuts, chuck, brisket, short rib, shank, etc., are best suited to methods that use liquid—stewing, braising and fricasseeing. Some portions of the flank, chuck and rump may be cooked by dry or moist methods.

Buying meat in quantity, whether family packs available at many supermarkets or a side of beef from a specialty market, can save money, for if handled properly, meat freezes well. All meat should be wrapped airtight for freezing; beef will keep up to nine months, pork, veal and lamb up to six months, variety meats about two months and ground meats for six weeks. Cured and smoked meats and sausages should be frozen no longer than one month. If possible, defrost all meats in the refrigerator.

For refrigeration, fresh meats should be wrapped loosely to ensure ventilation. Small cuts of beef can be stored two to three days and larger cuts four to five days. Veal, lamb and pork should be kept no more than two days, while innards, fresh sausage and ground meats should be used within twenty-four hours. Cured or smoked meats or sausages may be refrigerated up to seven days in the original wrapper. Be wary of any meat that becomes slimy to the touch or develops an off odor.

Though most cooks have a favorite way of preparing the many cuts of meat, the Cooking Guidelines that follow produce particularly flavorful results. Cook the larger cuts as suggested here, serve for dinner and then freeze the leftovers for another meal. Cooked meats are best if frozen no more than two months; defrost in the refrigerator.

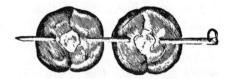

## COOKING GUIDELINES FOR BEEF

**COMPLEMENTARY SEASONINGS AND COMBINATIONS** Marjoram, chervil, rosemary, basil, thyme, savory, tarragon, mustard, cloves, horseradish, garlic, onion, sesame seeds, mushrooms, corn, tomatoes, potatoes, legumes.

**RUMP OR ROLLED POT ROAST** For a 3- to 4-pound roast. Combine 1 teaspoon dry mustard and 1/2 teaspoon each paprika, salt and crumbled dried dill. Toss in 1 teaspoon finely minced garlic and 1/2 teaspoon finely minced ginger root. Make a paste of this mixture with 3 tablespoons softened butter. Rub onto all sides of roast and sprinkle roast with freshly ground black pepper. Place meat on a double thickness of heavy-duty foil in a shallow baking pan. Bring foil up slightly to form a boat and pour in 1/2 cup dry white wine.

Strew sliced onion around meat and bring foil up to completely cover meat. Roast in a preheated 375°F oven 2 to 3 hours, depending upon size, or until fork tender. Make gravy from the pan juices.

**HAMBURGERS** For 1 pound ground chuck. Combine 1 egg, lightly beaten, 2 tablespoons Chili Sauce, 2/3 cup fresh or dry coarse bread crumbs or croutons, 1 teaspoon soy sauce, 1 teaspoon Worcestershire sauce, 1 to 2 garlic cloves, finely minced, 2 tablespoons grated onion and and juices and 1/4 cup milk. Let stand until bread has absorbed the milk. Add 1/2 teaspoon crumbled dried oregano, 1/2 teaspoon salt and 1/4 teaspoon freshly ground black pepper. Mix well and then mix in 1 pound ground chuck. Adjust seasonings (sauté a small amount, taste and adjust) and, if time allows, cover and refrigerate 3 to 4 hours. Form mixture into patties and broil or barbecue, cooking until meat is done to your liking.

*Beaten egg and bread crumbs are often leftover after breading meats. Beat them together, heat rich stock, and stir mixture in with a fork to form long strands. Alternately, add extra bread crumbs to form stiff mixture, form patties and fry with breaded meat.*

**BOILED BEEF** For a 3- to 4-pound beef brisket, bottom round or rump roast. Place meat in a Dutch oven or heavy saucepan just large enough to hold the meat and add chicken or pork stock to barely cover. Add 2 leeks, chopped, 1 parsley root, chopped (optional), 1 onion studded with 2 or 3 whole cloves, 1 carrot, chopped, 1 celery stalk and leaves, chopped, 10 black peppercorns, lightly crushed, 1 bay leaf, 3 parsley sprigs and 4 thyme sprigs. Cover, bring to gentle boil, lower heat and simmer 3 hours, or until meat is tender. Taste broth and add salt as needed. If not serving at once, let cool in liquid, then reheat in liquid when ready to serve. Strain liquid for gravy, or reserve for soup stock or cream sauces. Boiled beef is best if made 1 or 2 days before serving.

**BOILED TONGUE** For a 3-1/2- to 4-pound tongue. Soak smoked tongue in cold water to cover overnight. Drain and wipe with paper toweling. Cook smoked tongue and fresh tongue as for boiled beef, omitting carrot and adding 6 juniper berries, lightly crushed, and 1 lemon, sliced. Tongue is best if cooked 1 or 2 days before serving.

*Meats such as tongue and boiling beef require* slow *cooking to be tender.*

**CORNED BEEF** For a 3- to 3-1/2-pound brisket. Place brisket in a deep ceramic or glass container. Pour cold water over to completely cover. Strew over meat one of the following combinations: 1 to 2 teaspoons pickling spices and 1/2 to 1 lemon, sliced; 3 to 4 whole cloves, 1 bay leaf, broken, 6 black peppercorns, lightly crushed, 3 to 4 cardamom seeds, peeled, and rind of 1 lemon; or 6 allspice berries, lightly crushed, 4 whole cloves, 2 bay leaves, broken, and 1 lemon, sliced. Cover container and refrigerate 24 to 36 hours, turning meat occasionally. Remove from marinade and pat dry. Place fat side up in shallow baking pan and spread with Dijon-style mustard or a mixture of 2 parts French's mustard and 1 part prepared horseradish. Pat brown sugar over to make a coating 1/4 inch thick. Bake in preheated 350°F oven 1-1/2 to 2 hours, or until meat is fork tender. Let stand 15 to 20 minutes before carving.

## IDEAS FOR BEEF

● Combine crumbled blue cheese, softened butter, mashed anchovy fillets and chopped hard-cooked eggs. Spread on thinly sliced roast beef, roll and chill. Slice crosswise, garnish with parsley sprigs and serve as an hors d'oeuvre.

● Spread steak tartare between 2 thin slices of French bread. Freeze. Butter both sides of sandwich, broil, flip over and brown other side. Steak tartare should still be rare.

● Spread a layer of steak tartare 1/4 inch thick on split English muffin, spread a little Chili Sauce over and sprinkle with grated Cheddar or Monterey Jack cheese. Broil just until cheese is melted.

● Substitute cooked beef for the corned beef in Corned Beef Hash.

● Cover bottom of shallow baking dish with thin coating of Tomato Sauce and layer cooked beef slices on it. Top with layer of grated mozzarella cheese, then cooked eggplant slices and finally more grated cheese. Pour Tomato Sauce over the top, sprinkle with freshly grated Parmesan cheese and bake in a preheated 350°F oven 20 minutes, or until bubbly.

## INDEX TO RECIPES

*Avocado slices complement liver and onions. Toss into pan at the last minute and sauté briefly.*

## COOKING GUIDELINES FOR VEAL

**COMPLEMENTARY SEASONINGS AND COMBINATIONS** Marjoram, savory, oregano, basil, bay, thyme, saffron, lemon, garlic, onion, mushrooms, artichokes, asparagus, green beans, bulghur, noodles, potatoes, anchovy, ham.

**ROAST VEAL** For a 3-1/2- to 4-1/2-pound rolled leg of veal. Wipe veal roll with dampened paper toweling and make slashes all over the surface. Mash together 2 to 3 garlic cloves, minced, 3 tablespoons minced fresh parsley, 2 tablespoons minced green onion tops, 1 tablespoon minced shallots, 2 teaspoons minced fresh thyme and 1 tablespoon olive oil. Gradually stir in 1 tablespoon fresh lemon juice. Add 1/2 teaspoon

*each* dry mustard and freshly grated lemon rind, 1/4 teaspoon freshly ground white pepper and an additional 1/2 to 1 tablespoon olive oil. Rub this mixture into the veal roll, forcing it down into the slashes so flavors will penetrate. Drizzle an additional 1 or 2 tablespoons fresh lemon juice over, wrap in plastic wrap and refrigerate overnight. Remove veal roll from refrigerator 2 hours before cooking. Unwrap and place on a rack in a shallow baking pan. Roast in a preheated 300°F oven 35 to 40 minutes per pound, or until meat thermometer registers 170° to 175°F. Let stand 10 minutes before carving.

**BRAISED VEAL ROAST** For a 3- to 3-1/2-pound rolled shoulder of veal. In a Dutch oven, brown veal roast on all sides in equal parts butter and safflower oil. Remove meat and set aside. Adding more butter and/or oil as needed, brown chopped vegetables (see Mirepoix). Deglaze pan with 1/2 cup dry white wine. Return meat to pot

---

*When breading pounded veal or pork steaks, always dry on wire rack at room temperature 1 hour before browning. Coating will cling to meat better.*

---

and baste with juices. If your butcher has not tied a layer of fat on one side of roast, cover with 3 or 4 strips of pork fat back or bacon. Cover roast with foil, cover pot and place in lower third of a preheated 325°F oven. Cook, basting often, 35 to 40 minutes per pound, or until meat thermometer registers 170° to 175°F. During cooking, add more wine or veal or chicken stock, if needed.

**SWEETBREADS** For 2 pounds. Cover sweetbreads with ice water, changing water twice, for 30 minutes. Drain and place in saucepan with a mixture of 2 cups dry white wine, 2 large carrots, cut up, 2 celery stalks and leaves, cut up, 2 medium onions, quartered, 8 thyme or lemon thyme sprigs, 6 parsley sprigs, 1 teaspoon salt and 14 black peppercorns, lightly crushed. Pour boiling water over to barely cover, bring to gentle boil, cover saucepan, lower heat and simmer 10 to 15 minutes, depending upon size of sweetbreads. During cooking, turn sweetbreads over once. Remove from heat, tip lid and let cool in cooking liquid, then cover and refrigerate overnight to blend flavors. Remove sweetbreads, trim fat and membrane and pull apart into pieces. Strain cooking liquid and reserve. If freezing, place sweetbreads in jar and pour strained liquid in up to 1 inch from top of jar. Cover and freeze up to 2 months. Use cooking liquid for cream sauces or soups if not using in specific sweetbreads recipe.

## IDEAS FOR VEAL AND SWEETBREADS

● Combine diced cooked veal and thinly sliced onions sautéed in butter. Sprinkle with paprika and ground thyme. Drizzle Kitchen Bouquet or Maggi's Seasoning over, cook, stirring, 10 minutes and add veal or beef stock and dry white wine. Cook several minutes to heat, then thicken with cornstarch dissolved in cold water. Serve over cooked noodles.

● Spread toast with butter mixed with mashed anchovy fillets, dry mustard and ground oregano. Top with a slice of cooked veal and a slice of mozzarella cheese. Broil until cheese is melted.

● Combine cooked sweetbread pieces with diced cooked ham and chicken in Light or Medium Cream Sauce made with sweetbread cooking liquid. Spoon into buttered ramekins, sprinkle with Buttered Bread Crumbs or Parmesan Crumb Topping and bake in a preheated 350°F oven 15 minutes, or until heated through and bubbly.

● Dip cooked sweetbread pieces into egg beaten with fresh lemon juice, coat with Seasoned Bread Crumbs and brown on all sides in butter and safflower oil.

● Combine cooked sweetbread pieces with Quick Mushroom Sauce. Spoon into buttered ramekins and tuck dessert grapes around edges. Bake in a preheated 350°F oven 15 minutes, or until heated through and bubbly.

● Brown chopped onion, leeks and carrot in rendered chicken fat. Sprinkle with rice flour, stir in enough rich chicken or veal stock to make a soup and bring to boil. Add diced cooked potatoes and sweetbreads and bring back to boil. Add shredded cabbage and boil gently until cabbage is tender; adjust seasonings. Stir chopped tomato into soup just before serving.

● Combine cooked sweetbread pieces and Medium Cream Sauce made with sweetbread cooking liquid. Spoon into hollowed out tomatoes, top with Buttered Bread Crumbs and bake in a 350°F oven 10 to 15 minutes.

## INDEX TO RECIPES

*To save energy and assure proper cooking time, have meats at room temperature before cooking.*

## COOKING GUIDELINES FOR HAM

**COMPLEMENTARY SEASONINGS AND COMBINATIONS** Allspice, cloves, cardamom, nutmeg, mustard, horseradish, currant jelly, pineapple, orange, raisins, brown sugar, hard-cooked eggs, green vegetables, chicken, turkey, sweetbreads.

**BAKED HAM** For a 16- to 18-pound bone-in processed ham. Score ham diagonally across top and bake in a preheated 350°F oven 15 minutes. Remove from oven and insert a whole clove in each diagonal. Pack brown sugar over top surface of ham and arrange unpeeled orange slices on sugar. Return ham to oven for 10 minutes. Melt 1/4 pound butter with 1 teaspoon ground allspice and mix in two 6-ounce cans undiluted orange juice concentrate and 1-1/2 cups ginger ale. Remove ham from oven and carefully baste with the butter mixture. Lower oven heat to 325°F and return ham to oven. Continue baking 3 to 4 hours until done, basting with butter mixture every 15 to 20 minutes.

**BAKED HAM SLICE** For a slice approximately 1 inch thick. Place ham slice in baking dish with tight-fitting lid. Cover with sliced tart apples, sprinkle with a little brown sugar, ground cloves and freshly grated nutmeg, and pour in port wine to barely cover bottom of dish. Cover tightly and bake in a preheated 325°F oven 45 minutes or until tender, basting several times with juices and adding more port if needed.

## IDEAS FOR HAM

• Alternate cubes of cooked ham and pineapple chunks on skewers. Brush while barbecuing with a mixture of melted butter and orange liqueur.

• Place a slice of cooked ham on a toasted English muffin half. Top with a poached egg and cover with Basic Hollandaise.

• Place a slice of cooked ham on French Toast. Cover with Quick Mushroom Sauce.

• Spread *very* thin slices of cooked ham with softened cream cheese combined with minced fresh dill and freshly ground white pepper. Roll like a cigar, chill and serve as an hors d'oeuvre.

• Add finely minced cooked ham to Welsh Rabbit.

• Add coarsely ground cooked ham to biscuit dough.

## INDEX TO RECIPES

## COOKING GUIDELINES FOR PORK

**COMPLEMENTARY SEASONINGS AND COMBINATIONS** Rosemary, sage, oregano, marjoram, ginger root, soy sauce, Oriental sesame oil, garlic, onion, dried fruits such as prunes and pears, fresh fruits such as pears and apples, green vegetables, eggplant, tomatoes, mushrooms, lentils, tofu (bean curd), clams, prawns, ham.

**ROAST LOIN OF PORK** For a 3- to 4-pound pork loin. Mash together 1 teaspoon olive oil, 2 large garlic cloves, minced, 1 tablespoon minced fresh parsley and 1 teaspoon *each* minced fresh rosemary, fresh chives and freshly grated lemon rind. Gradually add 2 to 3 teaspoons more olive oil and then stir in 1 tablespoon grated onion and juices, 1/2 teaspoon salt and 1/4 teaspoon freshly ground black pepper. Wipe pork with dampened paper toweling and spread herb mixture over roast. Wrap roast in plastic wrap

and refrigerate 8 hours or overnight. Remove from refrigerator several hours before roasting. Unwrap, place on rack in shallow baking pan and cook in a preheated 350°F oven 30 to 45 minutes per pound, or until meat thermometer registers 180° to 185°F. Halfway through cooking, add 1 cup dry white wine or bourbon and baste frequently. If herb mixture appears to be browning too much, cover roast loosely with aluminum foil. Let roast stand 10 to 15 minutes at room temperature before carving. A boned and rolled pork roast may be prepared in the same manner. Increase the cooking time 5 to 10 minutes per pound.

## IDEAS FOR PORK

● Heat diced cooked pork and sautéed sliced mushrooms in Light or Medium Cream Sauce Enriched with Egg Yolk made with half pork stock. Serve on toasted cornbread.

● Combine sliced onion and green bell pepper sautéed in butter with diced cooked pork, chopped tomatoes, sugar, salt, freshly ground black pepper and chili powder. Simmer, covered, 45 minutes. Thicken with cornstarch dissolved in cold water and serve over cooked white or brown rice.

*When beating eggs to be used for coating meat to be fried, add 1 teaspoon fresh lemon juice for each egg.*

● Combine minced onion and celery sautéed in butter, cubed cooked pork, fresh or dry pumpernickel crumbs, salt and freshly ground black pepper. Moisten with flat beer, cover and bake in a preheated 375°F oven 30 minutes, adding more beer if needed. Serve on cooked pasta.

## INDEX TO RECIPES

## COOKING GUIDELINES FOR LAMB

**COMPLEMENTARY SEASONINGS AND COMBINATIONS** Rosemary, basil, oregano, mint, chervil, thyme, marjoram, lemon, parsley, chives, juniper berries, mustard, mint jelly, chutney, red wine, garlic, onion, artichokes, eggplant, tomatoes, grains, potatoes, lentils, garbanzo beans.

**ROAST LEG OF LAMB** For a 5- to 8-pound leg. Wipe roast with a dampened towel or paper toweling. Make 8 to 10 slits in the top and bottom of lamb leg and insert a sliver of garlic in each slit. Rub with crushed fresh rosemary or basil and fresh lemon juice. Sprinkle with salt and freshly ground black pepper. Wrap in plastic wrap and refrigerate overnight. Let come to room temperature before roasting. Unwrap and place on a rack in a shallow baking pan. Roast in a preheated 325°F oven 15 to 20 minutes per pound for medium rare, or until a meat thermometer registers 140° to 150°F, or 25 to 30 minutes per pound for well done, or until meat thermometer

*Roast whole head of garlic in a preheated 350°F oven 20 to 45 minutes (depending on size of head) until cloves are quite soft. Squeeze cloves onto French bread slices, crackers, or cooked vegetables and meats.*

registers 175° to 180°F. Alternately, insert garlic slivers as described. Make a paste of 5 tablespoons French's mustard, 3 tablespoons prepared horseradish and 1/2 teaspoon *each* salt and freshly ground black pepper. Coat lamb roast with paste and roast as described. If desired, halfway through cooking time for either method, add 1/2 to 1 cup rich lamb or beef stock, or dry red or white wine to pan. Baste roast frequently, adding more liquid as needed. Let roast stand 15 minutes before carving.

**BONED ROLLED LAMB ROAST** Roast as described for leg of lamb, increasing cooking time 5 to 10 minutes per pound.

## IDEAS FOR LAMB

● Heat slivered cooked lamb roast in a rich vegetable soup. Generously sprinkle soup with chopped fresh mint. Bring just to boil and serve at once.

● Heat chopped cooked lamb roast with cooked millet or barley, chopped beet greens, chopped tomatoes and seasonings as desired in a skillet until moisture evaporates.

● Sauté diced salt pork, minced onion and minced garlic until salt pork is crisp. Add cooked lentils and cubed cooked lamb roast. Moisten with rich lamb stock, cover and heat. Adjust seasonings and stir in minced fresh parsley.

● Heat lamb gravy with tomato paste and sautéed minced onions and sliced mushrooms. Add cubed cooked lamb roast, seasonings as desired and rich lamb stock if needed to moisten. Heat and serve over cooked rice or noodles.

## INDEX TO RECIPES

# RECIPES

# STOCKS & SOUPS

## STOCKS FROM LEFTOVER COOKED BONES

Most cooks know that the carcass of the Thanksgiving turkey makes a rich, flavorful stock, but using the bones of cooked poultry and meats to make this all-important ingredient should not end there. The carcass from Sunday's roast chicken or the bones from last night's pork chop or leg of lamb dinner will also make a delicious stock. Just freeze all of your leftover bones until there's time to make stock. You can even mix the bones in the kettle: a few chicken bones in a pork stock are good, or combine pork and beef bones. Chicken stock should, however, generally only be made with chicken bones and scraps, as its distinct flavor is important to the success of many dishes.

To improve the flavor of any stock, cut up the bones, if possible, and brown the vegetables and bones, preferably in rendered chicken fat, before adding the remaining ingredients. Once the stock is cooked and strained, boil it down to reduce the liquid and to concentrate the flavor, making what is called in this book rich stock. Because leftover bones are not as flavorful as fresh ones, you may add a good-quality bouillon cube or soup stock base during this reducing procedure to further intensify the bouquet of the stock.

Refrigerate the stock until you are ready to use it. If in a week's time you want to continue to refrigerate it, bring it to a boil, rejar and refrigerate again. The stock may also be frozen for up to three months, but be sure to leave head space to allow for expansion during freezing.

Do not defat stock until you are ready to use it, as the fat helps prevent spoilage. The fat solidifies on the surface of the stock once it has been refrigerated, and can then be easily lifted off and discarded. Also, never defat the stock before freezing it. When the stock is thawed, heat it, rejar and refrigerate until the fat solidifies, then lift off. If, however, you want to use freshly made stock immediately, skim off as much of the fat as possible with a shallow spoon and then float an ice cube on the surface to congeal the rest.

Some people clarify all of their stocks because they prefer a very clear liquid. Stocks made from leftover cooked bones are generally murkier in appearance than those made from fresh bones, so you may find you want to clarify them. Place the stock to be clarified in a saucepan. For each quart of stock, beat together one egg white, two tablespoons cold water and one crumbled egg shell and add to pan. Stir well, heat to boiling, boil two minutes, then remove from the heat and let stand, without stirring, twenty minutes. Pour through a strainer lined with dampened cheesecloth.

The following stock recipes use leftover cooked bones, but do not be limited by them. You can also combine cooked bones with uncooked bones and scraps. Freeze the wing tips, neck and tail of a whole chicken you are cutting into serving pieces and add them to your next batch of stock. Never throw out parsley and mushroom stems, vegetable peels, corn cobs and other vegetable scraps. Refrigerate or freeze them in a single container. Vegetable cooking water should also be refrigerated or frozen for adding to the stock pot.

# POULTRY STOCK

*Makes Approximately Three Quarts*

2 carrots, chopped
2 leeks, chopped (white and some green)
2 turnips, chopped
2 onions, unpeeled and quartered
2 garlic cloves, minced
3 to 4 tablespoons rendered chicken fat
1 turkey carcass, halved, or 2 chicken, duck or geese carcasses, plus any leftover scraps and giblets
6 parsley sprigs
1 thyme sprig
1 bay leaf
6 black peppercorns, lightly crushed
1/2 tablespoon salt
1/2 teaspoon poultry seasoning
1/2 teaspoon ground turmeric
3 quarts water

In a large soup kettle, brown all the vegetables and the garlic in rendered fat. Push the vegetables to one side and brown the carcass. Add all remaining ingredients, cover, bring slowly to rapid boil and skim off any surface scum. Lower heat and simmer, covered, 2 hours. Strain and adjust seasonings. Jar, cool, cover and refrigerate.

# ROAST BEEF STOCK

*Makes Approximately Two Quarts*

2 onions, chopped
2 carrots, chopped
2 celery stalks and tops, chopped
2 leeks, chopped
2 garlic cloves (optional)
3 tablespoons corn oil and/or rendered beef fat
6 or 7 cracked ribs of leftover rib roast of beef and any scraps, or bones from cooked pot roast, boiled beef, etc.
6 black peppercorns, lightly crushed
8 parsley sprigs
1 thyme sprig
1 marjoram sprig
1 bay leaf
1/2 tablespoon salt
1/2 cup mushroom stems, or 2 to 3 dried mushrooms, soaked to soften
2 quarts cold water

In a large soup kettle, brown all the vegetables and the garlic in oil and/or rendered fat. Push the vegetables to one side and brown the bones. Add all remaining ingredients, bring slowly to rapid boil and skim off any surface scum. Lower heat and simmer, covered, 2 hours. Strain and adjust seasonings. Jar, cool, cover and refrigerate.

**PORK STOCK** Follow directions for Roast Beef Stock, using leftover pork bones instead of beef bones; add 1 teaspoon sage and 1 oregano sprig.

**LAMB STOCK** Follow directions for Roast Beef Stock, using leftover leg of lamb bones and scraps instead of beef bones; add 1 rosemary sprig and 1 oregano sprig.

**GAME STOCK** Follow directions for Roast Beef Stock, using leftover venison bones, pheasant or partridge carcasses, or rabbit bones, plus scraps and giblets instead of beef bones. Substitute basil leaves for marjoram, and add 6 to 8 juniper berries, lightly crushed, and 3 to 4 whole cloves.

---

*Save potato peelings and add to stock pot for extra nutrients.*

## VEGETABLE STOCK FROM LEFTOVERS

Use twice as much liquid, either plain water or water leftover from steaming vegetables or boiling potatoes, as cooked or raw vegetables. Tomatoes, lettuce, parsnips, leeks, rutabagas, turnips, pods from shelled peas, green beans, carrots, onions, asparagus ends, green onion tops and mushroom stems would all be good additions. In a soup kettle, brown all the vegetables in safflower or corn oil. Add liquid and season with herbs and spices as desired. Cover, bring to boil, lower heat and simmer 2 hours. Strain and adjust seasonings, then reduce to concentrate flavor, if desired. Jar, cool, cover and refrigerate up to 3 days or freeze up to 1 month.

## FISH STOCK

This is an ideal way to use the scraps that remain when cutting up whole fish for cooking. Fish Stock should not be refrigerated for more than two days, or frozen for more than two months.

*Makes Approximately Four Cups*
2 cups water
2 cups dry white wine
2 pounds fish heads, bones, shells
   from any nonoily fish
1 onion, chopped
3 parsley sprigs
1 bay leaf
1 thyme sprig
2 tablespoons fresh lemon juice
1 teaspoon minced fresh tarragon
1 teaspoon freshly grated lemon
   rind
6 black peppercorns, lightly
   crushed
2 whole cloves
1/2 cup mushroom stems (optional)
1 teaspoon salt
1 tablespoon butter or safflower oil

Combine all ingredients in a soup kettle, cover, bring slowly to rapid boil and skim off any surface scum. Lower heat and simmer, covered, 45 minutes. Strain, jar, cool, cover and refrigerate or freeze.

## CELERY BROTH

If your household has a hard time using up a whole head of celery before it begins to wilt, this recipe will help solve the problem. Celery Broth can be used in place of any vegetable stock, and is a good base for the Rich-Stock Suggestions that follow.

*Makes Approximately Six Cups*
2-1/2 cups chopped celery and
   some leaves
1/2 cup chopped onion and/or
   white of leeks
2 large ripe tomatoes, chopped
3 tablespoons butter
6 cups rich chicken stock
1 bay leaf
3 parsley sprigs
Salt and freshly ground white
   pepper to taste
Celery salt to taste

In a soup kettle, cook celery, onion and tomatoes in butter, covered, until onions are soft. Add stock, bay leaf and parsley. Cover, bring to gentle boil, lower heat and simmer 20 minutes. Add salt, pepper and celery salt. Strain and adjust seasonings. Jar, cool, cover and refrigerate up to 3 days, or freeze for up to 1 month.

# RICH–STOCK SUGGESTIONS

● Bring 6 cups rich stock to boil, add 3 tablespoons each cooked julienned turnips and carrots, 1/2 cup cooked peas and 1/2 cup cut-up cooked green beans. Simmer until vegetables are heated through. Sprinkle with minced fresh chervil or parsley and garnish with lemon slices.

● Saute 1/2 cup sliced mushrooms in 1 tablespoon butter. Add to 6 cups rich chicken stock with 1 cup diced cooked chicken and 1/2 cup cooked rice or pasta. Reheat and season with fresh lemon juice. Garnish with watercress.

● Bring 6 cups rich chicken or beef stock to boil, add 1/2 cup cooked peas or asparagus tips and 1/2 cup shredded cooked chicken. Reheat and sprinkle with freshly grated Parmesan cheese and minced fresh parsley and/or chives.

● Heat 3 cups rich stock and 1 cup diced cooked vegetables and/or pasta or grains. In each of 2 soup bowls, place 2 to 3 teaspoons crumbled blue cheese. Pour hot soup over and sprinkle with minced fresh parsley and/or chives.

● Heat 3 cups rich stock, 1 or 2 cooked chicken gizzards, thinly sliced, 1 to 2 crêpes, thinly sliced, and 1/2 cup chopped cooked spinach, beet greens, Swiss chard or turnip greens. Garnish with chopped hard-cooked eggs and paprika.

● Heat 4 cups rich stock. In each of 4 bowls place a slice of slightly stale bread lightly browned in olive oil. Break a small egg onto each slice of bread (if you prefer a more solidly cooked egg, poach lightly first). Carefully pour hot soup over. Sprinkle with minced fresh Italian parsley and paprika.

● Heat 3 cups rich chicken or beef stock, 1/2 cup shredded cooked meat and 3/4 cup chopped cucumbers, sliced fresh mushrooms, shredded raw cabbage or spinach, and/or diced ripe tomatoes. Cover and simmer just until vegetables are tender. Season with fresh lemon juice, salt and freshly ground black pepper. Sprinkle with chopped green onion tops.

# ADDITIONS TO CLEAR SOUPS

The dumplings and balls that follow enhance the presentation of most clear soups. Cook a small amount of the mixture first so that you can taste and adjust the seasonings before cooking the entire batch.

## EGG DUMPLINGS

*Makes Approximately One Dozen*
3 hard-cooked egg yolks
1/4 teaspoon unbleached flour, or as needed
1 egg, lightly beaten
1/2 teaspoon salt
1/8 teaspoon freshly ground white pepper
1/8 teaspoon curry powder

Mash together cooked yolk and flour and mix in raw egg and seasonings, adding more flour as needed to make a workable dough. Form into small balls and drop into gently boiling salted water. Cook 5 minutes, or until balls rise to surface.

*If there's no cheesecloth on hand, use a large coffee filter for clarifying stock.*

## BREAD DUMPLINGS

*Makes Approximately One Dozen*
1 egg, lightly beaten
6 tablespoons fine dry bread
   crumbs, or as needed
1/4 teaspoon cornstarch
1/2 teaspoon milk
1 teaspoon finely minced fresh
   parsley
1/8 teaspoon salt
1/8 teaspoon freshly grated lemon
   rind
1/2 teaspoon grated onion

Mix together all ingredients, using
more bread crumbs if needed to
make a workable dough. Chill at
least 1 hour. Form into 12 small
balls and cook in simmering salted
water 3 minutes after balls rise to
the surface and puff up.

## ROYALES

*For Three to Four Cups Rich Stock*
1/2 cup chicken, veal or beef stock
1 garlic clove, minced
1 large parsley sprig
1 savory or oregano sprig
1/8 teaspoon paprika
1 egg
1 egg yolk
2 to 3 tablespoons any ground
   cooked vegetable, meat, poultry
   or game (optional)

Simmer stock, garlic, herbs and
paprika 10 minutes. Strain and
cool. Preheat oven to 350°F. Beat
together egg and egg yolk
and beat in strained stock. Sieve
into a buttered 4-inch-square shallow
dish and stir in ground vegetable.
Bake in preheated oven 20 minutes,
or until knife inserted in center
comes out clean. Cool, chill and
cut into small squares or other
decorative shapes.

## FORCEMEAT BALLS

*Makes Approximately Twenty-five*
2 hard-cooked egg yolks
1 teaspoon milk
3 tablespoons fine dry bread
   crumbs
1/2 cup ground cooked meat,
   poultry or game
1 egg, lightly beaten
1 teaspoon unbleached flour
1/4 teaspoon salt
1/8 teaspoon freshly ground white
   pepper

Mash hard-cooked yolks with milk
and mix with all remaining ingredients. Flour hands and form small
balls the size of a nutmeg. Drop
into gently boiling broth or salted
water and cook until balls rise to
surface.

## CHICKEN BALLS

For a main dish, form the chicken
mixture into two-inch balls, increase
cooking time to fifteen minutes
and serve with Mushroom Sauce
or Quick Mushroom Sauce.

*Makes Approximately Forty*
1-1/2 cups ground cooked chicken
   or turkey
2 tablespoons finely minced fresh
   parsley
1 egg, lightly beaten
1/2 cup fine dry bread crumbs
1 tablespoon freshly grated
   Parmesan or Romano cheese
1/4 teaspoon salt
1/4 teaspoon freshly ground black
   pepper

Mix together all ingredients, form
into balls the size of large marbles
and refrigerate several hours. Cook
in simmering salted water or broth
10 minutes.

## CREAM SOUPS FROM COOKED VEGETABLES

This basic recipe can be used to transform almost any cooked vegetable into a flavorful cream soup. If you prefer a grainy consistency, use a food processor to purée the soup; for a smoother texture, a blender works best. One-fourth to one-third cup cooked rice or potatoes or one recipe Egg Yolk Binder can be used as a thickener in place of the flour; milk and/or heavy cream can be substituted for part or all of the half-and-half cream; and vegetable cooking water can replace half of the stock. Cooked rice or pasta can be added to any of the cream soups, except potato, after they are puréed.

With the exception of the eggplant, all of the following soups can be served cold. Reduce the half-and-half cream measure to one-half cup and chill the finished soup. Add one-half cup heavy cream, adjust seasonings, chill well again, and then serve the soup in chilled bowls.

Additional vegetables that do not appear here may also be made into cream soups: carrots and other root vegetables, asparagus, peas, green beans and Swiss chard. For complementary herb suggestions, see the specific vegetable in the vegetable section.

Serve any of the cream soups with a bowl of plain yoghurt at table.

*Serves Three or Four*
1/4 cup chopped onion
1/4 cup chopped celery
1 garlic clove, minced
2 tablespoons chopped fresh parsley
1/2 teaspoon chopped fresh basil
1/2 teaspoon chopped fresh marjoram
1/4 teaspoon chopped fresh rosemary
1/8 teaspoon freshly grated nutmeg
1 bay leaf
1/4 teaspoon salt
1/8 teaspoon freshly ground black pepper
1-1/2 tablespoons butter and/or rendered chicken fat
1-1/2 tablespoons unbleached flour
3 cups rich chicken stock
2 cups chopped cooked broccoli
1 cup half-and-half cream
1-1/2 tablespoons tomato paste (optional)
Freshly grated Parmesan cheese

Cook onion, celery, garlic, herbs and seasonings in butter, covered, until soft. Sprinkle with flour and cook, stirring, 2 to 3 minutes, gradually adding 1-1/2 cups of the stock. Add broccoli, cover and cook until vegetables are very soft. Discard bay leaf. Purée and return to saucepan with the remaining 1-1/2 cups stock, cream and tomato paste, stirring to blend well. Heat without boiling, adjust seasonings and serve with Parmesan cheese.

**CAULIFLOWER** Omit nutmeg. Add while sautéing onion 1/2 teaspoon dry mustard and 1/4 teaspoon ground savory. When reheating, add 1/2 cup grated Cheddar cheese. Cook, stirring, until cheese is melted. Garnish with slivered black olives or tiny raw cauliflowerets.

**EGGPLANT** Omit nutmeg, basil, marjoram and rosemary. Sauté with onion 1/4 cup diced fresh mushrooms, a pinch of sugar and 1/4 teaspoon ground sage. Substitute lamb stock for the chicken stock and add the optional tomato paste and 1/4 cup dry red wine. Garnish with finely minced ripe tomato and pass a dish of plain yoghurt.

**LETTUCE** Increase butter measure to 2-1/2 tablespoons. Omit nutmeg, basil, marjoram and rosemary. Sauté with onion 2 to 3 cups shredded lettuce, 1/2 cup chopped watercress and 1/2 to 1 teaspoon minced fresh tarragon or 1/2 to 1 teaspoon curry powder.

**ZUCCHINI** Omit nutmeg. Sauté with onion a pinch of sugar. Garnish with lemon slices.

**SPINACH** Omit basil, marjoram and rosemary. Substitute green onions and tops for onion. Sauté with green onions a pinch of sugar and 2 tablespoons minced fresh dill. Just before serving season to taste with dry sherry. Garnish with chopped or sliced hard-cooked eggs and paprika.

**BUTTERNUT OR HUBBARD SQUASH** Omit nutmeg. Sauté with onion 3/4 cup chopped unpared apple. If desired, omit basil, marjoram and rosemary and sprinkle with 1 to 2 teaspoons curry powder; add a pinch of sugar. Garnish with Chiffonade of sorrel and spinach.

**POTATO** Sauté with onion 1/4 cup minced white of leek, 1-1/2 tablespoons minced carrots and 1/2 teaspoon Beau Monde seasoning. Substitute white pepper for black pepper. Sprinkle with chopped fresh chives and/or parsley and paprika.

---

*Heavy cream is salty, so adjust soup seasonings after the cream has been added.*

---

# CORN CHOWDER

*Serves Four to Six*

1/2 cup chopped onion
1 garlic clove, minced
1/2 teaspoon finely minced fresh sage
1/2 teaspoon finely minced fresh thyme
1/4 teaspoon finely minced fresh rosemary
2 tablespoons rendered chicken fat or butter
1/4 cup very finely minced red bell pepper or chopped pimientos
5 cups rich chicken stock
1-1/2 to 2 cups cooked corn kernels
1-1/2 to 2 cups cubed boiled potatoes
1/2 tablespoon Worcestershire sauce
Dash Tabasco sauce
1-1/2 cups half-and-half cream
Salt and freshly ground black pepper to taste
Chopped hard-cooked eggs
Minced fresh parsley
Paprika

Cook onion, garlic and herbs in rendered fat, covered, until onion starts to soften. Add bell pepper, stock, corn, potatoes, Worcestershire sauce and Tabasco. Bring to gentle boil, lower heat, cover and simmer 10 minutes. Add cream, reheat without boiling and season with salt and pepper. Sprinkle with eggs, parsley and paprika.

**VARIATION** Add with cream 1/2 to 1 cup cooked shredded zucchini.

# CREAM OF CELERY SOUP

*Serves Four to Six*

1 cup very finely minced celery
2 tablespoons very finely minced shallots
2 tablespoons butter
1/2 teaspoon celery salt
1/4 teaspoon freshly ground white pepper
1/8 teaspoon freshly grated nutmeg
2 tablespoons unbleached flour
4 cups Celery Broth
1 cup mashed potatoes (optional)
1/2 cup half-and-half cream
2 to 3 tablespoons sour cream
Fresh lemon juice to taste
Finely chopped celery leaves

Cook celery and shallots in butter, covered, until soft, sprinkling with seasonings as they cook. Sprinkle with flour and cook, stirring, 2 minutes. Gradually add broth and cook, stirring, until slightly thickened. Combine potatoes, cream and sour cream. Stir in and reheat without boiling. Season with lemon juice and adjust seasonings. Garnish with celery leaves.

# GREEN SOUP

For the small amounts of raw greens in the vegetable crisper.

*Serves Four to Six*
2 to 3 cups finely chopped sorrel, spinach, dandelion greens, kale, Swiss chard or any leafy vegetable in any combination
1/4 cup diagonally sliced celery (very thin slices)
1/2 cup slivered green onions and tops
1/4 cup minced fresh parsley
1/4 cup minced watercress
3 tablespoons butter
1 tablespoon unbleached flour
5 cups rich chicken or veal stock
2 egg yolks, lightly beaten
1 cup half-and-half cream
1 tablespoon fresh lemon juice
Salt and freshly ground white pepper to taste
Parmesan Croutons

Cook vegetables and herbs in butter, covered, just until celery is tender. Sprinkle with flour and cook, stirring, 2 to 3 minutes. Gradually add stock and cook, stirring, until slightly thickened. Combine egg yolks and cream. Whisk a little hot soup into cream mixture and return to remaining soup. Whisk over medium heat until thickened. Do not boil. Add lemon juice, salt and pepper. Pass a bowl of croutons.

# SPICY GAZPACHO

*Serves Four to Six*
2 cups stale French bread cubes, soaked in 3 cups water
4 teaspoons minced garlic
1/2 cup minced onion
4 ripe tomatoes, diced
3 tablespoons olive oil
3 tablespoons cider vinegar
1/2 teaspoon salt
1/4 teaspoon freshly ground black pepper
6 drops Tabasco sauce
1/8 teaspoon ground cumin
Diced green tomato or tomatillo (green husk tomato)
Coriander sprigs

In blender or food processor, purée bread and water, garlic, onion, ripe tomatoes, oil, vinegar, salt, pepper, Tabasco and cumin. Chill, adjust seasonings and serve in chilled bowls garnished with diced green tomato and coriander sprigs. Pass the peppermill.

# BREAD AND CABBAGE SOUP

*Serves Four to Six*
8 slices stale sourdough bread
3 to 5 garlic cloves, pressed
1-1/2 cups finely shredded cabbage
3/4 cup finely sliced onion
1 cup Tomato or Quick Tomato Sauce
1/2 teaspoon salt
1/4 teaspoon freshly ground black pepper
3 tablespoons freshly grated Romano cheese
3 tablespoons freshly grated Parmesan cheese
6 cups rich beef stock, or as needed
Minced fresh Italian parsley

Preheat oven to 375°F. Cover the bottom of a large Dutch oven or casserole (with tight lid) with bread, overlapping the slices. Layer the garlic, cabbage and onion on top of the bread. Spread Tomato Sauce over top and sprinkle with salt, pepper and cheeses. *Carefully* pour in stock without disturbing the layers. Cover and bake in preheated oven 45 minutes, checking after 30 minutes and adding extra stock if the soup appears to be too thick. Serve with a generous sprinkling of parsley.

# MINESTRONE

This well-known Italian vegetable soup is an excellent way to use up cooked legumes, vegetables and pasta. Vary the ingredients according to what's on your refrigerator shelf. Any leftover minestrone can be turned into one of the imaginative suggestions that follow.

*Serves Six to Eight*
1/2 cup olive oil
2 rosemary sprigs
2 garlic cloves
1/4 cup minced leek
1/4 cup minced carrot
1/4 cup minced celery
1/2 cup minced onion
2 strips bacon, diced
6 cups vegetable, beef or pork
   stock
3 large ripe tomatoes, peeled and
   chopped
1 cup coarsely chopped Swiss
   chard
2 cups shredded cabbage
1-1/2 cups cooked small white
   beans
1/2 cup coarsely cut cooked
   zucchini
1/2 cup coarsely cut cooked Italian
   green beans
1 cup cooked noodles or rice
Salt and freshly ground black
   pepper to taste
Minced Italian parsley, finely
   minced garlic and freshly grated
   Parmesan cheese at table

In a large soup kettle, heat together oil, rosemary and garlic cloves until garlic browns. Discard rosemary and garlic; pour off 1/4 cup of the oil and set aside. Add leek, carrot, celery, onion and bacon to kettle and sauté until vegetables are soft. Pour stock into kettle, bring to a boil and add tomatoes, Swiss chard and cabbage. Lower heat to simmer and cook for 10 minutes. Add small white beans, zucchini, green beans and noodles. Cook until heated through. Stir in reserved olive oil and season with salt and pepper. Serve with parsley, minced garlic and Parmesan cheese.

## TWO NEXT-DAY SUGGESTIONS

● Bring leftover minestrone to a boil. (If it is *very* thick, thin it slightly with stock.) In a large bowl, make a layer of 1- to 2-inch pieces of stale crusty coarse bread. Ladle hot minestrone over and repeat layers once or twice, as desired. Press top with a spatula or back of a spoon to firm contents. Let cool to room temperature and serve with olive oil, finely minced garlic, minced Italian parsley and Parmesan cheese at table.

---

*Flat-leaved (Italian) parsley has more flavor; curly-leaved parsley makes a more attractive garnish.*

● Arrange slices of stale crusty coarse bread on the bottom of a casserole and sprinkle generously with grated Parmesan cheese. Bring leftover minestrone to a boil and ladle hot soup over. Again sprinkle generously with cheese. Strew top with minced parsley and finely minced garlic and drizzle with olive oil. Bake in a preheated 350°F oven 20 to 30 minutes, or until top is nicely browned.

# PUMPKIN SOUP

Turn your Halloween jack-o'-lantern into this fragrant soup.

*Serves Three or Four*
1 tablespoon grated onion and
   juices
2 tablespoons *very* finely minced
   shallots
2 tablespoons butter
1 tablespoon unbleached flour
1/4 teaspoon granulated sugar
1/2 teaspoon ground ginger
1/4 teaspoon freshly grated nutmeg
1/4 teaspoon freshly ground white
   pepper
2 cups pumpkin purée
3 cups rich chicken stock
1 cup half-and-half cream
Salt
Parsley sprigs
Lemon or orange rind curls

Cook onion and shallots in butter, covered, 3 to 4 minutes until soft. Sprinkle with flour, sugar, ginger, nutmeg and pepper and cook, stirring, 2 minutes. Remove from heat and stir in pumpkin purée and stock. Return to heat and cook, stirring with wire whisk, until slightly thickened and smooth. Stir in cream, reheat without boiling and season with salt, if needed. Garnish with parsley and citrus curls.

**NOTE** If serving cold, reduce half-and-half cream measure to 1/2 cup. Chill, add 1/2 cup heavy cream, adjust seasonings and chill well. Serve in chilled bowls.

## SWEET POTATO SOUP

*Serves Two or Three*
3 tablespoons chopped green onion and tops
1/4 cup chopped celery and some leaves
2 teaspoons butter
2 teaspoons bacon drippings
3/4 cup mashed cooked sweet potatoes or yams
2-1/2 cups rich chicken stock
1/8 teaspoon freshly grated nutmeg
Salt and freshly ground black pepper to taste
Minced fresh parsley and/or chives
Sour cream

Sauté onion and celery in butter and bacon drippings until soft. Add sweet potatoes and 1 cup of the stock and purée in blender or food processor. Return to saucepan with remaining stock. Stirring often, bring almost to a boil. Season with salt and pepper and sprinkle with parsley. Pass the sour cream.

## BROWN LENTIL AND POTATO SOUP

A delicious main-meal soup with or without meat.

*Serves Four or Five*
1/4 cup finely minced onion
1/4 cup finely minced carrot
1/4 cup finely minced celery
1 garlic clove, minced
2 tablespoons bacon drippings
1/4 teaspoon ground thyme
1/2 teaspoon salt
1/4 teaspoon freshly ground black pepper
2 tablespoons tomato paste
5 cups lamb or beef stock
1-1/2 cups cooked lentils
1 cup diced boiled potatoes
1 cup shredded cooked lamb or beef (optional)
1/2 cup cooked shredded zucchini (optional)
1-1/2 tablespoons red-wine vinegar or dry red wine
Finely diced peeled ripe tomatoes
Slivered green onions

Lightly brown onion, carrot, celery and garlic in bacon drippings. Sprinkle with seasonings and stir in tomato paste and 1 cup of the stock. Cover and cook gently, stirring occasionally, 15 minutes. Add remaining stock, lentils, potatoes, meat and zucchini. Bring back to boil, lower heat, cover and simmer 5 minutes. Just before serving, adjust seasonings and stir in tomatoes. Sprinkle generously with green onions.

*Legume soups improve in flavor with reheating.*

# SPLIT PEA SOUP

The ham bone saved from a baked ham teams naturally with split peas for a delicious soup, but other legumes, such as garbanzo beans, lentils and small white beans, would also be good. If there is too little meat on the bone to add to the soup, stir in some sliced cooked sausage. Croutons and a bowl of freshly grated Parmesan cheese at table make good last-minute additions.

Since this recipe makes a sizable amount, you may want to freeze some of the soup. Just remember never to add the evaporated milk before freezing; mix it in when you are reheating the thawed soup for serving.

*Makes Approximately Three Quarts*
2 cups sliced onion
1 cup chopped carrots
3 garlic cloves, chopped
2 cups chopped celery and leaves
2 tablespoons rendered ham fat and/or butter
1 large ham bone
3 quarts water
2 cups green and/or yellow split peas
12 black peppercorns, lightly crushed
6 parsley sprigs
2 bay leaves
4 thyme leaves
4 oregano sprigs
Evaporated milk
Salt and freshly ground black pepper
Dry sherry (optional)

Brown onion, carrots, garlic, celery and leaves in rendered fat. Add ham bone, water, peas, peppercorns and herbs. Cover, bring to gentle boil, lower heat and cook, stirring occasionally, 3 to 4 hours, or until peas are very soft. Remove ham bone and reserve any meat still clinging to bone. Force soup mixture through food mill or sieve, pushing as much pulp through as possible. Jar, cool, cover and refrigerate or freeze. When ready to serve, remove any fat that has risen to top of soup. Reheat and thin with evaporated milk to desired consistency. Stir in reserved meat and season with salt and pepper. Just before serving add sherry to taste.

# GARBANZO BEAN SOUP

Another versatile soup. Add one-half to one cup diced cooked potatoes, cut-up green beans or peas when adding the garbanzo beans.

*Serves Four to Six*
2 cups cooked garbanzo beans
6 cups rich pork stock
1/2 cup chopped onion
1/4 cup chopped green bell pepper
1 to 2 garlic cloves, minced
2 to 3 tablespoons olive oil
1/8 teaspoon saffron threads (optional)
1/2 teaspoon paprika
1/2 teaspoon salt
1/4 teaspoon freshly ground black pepper
1 cup shredded cooked ham or pork roast
1 to 2 large ripe tomatoes, chopped
Minced fresh parsley and/or chives
Garlic Croutons

Purée 1/2 cup of the garbanzo beans with 1 cup of the stock. Sauté onion, bell pepper and garlic in oil until onion is soft. Sprinkle with seasonings and cook, stirring, 2 to 3 minutes. Add garbanzo purée, remaining 5 cups stock, remaining 1-1/2 cups garbanzo beans, ham and tomatoes. Bring to gentle boil, lower heat, cover and simmer 10 to 15 minutes. Adjust seasonings and sprinkle with parsley. Serve with croutons.

# CREAMY
# WHITE BEAN SOUP

*Serves Six*
1 cup chopped onion
1/2 cup chopped celery
1/2 cup chopped celery leaves
1/2 cup chopped carrot
1/2 cup coarsely chopped parsley
   with stems
2 teaspoons chopped fresh basil
2 tablespoons butter
2 tablespoons olive oil
6 cups veal and/or chicken stock
2 tablespoons tomato paste
1/4 teaspoon freshly ground white
   pepper
1-1/2 cups cooked small white
   beans
1 cup half-and-half cream
Salt
Fresh lemon juice
1 cup cooked peas or diced
   cooked vegetables
Chiffonade of sorrel and spinach, or
Slivered black olives

Cook onion, celery, celery leaves,
carrot, parsley and basil in butter
and oil, covered, 15 minutes; do
not brown. Add 2 cups of the
stock, the tomato paste, pepper
and beans. Cover and cook slowly
10 minutes or until the beans are
very soft. Purée in blender or food
processor and return to saucepan
with remaining 4 cups stock and
the cream. Heat and season to
taste with salt and lemon juice.

Add cooked vegetables and reheat.
Garnish with chiffonade.

# CURRIED
# LIMA BEAN SOUP

*Serves Two*
1/4 cup chopped onion
1 garlic clove, minced
1/2 teaspoon minced fresh thyme
2 tablespoons minced fresh parsley
1 teaspoon minced fresh basil
2 teaspoons butter and/or rendered
   chicken fat
1/4 to 1/2 teaspoon curry powder
1 cup cooked fresh or dried lima
   beans
1-1/4 cups chicken stock and/or
   cooking liquid from beans
1 small bay leaf
Salt and freshly ground black
   pepper to taste
1/4 to 1/3 cup half-and-half cream
Chopped hard-cooked egg
Minced fresh chives
Paprika

Cook onion, garlic, thyme, parsley
and basil in butter, covered, until
soft. Sprinkle with curry powder
and cook, stirring, 3 minutes. Add
beans, stock and bay leaf. Cook
over low heat 15 to 20 minutes
until beans are very soft. Discard
bay leaf and purée soup in blender
or food processor. Return to saucepan and add salt, pepper and
cream. Reheat and sprinkle with
chopped egg, chives and paprika.

# RICE AND VERMICELLI
# SOUP

*Serves Three or Four*
1/3 cup minced onion
1 garlic clove, minced
1/2 tablespoon butter
1/2 tablespoon olive oil
1 cup chopped peeled ripe
   tomatoes or Italian tomatoes
4 cups rich beef or chicken stock
2 cups Rice and Vermicelli Pilaf
1/4 cup minced fresh Italian
   parsley
1/4 teaspoon salt
1/8 teaspoon freshly ground black
   pepper
1 recipe Pilou (following)
Freshly grated Romano or
   Parmesan cheese

Sauté onion and garlic in butter
and oil until soft. Add tomatoes,
stock, pilaf, parsley, salt and pepper.
Cover and simmer 5 minutes until
thoroughly heated. Pour over Pilou
in soup tureen. Pass the grated
cheese.

**PILOU** In a soup tureen, beat 2 or
3 egg yolks until lemon colored
and slightly thickened. Drop by
drop, add 2-1/2 to 3 tablespoons
olive oil, beating constantly until
smooth and thickened, but not
quite as thick as mayonnaise.

# GRAIN AND ROOT VEGETABLE SOUP

A quick and easy way to use up any root vegetable—carrots, potatoes, celery root, turnips, parsnips—and that bowl of cooked grain or Grain Pilaf.

*Serves Four to Six*
1-1/2 to 2 cups diced root vegetables
2 large garlic cloves, minced
4 tablespoons rendered chicken fat and/or butter
6 to 8 cups stock
2 cups any cooked grain or Grain Pilaf
1 cup chopped ripe tomato
1/2 teaspoon salt
1/4 teaspoon freshly ground black pepper
1 cup milk or half-and-half cream
Minced fresh parsley and/or chives

Sauté vegetables and garlic in rendered fat until golden. Add stock, grain, tomato, salt and pepper. Simmer, covered, just until vegetables are starting to soften. Add cream, reheat, adjust seasonings and sprinkle with parsley.

---

*Add leftover cooked cereals, such as farina, Malt-O-Meal and Wheatina, to the stock pot or to a vegetable soup.*

---

# FISH CHOWDER

*Serves Five or Six*
1 cup minced white of leeks, onion or green onions, or a combination
1 to 2 garlic cloves, minced
1/4 pound salt pork, diced
3 tablespoons butter
3 cups rich chicken stock
1 bay leaf
1/4 teaspoon ground thyme
1/8 teaspoon ground allspice
1/4 teaspoon freshly ground black pepper
1/4 teaspoon celery salt
1 to 1-1/2 cups diced boiled potatoes
1 cup fish stock or bottled clam juice
1-1/2 cups milk
1/2 cup heavy cream
2 cups flaked cooked firm white fish
Salt to taste
Butter, cut into bits
Slivered green onions and tops
Paprika

Sauté leeks, garlic and salt pork in the 3 tablespoons butter until onion is soft. Add stock and seasonings, bring to gentle boil, lower heat, cover and simmer 10 minutes. Add potatoes, fish stock and milk and simmer 5 minutes. Add cream and fish and heat but do not boil. Season with salt, dot with butter bits and sprinkle with green onions and paprika.

# CURRIED TURKEY SOUP

*Serves Six*
1 cup chopped onion
1 to 2 garlic cloves, minced
3/4 to 1 cup chopped unpared tart apples
2 tablespoons rendered chicken fat or butter
2 teaspoons curry powder, or to taste
1/4 teaspoon ground cardamom, or to taste
6 cups rich turkey stock
1 cup cubed cooked turkey
3 egg yolks, lightly beaten
1 cup buttermilk
Salt and freshly ground white pepper to taste
Minced fresh parsley
Slivered blanched almonds, lightly browned in butter

Sauté onion, garlic and apple in rendered fat, sprinkling with curry powder and cardamom, until onion starts to soften. Add 1 cup of the stock, cover and simmer 20 minutes. Cool slightly and purée in blender or food processor. Return to saucepan, stir in remaining stock and bring to gentle boil. Beat together yolks and buttermilk, stir into stock mixture and season with salt and pepper. Bring just to boil, adjust seasonings and sprinkle with minced parsley. Pass the almonds.

# TURKEY SOUP WITH OYSTERS

*Serves Six*
2 cups diagonally sliced celery
1/2 cup chopped onion
1/2 cup chopped white of leeks
2 garlic cloves, minced
4 tablespoons butter and/or
    rendered chicken fat
2 cups diced cooked turkey
1/4 cup unbleached flour
2 cups milk or half-and-half cream
3 cups rich turkey stock
1/2 teaspoon freshly grated nutmeg
1/2 teaspoon freshly ground white
    pepper
1/2 teaspoon salt
1 to 2 teaspoons fresh lemon juice
2/3 cup cooked peas
1 tablespoon butter
1 pint shucked oysters
Minced fresh parsley or celery
    leaves

Sauté celery, onion, leeks and
garlic in butter and/or rendered
fat until onions are soft. Stir in
turkey and cook several minutes.
Sprinkle with flour and cook, stirring,
2 minutes. Gradually add milk and
stock and cook, stirring, until
smooth and thickened and heated
through. Add seasonings, lemon
juice and peas; keep warm. In a
skillet, heat 1 tablespoon butter
until foamy. Frizzle oysters and

their juices just until edges begin
to curl. Add to hot soup and serve
immediately with a generous
sprinkling of minced parsley.

# COCK-A-LEEKIE SOUP

*Serves Three*
2 cups minced white of leeks and
    a little light green
1 tablespoon rendered chicken fat
    or butter
3 cups rich chicken stock
1-1/2 cups cooked barley
1 cup shredded cooked chicken
1/2 cup half-and-half cream
Dash ground allspice
Salt and freshly ground white
    pepper to taste
Minced fresh parsley

Cook leeks in rendered fat, covered,
until starting to soften. Add stock
and barley, bring to gentle boil,
lower heat, cover and simmer 15
minutes. Add chicken, cream and
seasonings; bring just to boil and
adjust seasonings. Sprinkle with
minced parsley.

# SCOTCH BROTH

*Serves Three or Four*
1/2 cup diced white of leeks and
    a little light green
1/4 cup diced turnips
1/3 cup diced carrots
1/2 cup diced celery and leaves
1 tablespoon butter
1 tablespoon safflower oil
1/2 cup diced fresh mushrooms
1 cup shredded cooked lamb
3 cups lamb stock
1-1/2 cups cooked barley
Salt and freshly ground black
    pepper to taste
2 ripe tomatoes, peeled and diced
Minced fresh parsley

Lightly brown leeks, turnips, carrots
and celery in butter and oil. Add
mushrooms and cook, stirring, until
mushrooms are golden. Add lamb,
cover and cook over medium heat
2 minutes. Add stock and barley,
bring to gentle boil, lower heat,
cover and simmer 10 minutes.
Season with salt and pepper. Just
before serving stir in tomatoes.
Garnish with parsley.

## VARIATIONS
● Add with lamb 1/2 cup cooked
peas or cut-up cooked green beans.
● Add shredded cabbage last
5 minutes of cooking.

# SAUCES

The importance of preparing home-made sauces cannot be overstated. A good-tasting sauce makes all the difference when you are revitalizing leftovers. A can of white sauce off the market shelf just won't produce the same flavorful result.

In general, the sauces that follow do not use up leftovers, but many of the tomato-based recipes can be a boon to the cook who has a surplus of tomatoes. Freeze the tomatoes (see tomatoes in vegetable section) and prepare the sauces at your leisure. Then you can freeze the sauces for future use. This will make your homemade tomato sauces as easy to use as canned ones from the market, plus they will be free of preservatives and too much salt and sugar.

## TOMATO SAUCE

*Makes Three and One-half To Four Cups*

1 ham hock, approximately 1 pound
2 tablespoons butter
2 tablespoons olive oil
1/2 cup diced red or green bell pepper
1/2 cup diced onion and/or white of leeks
1/2 cup diced carrot
1/2 cup diced celery and leaves
3 garlic cloves, minced
2 teaspoons granulated or brown sugar
1 cup beef, chicken or veal stock
3 pounds ripe tomatoes, peeled and chopped (approximately 6 cups)
Bouquet garni of:
  3 thyme sprigs
  6 Italian parsley sprigs
  2 bay leaves
  2 whole cloves
  6 black peppercorns, lightly crushed
  1 to 2 dried chili peppers, seeded and lightly crushed
  1/2 orange with skin, cut up
1 teaspoon salt
Red wine vinegar to taste (optional)

In a large saucepan or skillet, brown ham hock in butter and oil on all sides. Remove and set aside. Add vegetables and garlic to skillet and cook, covered, until soft. Raise heat and stir in sugar. Cook, stirring, until well browned. Add stock and cook, stirring, several minutes. Force mixture through a food mill, or purée in a food processor or blender. Return to skillet and add reserved ham hock, tomatoes, bouquet garni, salt and red wine vinegar. Cover with tilted lid and cook, stirring often, 2 hours or until thickened. Discard bouquet garni. Remove ham hock, reserving meat for another use. Adjust sauce seasonings, jar, cool, cover and refrigerate up to 4 days; may be frozen up to 6 months.

---

*Freeze herbs in small containers or plastic wrap. Crumble into dishes while still frozen. Or blend herbs into a little water and freeze in ice cube trays. Pop out, bag and add to soups, sauces and stews; no need to defrost.*

---

## TOMATO PUREE

*Makes Approximately Two Cups*
Bouquet garni of:
   6 to 8 fresh basil leaves
   1 celery stalk and leaves, cut up
   6 whole allspice, lightly crushed
1 recipe Tomato Sauce

Add bouquet garni to Tomato Sauce and cook, stirring occasionally, 3 to 4 hours, or until mixture is the consistency of barely whipped cream. Discard bouquet garni, jar, cool, cover and refrigerate up to 5 days; may be frozen up to 4 months.

## TOMATO PASTE

*Makes Approximately One-half Cup*
Bouquet garni of:
   1 celery stalk and leaves, cut up
   2 large oregano sprigs
   2 bay leaves
   6 to 8 large fresh basil leaves
   6 whole allspice, lightly crushed
   2 bay leaves
   12 Italian parsley sprigs
1 recipe Tomato Purée

Add bouquet garni to Tomato Purée and cook, stirring often, until very thick. Discard bouquet garni and adjust seasonings. Jar, cool, cover and refrigerate up to 3 days; may be frozen up to 1 month.

## MARINARA SAUCE

*Makes One Quart*
1 cup chopped onions
3/4 cup chopped green bell pepper
4 to 6 garlic cloves, minced
2 tablespoons olive oil
2 teaspoons butter
1/4 teaspoon granulated sugar
3 pounds ripe tomatoes, peeled and chopped (approximately 6 cups)
1/2 teaspoon salt
1/4 teaspoon freshly ground black pepper
3/4 cup chopped fresh basil

Sauté onions, bell pepper and garlic in oil and butter until softened. Sprinkle with sugar and cook, stirring, 2 to 3 minutes to brown lightly. Add remaining ingredients, bring to gentle boil, stir well, lower heat and cook, stirring occasionally, until reduced to 1 quart. Jar, cool, cover and refrigerate up to 5 days; may be frozen up to 2 months.

## CREOLE SAUCE

*Makes Approximately Two Cups*
1/3 cup diced onion
1/3 cup diced green bell pepper
1/3 cup diced celery
3 to 4 garlic cloves, minced
1 tablespoon butter
1 tablespoon bacon drippings
1/2 teaspoon granulated or brown sugar
1-1/2 pounds ripe tomatoes, peeled and chopped (approximately 3 cups)
1 tablespoon tomato paste
Bouquet garni of:
   1 bay leaf
   3 parsley sprigs
   3 thyme sprigs
   4 basil leaves
1 to 3 dried red chili peppers, seeded and lightly crushed
6 to 8 pimiento-stuffed olives, halved
1 teaspoon Worcestershire sauce (optional)
Salt and freshly ground black pepper to taste
Tomato juice, if needed

Cook onion, bell pepper, celery and garlic, covered, in butter and bacon drippings until soft. Sprinkle with sugar, raise heat and stir to brown lightly. Add tomatoes, tomato paste, bouquet garni and chili peppers. Lower heat and cover with slightly tilted lid. Cook, stirring often, 1 hour or until reduced and thickened. Discard bouquet garni. Add olives, Worcestershire sauce, salt and pepper. If thinner sauce is preferred, thin with tomato juice. Jar, cool, cover and refrigerate up to 5 days; may be frozen up to 4 months.

# FRESH TOMATO SAUCE

*Makes Approximately Two Cups*
1/3 cup chopped onion
1 large garlic clove, minced
3 tablespoons butter
1/2 teaspoon sugar
1 pound ripe tomatoes, chopped
   (approximately 2 cups)
Bouquet garni of:
   3 parsley sprigs
   1 bay leaf
   1/4 orange
   1 thyme sprig
   4 black peppercorns, lightly
      crushed

Sauté onion and garlic in 2 tablespoons of the butter until softened. Sprinkle with sugar and cook, stirring, 2 to 3 minutes. Add tomatoes and bouquet garni. Cook, stirring occasionally, 20 minutes. Discard bouquet garni and just before serving swirl in remaining butter. Sauce may be refrigerated up to 3 days.

# QUICK TOMATO SAUCE

The yield for this recipe depends upon how many of the optional vegetables you add. Good on almost everything from pasta to omelets.

*Makes Approximately Two Cups*
2 large garlic cloves, minced
1 cup chopped onions (optional)
1/2 cup sliced celery and some
   leaves (optional)
1/4 cup chopped green bell pepper
   (optional)
1 to 1-1/2 tablespoons butter
1 to 1-1/2 tablespoons olive oil
1/4 teaspoon granulated sugar
1 pound ripe tomatoes, chopped
   (approximately 2 cups)
1 tablespoon minced fresh basil
1 tablespoon minced fresh oregano
Salt and freshly ground black
   pepper to taste

Sauté garlic, onions, celery and bell pepper in butter and oil until slightly softened. Add remaining ingredients and cook, stirring occasionally, 15 to 20 minutes. Jar, cool, cover and refrigerate up to 3 days; may be frozen up to 1 month.

# MEXICAN QUICK TOMATO SAUCE

*Makes Approximately Two Cups*
3/4 cup chopped onion
2 large garlic cloves, minced
2 tablespoons peanut oil
1 pound ripe tomatoes, chopped
   (approximately 2 cups)
1 to 2 fresh hot chili peppers,
   seeded and diced
1/2 teaspoon ground cumin
1 tablespoon minced fresh oregano
Salt and freshly ground black
   pepper to taste
2 teaspoons chopped fresh
   coriander

Sauté onion and garlic in oil until soft. Add tomatoes, chili peppers and seasonings. Cook, stirring occasionally, 15 to 20 minutes. Stir in coriander. Jar, cool, cover and refrigerate up to 3 days; may be frozen up to 1 month.

---

*No fresh herbs in your garden? Use 1/3 to 1/2 the amount of dried.*

---

# CREAMY QUICK TOMATO SAUCE

A delicious last-minute sauce that is good on freshly cooked vegetables, spooned over sliced hard-cooked eggs atop toasted English muffins, or used as the liquid for poaching eggs.

*Makes Approximately Two-thirds Cup*
1 tablespoon butter
1 large ripe tomato, chopped
   (approximately 1 cup)
1/4 teaspoon crumbled dried basil
1/4 teaspoon salt
Pinch granulated sugar
1/8 teaspoon freshly ground black
   pepper
1/3 cup heavy cream

Melt butter, add tomato and seasonings and cook, stirring, 5 minutes. Add cream, reheat and adjust seasonings. May be refrigerated up to 3 days; reheat gently.

# CREAM SAUCES

Cream sauce, also called white or béchamel sauce, can be made with milk, cream and/or stock. To prepare, melt butter and/or rendered chicken fat in a skillet or saucepan until bubbly. Sprinkle with flour and cook, stirring, two to three minutes to cook away the raw taste of the flour, but do not brown. This cooked butter and flour mixture is called a roux. Now gradually add the liquid, cooking and stirring until the mixture is smooth and thickened. It is not necessary to heat the liquid before adding it, though heated liquid helps keep the sauce from lumping. If using cold liquid, remove the roux from the heat, add the liquid, stirring it in well, then return to the heat and proceed.

To impart more flavor to any cream sauce, add a small onion studded with one or two whole cloves, mushroom stems, a lightly bruised garlic clove, a bay leaf and/or parsley sprigs to the liquid, heat slowly four to five minutes, and then strain the liquid into the roux. Add salt and white pepper and any other seasonings at the end of the thickening process.

The following basic cream sauce recipes and variations each make approximately one cup. If you are making cream sauce to use up extra cream, the sauce may be frozen up to two months. (See general directions for freezing.) The sauce will separate during freezing; when reheating defrosted sauce, adjust consistency with additional fresh cream.

**LIGHT CREAM SAUCE** Use 2 tablespoons butter and/or rendered chicken fat, 1-1/2 to 2 tablespoons unbleached flour and 1 cup liquid. Proceed as directed for making cream sauce.

**MEDIUM CREAM SAUCE** Use 3 tablespoons butter and/or rendered chicken fat, 3 tablespoons unbleached flour and 1 cup liquid. Proceed as directed for making cream sauce.

**HEAVY CREAM SAUCE** Use 3 tablespoons butter and/or rendered chicken fat, 1/3 cup unbleached flour and 1 cup liquid. Proceed as directed for making cream sauce.

**ENRICHED CREAM SAUCE** Combine 1 recipe Light or Medium Cream Sauce made with stock and 1/4 cup heavy cream. Cook over medium-low heat, stirring often, until reduced to 1 cup.

**CREAM SAUCE ENRICHED WITH EGG YOLK** Prepare 1 recipe Light or Medium Cream Sauce. Beat about 1/4 cup heated cream sauce into 1 egg yolk, lightly beaten, then whisk mixture into remaining 3/4 cup cream sauce. Cook over medium-low heat, stirring constantly, until thickened. Do not allow to boil.

**EGG CREAM SAUCE** In a blender or food processor, blend 1 hard-cooked egg yolk, chopped, and liquid to be used in 1 recipe Light Cream Sauce. Proceed as directed for making cream sauce.

**SHALLOT CREAM SAUCE** Cook 1 tablespoon minced shallot and 1/2 cup dry white wine until reduced to 2 tablespoons. Add 1 recipe Medium Cream Sauce made with chicken stock and cook, stirring often, 4 to 5 minutes. Remove from heat and add 1 teaspoon fresh lemon juice and salt and freshly ground white pepper to taste.

**CURRY CREAM SAUCE** Add 1/2 teaspoon curry powder when adding flour to pan in 1 recipe Light or Medium Cream Sauce.

**CHEESE SAUCE** Prepare 1 recipe Light or Medium Cream Sauce. Beat about 1/4 cup heated cream sauce into a mixture of 1 egg yolk beaten with 2 tablespoons half-and-half cream, then whisk mixture into remaining 3/4 cup cream sauce. Cook over medium-low heat until thickened, add 2 tablespoons *each* freshly grated Parmesan and

Gruyère cheese and cook, stirring, just until cheeses are melted. Do not allow to boil.

**CHEDDAR CHEESE SAUCE** Substitute 1/3 to 1/2 cup grated sharp Cheddar cheese for the Parmesan and Gruyère cheeses in Cheese Sauce.

**TOMATO CHEESE SAUCE** Combine 1 recipe Cheese Sauce or Cheddar Cheese Sauce and 1/2 cup chopped ripe tomatoes and heat gently.

## ADDITIONS TO FINISHED CREAM SAUCE

Any of the following may be stirred into thickened cream sauce.

**HERBS AND SPICES** Salt, freshly ground white pepper, freshly grated nutmeg, celery salt, ground herbs and/or spices, crumbled dried herbs, chopped fresh herbs, paprika, dry mustard, saffron threads.

**LIQUID SEASONINGS** Dry sherry, Worcestershire sauce, Tabasco sauce, fresh lemon juice, onion juice.

**OTHER ADDITIONS** Freshly grated lemon rind, drained capers, minced gherkins and a little juice, chopped anchovy fillets or anchovy paste, chopped hard-cooked eggs and chopped pimiento.

## BASIC HOLLANDAISE

Hollandaise sauce made by hand will be less stable than hollandaise made in a blender or food processor. Both may be kept warm over hot (not boiling) water up to ten minutes, but neither will reheat well. Any extra sauce may be jarred, covered and refrigerated up to three days. To use refrigerated sauce, spoon small amounts on hot foods and let the sauce melt. The hand method will yield approximately two-thirds cup, the blender method three-fourths cup.

**BLENDER METHOD**
1/4 pound butter
2 egg yolks
1 tablespoon fresh lemon juice
1/4 teaspoon salt
1/8 teaspoon paprika
1/8 teaspoon freshly ground white pepper
1/8 teaspoon freshly grated lemon rind (optional)
1 to 2 drops Tabasco sauce (optional)

Cut butter into pieces and melt until hot but not browned. Place all other ingredients in a blender or in the bowl of a food processor with metal blade in place. On low speed, blend 2 to 3 seconds. In thin, steady stream, pour in heated butter. Adjsut seasonings.

**HAND METHOD**
1 egg, chilled
1-1/2 tablespoons fresh lemon juice, chilled
1/8 teaspoon salt
Dash paprika and freshly ground white pepper
4 tablespoons butter, chilled

In a heavy Teflon-type pan or the top pan of a double boiler, beat egg lightly and blend in lemon juice and seasonings. Place pan on low heat, or bring water in bottom of double boiler to a bare simmer (do not allow to boil at any time). Add butter and cook, stirring constantly, until butter is melted and sauce is thickened. Adjust seasonings.

**HERB HOLLANDAISE** Stir into Basic Hollandaise 1 tablespoon minced fresh chives, 2 teaspoons finely minced shallots, 1 tablespoon minced fresh parsley and 2 tablespoons minced watercress leaves.

**BEARNAISE SAUCE** In a saucepan, combine 1-1/2 tablespoons white wine vinegar, 1-1/2 tablespoons dry white wine, 1/2 teaspoon minced shallots, 1/2 teaspoon finely minced fresh parsley and 1/2 teaspoon finely minced fresh tarragon. Bring to boil and, stirring occasionally, reduce to 1-1/2 tablespoons; cool and chill. Use in place of the lemon juice in Basic Hollandaise.

## LOW-CALORIE HOLLANDAISE

If you like hollandaise sauce, but can't afford the calories, here is a low-calorie alternative. It is delicious on any firm green vegetable, can be served hot or cold and reheats easily in a double boiler.

*Makes Approximately*
*One and One-fourth Cups*
2 eggs
1 cup plain yoghurt
1/2 teaspoon salt
1/8 teaspoon freshly ground white
    pepper
1/8 teaspoon freshly grated nutmeg
1 to 3 drops Tabasco sauce
1/2 teaspoon freshly grated lemon
    or orange rind

In the top pan of a double boiler, lightly whisk the eggs until they are just blended. Place over bottom pan of simmering water and whisk in the yoghurt, salt, pepper and nutmeg. Cook, whisking almost constantly, until mixture is thickened to the consistency of whipped cream, about 10 to 15 minutes. Stir in Tabasco and lemon rind and adjust seasonings.

*If you are out of Tabasco sauce, substitute a dash of cayenne pepper.*

## BROWN SAUCE

Though this sauce is time-consuming to prepare, it is well worth the effort. It can be added to homemade corned beef hash, used in meat pies, spooned over meatloaf and is the basis of Mushroom Sauce. You may also reduce it to a concentrate for adding to stocks and sauces to enhance their flavor.

*Makes Approximately Four Cups*
1 carrot, chopped
1 onion, chopped
1/2 cup rendered beef or pork fat
1/2 cup unbleached flour
2 quarts rich beef stock
2 garlic cloves, lightly mashed
Bouquet garni of:
    2 celery stalks and leaves
    3 parsley sprigs
    1 thyme sprig
    1 bay leaf
1/2 cup Tomato Purée or tomato
    juice

In a large saucepan, sauté carrot and onion in fat until just starting to brown. Sprinkle with flour and cook, stirring, until mixture is a light hazelnut color. Add 2 cups of the stock and cook, stirring, until thickened. Stir in 4 cups of the remaining stock, add garlic and bouquet garni, bring to boil, lower heat and cook, stirring often, over medium-low heat 1 hour or until mixture is reduced to 3 cups. Skim off any fat that rises to surface during cooking. Mix in Tomato Purée, then strain. Return to saucepan and add remaining 2 cups stock. Cook, stirring occasionally, until reduced to 4 cups. Jar, cool, cover and refrigerate up to 1 week, or freeze up to 6 months.

## QUICK BROWN SAUCE

If the traditional Brown Sauce recipe looks too formidable, you can make a quick version. Boil 2 cups of canned beef broth 15 minutes. Dissolve 2 teaspoons arrowroot in 3 tablespoons cold water and stir into the stock. Reduce heat to low and cook, stirring, until thickened. Add 1/2 cup diced tomatoes, cook 10 minutes and strain.

## MUSHROOM SAUCE

*Makes Approximately*
*One and One-half Cups*
2 to 3 tablespoons butter and/or
   rendered chicken fat
3/4 pound fresh mushrooms, sliced
1/4 teaspoon salt
1/4 teaspoon crumbled dried
   oregano
1/8 teaspoon freshly ground white
   pepper
1/8 teaspoon garlic powder
Dash cayenne pepper
2 tablespoons minced shallots
1/2 cup dry white wine, dry sherry
   or Madeira wine
1 cup Brown Sauce
1 teaspoon minced fresh tarragon
   (optional)
1 tablespoon minced fresh parsley

In a large skillet, melt butter until
foamy. Add mushrooms, sprinkle
with seasonings and cook over
medium-high heat, stirring often,
until mushrooms are golden. Add
shallots, mix well, sauté 1 minute
and stir in wine. Raise heat and,
watching carefully, reduce liquid
by half. Blend in Brown Sauce and
tarragon; cook, stirring often, 5 to
10 minutes to blend flavors. Adjust
seasonings and stir in minced
parsley. If making ahead, reheat in
top of double boiler over simmering
water or in a Teflon-type skillet.

## QUICK MUSHROOM SAUCE

*Makes Approximately Two Cups*
3/4 pound fresh mushrooms, sliced
1/4 cup sliced green onions
2 tablespoons butter
2 tablespoons olive oil
1/2 teaspoon crumbled dried
   oregano
1/2 teaspoon salt
1/4 teaspoon freshly ground black
   pepper
1/4 teaspoon garlic powder
Dash cayenne pepper
2 tablespoons unbleached flour
1/2 cup dry Marsala or white wine
1/2 cup half-and-half cream, or
   as needed

Sauté mushrooms and onions in
butter and oil, sprinkling with
seasonings while stirring, until
mushrooms are golden. Sprinkle
with flour and cook, stirring, 2 to 3
minutes, then gradually mix in
wine and cream. Cook, stirring,
until thickened, adding more cream
if needed; adjust seasonings.

## GRAVY

Gravy is a sauce made from the
pan juices of roasted or braised
meats and poultry. The juices are
defatted and seasoned and then
served either plain, combined with
dry white wine and/or complementary stock, or thickened and
combined with stock or equal
parts stock and half-and-half cream.
A little dry sherry or dry vermouth
may be added to thickened gravies,
and sour cream may be stirred
into them at the end of cooking.
Flour, ground walnuts or fine dry
bread crumbs or cornstarch may
be used as thickeners. Suggested
seasonings include ground herbs,
chicken or beef stock base or
Marmite, Kitchen Bouquet, Worcestershire sauce, Maggi's seasoning,
fresh lemon juice, salt and freshly
ground black or white pepper. If
desired, gravy may be strained
just before serving to remove large
pan scrapings.

To serve pan juices, pour juices
into a large measuring cup and let
stand until the fat rises to the
surface. Spoon off as much fat as
possible into a container. Then
either whisk a chilled lettuce leaf
across the surface or float an ice
cube on top of the defatted juices;
any remaining fat will adhere to
the leaf or ice. (Reserve fat,
excluding lamb, to use in recipes
calling for rendered fat.) Season
juices to taste and return to
roasting pan. Place pan over medium
heat and heat juices, stirring in
any bits clinging to the bottom of
the pan and adding dry white wine
and/or stock to make quantity of
gravy desired. Adjust seasonings.

To make gravy thickened with
flour, remove all fat from pan

juices as directed. For 2 cups of gravy, return 3 tablespoons of fat to the roasting pan and place over medium heat. Sprinkle 2-1/2 to 3 tablespoons unbleached flour over the fat and cook, stirring up any bits on bottom of pan, 2 to 3 minutes. Add stock or stock and cream to pan juices to measure 2 cups and season as desired. Gradually add liquid to roasting pan and cook, stirring, until smooth and thickened. If gravy thickens too much, add additional stock or some sour cream to achieve desired consistency. Adjust seasonings.

To make gravy thickened with cornstarch, remove all fat from pan juices as directed and add stock or equal parts stock and cream to juices to measure 2 cups and season to taste. If desired, return 1 tablespoon fat to the roasting pan, then place pan over medium heat. Pour in liquid, heat just to simmer and stir in mixture of 1-1/2 tablespoons cornstarch dissolved in 1/3 cup water. Cook, stirring, until thickened, adding additional liquid or sour cream if needed to thin gravy. Cornstarch-bound gravies should not be over-cooked. Adjust seasonings.

*Arrowroot may be substituted for cornstarch in gravies, but can't be reheated. Dissolve in cold liquid, as for cornstarch, before using.*

## ONION SAUCE

Especially good with roasted meats.

*Makes Approximately One Cup*
2 medium onions, thinly sliced
4 tablespoons butter
2 teaspoons granulated sugar
2 teaspoons unbleached flour
1 cup chicken or beef stock
1/4 cup Madeira wine
Salt and freshly ground black
    pepper to taste

Sauté onions in butter, stirring often, until softened. Sprinkle with sugar and, stirring often, cook over very low heat 30 minutes. Raise heat slightly and sprinkle flour into pan. Cook, stirring, 3 minutes, then gradually blend in stock. Cook, stirring often, 10 minutes. Blend in Madeira and continue cooking and stirring until thickened to desired consistency. Season with salt and pepper.

## SHALLOT–
## RED WINE SAUCE

Especially good on roast beef, meatloaf or beef meatballs.

*Makes Two-thirds Cup*
1/3 cup minced shallots
1 teaspoon butter
1 teaspoon safflower oil
2 tablespoons dry red wine
1/2 cup beef broth

Cook shallots in butter and oil, covered, until starting to soften. Uncover, add wine and beef broth and cook, stirring occasionally, until reduced to 2/3 cup. If not using immediately, jar, cool, cover and refrigerate up to 3 days; reheat gently before serving.

## WINE SAUCE

Serve with fish or shellfish.

*Makes Approximately*
*One and One-half Cups*
3 tablespoons unsalted butter
3 tablespoons unbleached flour
1-1/2 cups dry white wine
1/2 cup heavy cream
1 cup finely shredded Emmenthaler
    or Gruyère cheese
2 tablespoons minced fresh chives
2 tablespoons minced fresh parsley
1 teaspoon minced fresh tarragon
Salt, freshly ground white pepper
    and paprika to taste

Melt butter, sprinkle with flour and cook, stirring often, until the color of brown wrapping paper. Gradually add wine; cook and stir 5 minutes or until thickened and reduced by about 3 tablespoons. Add cream and heat without boiling. Add cheese, stir to melt and add herbs and seasonings.

## LEEK SAUCE

Serve this rich sauce with any cooked meat. It may be made ahead and reheated in a double boiler or Teflon-type pan, or in a microwave oven, then thinned with a little milk if needed.

*Makes Approximately One and Three-fourths Cup*
1-1/2 cups very thinly sliced leeks (white and a little light green)
2 tablespoons butter
2 tablespoons unbleached flour
1/4 teaspoon salt
1/4 teaspoon dry mustard
1/8 teaspoon freshly ground white pepper
1 cup rich chicken or veal stock
1/2 cup milk, or as needed
1 medium tomato, diced (optional)

Cook leeks, covered, in butter until soft. Sprinkle with flour and seasonings and cook, stirring, 2 to 3 minutes. Gradually add stock and milk and cook over medium heat, stirring, until thickened. Adjust seasonings and stir in tomato. Cook, stirring, just until heated.

---

*A pinch of salt in the bottom of a double boiler helps water to boil more rapidly.*

---

## SAGE SAUCE

Gently reheat any sliced cooked meats, especially pork roast, in this easy-to-prepare sauce.

*Makes Approximately One Cup*
1 cup finely minced onion
1 to 2 tablespoons finely minced fresh sage
2 tablespoons butter
1/3 cup fine dry bread crumbs
2/3 cup rich pork or beef stock
Salt and freshly ground black pepper to taste

Cook onion and sage in butter, covered, until onion is soft. Add bread crumbs and cook, stirring, 5 minutes. Blend in stock and cook, stirring, until heated through. Season with salt and pepper.

## MUSTARD SAUCE

For ham, tongue, or corned beef; serve meat and sauce hot or at room temperature.

*Makes Approximately One Cup*
2 teaspoons French's dry mustard
1 teaspoon granulated sugar
1/4 teaspoon salt
2 tablespoons unbleached flour
3/4 cup water
2 tablespoons cider vinegar
2 egg yolks, lightly beaten
2 tablespoons butter, melted
1 tablespoon brown sugar

In the top pan of a double boiler or in a heavy saucepan, combine mustard, granulated sugar, salt and flour. Combine water and vinegar. Stirring with a whisk or wooden spoon, gradually add water-vinegar mixture to mustard mixture. Place over simmering water, or over medium heat if using a saucepan, and cook, stirring almost constantly, until smooth and slightly thickened. Whisk about 1/3 cup of mixture into egg yolks and blend well, then whisk into remaining mustard mixture and blend in butter and brown sugar. Cook, stirring, until thickened. Do not allow to boil. If not using immediately, jar, cool, cover and refrigerate up to 3 weeks. If serving hot, reheat gently.

## SWEET AND SOUR SAUCE

Use in place of chutney with cold roast chicken, duck or pork.

*Makes Approximately One Cup*
2 tablespoons cornstarch
1 cup cold water
2 tablespoons catsup
2 tablespoons granulated sugar
1 tablespoon cider vinegar
1/4 teaspoon ground ginger
Dash salt
1-1/2 tablespoons Oriental plum sauce (optional)

In a saucepan, dissolve cornstarch in water. Blend in catsup, sugar, vinegar, ginger and salt. Cook, stirring, until mixture is heated and thickened. Adjust seasonings, adding more vinegar and/or ginger to taste. Add plum sauce and reheat. If making ahead, reheat just to serving temperature; do not overheat.

## HERB SAUCE

Serve on cooked vegetables such as asparagus, broccoli or cauliflower, or on crisp lettuce leaves.

*Makes Approximately One-half Cup*
3 tablespoons olive oil
1/2 cup coarsely chopped fresh
   parsley
1/4 cup chopped green onions and
   tops
1 teaspoon chopped fresh basil
1 garlic clove, chopped
2 tablespoons fresh lime or lemon
   juice
1 anchovy fillet, or 1/2 to 1 teaspoon anchovy paste
1/2 teaspoon salt
1 hard-cooked egg, chopped
Freshly ground black pepper to
   taste

In a blender or food processor, combine all ingredients and blend until smooth. Jar, cover and refrigerate up to 5 days.

## BLACK BEAN SAUCE

The black bean sauce used here is available in jars and cans in Oriental markets and some super-markets. Thinly sliced cooked meat or poultry can be added to this sauce, the pan covered and the meat slowly reheated. You will need only a small amount of the sauce, as it is quite pungent. Steamed white rice is the perfect accompaniment.

*Makes Approximately One-third Cup*
1/4 cup black bean sauce
6 to 7 tablespoons chicken stock
1 to 2 garlic cloves, lightly crushed
1 to 2 slices ginger root
1 to 2 teaspoons dry sherry
Pinch sugar, or to taste
Cayenne pepper to taste (optional)

In a medium skillet, combine black bean sauce, chicken stock, garlic and ginger root. Cover, bring to simmer and cook 5 minutes. Discard garlic and ginger root. Add sherry, sugar and cayenne and mix well.

## YOGHURT SAUCE

Dolmas or tiny lamb or veal meat-balls are excellent dipped into this fresh-tasting sauce.

*Makes Approximately One Cup*
1 cup plain yoghurt
2 tablespoons fresh lemon juice,
   or to taste
2 tablespoons minced fresh mint,
   or to taste
1 teaspoon finely minced garlic,
   or to taste

Combine all ingredients and mix well. Jar, cover and refrigerate up to 1 week.

## ANCHOVY–EGG SAUCE

For poached fish, artichokes or steamed broccoli or asparagus.

*Makes Approximately One-third Cup*
3 hard-cooked eggs
1/2 tablespoon heavy cream
2 to 3 anchovy fillets, mashed
2 drops Tabasco sauce
1/2 teaspoon Worcestershire sauce
3 to 4 tablespoons Basic
   Mayonnaise

Force eggs through a 1/8-inch mesh sieve and blend in remaining ingredients in order given. Adjust seasonings, jar, cover and refrigerate up to 5 days.

## REMOULADE SAUCE

Though this sauce is traditionally made with fresh chervil, if chervil is unavailable double the amount of parsley used. You may use the type of pickle you prefer—dill, sour, sweet. This versatile sauce is equally good on cold meats, poultry, fish, and shellfish.

*Makes Approximately*
*One and One-third Cups*
1 cup Basic Mayonnaise
2 shallots, finely minced
3 tablespoons finely minced pickles, well drained
2 to 3 teaspoons well-drained capers, minced
2 to 3 teaspoons Dijon-style mustard
1 tablespoon mixed minced fresh parsley, tarragon and chervil
1 to 2 anchovy fillets, finely minced, or 1/2 to 1 teaspoon anchovy paste
1 teaspoon fresh lemon juice, or to taste
Pinch granulated sugar
Salt and freshly ground black pepper to taste
3 large pitted black olives, minced (optional)
1 to 2 teaspoons minced fresh chives (optional)
Heavy cream, if needed

Combine all ingredients, except heavy cream, and mix well. Adjust seasonings and if mixture is too thick, blend in a little cream. Jar, cover and refrigerate up to 4 days.

## HORSERADISH SAUCE

The perfect accompaniment to cold roast or corned beef.

*Makes Approximately*
*Three-fourths Cup*
1/2 cup sour cream
2 tablespoons prepared horseradish
1/2 teaspoon granulated sugar
1 small tart apple, pared and grated
1/4 teaspoon ground savory
1 to 2 teaspoons fresh lemon juice
1/2 teaspoon freshly grated lemon rind
Dash cayenne pepper

Combine all ingredients and mix well. Adjust seasonings to taste. Jar, cover and refrigerate up to 3 days.

## TOMATO CATSUP

*Makes Approximately*
*Three-fourths Cup*
Bouquet garni of:
   6 to 8 large fresh basil leaves
   1 celery stalk and leaves, cut up
   6 whole allspice, lightly crushed
   1 to 3 dried red chili peppers, seeded if desired and lightly crushed
   One 1-inch stick cinnamon
   1 teaspoon celery seeds
   1 teaspoon mustard seeds
1 recipe Tomato Purée
1 tablespoon honey or 2 tablespoons brown sugar
2 tablespoons cider vinegar

Add bouquet garni to Tomato Purée and cook, stirring occasionally, until reduced by half. Stir in honey and cook, stirring often, until very thick. Discard bouquet garni and stir in vinegar. Continue cooking, stirring often, until of desired thickness. Adjust with more honey and/or vinegar and cook to blend flavors. Jar, cool, cover and refrigerate up to 3 days, or freeze up to 1 month.

---

*Soak lemons, limes and oranges in warm water before juicing. You'll extract more juice, more easily.*

---

# CHILI SAUCE

*Makes Approximately Two Cups*
2-1/2 to 3 pounds ripe tomatoes
1 cup chopped onion
1/2 cup chopped green bell pepper
1/2 cup cider vinegar
1 tablespoon honey
1 teaspoon mustard seeds
1 teaspoon salt
1/2 teaspoon crushed dried hot
   red chili pepper
1/2 teaspoon minced garlic
1/2 teaspoon minced ginger root
1/4 teaspoon freshly grated nutmeg
1/4 teaspoon ground coriander
2 whole cloves

Peel and chop tomatoes to measure 5 cups. In a large saucepan, combine tomatoes with all remaining ingredients. Bring to gentle boil, lower heat and simmer gently, stirring often, 2-1/2 hours or until thickened. Increase heat for final 10 minutes of cooking time. Jar, cool, cover and refrigerate up to 5 days, or freeze up to 2 months.

# TOMATILLO SAUCE

A spicy-hot table sauce that is especially good on tacos, enchiladas and refried beans. Tomatillos are a type of green tomato with a husk that must be removed before the fruit can be eaten. They can be found both canned and fresh in Latin American markets and some supermarkets.

*Makes Approximately Three Cups*
1-1/2 pounds fresh tomatillos,
   husked, or 2-1/2 cups well-
   drained canned tomatillos
1 medium white onion, cut up
4 garlic cloves
3 or 4 fresh hot green chili
   peppers, seeded if desired
1/4 cup fresh coriander leaves
1/2 teaspoon salt
1/4 teaspoon sugar

If using fresh tomatillos, simmer in salted water about 10 minutes, or until tender; drain well. Combine all ingredients in a blender and blend until smooth (or you may leave it somewhat coarse if you prefer). Taste and adjust seasonings. Jar, cover and refrigerate up to 2 weeks.

# UNCOOKED TOMATO SAUCE

Another table sauce that goes well with any tortilla dish. Let stand for an hour or so before eating so that the flavors blend.

*Makes Approximately*
*One and One-half Cups*
3 medium ripe tomatoes
1 small white onion
2 garlic cloves
3 tablespoons coriander leaves
3 or 4 fresh hot green chili
   peppers, seeded if desired
1 tablespoon fresh oregano leaves
1/2 teaspoon salt
1/4 cup water

Mince the tomatoes, onion, garlic, coriander, chilis and oregano and combine in a bowl. Add salt and water and mix well. Jar, cover and refrigerate up to 2 days.

# HOMEMADE MUSTARD

This Russian-style mustard depends on a large measure of sugar for the best result. If, however, you prefer a hotter, tarter mustard, reduce the sugar measure to taste.

*Makes Approximately One-half Cup*
1/2 cup dry mustard
1 cup granulated sugar
1/4 teaspoon salt
3/4 cup boiling water, or as needed
1 teaspoon distilled white vinegar
1 tablespoon corn oil

Combine mustard, sugar and salt. Stirring constantly, pour in 3/4 cup boiling water, blending to form a paste and adding more water if needed. Add vinegar and corn oil, blending in well. Jar, cover and refrigerate up to 1 month.

# SPREADS, DIPS & SANDWICH FILLINGS

## CHICKEN LIVER PATE

*Makes Approximately One Cup*
6 to 8 chicken livers, halved
   (about 1/2 pound)
Dry sherry
1/2 cup chopped onion
1 garlic clove, minced
1-1/2 tablespoons rendered
   chicken fat
3 tablespoons butter
1/2 teaspoon salt
1/4 teaspoon ground turmeric
1/4 teaspoon freshly ground black
   pepper
1/8 teaspoon freshly grated nutmeg
1 tablespoon dry sherry, brandy or
   white port wine
1 hard-cooked egg, yolk and
   white sieved separately
Slivered or halved black olives
Parsley sprigs

Marinate livers in sherry to cover
2 to 4 hours. Drain and pat dry.
Sauté onion and garlic in rendered
fat and 1-1/2 tablespoons of the
butter until soft. Add livers, sprinkle
with seasonings and cook, stirring,
until livers stiffen and are just
cooked through. Do not overcook.
Purée liver mixture in blender or
food processor. Cut remaining
butter into small bits and add with

1 tablespoon sherry to blender.
Purée until smooth, adjust seasonings
and pack into an oiled mold.
(Prepare mold with Lecithin Oil, if
possible.) Cover with plastic wrap
and refrigerate up to 3 days.
Unmold onto serving plate and
decorate with eggs and black olives.
Garnish with parsley sprigs.

## HAM AND BLUE CHEESE MOUSSE

*Makes Approximately Two Cups*
1 tablespoon unflavored gelatin
3 tablespoons cold water
1 cup crumbled gorgonzola or
   Roquefort cheese
1/2 cup coarsely ground cooked
   ham
4 ounces cream cheese, softened
3/4 cup heavy cream
1/2 teaspoon onion powder
1/4 teaspoon garlic powder
1/4 teaspoon freshly ground white
   pepper
Salt to taste
2 tablespoons minced fresh chives
1 egg white
Pinch cream of tartar
Pimiento-stuffed olives

Sprinkle gelatin over water and let
soften. Dissolve over hot water.
Combine gorgonzola cheese, ham,
cream cheese, heavy cream, seasonings and chives. Adjust seasonings and stir in gelatin. Beat egg
white and cream of tartar until
stiff but not dry. Fold into cheese
mixture and pack into a 2- to 3-
cup mold lightly brushed with
Lecithin Oil or safflower oil. Cover
with plastic wrap and refrigerate
at least 4 hours until stiff. Unmold
on serving plate and decorate with
sliced and diced pimiento-stuffed
olives.

## HUMMUS
(Garbanzo Bean Spread)

This popular Middle Eastern dish
will taste best if you have cooked
the garbanzo beans in well-seasoned
water or stock. Add the bean
cooking liquid to the purée until it
is the consistency you like. It
should be smooth and somewhat
thick, but thin enough to form into
a shallow oval or circle on a plate.

*Makes Approximately
One and One-third Cups*
1 large garlic clove, minced
1 tablespoon minced fresh parsley

1/4 to 1/2 teaspoon salt
1/4 teaspoon freshly ground black
    pepper
Dash cayenne pepper
1 cup cooked garbanzo beans
Liquid from cooking beans
    as needed
1/3 cup tahini (sesame seed paste)
2 to 3 tablespoons fresh lemon or
    lime juice, or to taste
1/2 to 1 tablespoon olive oil
Paprika
Minced fresh parsley
Warmed pita bread, broken into
    pieces

In mortar and pestle, mash garlic, 1 tablespoon parsley, salt, black pepper and cayenne pepper; set aside. Reserve 6 to 8 whole garbanzo beans. In a blender or food processor, purée remaining garbanzo beans, adding a little cooking liquid if needed. Blend in garlic mixture, tahini and lemon juice, adding cooking liquid to desired consistency. Adjust seasonings and with spatula spread about 1 inch thick on serving plate, forming an oval or circle. Make a shallow indentation in center. (If making ahead, at this point cover tightly with plastic wrap and refrigerate. Let come to room temperature before serving.) Pour oil into hollow and sprinkle surface of purée with paprika. Decorate with minced parsley and reserved whole garbanzo beans. Serve with pita bread.

# EGGPLANT SPREAD

When a half eggplant remains from making Oriental Eggplant Salad, prepare this smooth, Provençal-style dip. Accompany with a thinly sliced French baguette.

*Makes Approximately*
*One and One-half Cups*
1/2 globe eggplant, peeled
    (about 1/2 pound)
Salt
Olive oil
1/2 cup finely minced onion
2 garlic cloves, finely minced
1 medium ripe tomato, finely
    diced and drained (optional)
1/2 teaspoon salt
1/4 teaspoon freshly ground
    black pepper
Cayenne pepper to taste
1 tablespoon fresh lemon juice
2 tablespoons minced fresh
    parsley
Anchovy fillets
Red bell pepper rings or halved
    cherry tomatoes

Cut eggplant in thin slices lengthwise, sprinkle slices with salt and let stand 1 hour. Preheat oven to 375°F. Rinse slices and pat dry, then place on a baking sheet and brush with olive oil. Bake eggplant 30 minutes, or until very soft to the touch. Let cool and mash with a fork or force through a sieve. Combine eggplant with onion, garlic, diced tomato, salt, black pepper, cayenne pepper and lemon juice and mix well. Add olive oil to thin mixture to desired consistency. Taste and adjust seasonings. Mound on a plate, sprinkle with parsley and garnish with anchovy fillets and bell pepper rings.

# TOMATILLO SPREAD

*Makes Approximately*
*Two-thirds Cup*
2 ounces cream cheese,
    softened
1/4 cup sour cream
6 tablespoons Tomatillo
    Sauce, drained
1/3 cup chopped roasted
    peanuts
1/4 cup chopped pimiento
    stuffed olives
1/8 to 1/4 teaspoon salt
Dash freshly ground black
    pepper

Combine all ingredients and mix well. Taste and adjust seasonings. Cover and refrigerate up to 2 days.

---

*Store unpeeled garlic cloves in the freezer for easier peeling and chopping, but never more than 2 to 3 weeks.*

---

## POTATO–GARLIC SPREAD

This recipe is for garlic lovers. Plan ahead when boiling potatoes for dinner and cook enough extra to make this spread. Rice the potatoes while they are still hot; the next day, make the spread and serve with thinly sliced small French bread rounds. The spread will keep for several days in the refrigerator; or heat the leftover spread with enough stock to make a sauce consistency and serve spooned over cooked fish or vegetables.

*Makes Approximately*
*One and One-fourth Cups*
3 to 4 garlic cloves
1/4 teaspoon salt
1 cup riced boiled potatoes
1/3 cup olive oil
2 tablespoons fresh lemon or
   lime juice

In a blender or a food processor fitted with a metal blade, finely mince the garlic with the salt. Add potatoes and mix with on and off pulses, being careful not to let the potatoes get gummy. With motor running, add oil alternately with lemon juice. Remove to bowl and stir well. Adjust seasoning with salt.

## LAYERED BEAN DIP

*Serves Eight*
2/3 cup Refried Beans
3/4 cup Tomatillo Sauce,
   drained
1/3 cup sour cream
1/2 avocado, mashed with
   1 teaspoon fresh lemon juice
1 medium ripe tomato, finely
   diced and drained
1/4 cup minced green onions
   and tops
1/4 small head iceberg lettuce,
   very finely shredded
1/4 to 1/3 cup finely shredded
   Monterey Jack cheese
Halved black olives
Corn chips (preferably
   homemade)

Combine beans and 1/2 cup of the Tomatillo Sauce, mix well and spread in center of a shallow platter. Spoon sour cream on top, and then spoon remaining 1/4 cup Tomatillo Sauce on top of sour cream. Spread avocado on sauce layer and strew with tomato, green onion and lettuce. Sprinkle cheese evenly over top and decorate with black olives. Surround with corn chips.

## SANDWICH SALAD SPREADS

All of the following salads may be made into sandwiches or served as a spread for crackers. They may also be used for stuffing cold vegetables, such as tomatoes, small beets, brussels sprouts and artichoke bottoms.

## EGG SALAD

*Makes Approximately One-half Cup*
3 hard-cooked eggs, finely
   chopped
3 to 4 tablespoons *finely*
   minced celery
1 tablespoon *finely* minced bell
   pepper
2 tablespoons minced pimiento-
   stuffed olives
Mustard Mayonnaise to bind

Combine all ingredients and mix well. Cover and refrigerate up to 24 hours.

## CHICKEN OR TURKEY SALAD

*Makes Approximately One Cup*
3/4 cup *finely* minced cooked
   chicken or turkey
2 tablespoons *finely* minced celery
2 tablespoons *finely* chopped tart
   apple
1 tablespoon chopped blanched
   almonds
1 hard-cooked egg, chopped
   (optional)
Curry Mayonnaise to bind

Combine all ingredients and mix
well. Cover and refrigerate up to
24 hours.

## HAM SALAD

*Makes Approximately
Three-fourths Cup*
1/3 cup *finely* minced cooked
   ham
1/3 cup grated white Cheddar
   or shredded Monterey Jack
   cheese
2 tablespoons Mustard
   Mayonnaise
2 tablespoons sour cream
1 teaspoon fresh lemon juice
1/2 teaspoon chopped fresh
   basil, oregano or chives
1 teaspoon chopped fresh parsley
Salt and freshly ground white
   pepper to taste

Combine all ingredients and mix
well. Cover and refrigerate up to
24 hours.

### VARIATIONS

- Substitute for the ham, cooked
corned beef, tongue, veal, beef.
- Add 1 hard-cooked egg, chopped,
and *finely* minced celery and leaves.
- Add minced green or red bell
pepper and chopped black olives.

## SALMON SALAD

*Makes Approximately
Three-fourths Cup*
2/3 cup flaked cooked salmon
2 tablespoons Basic
   Mayonnaise
1 tablespoon finely chopped
   green onion and tops
1 teaspoon fresh lemon juice,
   or to taste
1 teaspoon drained capers
Salt and freshly ground black
   pepper to taste

Combine all ingredients and mix
well. Cover and refrigerate up to
24 hours.

---

*Treat your chopping boards with
linseed oil to keep a good finish:
rub in, let stand 1 to 2 hours,
then rub off with a coarse cloth.*

---

## OLIVE SALAD

*Makes Approximately
Three-fourths Cup*
1/2 cup chopped black olives
2 hard-cooked eggs, chopped
1/4 cup *finely* minced onion
1/4 cup shredded Monterey Jack
   cheese
2 teaspoons minced fresh chives
Basic Mayonnaise to bind
Salt, paprika and freshly ground
   black pepper to taste

Combine all ingredients and mix
well. Cover and refrigerate up to
2 days.

## SANDWICH SPREAD SUGGESTIONS

**ANCHOVY AND EGG** Toss chopped
hard-cooked eggs with chopped
anchovy fillets; bind with Lemon
Mayonnaise.

**EGG** Combine Curry Mayonnaise
with minced celery and onion, dry
mustard, Tabasco sauce, minced
fresh parsley and chopped hard-
cooked eggs.

**CUCUMBER** Lightly salt thick
cucumber slices, drain in colander
and pat dry. Mince and combine
with sieved hard-cooked eggs and
minced radishes, watercress, green

onions, and fresh dill, salt, freshly ground white pepper and Mustard Mayonnaise to bind.

**HAM AND EGG** Combine equal parts coarsely ground cooked ham and sieved hard-cooked eggs, drained capers, salt, freshly ground white pepper and Mustard Mayonnaise to bind.

**HAM AND OLIVE** Combine equal parts minced cooked ham and chopped black olives; bind with Basic Mayonnaise.

**HAM AND CHICKEN** Combine equal parts minced cooked ham and chicken, finely chopped Brazil nuts, finely minced gherkins, Lemon Mayonnaise to bind.

**HAM** Combine minced cooked ham, minced fresh parsley and pickles, tomato paste and Mustard or Lemon Mayonnaise to bind.

**BEEF** Combine finely minced cooked beef, chopped hard-cooked eggs, minced fresh parsley, grated onion, Dijon-style mustard and Sour Cream Dressing to bind. Prepare open-faced sandwiches and garnish with lumpfish caviar.

**TONGUE** Combine minced cooked tongue, chopped pimiento-stuffed olives, minced fresh parsley, chopped

hard-cooked egg and Horseradish Sauce to bind.

**TONGUE AND CHICKEN OR TURKEY** Combine equal parts minced cooked tongue and chicken or turkey, softened butter, Dijon-style mustard, salt and freshly ground black pepper.

**CHICKEN OR TURKEY** Combine coarsely ground cooked chicken or turkey, softened cream cheese, finely chopped blanched almonds, chopped chutney, salt, freshly ground white pepper and Curry Mayonnaise to bind.

**SALMON** Soften cream cheese with Curry Mayonnaise; add minced fresh chives and dill or watercress and with fork blend in flaked cooked salmon.

**SALMON OR WHITE FISH** Combine flaked cooked salmon or white fish, chopped hard-cooked eggs, finely minced celery and/or cucumber, minced fresh parsley, chopped drained capers, Seafood Seasoning, salt, freshly ground white pepper, Lemon Mayonnaise to bind.

**CREAM CHEESE** Combine softened cream cheese with minced bell peppers and black olives, grated onion, salt and freshly ground black pepper.

## BROILED SANDWICH SUGGESTIONS

Toast one side of bread slices. Spread untoasted side with one of the following mixtures and broil until bubbly.

**HAM OR TONGUE** Toss together minced cooked ham or tongue, chopped chutney, grated mild cheese, chopped ripe olives. Top with a sprinkling of freshly grated Parmesan cheese.

**TURKEY OR CHICKEN** Combine minced cooked turkey or chicken, mashed avocado, grated onion, fresh lemon juice and freshly ground white pepper. Top with a slice of Monterey Jack cheese.

**FISH OR SHELLFISH** Toss together flaked cooked firm white fish or shellfish, grated Cheddar cheese, chopped hard-cooked eggs, grated onion, fresh lemon juice, minced fresh parsley and sour cream to bind. Sprinkle with paprika.

**FISH OR SHELLFISH** Toss together flaked cooked firm white fish or shellfish, grated Gruyère cheese, minced green onions and tops, fresh lemon juice, garlic salt, freshly ground white pepper and Sour Cream Dressing to bind. Sprinkle with grated Gruyère cheese.

# FELAFEL
## (Garbanzo Bean Patties)

Tuck these flavorful rounds into warm pita bread and serve with an assortment of condiments—finely chopped onions, cucumbers, bell peppers and ripe tomatoes and plain yoghurt or Yoghurt Sauce— for diners to add as desired.

*Makes Fourteen To Sixteen Patties*
1/4 cup fine bulghur
1/4 cup fresh lemon juice
1 or 2 slices stale coarse white bread, broken into pieces
2 garlic cloves, minced
1/2 teaspoon salt
1/4 to 1/2 teaspoon ground cumin
1/4 teaspoon ground turmeric
1/8 teaspoon cayenne pepper
2 cups cooked garbanzo beans
2 tablespoons finely minced fresh coriander
2 tablespoons peanut oil, or as needed

Combine the bulghur and lemon juice in a bowl and let stand 20 minutes. Soak the bread in water to cover 5 minutes, then remove and squeeze dry. In a mortar, combine garlic, salt, cumin, turmeric and cayenne and mash together until well blended. Put the garbanzo beans in a mixing bowl and mash with a fork until smooth. Add the bulghur and lemon juice, soaked bread, garlic mixture and coriander. Mix with a fork until well blended. Taste and adjust seasonings. With your hands, form the garbanzo mixture into 2-inch patties about 1/2 inch thick. Heat oil in a skillet, add as many patties as will fit comfortably and fry until golden on both sides, turning once. Remove and keep warm in moderate oven. Fry remaining patties, adding oil to pan as needed. Serve hot in pita bread with condiments.

# PITA BREAD FILLING SUGGESTIONS

Warm pita bread in a moderate oven. Serve suggested ingredients in individual dishes at table for each diner to add as desired.

**ROAST BEEF** Thinly sliced roast beef, mango chutney, minced onion, sour cream or plain yoghurt, sliced cucumbers, thinly sliced red or green bell peppers.

**MEATLOAF** Crumbled Meatloaf heated in Quick Tomato Sauce, chopped ripe tomatoes, pine nuts,

---

*Fresh coriander has aliases— Chinese parsley and cilantro.*

---

shredded lettuce or spinach leaves, grated Cheddar or Monterey Jack cheese, halved black olives, chopped cooked artichoke hearts or bottoms, plain yoghurt.

**PORK** Shredded cooked pork roast, finely julienned bamboo shoots and water chestnuts heated in a little stock, lightly scrambled eggs, shredded Napa cabbage, soy sauce.

**LAMB** Shredded cooked lamb roast or lamb kebabs heated in a little stock, cooked garbanzo beans and minced onion marinated in Basic Vinaigrette, minced ripe tomato, cucumber, green bell pepper, zucchini and fresh parsley in any combination, Yoghurt Sauce with extra minced fresh mint and fresh lemon juice, Armenian string cheese or grated Monterey Jack cheese.

**LAMB** Heated lamb meatballs or stew, minced fresh mint, minced garlic, chopped ripe tomatoes, minced hot chili peppers, plain yoghurt, shredded lettuce, diced avocado brushed with fresh lemon juice.

**TONGUE** Julienned boiled tongue, zucchini and tomatoes (well drained) marinated in Basic Vinaigrette, minced fresh parsley, slivered green onions, slivered black olives, Yoghurt Sauce.

## CROISSANT AND ROLL FILLING SUGGESTIONS

Split croissants lengthwise and split rolls. Fill and serve at room temperature or heat in a 350°F oven.

**VEGETABLE** Crisply cooked julienned vegetables in Wine Sauce. Heat.

**BEEF, PORK OR VEAL** Julienned cooked beef, pork or veal roast, crumbled crisply cooked bacon, thinly sliced sweet red or white onion, Mushroom Sauce. Heat.

**FISH OR SHELLFISH** Flaked cooked firm white fish or salmon or minced shellfish in Curry Cream Sauce. Heat.

**LIVER** Chopped cooked chicken livers or calves' liver, sautéed minced mushrooms, chopped hard-cooked eggs, minced fresh parsley and chives, Shallot Cream Sauce to bind. Heat.

**FISH** Flaked cooked firm white fish or salmon, minced green onions and tops, minced water chestnuts, diced avocado tossed in fresh lemon juice, Curry Mayonnaise to bind.

**TURKEY OR CHICKEN** Thinly sliced cooked turkey or chicken, sliced radishes, crumbled crisply cooked bacon, Curry Mayonnaise to bind, shredded lettuce.

**SALMON SPREAD** Salmon Spread, fresh bean sprouts, sliced hard-cooked eggs, sprinkling of minced fresh chives and paprika.

**BLUE CHEESE** Shredded lettuce, chopped hard-cooked egg, diced avocado tossed in fresh lemon juice, crumbled gorgonzola or Roquefort cheese, Lemon Mayonnaise to bind.

## TORTILLA FILLING SUGGESTIONS

To heat tortillas, wrap in foil and heat in 350°F oven ten to fifteen minutes, or heat on a lightly greased skillet, turning once. Tortillas may also be heated in their original wrapper (pierce in several places with tines of fork) in a microwave oven on Hi, rotating halfway through two- to three-minute timing.

**PORK** Sauté minced onion and garlic in oil until soft. Add diced or slivered cooked pork roast and ground cumin, crumbled dried oregano, diced canned green chili peppers, salt and freshly ground black pepper. Moisten with stock, spoon into warm tortillas and serve with Tomatillo Sauce, shredded lettuce and sour cream.

**CHICKEN** Sauté chopped green onions in oil and add diced or shredded cooked chicken, chopped ripe tomato to moisten, diced canned green chili peppers, minced fresh coriander, salt and freshly ground black pepper. Spoon into warm tortillas and serve with Uncooked Tomato Sauce, sour cream and avocado cubes tossed with fresh lemon juice.

**RICE** Combine equal amounts heated cooked rice and shredded Monterey Jack cheese and pumpkin or sunflower seeds to taste. Fill warm tortillas, fold in half and place in 350°F oven to melt cheese and crisp the tortillas.

**HAM** Sauté diced cooked ham in half oil and half butter. Beat eggs and combine with shredded Monterey Jack or Muenster cheese, diced canned green chili peppers, salt, freshly ground black pepper and crumbled dried oregano. Add eggs to skillet with ham and cook until soft. Spoon into warm tortillas and serve with Uncooked Tomato Sauce and avocado slices tossed with fresh lemon juice.

# SALADS & SALAD DRESSINGS

Salad ingredients are an important part of any planned leftovers schedule. When steaming vegetables for dinner, put in some extra for the next day's salad. Remove the salad vegetables from the steamer while they are still very crisp, let cool and refrigerate; or, for additional flavor, dress the vegetables with a vinaigrette while they are still hot. Pasta, rice and legumes, even meats and poultry, can all be "planned" for salads in this same way.

Any meats you use should be juicy and attractive in appearance. Never try to disguise overcooked, dried-out meats by putting them in salads. Fish and shellfish should be treated gently, tossed in at the last moment and mixed with seasonings that will not overpower their delicate flavor.

Always remember to bring any vinaigrette-type dressing to room temperature before tossing with a salad. These dressings, especially those made with olive oil, thicken under refrigeration.

## SALAD HINTS

● Wash greens, dry thoroughly with paper toweling, or spin dry, wrap in terry towel and refrigerate several hours before using.

● Tear, rather than cut, lettuce, unless using for a bed, in which case, shred.

● Rub salad bowl with a cut garlic clove.

● If using a heavy dressing such as mayonnaise, toss lettuce with oil before adding dressing or it will not cling to leaves.

● Oil from marinated artichoke hearts or bottoms may be used as the oil in salad dressings.

● When making tossed salads, reserve a few of the ingredients to use as garnish after tossing.

*Color and texture are important to every dish, but especially salads.*

● If dressing salad from cruets, add oil first, toss to coat leaves, then add vinegar.

● Use vegetables in salad that avoid repetition with meat and complement vegetable side dishes.

● Avocado, raw mushrooms, and fruits such as pears, apples and bananas should be rubbed with fresh lemon juice to prevent discoloration.

● Salads should be combined and tossed just before serving.

● Sprinkle chopped hard-cooked eggs and/or minced fresh chives and/or parsley on salad after tossing.

● When planning salad ingredients, consider eye appeal, color and texture.

● If serving croutons with tossed salad, strew over after tossing or serve on the side.

## CHICKEN FRUIT SALAD

This versatile salad can be adapted to a wide variety of ingredients. Use celery, jicama and/or sunchokes in place of the water chestnuts. Choose from a large array of fruits: halved seedless grapes, diced papaya, pineapple, apple, melon, avocado, mango and peach. For the walnuts, substitute chopped cashews or pecans or lightly toasted slivered blanched almonds.

*Serves Two or Three*
2 cups diced cooked chicken
1/4 cup diced water chestnuts
1/4 cup raisins or chopped dates
1-1/2 cups mixed fresh fruits
1/2 tablespoon fresh lemon juice
2 tablespoons grated fresh or
　unsweetened dried coconut
2 tablespoons chopped walnuts
1 cup plain yoghurt
2 tablespoons Basic Mayonnaise
1/2 tablespoon honey, or 2 table-
　spoons chopped chutney (optional)
1 to 2 teaspoons minced fresh
　dill or tarragon
Salt and freshly ground white
　pepper to taste
Lettuce leaves
Watercress sprigs, bell pepper
　rings or pomegranate seeds

Toss together the chicken, water chestnuts, raisins, fruits, lemon juice, coconut and nuts. Chill. One hour before serving, combine yoghurt, mayonnaise, honey and seasonings. Toss with chicken-fruit mixture and chill. To serve, mound on lettuce leaves and garnish with watercress.

## ORIENTAL CHICKEN SALAD

*Serves Three or Four*
2 cups shredded cooked chicken
2 tablespoons hoisin sauce
3 tablespoons finely chopped
　peanuts
3 tablespoons toasted sesame
　seeds
1/2 cup slivered green onions
4 ounces fine rice sticks*
Peanut oil for deep frying
Shredded lettuce or Napa cabbage
Oriental sesame oil
Shrimp chips, deep fried (optional)
Coriander sprigs

---

*To toast sesame seeds, put in shallow metal pan in 350°F oven just until golden, or toast on stove top in a cast-iron pan. Watch carefully.*

---

Toss chicken with hoisin sauce to coat well. Add 2 tablespoons of the peanuts, 2 tablespoons of the sesame seeds and the green onions and toss well. In a large skillet, heat oil to a depth of 1/2 inch to 375°F. A few handfuls at a time, add rice sticks to oil and deep fry until they expand and just start to turn golden. This will take only a few minutes. Remove rice sticks with slotted utensil and drain on crumpled paper toweling. Repeat with remaining rice sticks until all are cooked. Toss about one-third of the rice sticks with the chicken mixture. Arrange lettuce on a large platter and layer half of chicken mixture on top. Sprinkle with half of the remaining rice sticks, top with remaining chicken mixture and then strew remaining peanuts and sesame seeds over. Drizzle with sesame oil and top with remaining rice sticks. Arrange shrimp chips around salad and garnish with coriander sprigs.

*Rice sticks, also called py mei fun, are very thin, rice-flour noodles available in Oriental markets and some supermarkets. They are sold by weight, packaged in cellophane.

## POULTRY SALAD SUGGESTIONS

**CHICKEN** Julienned cooked chicken marinated with coarsely grated raw carrots and Monterey Jack cheese in Basic Vinaigrette made with white wine vinegar and seasoned with ground mace and cloves. Toss with torn spinach leaves. Serve with sprinkling of freshly ground black pepper and chopped hard-cooked eggs.

**CHICKEN OR TURKEY** Thinly sliced cooked chicken or turkey, thinly sliced avocado rubbed with fresh lemon juice, slivered celery hearts or celery root, watercress leaves, sliced hard-cooked eggs. Arrange on lettuce leaves, garnish with tomato wedges and serve with Blue Cheese Dressing on the side.

**TURKEY** Diced cooked turkey, minced water chestnuts, minced bamboo shoots, coarsely chopped peanuts, chopped watercress, Oriental Dressing. Serve on shredded Napa cabbage with garnish of coriander sprigs.

**TURKEY AND HAM** Julienned cooked turkey and ham, tomato wedges, sliced sweet red or white onion, diced cooked artichoke hearts, strips of medium-sharp Cheddar cheese, Lemon Vinaigrette. Serve on lettuce and garnish with stuffed egg halves and parsley sprigs.

**TURKEY OR CHICKEN** Diced cooked turkey or chicken, diced canned mild green chili peppers, grated Monterey Jack cheese, toasted pine nuts, Herb Vinaigrette made with fresh tarragon.

**TURKEY OR CHICKEN** Diced cooked turkey or chicken, diced cooked ham, diced unpared tart apples, chopped celery. Serve on lettuce leaves and top with Avocado Dressing. Garnish with watercress or parsley sprigs.

**TURKEY, CHICKEN OR DUCK** Shredded cooked turkey, chicken or duck, diagonally sliced celery, toasted slivered blanched almonds, bell pepper strips, Blue Cheese Mayonnaise. Serve on lettuce leaves and garnish with pimiento strips.

**DUCK** Julienned cooked duck, Hoisin Dressing, orange or mandarin orange sections, minced green onions, chopped walnuts. Serve on bed of fresh spinach leaves and sprinkle with toasted sesame seeds or chopped fresh parsley.

---

*Freeze meats and poultry until* just firm *for easier slicing.*

---

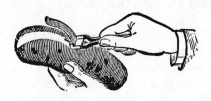

## FISH POTATO SALAD

*Serves Three or Four*
1/3 cup Basic Mayonnaise
2 tablespoons Garlic Olive Oil
1/2 cup finely chopped fresh sorrel (optional)
3 tablespoons minced fresh parsley
1 tablespoon minced fresh chives
2 teaspoons minced fresh dill
2 teaspoons fresh lemon juice, or to taste
1-1/2 to 2 cups diced boiled potatoes
1 cup chopped ripe tomatoes
1/2 cup flaked cooked firm white fish or salmon
Salt and freshly ground white pepper to taste
Lettuce leaves
Parsley sprigs
Lemon wedges

Combine mayonnaise, oil, herbs, lemon juice, potatoes and tomatoes. Toss to blend well and refrigerate several hours. Toss in fish and season with salt and pepper. Mound on lettuce leaves and garnish with parsley and lemon wedges.

## SUGGESTED ADDITIONS TO POTATO SALAD

The following are suggestions for additions to your own favorite basic potato salad recipe. Add them, toss with the suggested dressing or one of your own choice and stir in Basic Vinaigrette if mixture is too full-bodied.

**BEET** Slivered cooked beets, chopped celery, Sour Cream Dressing. Serve on lettuce leaves and sprinkle with chopped hard-cooked eggs.

**ROAST BEEF** Julienned cooked roast beef, cooked lima beans or cut-up green beans, thinly sliced red or white sweet onion, minced fresh parsley, Green Mayonnaise.

**POT ROAST** Shredded cooked pot roast, ham, tongue or corned beef, minced celery and bell pepper, chopped fresh chives, Mustard Mayonnaise.

**PRAWN OR FISH** Diced cooked prawns or flaked cooked firm white fish, toasted chopped blanched almonds, minced fresh dill, Shallot Vinaigrette.

**PORK OR VEAL ROAST** Cubed cooked pork or veal roast, chopped tart unpared apple, cucumber and celery, Blue Cheese Mayonnaise.

**TURKEY** Cubed cooked turkey, chopped green onions and tops, slivered black olives, Curry Mayonnaise.

## SEAFOOD SALAD SUGGESTIONS

**PRAWN OR FISH** Chopped cooked prawns or flaked cooked firm fish, cut-up cooked green beans, sliced hard-cooked eggs, slivered black olives, Garlic Vinaigrette. Garnish with pimiento strips.

**PRAWN OR FISH** Diced cooked prawns or flaked cooked firm fish, minced water chestnuts, cooked asparagus tips, chopped hard-cooked eggs. Arrange on Romaine lettuce and garnish with tomato wedges or halved cherry tomatoes. Serve with Mustard Vinaigrette on the side.

**FISH** Flaked cooked firm white fish, chopped green onions and celery, halved seedless green grapes, Hoisin Dressing. Serve on bed of watercress.

---

*Don't be fooled by an onion's color. Red does not necessarily mean sweet.*

---

## MARINATED BEEF SALAD

*Serves Two*

2 to 4 slices boiled beef
1/3 cup Garlic Vinaigrette
Romaine lettuce
1/3 cup sliced green onions and
   tops
2 hard-cooked eggs, chopped
2 tablespoons capers, drained
4 anchovy fillets

Marinate beef in vinaigrette 1 hour at room temperature, turning several times. Shred or tear lettuce and place on serving plate. Lift beef from vinaigrette and arrange on lettuce. Sprinkle with onions, eggs and capers. Garnish with anchovy fillets.

## TONGUE SALAD

*Serves Two*

4 to 6 thin slices boiled tongue
1/3 cup Mexican Dressing
Romaine or red leaf lettuce
1 medium ripe tomato, sliced
1/2 sweet red or white onion,
   thinly sliced
1/2 green or red bell pepper,
   thinly sliced
3 tablespoons sliced pimiento-
   stuffed green olives
Salt and freshly ground black
   pepper to taste
Minced fresh coriander

Marinate tongue in 2 tablespoons of the dressing 1 hour at room temperature, turning several times. Line a serving plate with lettuce leaves. Arrange tongue slices on lettuce and arrange in layers on top the tomato, onion, bell pepper and olives. Season with salt and pepper and pour remaining dressing over the top. Garnish with minced coriander.

## MEAT SALAD SUGGESTIONS

**CORNED BEEF** Julienned corned beef, potatoes and beets and shredded cabbage from New England boiled dinner, thinly sliced unpared apples, Mustard Vinaigrette. Serve on lettuce leaves.

**ROAST BEEF** Sliced cooked roast beef cut into strips and marinated in Basic Vinaigrette made with wine vinegar at least 1 hour. Toss with sliced pimiento-stuffed olives, sliced sweet red or white onion, broken Romaine lettuce.

**ROAST OR BOILED BEEF** Julienned roast or boiled beef marinated in Mexican Dressing 1 hour, strips of Monterey Jack or Cheddar cheese, cooked kidney or garbanzo beans, diced avocado, chopped green onions and tops, crushed corn chips. Serve on shredded iceberg lettuce with garnish of halved black olives and chopped fresh coriander.

**BEEF STEAK** Cooked beef steak sliced thinly on diagonal and marinated, covered, 1 hour in Oriental Dressing. Toss with chopped ripe tomatoes, thinly sliced sweet red or white onion, minced garlic, chopped fresh parsley and chives. Serve on lettuce, if desired.

**VEAL** Shredded cooked veal roast, diced avocados, Walnut Oil Dressing on Bibb lettuce. Garnish with chopped walnuts lightly browned in olive oil.

**LAMB** Shredded cooked lamb roast, slivered black olives, coarsely grated raw carrot, celeriac or turnips, thinly sliced sweet red or white onion, minced garlic, Mustard Vinaigrette.

---

*For just a trace of garlic flavor, rub salad bowl with a cut garlic clove.*

---

**LAMB** Cubed cooked lamb roast, fresh pineapple chunks, diced celery, mandarin orange sections, Lemon Mayonnaise seasoned with ground ginger, freshly grated nutmeg and freshly ground white pepper.

**PORK** Julienned cooked pork roast and ham, torn lettuce leaves, slivered cucumber, bell pepper and radishes, Shallot Vinaigrette. Garnish with thin strips of provolone or Cheddar cheese.

**PORK ROAST OR HAM** Julienned cooked pork roast or ham, sliced fresh mushrooms rubbed with fresh lemon juice or softened and slivered dried shiitake mushrooms, chopped fresh parsley, Miso Dressing.

**HAM OR TONGUE** Julienned cooked ham or tongue, cooked asparagus tips, sliced water chestnuts or raw sunchokes or jicama, chopped watercress, Mustard Vinaigrette. Serve on lettuce leaves and garnish with toasted sesame seeds.

**HAM OR TONGUE** Julienned cooked ham or tongue, slivers of pickles, diced unpared apples, slivered black olives, sliced radishes, Basic Vinaigrette. Serve on lettuce with garnish of watercress sprigs and sliced hard-cooked eggs with or without a dab of lumpfish caviar.

## MIXED VEGETABLE SALAD

*Serves Four to Six*
1 cup cooked peas
1 cup diced cooked carrots
1 cup diced cooked potatoes
1/2 cup diced cooked beets
4 green onions and some green, thinly sliced
1 large apple, unpared and diced
1/4 teaspoon salt
1/8 teaspoon freshly ground black pepper
1/8 teaspoon paprika
1 tablespoon Homemade Mustard
1/4 cup corn oil
1 tablespoon granulated sugar
1/4 cup sour cream
Lettuce leaves
Minced fresh parsley
Chopped hard-cooked eggs

In a large bowl, toss together the vegetables, apple and seasonings. Make a paste of the mustard, 2 tablespoons of the oil and the sugar. Stir in remaining 2 tablespoons oil, mixing well, and toss into vegetables to coat well. Adjust seasonings. Cover and refrigerate overnight, stirring occasionally. One hour before serving, mix in sour cream. To serve, mound on lettuce leaves and sprinkle with minced parsley. Garnish with chopped eggs.

## ORIENTAL EGGPLANT SALAD

Households of two often find themselves with half of an eggplant remaining in the vegetable crisper. This easy, delicious salad makes a complete meal with a simple stir fry and steamed rice.

*Serves Two*
1/2 globe eggplant, unpeeled
1/2 cup shredded cooked pork roast
1/3 cup Oriental Dressing
1 tablespoon minced green onion
1 tablespoon minced fresh coriander

Steam the eggplant over gently simmering water until it can be easily pierced with a fork. Remove from the steamer, cut into thick slices lengthwise and refrigerate until well chilled. With a sharp knife, shred the eggplant slices into long, thin strips. Arrange eggplant on a plate and top with shredded pork. Pour the salad dressing over the top and toss carefully to mix well. Garnish with green onion and coriander.

---

*Don't let dried herbs and spices sit on the shelf too long; they lose their pungency.*

---

## VEGETABLE SALAD SUGGESTIONS

**GREEN BEAN** Cooked green beans marinated in Oriental Dressing. Serve on lettuce leaves and sprinkle with toasted sesame seeds.

**BEET** Julienned cooked beets, chopped hard-cooked eggs, chopped pickles, Basic Mayonnaise mixed with a little pickle juice. Serve on lettuce and sprinkle with chopped fresh parsley and chives.

**BROCCOLI** Cooked broccoli flowerets, Anchovy Vinaigrette with minced garlic. Serve on lettuce leaves with garnish of anchovy fillets.

**ASPARAGUS** Cooked asparagus tips, sliced raw mushrooms rubbed with fresh lemon juice, minced green onions and tops, Yoghurt Dressing for Green Salads made with chopped fresh dill. Serve on lettuce with garnish of sieved hard-cooked eggs.

**CAULIFLOWER** Cooked cauliflowerets. Serve on shredded lettuce, top with Miso Dressing and sprinkle with chopped green onions and tops.

**CARROT** Julienned cooked carrot, grated onion, Basic Vinaigrette. Just before serving, toss in chopped hard-cooked eggs, mound on lettuce and garnish with sliced Red Eggs and minced fresh parsley.

**CELERY ROOT** Julienned cooked celery root, chopped fresh sorrel, finely minced celery, chopped hard-cooked eggs, flaked cooked salmon, salt, white pepper, Basic Vinaigrette as needed to moisten. Serve on lettuce with garnish of parsley sprigs and lemon wedges.

## TWO LENTIL SALADS

If lentils have been part of your planned leftovers schedule, these salads, each designed to serve two, are perfect ways to use them. Prepare as directed, then mound on lettuce leaves and garnish with chilled steamed vegetables, such as broccoli flowerets, cauliflowerets, asparagus tips, and green beans, or raw vegetables, such as bell pepper rings or carrot curls. If your refrigerator is shy of vegetable garnishes, simply sprinkle with minced fresh parsley and chopped hard-cooked eggs.

1-1/2 cups cooked lentils
1/3 cup Mustard Vinaigrette
1 small sweet red onion, very
   thinly sliced

Toss lentils with dressing to coat well. Toss in onion slices and refrigerate at least 3 to 4 hours, stirring occasionally. (Flavor will be best if refrigerated for 3 days before serving.)

3 tablespoons safflower oil
2 tablespoons red wine vinegar
1/4 to 1/2 teaspoon granulated
   sugar
1/2 teaspoon salt
1/4 teaspoon freshly ground black
   pepper
1-1/3 cups cooked lentils
1/4 cup finely minced onion
3 tablespoons minced green onion
   tops, or 2 tablespoons minced
   fresh chives
1 or 2 ripe tomatoes, cut up

Combine oil, vinegar, sugar, salt and pepper and mix well. Toss in lentils, onion and green onion tops. Adjust seasonings and chill 3 hours. Just before serving, toss in tomatoes.

## GARBANZO BEAN SALAD

Any diced cooked meat or poultry can be added to this Mediterranean-inspired salad.

*Serves Two or Three*
2 cups cooked garbanzo beans
1/2 cup Quick Tomato, Marinara
   or Creole Sauce
1/4 cup Mustard Vinaigrette made
   with red wine vinegar
1 teaspoon very finely minced
   garlic
2 tablespoons finely minced red or
   white onion
2 tablespoons finely minced
   Italian parsley
1 teaspoon finely minced fresh
   oregano or basil
Salt and freshly ground black
   pepper to taste
Lettuce leaves
Ripe-tomato wedges or halved
   cherry tomatoes

Toss together all ingredients except lettuce and tomato wedges. Cover and refrigerate 3 hours, stirring occasionally. To serve, mound garbanzo bean mixture on lettuce leaves and garnish with tomato wedges.

*Bring vinaigrette dressing to room temperature before adding to salads, as the oil thickens when chilled.*

## BEAN–POTATO SALAD

*Serves Four*

1/3 cup olive oil
2 to 3 tablespoons fresh lemon
 juice
1 teaspoon Dijon-style mustard
3 tablespoons minced fresh parsley
2 tablespoons minced fresh chives
1 teaspoon minced fresh basil
1/2 teaspoon finely minced garlic
1/2 cup minced sweet red or
 white onion
3 cups cooked small white beans
1 cup diced boiled potato
Salt and freshly ground black
 pepper to taste
1 or 2 hard-cooked eggs, chopped
Butter lettuce leaves
Tomato wedges

Combine oil, lemon juice, mustard,
herbs, garlic and onion. Mix well
and toss in beans and potato.
Season with salt and pepper, cover
and refrigerate 3 hours, stirring
occasionally. Adjust seasonings and
toss in chopped eggs. To serve,
mound bean-potato mixture on
butter lettuce leaves and garnish
with tomato wedges.

*For a balanced meatless meal,
serve yoghurt or other dairy
product with a legume and grain
dish.*

## WHITE BEAN SALAD

*Serves Two*

2 cups cooked small white beans
1 cup julienned cooked lamb roast
2 teaspoons finely minced garlic
2 teaspoons chopped fresh oregano
1/3 to 1/2 cup Lemon Vinaigrette
1 small red onion, thinly sliced
3 cups shredded fresh spinach
Salt to taste
Tomato wedges or halved cherry
 tomatoes
Freshly ground black pepper

Combine beans, lamb, garlic, oregano
and 1/3 cup of the vinaigrette.
Toss to mix well, adding more
vinaigrette if needed. Refrigerate
2 to 3 hours. Toss in onion,
spinach and salt. Mound on plates
and surround with tomato wedges.
Pass the peppermill.

## LEGUME SALAD SUGGESTIONS

Refrigerate legumes and dressing
for up to three hours before
adding remaining ingredients.

**GARBANZO OR KIDNEY BEAN**
Cooked garbanzo or kidney beans,
Basic Vinaigrette made with red
wine vinegar, fresh lemon juice
and mixed fresh herbs. Toss with
strips of medium-sharp Cheddar
or Monterey Jack cheese, slivered
black olives, chopped ripe tomatoes,
thinly sliced sweet red or white
onions.

**KIDNEY BEAN** Cooked kidney
beans, Mexican Dressing. Toss in
chopped ripe tomatoes, shredded
Cheddar cheese, sliced green onions
and tops. Serve on lettuce leaves
surrounded with avocado slices.

**RED BEAN** Cooked red beans,
cooked white rice, chopped onion,
Garlic Vinaigrette. Toss in chopped
fresh parsley and freshly grated
Parmesan cheese.

**LENTIL OR SMALL WHITE BEAN**
Cooked lentils or beans, Oriental
Dressing. Toss with diced ripe
tomatoes, sliced fresh mushrooms,
diced mild cheese or cooked ham,
chopped green onions. Serve on
bed of lettuce and garnish with
halved black olives and parsley
sprigs.

**LENTIL OR SMALL WHITE BEAN**
Cooked lentils or beans, Mustard
Vinaigrette. Toss with chopped
cucumber, chopped celery, shredded
carrots, sliced green onions and
tops, fennel seed or chopped fresh
fennel feathers. Stuff cooked jumbo
pasta shells. Serve in lettuce cups
with garnish of chopped fresh
parsley and halved cherry tomatoes.
Pass extra dressing.

# MACARONI SALAD

Cooked vegetables—chopped broccoli, cut-up green beans, peas—may be used in place of the raw minced vegetables. The addition of diced cooked ham, chicken or turkey makes this salad a complete meal.

*Serves Three or Four*
1/2 cup Quick Tomato or Marinara Sauce
1/4 cup Basic Mayonnaise
1/4 cup minced bell pepper
1/4 cup minced fresh Italian parsley
1/4 cup minced celery and some leaves
6 to 8 large pitted black olives, slivered
1/2 teaspoon salt
1/4 teaspoon chili powder and/or crumbled dried oregano or tarragon
Freshly ground black pepper
2 cups cooked elbow or salad macaroni
Lettuce leaves
Tomato wedges or halved cherry tomatoes

Combine sauce, mayonnaise, bell pepper, parsley, celery, olives and seasonings. Toss in macaroni to thoroughly coat and refrigerate 2 to 3 hours. To serve, mound macaroni mixture on lettuce leaves and garnish with tomato wedges. Grind over additional pepper.

# COCKSCOMB PASTA SALAD

If cockscomb pasta cannot be found, use elbow or salad macaroni, fusilli or small shells. Tongue, beef, lamb, pork or ham can be a stand-in for the turkey.

*Serves Three or Four*
2/3 cup julienned cooked turkey
2 tablespoons Basic Vinaigrette made with red wine vinegar
1/4 cup sour cream
1/4 cup Basic Mayonnaise
1/4 cup minced fresh Italian parsley
1/4 cup minced celery and tender leaves
3 tablespoons chopped pimientos or minced bell pepper
2 cups cooked cockscomb pasta
2/3 cup julienned Monterey Jack or fontina cheese (about 3 ounces)
Salt and freshly ground black pepper to taste
Lettuce leaves
Halved black olives

Marinate turkey in vinaigrette at room temperature, stirring occasionally, at least 1 hour. Combine sour cream, mayonnaise, parsley, celery and pimientos. Toss with pasta to coat well, then add turkey mixture, cheese and seasonings and toss again. Cover and refrigerate 2 to 3 hours. To serve, mound turkey mixture on lettuce leaves and garnish with olives.

# ORIENTAL NOODLE SALAD

Fresh bean sprouts, cubed pineapple or cooked peas or snow peas are good additions to this summertime salad.

*Serves Two*
2 cups cooked Chinese-style noodles
1/2 cup finely diced cooked pork roast
2 tablespoons diced water chestnuts
2 tablespoons diced bamboo shoots
1/4 cup minced celery
3 tablespoons coarsely chopped unsalted peanuts
2 tablespoons chopped fresh coriander
1/3 cup Oriental Dressing without sesame seeds, or Hoisin Dressing
Shredded Chinese cabbage
1 teaspoon toasted sesame seeds

Combine all ingredients except cabbage and sesame seeds. Toss well, cover and refrigerate 3 hours. To serve, mound on shredded cabbage and sprinkle with sesame seeds.

# SOMEN NOODLE SALAD

*Serves Two*
2 cups cooked somen noodles*
3 tablespoons Oriental Dressing, with optional garlic and ginger
One 2-inch-square frozen tofu (bean curd), thawed and well drained
2/3 cup shredded cooked chicken
4 to 6 tender young watercress sprigs
1/3 cup slivered green onions and tops
1/2 recipe Egg Garnish

Toss noodles with 1 tablespoon of the dressing. Crumble the bean curd and toss with 1/2 tablespoon of the dressing. Let noodles and tofu stand for 20 minutes. Arrange noodles on a platter. Arrange on the noodles the chicken, watercress sprigs, green onions, egg slivers and crumbled tofu. Drizzle remaining dressing over.

*Somen noodles are very thin wheat noodles. They are available dried, packaged in cellophane, in Japanese markets.

---

*Store cooked pasta in water to cover in the refrigerator up to 3 days. Drain well and pat dry before using for salads.*

---

# PASTA SALAD SUGGESTIONS

Refrigerate pasta and dressing for up to three hours before adding remaining ingredients.

**FISH** Cooked pasta, Avocado Dressing. Toss in flaked cooked firm white fish, sliced hard-cooked eggs, tomato wedges, cut-up cooked green beans.

**CHICKEN** Cooked cockscomb pasta, diced cooked chicken, Mustard Vinaigrette. Toss in grated Gruyère, Emmenthaler, Monterey Jack, Jarlsberg or mozzarella cheese, slivered ripe olives, julienned green bell pepper, torn Romaine lettuce leaves.

**BROCCOLI OR ASPARAGUS** Cooked medium shells, Anchovy Mayonnaise. Toss in broccoli flowerets or asparagus tips, halved black olives, coarsely chopped ripe tomato, minced fresh parsley.

**FETA CHEESE** Cooked fusilli, Garlic Vinaigrette. Toss in shredded raw spinach, shredded sweet red or white onion, julienned ripe tomatoes, chopped fresh basil, crumbled feta cheese. Garnish with minced fresh parsley.

---

# RICE SALAD

Use chicken, turkey or duck in place of the ham.

*Serves Three or Four*
2 cups cooked white or brown rice
1/2 cup diced cooked ham
3/4 cup Mustard or Curry Mayonnaise
1/2 cup Creole, Quick Tomato or Chili Sauce
1/3 cup chopped green onions and tops
1/4 cup sliced black or pimiento-stuffed olives (optional)
1 cup diagonally sliced celery
2 hard-cooked eggs, chopped
4 to 6 radishes, sliced
1/2 cucumber, peeled, seeded and diced
Lettuce leaves
Green bell pepper rings
Tomato wedges

Combine rice, ham, mayonnaise, Creole Sauce, onions, olives and celery. Refrigerate 3 hours. Just before serving, toss in eggs, radishes and cucumber. Line a large shallow salad bowl with lettuce leaves and mound rice mixture on lettuce. Garnish with pepper rings and tomato wedges.

---

*When a recipe says "toss in," lightly lift and turn the ingredients with a fork. Do not stir.*

# BROWN RICE MIDDLE EASTERN SALAD

*Serves Four*
1/4 cup olive oil
1/4 cup fresh lemon or lime juice
1 teaspoon salt
2 cups cooked brown rice
2 medium ripe tomatoes, peeled and finely chopped
1 cup chopped green onions and tops
1/2 cup chopped fresh mint
1/2 teaspoon finely minced garlic
Romaine lettuce leaves

Combine oil, lemon juice and salt and stir well. Combine rice and oil mixture and toss to mix well. Refrigerate 3 hours. Just before serving, toss together tomatoes, green onions, mint, garlic and rice mixture. Arrange lettuce leaves in shallow salad bowl and mound rice mixture in center.

# RICE SALAD SUGGESTIONS

Combine cooked white or brown rice, and meat or poultry if using, with dressing and refrigerate up to three hours before adding remaining ingredients.

**TURKEY OR CHICKEN** Cooked rice, diced cooked turkey or chicken, Yoghurt Dressing for Green Salads. Toss in torn spinach leaves, watercress leaves, chopped green onions and tops, fresh snow peas and/or bean sprouts, halved seedless grapes.

**FRUIT AND VEGETABLE** Cooked rice, Blue Cheese Vinaigrette. Toss in orange sections, chopped unpared apple, chopped celery, onion and cucumber, grated carrots, halved seedless grapes, raisins and chopped toasted almonds, pecans or cashews.

**FRUIT** Cooked rice, Yoghurt Dressing for Fruit Salads. Toss in diced fresh fruit such as firm pears, apples, tangerines, melons, halved seedless grapes, shredded unsweetened coconut. Garnish with fresh mint sprigs.

**EGG** Cooked rice, Anchovy Mayonnaise. Toss in chopped hard-cooked eggs, sliced celery, sliced cucumber, slivered black olives, coarsely chopped ripe tomatoes, chopped fresh parsley and/or watercress.

**PORK ROAST OR HAM** Cooked rice, slivered cooked pork roast or ham, Oriental Dressing. Toss in raw snow peas, chopped water chestnuts, minced fresh coriander.

**LAMB ROAST** Cooked rice, shredded cooked lamb roast, Curry Mayonnaise. Toss in shredded Gruyère or fontina cheese, thinly sliced sweet red or white onion, chopped fresh chives.

**HERB** Cooked rice, Herb Mayonnaise. Toss in chopped fresh sorrel, chopped watercress leaves, sliced raw mushrooms, thinly sliced unpared tart apple. Garnish with anchovy fillet.

# BULGHUR SALAD

*Serves Four to Six*
2 cups cooked bulghur
1/4 cup sliced green onions and tops
1/2 cup cooked peas
1/2 cup cooked corn kernels
1/4 cup minced green or red bell pepper
1 tablespoon minced fresh coriander
2 tablespoons minced fresh parsley
1/3 cup Mustard Vinaigrette made with red wine vinegar
Ground cumin, salt and freshly ground pepper to taste
Lettuce leaves
Tomato wedges
Grapefruit sections

Toss together bulghur, green onions, peas, corn, bell pepper, coriander and parsley. Add vinaigrette and seasonings and toss gently. Refrigerate three hours. Adjust seasonings and mound bulghur mixture on lettuce leaves. Garnish with tomato wedges and grapefruit sections.

The following two recipes turn the lowly hard-cooked egg into a colorful addition to potato and other vegetable salads and to platters of cold cuts.

# RED EGGS

Cooked beets may also be heated in this pickling liquid.

*Makes Eight Eggs*
1 cup beet juice*
1 cup cider vinegar
1 garlic clove, lightly mashed
1 small onion, sliced
1 small bay leaf
2 tablespoons granulated sugar
3/4 teaspoon salt
1/4 teaspoon ground cloves
1/4 teaspoon ground allspice
1/4 teaspoon freshly grated nutmeg
8 hard-cooked eggs, shelled

Combine all ingredients except eggs. Bring to boil, lower heat and simmer 10 minutes. Pour beet juice mixture over eggs and let stand at least 4 hours. Jar, cover and refrigerate up to 1 week. The longer the eggs stay in the pickling mixture, the spicier they will be.

*Water in which 3 to 4 beets have been cooked.

# TEA EGGS

*Makes Eight Eggs*
1 cup strong tea
3/4 cup cider vinegar
1 tablespoon granulated sugar
1/2 teaspoon salt
3 slices ginger root
8 hard-cooked eggs, shelled

Bring all ingredients, except eggs, to rapid boil. Remove from heat and cool slightly. Place eggs in jar, pour tea mixture over, cool, cover and refrigerate 2 to 6 days.

# SALAD DRESSINGS

With the exception of a bit of blue cheese or cream cheese or perhaps a hard-cooked egg, salad dressings themselves will not clear leftovers out of your refrigerator. But they can give a special lift to the salads and cold vegetable dishes you create with leftovers. These dressings are so good, however, they shouldn't be relegated to this role alone. Use them on all of your salads.

# BASIC VINAIGRETTE

*Makes Approximately One Cup*
1/4 cup red or white wine vinegar or cider vinegar
2/3 cup olive oil
1/4 teaspoon salt
1/8 teaspoon freshly ground black pepper

In a jar with tight lid, combine all ingredients, cover and shake to mix thoroughly. Adjust seasonings to taste and refrigerate up to 2 weeks.

**LEMON VINAIGRETTE** Substitute for the vinegar in Basic Vinaigrette 1/3 cup fresh lemon or lime juice.

**HERB VINAIGRETTE** Add to Basic or Lemon Vinaigrette 1 tablespoon chopped fresh herbs or 1/2 tablespoon crumbled dried herbs, or to taste.

**MUSTARD VINAIGRETTE** Add to Basic Vinaigrette 1/2 teaspoon dry mustard, Homemade Mustard or Dijon-style mustard, or to taste.

**GARLIC VINAIGRETTE** Add to Basic, Lemon or Mustard Vinaigrette 1 teaspoon finely minced garlic and 1/4 teaspoon crumbled thyme.

**ANCHOVY VINAIGRETTE** Add to Basic or Lemon Vinaigrette 1/2 to 1 teaspoon mashed anchovy fillets or anchovy paste.

**BLUE CHEESE VINAIGRETTE** Substitute walnut oil for olive oil in Basic Vinaigrette. Use cider vinegar and add 1/2 teaspoon minced fresh thyme and 2 to 3 tablespoons crumbled gorgonzola or Roquefort cheese.

**SHALLOT VINAIGRETTE** Add to Basic or Lemon Vinaigrette 1-1/2 tablespoons finely minced shallots.

**SUGGESTED ADDITIONS TO BASIC OR LEMON VINAIGRETTE**

● One tablespoon chopped pimiento.
● One to 2 tablespoons freshly grated Parmesan or Romano cheese.
● One to 2 hard-cooked eggs, chopped, and 4 to 6 pimiento-stuffed olives, sliced.
● One-half avocado, mashed.
● Three to 4 tablespoons toasted sesame seeds.
● Grated onion to taste.
● One teaspoon grated onion, 1/2 teaspoon dry mustard, 2 teaspoons celery seeds, granulated sugar to taste.
● One tablespoon poppy seeds, 1/2 teaspoon Dijon-style mustard and 1 teaspoon minced garlic.

● One tablespoon well-drained capers and 2 teaspoons minced fresh parsley.
● Two tablespoons Chili Sauce and 1 tablespoon minced watercress.
● One-half teaspoon curry powder, 2 tablespoons chopped chutney and 1 hard-cooked egg, chopped.
● Two tablespoons minced shallots, 1 tablespoon minced sweet red or white onion, 1 medium ripe tomato, minced, 1/2 teaspoon minced fresh tarragon and 1 teaspoon dry mustard.

## LEMON–GARLIC DRESSING

*Makes Approximately One-half Cup*
1 hard-cooked egg
3 tablespoons fresh lemon juice
1/4 cup safflower or olive oil
1 tablespoon finely minced onion, or to taste
1/2 teaspoon finely minced garlic, or to taste
Salt and freshly ground white pepper to taste

Separate egg yolk and white. Force yolk through a sieve and combine with remaining ingredients. Chop egg white and stir in to blend well. Jar, cover and refrigerate up to 4 days.

**VARIATION** Mash with egg yolk 1 to 1-1/2 tablespoons crumbled blue cheese.

## WALNUT OIL DRESSING

*Makes Approximately Three-fourths Cup*
1/2 cup walnut oil
1 teaspoon German-style mustard or Homemade Mustard
1/2 teaspoon salt
1/4 teaspoon granulated sugar
1/4 teaspoon freshly ground black pepper

Combine all ingredients and mix well. Jar, cover and refrigerate up to 10 days.

## MEXICAN DRESSING

*Makes Approximately One Cup*
1/2 cup olive oil
1/4 cup red wine vinegar
2 tablespoons fresh lemon juice
1 garlic clove, minced
2 tablespoons minced onion
1/4 teaspoon ground cumin
1 dried red chili pepper, seeded and crushed
Salt and freshly ground black pepper to taste

Combine all ingredients and mix well. Jar, cover and refrigerate up to 1 week.

## ITALIAN DRESSING

*Makes Approximately One Cup*
1/2 cup olive oil
1/4 cup red wine vinegar
2 tablespoons fresh lemon juice
2 tablespoons grated or finely
    minced onion
1 tablespoon freshly grated
    Parmesan cheese
1 garlic clove, minced
1 teaspoon salt
2 teaspoons minced fresh basil
2 teaspoons minced fresh oregano
1/2 to 1 dried red chili pepper,
    seeded and crushed (optional)
Salt and freshly ground black
    pepper to taste

Combine all ingredients and mix
well. Jar, cover and refrigerate up
to 1 week.

## ORIENTAL DRESSING

*Makes Approximately One-third Cup*
1/4 cup rice vinegar
4 teaspoons soy sauce
4 teaspoons sesame or safflower oil
1 teaspoon honey
1/2 teaspoon dry mustard
1/4 teaspoon salt, or to taste
1/4 teaspoon finely minced ginger
    root (optional)

1/4 teaspoon finely minced garlic
    (optional)
2 teaspoons lightly toasted sesame
    seeds
Dash Oriental sesame oil
Freshly ground black pepper
    to taste

Combine all ingredients and mix
well. Jar, cover and refrigerate up
to 1 week.

## HOISIN DRESSING

Try this dressing on sliced jicama
or a salad of chicken and crisp
snow peas.

*Makes Approximately
Two-thirds Cup*
1/4 cup hoisin sauce
1/4 cup fresh lemon or lime juice
3 tablespoons corn oil
1/4 to 1/2 teaspoon very finely
    minced garlic
1/4 to 1/2 teaspoon very finely
    minced ginger root
4 drops Oriental sesame oil, or to
    taste

Combine all ingredients and mix
well. Jar, cover and refrigerate up
to 10 days.

## MISO DRESSING

Chilled iceberg lettuce is the perfect
complement to this unusual dressing;
it is also good on cooked cauliflower,
asparagus and green beans. If
possible, prepare the dressing and
serve it at once.

*Makes Approximately
One-third Cup*
2 tablespoons red or white miso
1 teaspoon rice vinegar
1/4 teaspoon brown sugar
2 tablespoons peanut oil
3 drops Oriental sesame oil
2 tablespoons ice water

Into medium bowl, sieve miso and
gradually blend in vinegar, sugar
and oils. Blend thoroughly and
whisk in water. Jar, cover and
refrigerate up to 1 week.

## TOFU DRESSING

Use on crisp greens, hard-cooked
eggs, sliced tomatoes, cooked firm
green vegetables, and as a dip for
raw vegetables.

*Makes Approximately
Three-fourths Cup*
2/3 cup mashed firm or soft tofu
   (bean curd)
1 tablespoon chopped fresh parsley
1 tablespoon chopped fresh chives
3-1/2 tablespoons fresh lemon
   juice
2 tablespoons safflower oil
1 or 2 drops Oriental sesame oil
   (optional)
1/2 teaspoon salt
1/4 teaspoon freshly ground white
   pepper
1/2 tablespoon red or white miso,
   or 1 teaspoon soy sauce
1/2 teaspoon minced ginger root
   (optional)

Place all ingredients in a blender
or food processor and purée until
well mixed, smooth and creamy.
Adjust seasonings. Jar, cover and
refrigerate up to 10 days.

## VARIATIONS

● Season with curry powder to
taste.
● Add crumbled blue cheese to
taste.
● Before adding other ingredients
purée in blender 1 to 2 garlic
cloves.
● Add freshly grated Parmesan
cheese to taste.
● Add 2 tablespoons Tomato
Purée.

## AVOCADO DRESSING

This very creamy dressing is
delicious on sliced tomatoes or on
a fish or shellfish salad; add Basic
Vinaigrette for a thinner consistency.
For a simpler version of avocado
dressing, mash avocado with Lemon
Vinaigrette to taste.

*Makes Approximately One Cup*
1 slice ginger root
1 garlic clove
One-half ripe avocado
2 to 3 tablespoons fresh lemon or
   lime juice
2 tablespoons sour cream
1 tablespoon olive oil
Salt and freshly ground white
   pepper to taste
Paprika to taste

In a blender or food processor,
mince the ginger root and garlic
very finely to measure about 1/4
teaspoon each. Add remaining ingredients and blend until smooth and
creamy. Adjust seasonings, jar,
cover and refrigerate up to 3 days.

## SOUR CREAM DRESSING

Reminiscent of a very light-bodied
mayonnaise, this tangy dressing is
especially good with artichokes
and as a dip for raw vegetables.

*Makes Approximately
Three-fourths Cup*
2 hard-cooked egg yolks
1 tablespoon safflower oil
2 tablespoons fresh lemon juice
1/4 cup sour cream
1/4 cup Basic Mayonnaise
Salt and freshly ground white
   pepper to taste

Mash egg yolks with oil. Blend in
lemon juice until well mixed. Add
remaining ingredients. Jar, cover
and refrigerate up to 1 week.

### SUGGESTED ADDITIONS TO
SOUR CREAM DRESSING

● One tablespoon minced fresh
parsley and/or chives.
● One-fourth teaspoon each garlic
powder and paprika.
● One-half teaspoon curry powder.
● One teaspoon prepared horseradish
● One teaspoon Dijon-style
mustard.
● One hard-cooked egg white,
chopped.

# BASIC MAYONNAISE

Mayonnaise can be made by hand or in a blender or food processor. The hand method produces a soft mayonnaise that will keep, covered, in the refrigerator three to six days. Mayonnaise made in a blender is more stable and will keep up to ten days; it can be used in most recipes calling for commercial mayonnaise. With either method, it is important that the eggs are fresh and all of the ingredients and utensils are at room temperature. Sandwich spreads, stuffed eggs, potato salads and other dishes made with homemade mayonnaise should always be refrigerated and never kept longer than twenty-four hours.

### HAND METHOD

Use a wooden bowl, just large enough to hold the finished mayonnaise, and a wooden spoon. Add oil drop by drop, beating in gently in a circular motion always in the same direction. Never add more oil until the previous oil is completely absorbed. If the mayonnaise should curdle because the oil is added too quickly, gradually stir the curdled mayonnaise into a fresh lightly beaten egg yolk. Then add oil, vinegar and seasonings as if making a new batch.

*Makes One Cup*
1 cup olive or safflower oil
2 egg yolks
1 to 2 teaspoons cider, tarragon or wine vinegar
1/2 teaspoon salt
1/4 teaspoon freshly ground white pepper
1/4 teaspoon paprika
Dash cayenne pepper (optional)

Measure oil into a cup with a spout or into a squeeze bottle. Beat yolks until thick and lemon colored. A drop at a time, stir in 1/2 cup of the oil. Add half the vinegar, stirring constantly, and stir in seasonings. Gradually add remaining oil and then remaining vinegar. Adjust seasonings to taste.

### BLENDER METHOD

*Makes Approximately One and One-fourth Cups*
1 egg
1 egg yolk
1/2 tablespoon cider, tarragon or wine vinegar
1/2 teaspoon salt
1/4 teaspoon freshly ground white pepper
1/4 teaspoon paprika
Dash cayenne pepper (optional)
1 cup olive or safflower oil

In a blender or bowl of a food processor fitted with steel blade, place egg, egg yolk, vinegar and seasonings. Blend just until mixed. With motor running, slowly pour in oil in a thin, steady stream. Adjust seasonings, jar, cover and refrigerate.

**LEMON MAYONNAISE** Substitute 1/2 tablespoon fresh lemon juice for the vinegar in Basic Mayonnaise.

**MUSTARD MAYONNAISE** Add to Lemon Mayonnaise 1/2 to 1 teaspoon dry mustard.

**GARLIC MAYONNAISE (AIOLI SAUCE)** Add to Lemon Mayonnaise 3 to 4 garlic cloves, *very* finely minced.

**CURRY MAYONNAISE** Add to Basic Mayonnaise or Lemon Mayonnaise 1/2 teaspoon curry powder and 1 teaspoon honey (optional).

**ANCHOVY MAYONNAISE** Add to Basic Mayonnaise 1/2 teaspoon mashed anchovy fillet or anchovy paste.

**GREEN MAYONNAISE** Add to Basic Mayonnaise or Lemon Mayonnaise 1/4 cup *each* firmly packed chopped watercress leaves and spinach leaves, blanched, well-drained and crushed in mortar and pestle.

**HERB MAYONNAISE** Add to Lemon Mayonnaise 1 teaspoon finely minced fresh basil, dill, parsley, chives, and thyme in any combination.

**HORSERADISH MAYONNAISE** Add to Basic Mayonnaise grated fresh or prepared horseradish to taste.

**TOMATO MAYONNAISE** Add to Basic Mayonnaise 1 to 2 tablespoons Tomato Purée.

**BLUE CHEESE MAYONNAISE** Add to Lemon Mayonnaise 2 to 3 tablespoons crumbled gorgonzola or Roquefort cheese.

## CREAM CHEESE DRESSING

A good way to use up a small amount of cream cheese. This dressing, which can be easily doubled, complements cooked green vegetables and green salads.

*Makes Approximately One-fourth Cup*
1-1/2 ounces cream cheese, softened
1/4 cup Basic Vinaigrette
1 teaspoon minced fresh chives
1 teaspoon minced fresh parsley

Mash cream cheese with a little vinaigrette to make a paste. Blend in remaining vinaigrette, chives and parsley. Use immediately or jar, cover and refrigerate up to 2 days.

## BLUE CHEESE DRESSING

Serve on avocados, endive or salad greens, or on cooked broccoli or cauliflower.

*Makes Approximately Two-thirds Cup*
1/4 to 1/3 cup crumbled gorgonzola or Roquefort cheese
1/4 cup Basic Mayonnaise
1/2 cup buttermilk
2 tablespoons minced fresh parsley
Salt and freshly ground white pepper to taste

Combine all ingredients and blend until smooth. Jar, cover and refrigerate up to 1 week.

## YOGHURT DRESSING FOR GREEN SALADS

Try on any lettuce, on sliced cucumbers, or on a salad of cucumber, tomato, celery and bell pepper.

*Makes Approximately Two-thirds Cup*
1/4 cup plain yoghurt
1/4 cup safflower oil
2 tablespoons cider vinegar
2 tablespoons minced fresh herbs
1/4 teaspoon salt, or to taste
Freshly ground black pepper to taste
Dash cayenne pepper (optional)

Beat together yoghurt and oil until creamy. Mix in remaining ingredients. Adjust seasonings, jar, cover and refrigerate up to 10 days.

## YOGHURT DRESSING FOR FRUIT SALADS

If you have been using fruit-flavored yoghurt on your fruit salads, add mashed fresh berries, peaches, or other fruit to this dressing for a superior substitute.

*Makes Approximately One-half Cup*
1/3 cup plain yoghurt
2 tablespoons fresh lemon juice
2 teaspoons mild honey
1 teaspoon minced fresh mint
1/8 teaspoon ground cinnamon, or to taste
1/8 teaspoon freshly grated nutmeg or to taste
1/8 teaspoon ground ginger, or to taste
1/4 teaspoon pure vanilla extract

Combine all ingredients and mix well. Adjust seasonings, jar, cover and refrigerate up to 5 days.

# VEGETABLES

## COOKED–VEGETABLE PUREES

Most cooked vegetables may be puréed in a blender (for a smooth consistency), a food processor (for a coarser consistency), or a food mill (for a fluffy consistency), heated with cream and served as an elegant and colorful vegetable side dish, as a filling for crêpes or omelets, or as the base for a soufflé.

Purée about 2 cups of the coarsely cut vegetable or a combination, adding a little rich stock if needed for moisture. In a Teflon-type skillet, gently heat 2 cups purée, 1 to 2 tablespoons butter and 2 to 3 tablespoons heavy cream (or use olive oil to taste in place of the butter and rich stock to thin for the heavy cream). Cook gently until heated through and add seasonings of choice. (Refer to specific vegetables in the vegetable section for seasoning suggestions.) Garnish with slivered blanched almonds that have been browned in butter, or if color is needed, with chopped fresh chives, parsley or coriander.

**VEGETABLES AND VEGETABLE COMBINATIONS SUITABLE FOR PUREEING** Broccoli, peas, lettuce, peas and lettuce, carrots, carrots and turnips, carrots and sunchokes, green beans, pumpkin, winter squashes, asparagus, eggplant, chestnuts, beet greens, spinach, Swiss chard, parsnips, cauliflower.

## LENTIL CAKES

*Makes Six Cakes*
1-1/2 cups cooked lentils
1/3 cup finely minced sweet red or white onion
1 tablespoon minced fresh parsley and/or chives
1/4 teaspoon salt
1/8 teaspoon freshly ground black pepper
Dash cayenne pepper
1 egg, lightly beaten
Fine dry bread crumbs
Corn oil

Mash lentils and mix well with onion, chives and seasonings. Chill well and form into 6 flat patties. Dip in egg and coat well with bread crumbs. Let dry on wire rack 1 hour. Brown well on both sides in oil, turning only once.

## RICE CAKES

Good served plain or with Mushroom or Quick Mushroom Sauce.

*Makes Approximately Six Cakes*
1 cup cooked brown or white rice
2 eggs, lightly beaten
1/2 cup chopped cooked Swiss chard or spinach, or scraped cooked corn
1/4 cup milk
2 tablespoons unbleached flour
1 tablespoon minced fresh parsley
1/4 teaspoon salt
1/8 teaspoon freshly ground black pepper
1/8 teaspoon freshly grated nutmeg
Butter and peanut oil for browning

Combine all ingredients except butter and oil. Heat equal amounts butter and oil on griddle or skillet. Ladle batter in, forming cakes approximately 5 inches in diameter and pulling egg up and around cake. Brown well, turning only once and adding additional butter and oil if needed.

# POTATO CAKES

*Makes Eight Cakes*
2 tablespoons minced onion
1 garlic clove, minced
3 tablespoons butter
2 cups mashed potatoes
2 tablespoons minced fresh parsley
and/or chives
1/4 teaspoon salt
1/4 teaspoon celery salt
1/4 teaspoon paprika
1/4 teaspoon freshly ground white
pepper
6 tablespoons freshly grated
Parmesan cheese
2 egg yolks, lightly beaten
Fine dry bread crumbs
Butter for browning

Sauté onion and garlic in 3 tablespoons butter until soft. Beat potatoes with onion mixture, parsley, seasonings, cheese and egg yolks. Stir in bread crumbs, if needed to bind. Chill well and form into 8 flat patties. Coat well with fine dry bread crumbs and let dry on wire rack 30 minutes. Brown on both sides in butter, turning once.

# CORN FRITTERS

These fritters may be made with half corn and half minced cooked ham or corned beef. Serve with honey or maple syrup, or as an accompaniment to meat or poultry entrées.

*Makes Approximately
Twelve Fritters*
1 egg, lightly beaten
1/4 cup milk, or as needed
1/3 cup unbleached flour
1 teaspoon baking powder
1/4 teaspoon granulated sugar
1/2 teaspoon salt
1/4 teaspoon freshly ground black
pepper
1/4 teaspoon crumbled dried
oregano
1-1/2 cups scraped cooked corn
1 tablespoon butter, or as needed
1 tablespoon corn oil, or as needed

Beat together egg and milk. Combine flour, baking powder, sugar and seasonings. Blend into egg mixture and stir in corn. Add additional milk if mixture seems too thick. Heat butter in a heavy skillet. Drop batter by spoonfuls onto hot skillet, pressing gently to form cakes about 3-1/2 inches in diameter; do not crowd pan. Brown on both sides, turning only once and adding additional butter and oil as needed. Serve immediately.

# SWISS CHARD FRITTERS

*Makes Approximately Sixteen Fritters*
3/4 cup milk
1/2 cup unbleached flour
1 egg
1/4 teaspoon finely minced fresh
rosemary
1/4 teaspoon granulated sugar
1/4 teaspoon salt
1/8 teaspoon freshly ground black
pepper
1 cup well-drained, firmly packed,
finely chopped cooked Swiss chard
1 to 2 tablespoons butter, or
as needed
1 to 2 tablespoons Brown Butter

In a blender or food processor, blend milk, flour, egg, rosemary, sugar, salt and pepper. Stir in chard (do not blend). Heat butter in a heavy skillet. Drop batter by spoonfuls onto hot skillet, pressing gently to form cakes about 3-1/2 inches in diameter; do not crowd pan. Brown on both sides, turning only once and adding additional butter as needed. Drizzle Brown Butter over each fritter and serve immediately.

*Out of whole milk? Add 1 tablespoon noninstant nonfat milk powder and 1 to 2 teaspoons safflower oil to each cup of nonfat milk.*

## LARGE CRISPY POTATO CAKE

*Serves Three or Four*

3 cups loosely packed, coarsely shredded,* boiled and chilled potatoes
1/2 cup shredded onion (optional)
2 tablespoons butter, or as needed
1 tablespoon safflower oil, or as needed
1/4 teaspoon salt
3 tablespoons half-and-half cream
2 tablespoons butter, cut into bits

Combine potatoes and onion. Heat 2 tablespoons butter and the oil in a heavy 10-inch skillet and add potatoes. Sprinkle with salt and press into a flat cake 1/2 inch smaller in diameter than the skillet. Cook over medium heat 25 minutes, or until bottom is crusty, adding more butter and/or oil if needed. Drizzle cream over evenly and dot with butter bits. Continue cooking 10 minutes. Flip onto a serving plate crusty side up.

*Available in specialty cookware shops, the Swiss-made Rösti grater, with holes about 3/8 inch wide, shreds foods more coarsely than the standard kitchen grater, which has openings of only about 1/4 inch. The Rösti is excellent for shredding vegetables for sautéing and is essential for this recipe.

## POTATO DUMPLINGS

Serve these dumplings in soup, or reheat gently in butter and serve sprinkled with chopped fresh parsley and chives.

*Makes Fourteen to Sixteen Dumplings*

1 egg, lightly beaten
1/4 teaspoon ground thyme
1/2 teaspoon salt
1/8 teaspoon freshly ground white pepper
1 tablespoon finely minced fresh parsley
1-1/2 cups grated boiled or baked potatoes
2 tablespoons unbleached flour
1/4 teaspoon baking powder
14 to 16 Seasoned Croutons

Have a large kettle of gently boiling salted water ready. Combine egg, seasonings, parsley and potatoes. Combine flour and baking powder and stir into potato mixture. Around each crouton form a ball of potato mixture about the size of a walnut. Drop a few at a time into gently boiling water. (If kettle is large enough, all dumplings may be cooked at once.) When dumplings rise to surface, cover and cook 5 to 7 minutes. Never let water reach hard boil. Remove with slotted spoon, draining well.

## MASHED POTATO MOUNDS

*Serves Six*

2-1/2 cups mashed potatoes
1/4 teaspoon salt
1/4 teaspoon garlic powder
1/4 teaspoon onion powder
1/2 teaspoon paprika
3 tablespoons minced green onion tops
3 tablespoons minced fresh parsley
2 eggs, separated
1 egg white
1/8 teaspoon cream of tartar
2 tablespoons Basic Mayonnaise
1 teaspoon fresh lemon juice

Preheat oven to 350°F. Combine potatoes, seasonings, green onion tops, parsley and egg yolks. Beat well and spoon 6 mounds onto a buttered baking sheet. Beat together egg whites and cream of tartar until stiff but not dry. Combine mayonnaise and lemon juice and fold into egg white. Spread some of the egg white on each mashed potato mound. Bake 10 to 15 minutes until heated and browned.

**VARIATION** Decrease potato measurement to 2 cups. Add 1/2 cup coarsely ground or finely minced cooked corned beef, pot roast, lamb, poultry, or minced cooked vegetable, such as broccoli or spinach.

# CARROT PUFFS

Scraped corn kernels or mashed squash (acorn, butternut or Hubbard) can also be used to make these puffs. If preparing them with corn, use ground thyme or sage in place of the cloves.

*Makes Approximately*
*Two Dozen Puffs*
1 cup mashed cooked carrots
1 cup unbleached flour
1 teaspoon baking powder
1 egg, lightly beaten
1 tablespoon minced fresh parsley
1/4 teaspoon salt
1/4 teaspoon ground cloves
1/8 teaspoon freshly ground white
  pepper
Peanut oil for deep frying
Powdered sugar (optional)

Combine carrots, flour, baking powder, egg, parsley and seasonings. Chill. Heat at least 2 inches of oil in fryer or saucepan to 375°F. Drop carrot mixture by spoonfuls into hot oil; do not crowd pan. Turning once, cook until golden. Lift out with slotted utensil and drain on paper toweling. Dust with powdered sugar and serve immediately.

# CORN CASSEROLE

*Serves Two or Three*
1/3 cup toasted slivered blanched
  almonds
3/4 cup grated Gruyère cheese
3/4 cup cooked corn kernels
1/4 cup finely chopped green
  onions and tops
1 tablespoon chopped pimientos
1/2 cup milk, or 1/4 cup *each* half-
  and-half cream and chicken stock
1 egg, lightly beaten with 1 egg yolk
1/4 teaspoon salt
1/4 teaspoon dry mustard
1/4 teaspoon crumbled dried
  oregano or basil
1/8 teaspoon freshly ground black
  pepper

Preheat oven to 350°F. Set aside 2 tablespoons of the almonds and 1/4 cup of the cheese. Combine all remaining ingredients and transfer to a buttered 6-inch soufflé dish or small casserole. Sprinkle with reserved cheese and almonds. Bake in preheated oven 40 to 45 minutes, or until cake tester inserted in center comes out clean.

---

*Don't discard the milk you used to cook those old ears of corn. Add to a pot of corn chowder.*

# SCALLOPED CORN AND TOMATOES

*Serves Three or Four*
2 tablespoons minced onion
2 tablespoons minced green bell
  pepper
3 tablespoons butter
1-1/4 cups chopped ripe tomatoes
1/2 to 2/3 cup cooked corn kernels
2 tablespoons slivered ripe olives
1 teaspoon granulated sugar
1/4 teaspoon salt
1/4 teaspoon crumbled dried
  oregano or sage
1/8 teaspoon freshly ground black
  pepper
1/2 cup cubed stale bread
1/4 cup Parmesan Crumb Topping

Preheat oven to 350°F. Sauté onion and bell pepper in 2 tablespoons of the butter until softened. Combine with tomatoes, corn, olives, sugar, seasonings and bread. Adjust seasonings and transfer to shallow baking dish. Sprinkle evenly with crumb topping. Dot with remaining 1 tablespoon butter and bake in preheated oven 15 to 20 minutes, or until heated through and lightly browned.

## STUFFED VEGETABLES

The vegetable, normally relegated to an accompanying role, can be the main feature of any meal when it is stuffed, and leftovers from last night's entrée can become the filling for tonight's stuffed vegetable dinner.

Stuffed vegetables are basically of two types: the leaf type in which leaves are wrapped around filling and the rolls are cooked in stock or tomato sauce on the stove top, and the hollowed-out type in which the pulp is removed from the vegetable, the vegetable is filled and then either baked or steamed.

It is important always to use fresh seasonal vegetables for stuffing, for they have the best flavor. The baking dish must be just large enough to hold the vegetables close together for best cooking. The following recipes can all be made in advance and refrigerated, covered, for up to twenty-four hours before cooking, which makes this an ideal entrée for the busy cook. Be sure, however, to bring the dish to room temperature before baking.

In general, the fillings given here are interchangeable, so use your imagination. Also, any Grain Pilaf can be combined with diced vegetable pulp for stuffing vegetables.

## STUFFED MUSHROOMS

To prepare 8 to 12 large mushrooms for stuffing, brush well to clean. Snap off stems. Brush caps with melted butter and fresh lemon juice; set aside. Finely chop stems and sauté with 2 tablespoons finely minced onion and 1 teaspoon finely minced garlic in 2 to 3 teaspoons butter. Combine this mixture with suggested fillings below. Place filled caps close together in buttered shallow baking dish. Bake in a preheated 400°F oven 10 to 15 minutes until mushrooms are just tender and filling is browned.

**HAM AND/OR SWEETBREADS** Three-fourths cup ground cooked ham and/or finely minced cooked sweetbreads, 1/4 cup sour cream, 1 tablespoon *each* minced fresh parsley and chives, salt, freshly ground black pepper and dry mustard to taste.

**SPINACH OR SWISS CHARD** Three-fourths cup creamed spinach or Swiss chard, 1 to 2 teaspoons grated onion, and freshly grated nutmeg, salt and freshly ground black pepper to taste. Top with fresh bread crumbs and sprinkle with paprika.

**BREAD CRUMB** One-half cup dry bread crumbs, 1/4 cup finely chopped blanched almonds, pecans or walnuts, and minced fresh basil, finely minced garlic, salt, freshly ground black pepper and paprika to taste and half-and-half cream to moisten. Sprinkle with freshly grated Parmesan or Romano cheese and paprika.

**FISH** One egg, lightly beaten, 1 cup flaked cooked firm white fish, 1 tablespoon Basic Mayonnaise, 1 tablespoon finely minced green onion, fresh lemon juice, salt, crumbled dried oregano and cayenne pepper to taste, and 1 to 2 tablespoons fresh bread crumbs to bind. Fill and top with 2 tablespoons fresh bread crumbs mixed with 2 tablespoons melted butter. Sprinkle with paprika.

**LAMB** Three-fourths cup ground cooked lamb, 1/4 cup finely chopped cooked Swiss chard, 1/4 cup Tomato Sauce. Fill, top with finely grated Gruyère cheese.

**CHICKEN LIVER** Three chopped cooked chicken livers, 2 tablespoons melted butter, 3 tablespoons minced fresh parsley, 1 tablespoon grated onion, 2 tablespoons minced shallots, 1/4 cup dry bread crumbs, salt, freshly ground black pepper and crumbled dried oregano to taste and stock to moisten. Fill, sprinkle with freshly grated Parmesan cheese and dot with butter.

# DOLMAS

To most people, dolmas are grape leaves wrapped around a filling of raw ground lamb. Other leaves and fillings will, however, work equally well. Swiss chard, cabbage, large spinach, nasturtium and tender young grape leaves straight from the vine may be used in place of the brined grape leaves (available in jars), and cooked meats and grains may be used as fillings. All of these leaves, unlike the brined vine leaves, must be blanched one minute and then drained well before use. (The leaves may also be blanched on Hi in a microwave oven about thirty seconds; do not leave too long or they will "cook.") Also, always remember to place any leaf *rib side up* on the work surface before filling.

Uncooked dolmas may be sheet frozen and kept up to one month. Defrost in the refrigerator and cook as directed in the recipe. Any of the suggested leaves may be substituted for the brined grape leaves in this recipe, except cabbage leaves, which are best when cooked in a smooth tomato sauce or in tomato juice rather than stock.

*If you don't have the particular cheese called for in a recipe on hand, see the section on cheeses for an alternative.*

*Filling for Approximately Three Dozen Leaves*
1/2 cup minced green onions and tops
1 teaspoon minced garlic
1 to 2 tablespoons olive oil
1-1/2 cups crumbled cooked lamb or beef patties
1 cup cooked white or brown rice
1 cup cooked garbanzo beans, lightly mashed
3 tablespoons minced fresh parsley
1/2 teaspoon crumbled dried oregano
1/2 teaspoon crumbled dried basil
1/2 teaspoon salt
1/4 teaspoon freshly ground black pepper
3 tablespoons fresh lemon juice
1 cup finely chopped ripe tomatoes
Grape leaves
Beef broth or consommé
Yoghurt Sauce

Sauté onions and garlic in oil 2 to 3 minutes. Add lamb, rice, garbanzo beans, herbs, salt and pepper. Cook, covered, 3 minutes. Uncover and add 1 tablespoon of the lemon juice and the tomatoes. Cook, stirring, until moisture from tomatoes has been absorbed. Adjust seasonings.

Unwrap grape leaves and rinse with cold water. Pat dry, remove tough stems and place on work surface rib side up. Place 1 to 3 tablespoons filling on stem end (amount depends upon size of leaves) and roll up jelly-roll fashion, folding sides in as you roll. Place seam side down in heavy shallow saucepan or skillet. Combine beef broth with remaining 2 tablespoons fresh lemon juice, add to saucepan, place a plate on top of rolls to weigh down and bring broth to gentle boil. Lower heat and simmer 15 to 20 minutes, depending on size of rolls. Remove rolls to wire rack and cool. Serve at room temperature with Yoghurt Sauce.

**NOTE** If serving dolmas hot, beat 1 egg yolk, beat in a little of the hot beef broth and then whisk mixture into 1-1/2 to 2 cups hot broth. Cook gently, stirring, until thickened. Serve with sour cream on the side.

## STUFFED RIPE TOMATOES

To prepare tomatoes for stuffing, cut 1/2 inch off top of tomatoes. Scoop out pulp, leaving a shell 1/3 inch thick. Sprinkle insides lightly with salt and freshly ground black pepper and turn upside down on wire rack to drain. Chop tops and tomato pulp and drain well. Set aside. Each of the following recipes will fill 2 large tomatoes.

1 tablespoon Brown Butter
2/3 cup cooked orzo
Reserved chopped tomato pulp
1/4 cup shredded bel paese cheese
1 teaspoon minced fresh basil
2 teaspoons minced fresh parsley
Salt and freshly ground black
    pepper to taste
Paprika

Preheat oven to 350°F. Combine butter, orzo, 6 tablespoons of the tomato pulp, 3 tablespoons of the cheese, basil, parsley and salt and pepper. Adjust seasonings and mound into prepared tomato shells. Line a shallow baking pan just large enough to hold tomatoes close together with remaining tomato pulp. Place filled tomatoes on pulp and sprinkle remaining 1 tablespoon cheese over tops. Sprinkle with paprika and bake in preheated oven 10 minutes until just tender and filling is heated.

2 tablespoons minced onion
1 garlic clove, finely minced
2 teaspoons butter
1/4 to 1/2 teaspoon dry mustard
1 tablespoon minced green onion
    tops
Reserved chopped tomato pulp
1/4 cup shredded cooked chicken
1/4 cup cooked wheat berries
2 tablespoons shredded fontina
    cheese
1 tablespoon minced fresh parsley

Preheat oven to 350°F. Cook onion and garlic in butter, covered, until soft. Sprinkle with mustard and cook, stirring, 2 minutes. Add green onion tops, 2 tablespoons of the tomato pulp, the chicken and wheat berries. Cook, stirring, several minutes and mix in cheese. Mound into prepared tomato shells. Line a shallow baking dish just large enough to hold tomatoes close together with remaining tomato pulp. Place tomatoes on pulp and bake in preheated oven 10 minutes until just tender and filling is heated. Sprinkle with parsley.

1/2 cup Light Cream Sauce
1 egg yolk, lightly beaten
Reserved chopped tomato pulp
1/2 cup diced cooked potatoes
1/4 cup diced mozzarella cheese
Salt, freshly ground white pepper
    and freshly grated nutmeg
    to taste
1/4 cup Seasoned Bread Crumbs

Preheat oven to 350°F. Heat cream sauce and beat a small amount into egg yolk, then whisk mixture into remaining cream sauce. Cook, stirring, until thickened; do not allow to boil. Add reserved tomato pulp, potatoes, mozzarella, and salt, pepper and nutmeg. Mound into prepared tomato shells. Line the bottom of a shallow baking dish just large enough to hold tomatoes close together with bread crumbs. Place filled tomatoes on bread crumbs and bake in preheated oven 10 minutes until just tender and filling is heated.

## TOMATO FILLING SUGGESTIONS

**HASH** Corned Beef (or beef or turkey) Hash or Fish Hash. Top with grated Cheddar cheese.

**CREAMED CORN** Creamed corn, tomato pulp, coarse dry bread crumbs, chopped pimientos, minced green onion tops.

**RICE** Cooked rice, chopped cooked spinach, freshly grated Parmesan cheese, crumbled dried oregano, tomato pulp as needed, salt and freshly ground black pepper.

**RICE** Curried Brown Rice. Top with freshly grated mild cheese.

**WILD RICE** Cooked wild rice, shredded cooked poultry or game, minced fresh parsley and chives. Top with freshly grated mild cheese.

## STUFFED GREEN TOMATOES

To prepare green tomatoes for stuffing, steam or parboil until *barely* fork tender, about 3 minutes. Cut 1/2 inch off top of tomatoes. Cut out pulp, leaving a shell about 1/3 inch thick. Sprinkle inside of tomatoes lightly with salt and turn upside down on wire rack to drain. Chop pulp and top, drain and set aside.

*Filling for Two Large Tomatoes*
Reserved chopped tomato pulp
1/2 teaspoon finely minced garlic
2 tablespoons chopped fresh
   parsley
2 tablespoons chopped fresh chives
1/2 cup shredded cooked pork
   roast
1/4 cup shredded Monterey Jack
   cheese

3 tablespoons coarse whole-grain
   bread crumbs
1/4 to 1/2 teaspoon crumbled
   dried sage
1 teaspoon fresh lemon juice
Salt and freshly ground black
   pepper to taste
Dash cayenne pepper
2 tablespoons Parmesan Crumb
   Topping
Paprika

Preheat oven to 350°F. Combine chopped pulp, garlic, parsley, chives, pork, Monterey Jack cheese, bread crumbs, sage, lemon juice, salt, pepper and cayenne pepper. Fill prepared shells and top with Parmesan topping; sprinkle with paprika. Bake in preheated oven 15 to 20 minutes until tomatoes are tender.

## STUFFED BELL PEPPERS

To prepare bell peppers for stuffing, parboil or steam 2 minutes until *barely* fork tender. Cut off stem end and remove ribs and seeds. Place peppers upside down on a wire rack. Mince the flesh around the stem and set aside.

*Filling for Two Bell Peppers*
1/3 cup minced onion
1 garlic clove, minced
1 tablespoon peanut oil
Reserved minced pepper tops
3/4 cup shredded cooked pot roast
1 cup cooked bulghur
1/3 cup shredded sharp Cheddar
   cheese
1 egg, lightly beaten
1/2 teaspoon crumbled dried
   oregano
Salt and freshly ground black
   pepper to taste
1 cup Tomato Sauce
2 tablespoons Parmesan
   Crumb Topping
Paprika

Preheat oven to 350°F. Sauté onion and garlic in oil until starting to soften. Add reserved minced pepper and cook, covered, 3 minutes. Add pot roast and cook, stirring, 1 to 2 minutes. Remove from heat and add bulghur, cheese, egg and seasonings. Cover bottom of shallow baking dish just large enough to hold peppers close together with Tomato Sauce. Stand peppers on sauce and sprinkle with Parmesan topping and paprika. Bake in preheated oven 15 minutes, or until fork tender.

---

*A bumper crop of lemons or limes? Squeeze, jar and freeze juice up to 3 months.*

# STUFFED APPLES

To prepare apples for stuffing, steam 10 minutes. Cut 1 inch off top and scoop out apple flesh, leaving a shell 1/3 inch thick. Quickly rub inside of apple with fresh lemon juice and set aside. Dice the flesh and toss with fresh lemon juice. Set aside.

*Filling for Two Large, Tart Apples*
2 tablespoons minced onion
1-1/2 tablespoons butter
Reserved diced apple flesh
1/4 to 1/2 teaspoon curry powder
1/4 cup cooked lentils and/or rice
Salt and freshly ground black
   pepper to taste
2 to 3 tablespoons water
1 tablespoon dry white wine or
   dry sherry
1 tablespoon minced fresh parsley

Preheat oven to 350°F. Cook onion in 2 teaspoons of the butter, covered, until just starting to soften. Add 1/4 cup of the reserved apple flesh, sprinkle with curry and cook, stirring, 2 minutes. Add lentils, heat, sprinkle with salt and pepper and adjust seasonings to taste. Mound filling into prepared apple shells. Line a shallow baking dish just large enough to hold apples close together with the remaining apple flesh. Drizzle water and wine over and place apples in dish. Dot apples with remaining butter and bake in preheated oven 30 minutes, or until tender. Sprinkle with parsley.

# STUFFED ONIONS

To prepare onions for stuffing, peel and cut 1/2-inch slice off top. Steam or parboil in salted water 4 to 5 minutes until *barely* fork tender. Remove centers, leaving a shell about 1/3 inch thick. Sprinkle insides of shells lightly with salt and turn upside down on wire rack. Finely mince centers and set aside.

*Filling for Three Large Onions*
1/2 cup reserved minced onion
1 cup cooked barley
1/2 cup shredded cooked lamb
1/4 cup Tomato Sauce
1/2 teaspoon salt
1/4 teaspoon granulated sugar
Pinch cayenne pepper
Freshly ground black pepper
   to taste
Stock

Preheat oven to 350°F. Combine all ingredients, except stock, adjust seasonings and mound into prepared onion shells. Arrange close together in a shallow baking dish and pour in stock to come 1/2 inch up sides of dish. Bake in preheated oven 20 minutes, or until fork tender and filling is heated.

# STUFFED ZUCCHINI

To prepare zucchini for stuffing, cut off and discard stem and blossom ends. Steam 3 minutes until *barely* fork tender. Halve lengthwise and remove any large seeds. Carefully scoop out pulp, leaving a shell 1/4 inch thick. Place shells upside down on a wire rack to drain. Dice pulp and set aside. Each of the following recipes will fill two 6- to 7-inch zucchini.

Reserved diced zucchini pulp
2 garlic cloves, minced
1 teaspoon finely minced fresh
   thyme
1 cup Quick Tomato or Marinara
   Sauce
2 ounces cream cheese, softened
2/3 cup crumbled cooked meatloaf
   or beef patties
2 tablespoons minced pimiento-
   stuffed olives
Salt and freshly ground black
   pepper to taste
1/4 cup freshly grated Parmesan
   cheese
Paprika

In a heavy skillet, cook reserved zucchini pulp, garlic and thyme, covered, until slightly softened. Remove 1/4 cup and set aside. Combine remaining pulp mixture with 2/3 cup of the tomato sauce and use to line the bottom of a shallow baking dish just large enough to hold zucchini close together. Preheat oven to 350°F. Mash the cream cheese with remaining tomato sauce and with a fork stir in meatloaf, the 1/4 cup reserved zucchini-garlic mixture and the olives. Season with salt and pepper and mound into prepared shells. Sprinkle evenly with cheese and paprika and arrange on the bed of tomato mixture. Bake in preheated oven 15 to 20 minutes, or until zucchini is tender.

1/2 cup chopped onion
2 garlic cloves, minced
Reserved diced zucchini pulp
2 ripe tomatoes, chopped
1/2 cup cooked lentils
1 egg, lightly beaten
1/2 cup finely shredded Gruyère
   cheese
3 tablespoons Tomato Purée
1/4 teaspoon ground cumin
Salt and freshly ground black
   pepper to taste
Pinch cayenne pepper
Paprika

In a heavy skillet, cook onion and garlic with reserved pulp, covered, until slightly softened. Remove 1/4 cup and set aside. Combine remaining pulp mixture with the tomatoes and use to line the bottom of a shallow baking dish just large enough to hold zucchini

close together. Preheat oven to 350°F. Combine lentils, egg, 3 tablespoons of the cheese, the 1/4 cup reserved zucchini-onion mixture, the Tomato Purée, cumin, salt and peppers. Mound into prepared zucchini shells and sprinkle with remaining cheese and the paprika. Bake in preheated oven 15 to 20 minutes, or until zucchini is tender.

## STUFFED SCALLOP SQUASH

Steam squash 4 to 5 minutes until *barely* fork tender. With a sharp knife, slice off a 1-1/2-inch in diameter disc from the top of each, cutting into the squash as if for the cap of a jack-o'-lantern. Scoop out and discard any large seeds and stringy pulp. Remove tender pulp, leaving a 1/4-inch shell. Dice pulp and set aside.

*Filling for Six Small Squash\**
1/4 cup minced onion
1 garlic clove, minced
2 tablespoons butter
1/2 cup minced cooked tongue
Reserved diced pulp
1/2 cup coarse dry bread crumbs
1/3 cup shredded mozzarella or
   fontina cheese
1/4 cup cooked peas
1/2 teaspoon crumbled dried
   savory
2 tablespoons minced fresh parsley
Salt and freshly ground black
   pepper to taste
2 tablespoons freshly grated
   Parmesan cheese
Paprika

Preheat oven to 350°F. Sauté onion and garlic in butter until just starting to soften. Add tongue and reserved pulp. Cook, covered, 1 to 2 minutes. Stir well and remove from heat. With a fork toss in bread crumbs, mozzarella cheese, peas, herbs, and salt and pepper. Mound in prepared squash shells and sprinkle evenly with Parmesan cheese and paprika. Bake in preheated oven 15 to 20 minutes, or until fork tender.

\*If your scallop squash are home grown, they may be considerably larger than store bought, in which case this amount of filling would be sufficient for only 3 or 4.

## STUFFED ACORN SQUASH

To prepare squash for stuffing, halve lengthwise and place cut side down in buttered shallow baking dish. Bake in a preheated 400°F oven 30 minutes.

*Filling for One Squash*
2 tablespoons finely minced green onion and tops
1 small garlic clove, minced
2 tablespoons butter
1-1/2 cups cooked millet
1/2 cup minced cooked ham
2 tablespoons fresh parsley
2 tablespoons chopped walnuts
2 tablespoons dried currants
1/4 teaspoon ground ginger
1/4 teaspoon ground allspice
Salt and freshly ground black pepper to taste
2 teaspoons fresh lemon juice
2 teaspoons honey
2 tablespoons dry sherry

Preheat oven to 400°F. Sauté onion and garlic in butter 2 minutes. Toss in millet, ham, parsley, walnuts, currants, seasonings, lemon juice and honey. Adjust seasonings and mound into prepared shells. Place shells close together in shallow baking dish, add sherry to dish and pour in water to come 1/2 inch up sides of dish. Bake in preheated oven 30 minutes, basting with juices several times, or until fork tender.

## STUFFED CHAYOTE SQUASH (Merliton)

Halve chayote squash lengthwise. Steam 35 minutes or until fork tender. Scoop out and discard any seeds and stringy pulp. Remove tender pulp, leaving a 1/4-inch shell. Dice the pulp and set aside.

*Filling for Two Chayote Squash (Twelve Ounces Each)*
Reserved diced pulp
1-1/2 tablespoons bacon drippings
1 cup Tomato Sauce
1/2 cup minced onion
1 large garlic clove, minced
3/4 cup coarsely ground cooked ham
1 egg, lightly beaten
1/2 cup cooked corn kernels or scraped corn
1/2 cup cubed cornbread (1/3-inch cubes) or coarse dry bread crumbs
1/8 to 1/4 teaspoon cayenne pepper
Salt and freshly ground black pepper to taste
1/4 cup grated Tillamook cheese
Paprika

Preheat oven to 350°F. Sauté reserved pulp in 1 tablespoon of the bacon drippings until soft. Remove from pan, mix with 1/2 cup of the Tomato Sauce and use to line the bottom of a shallow baking dish just large enough to

hold the chayote close together. Sauté onion and garlic in remaining 1/2 tablespoon bacon drippings until soft. Add ham and stir until well mixed. Remove from heat and stir in egg, corn and remaining 1/2 cup Tomato Sauce. With a fork, toss in cornbread and seasonings. Mound into prepared squash shells and sprinkle with cheese and paprika. Bake in preheated oven 15 to 20 minutes, or until squash is tender.

## TWICE–BAKED POTATOES

Cut 2 large freshly baked potatoes in half lengthwise if potatoes are broad, or cut a thin slice off the top if potatoes are long and slender. (Save the slice and fry it for breakfast the next morning.) Carefully scoop out pulp, leaving a shell about 3/8 inch thick. Mash pulp while still hot and with fork stir in 1/3 cup low-fat cottage cheese, sour cream, plain yoghurt, buttermilk, half-and-half cream, or a combination of cream and stock. Toss in 1/3 to 2/3 cup of one of the following filling suggestions and season with salt and freshly ground black pepper. Mound into reserved shells and place on a baking sheet. Sprinkle with grated cheese and/or paprika, or dot with butter and sprinkle with paprika. Bake in a preheated 350°F oven 15 minutes, or until heated through and lightly browned. Serve each person a whole potato as a main dish, or a half potato as a side dish.

## POTATO FILLING SUGGESTIONS

● Crumbled cooked meatloaf, diced jalapeño peppers.

● Shredded cooked chicken, turkey or game, sautéed minced green onions and tops, cooked peas.

● Chopped mild green chili peppers and grated sharp Cheddar cheese.

● Flaked cooked firm white fish, sautéed diced bell peppers and onions, minced fresh chives and parsley.

● Mashed ripe avocado, fresh lemon juice, minced fresh chives.

● Sautéed minced celery, minced fresh parsley, grated Gruyère cheese.

● Hard-cooked egg yolks mashed with anchovy paste or anchovy fillets, minced fresh parsley, minced hard-cooked egg whites.

● Flaked crab meat, grated onion, grated Cheddar cheese.

● Minced onions sautéed in butter, grated Monterey Jack cheese, minced fresh parsley and chives, chopped walnuts, sunflower seeds.

● Crumbled blue cheese, minced fresh chives and parsley, mashed garlic.

● Cubed Muenster cheese, minced fresh parsley, paprika.

● Grated sharp Cheddar cheese, ground cumin, minced garlic, butter.

● Chopped cooked spinach or other greens, grated Gruyère cheese, freshly grated nutmeg, chopped mild green chili peppers.

● Diced bell peppers, onion and garlic sautéed in olive oil, minced cooked lamb roast, chopped ripe tomatoes, crumbled dried basil, Tabasco sauce.

● Diced cream cheese or crumbled feta cheese, fresh lemon juice, minced fresh chives.

● Lumpfish caviar, chopped hard-cooked eggs, butter, heavy cream.

## STUFFED EGGPLANT

Halve eggplant lengthwise. Steam 4 minutes until barely fork tender. Scoop out pulp, leaving a 1/4-inch shell. Chop pulp to measure 1 cup and set aside. (Remaining pulp may be steamed until tender and used to make Oriental Eggplant Salad or Eggplant Spread.)

*Filling for One One-pound Eggplant*
1/2 cup minced onion
2 garlic cloves, minced
2 tablespoons olive oil, or as needed
1 cup reserved chopped eggplant pulp
1 cup cooked fusilli or shell macaroni
1/3 cup slivered black olives
1 large tomato, chopped
1/2 cup crumbled feta cheese
3/4 teaspoon crumbled dried basil
3 tablespoons minced fresh parsley
1 egg, lightly beaten
Salt and freshly ground black pepper to taste
1/4 cup Parmesan Crumb Topping

Preheat oven to 350°F. Sauté onion and garlic in olive oil, covered, until starting to soften. Add eggplant pulp and cook, stirring, several minutes, then add fusilli, olives, and tomato. Remove from heat and stir in feta cheese, basil, parsley, egg and salt and pepper. Adjust seasonings and mound into prepared eggplant shells. Sprinkle with Parmesan topping and place close together in shallow baking dish. Pour in hot water to come 1/2 inch up sides of dish. Bake in preheated oven 25 to 30 minutes, or until fork tender.

# EGG DISHES

## BASIC METHOD FOR OMELETS

The role of the omelet in solving the problem of leftovers is obvious. Extra eggs, egg yolks and egg whites can make the omelet itself, and an endless list of small amounts of cooked vegetables, meats, seafood and grains can become the filling.

Prepare the filling so that it is completely ready. This way you are not in danger of overcooking the omelet. Most fillings, other than cheese, should be warmed before they are added. For two persons, you will need four eggs, plus any extra yolks or whites, and one-half to one cup of filling. In a small, deep bowl, beat the eggs with a wire whisk until they are blended but not frothy. Beat in three tablespoons of cold water, milk, half-and-half cream or heavy cream, salt and freshly ground black or white pepper to taste, and minced fresh herbs, if desired. Complementary herbs would be parsley, chives or watercress or sorrel leaves. The cold liquid helps to lighten the eggs as they cook. You may also separate the eggs: beat the cold liquid and seasonings into the yolks and beat the whites,

with a pinch of cream of tartar or baking soda to lighten them, until stiff but not dry. Stir one-fourth of the whites into the yolks, then carefully fold in the remaining whites.

Heat a nine- or ten-inch skillet or omelet pan over medium-high heat and add two to three teaspoons butter or half butter and half safflower oil. Tilt the pan to evenly cover the surface. There should be enough butter in the pan so that the egg mixture "floats" on the butter when it is added, and the pan should be quite hot. To test, flick a few drops of water into the pan; if they sizzle, it is ready. Pour in the egg mixture and tilt the pan to evenly cover the surface. Wait sixty seconds, then lower the heat to medium low. Cook, tipping the pan in a circular motion and loosening the edges of the egg with a thin spatula or knife to let the uncooked portion flow under. When the omelet begins to set on top but is still quite soft, gently score it across the center,

---

*Eggs separate most easily when cold from the refrigerator.*

place the filling on one-half, and fold over the other half. Lifting with a spatula, slide the omelet onto a serving plate and divide into two portions. Ideally, the bottom of the omelet will be lightly golden and the inside will be moist but not runny.

For a lighter omelet, heat the pan and add the egg mixture as directed. Cover and cook over low heat until the bottom is set, about five minutes. (Do not tilt the pan as the omelet cooks.) Uncover, gently score the omelet across the center, place the filling on one-half and bake in a preheated 350°F oven five minutes. Remove from the oven, fold in half and slide onto a serving plate.

If you prefer, you need not fold the omelet, whether cooked completely on the stove top or partially in the oven. Spread the filling over the entire surface at the same point you would add filling for a folded omelet and continue to cook as directed. When ready to serve, slide the unfolded omelet onto a plate and cut into wedges.

Specific methods are given with the following omelet recipes, but any of these preparations and cooking methods may be used.

## PORK AND ZUCCHINI OMELET

*Serves Two*
1/2 cup shredded cooked pork
    roast
1/2 cup cooked shredded zucchini
1/4 teaspoon crumbled dried
    oregano or thyme
1 tablespoon stock
3 to 4 teaspoons butter
Salt and freshly ground black
    pepper for filling
4 eggs, lightly beaten
1 tablespoon milk or half-and-
    half cream
1/8 teaspoon salt
Dash freshly ground black pepper
1/2 to 2/3 cup shredded Monterey
    Jack, fontina or sharp Cheddar
    cheese
Minced fresh parsley

Preheat oven to 350°F. In a heavy
skillet, combine pork, zucchini,
oregano, stock, 1 teaspoon of the
butter and salt and pepper to
taste. Cover and place over medium-
low heat until heated through;
keep warm. Beat eggs with milk,
1/8 teaspoon salt and dash pepper.
In a 9- or 10-inch skillet, melt the
remaining 2 to 3 teaspoons butter.
Cook and fill the omelet as directed
in Basic Method for Omelets,
cooking on the stove top first and
then in the preheated oven. About
1 minute before the omelet is
ready, remove from the oven,
sprinkle the cheese over the filling
and return to the oven until cheese
is melted. Quickly fold over and
turn out onto serving plate. Sprinkle
with minced parsley.

## CHICKEN LIVER OMELET

*Serves Two*
4 chicken livers, cut into bite-
    size pieces
Dry sherry
3 tablespoons minced green onions
    and some tops
2 tablespoons butter
1/2 teaspoon salt
1/8 teaspoon ground turmeric
1/4 teaspoon freshly ground white
    pepper
4 eggs, separated
Pinch baking soda
2 tablespoons milk or half-and-
    half cream
Mushroom Sauce

Marinate livers in sherry to cover
1 to 2 hours. Drain and pat dry.
Sauté onions in 1 tablespoon butter,
covered, 2 to 3 minutes. Remove
cover, raise heat slightly and add
livers. Sauté, stirring and sprinkling
with 1/4 teaspoon of the salt, the
turmeric and 1/8 teaspoon of the
pepper, just until livers stiffen and
are barely cooked through. Do not
overcook. Keep warm. Beat egg
whites and baking soda until stiff
but not dry. Beat egg yolks until
lemon colored, then beat in milk
and remaining salt and pepper.
Combine yolks and whites as
described in Basic Method for
Omelets. Melt remaining tablespoon
butter in a 9- or 10-inch skillet
and cook, fill and fold omelet as
directed in basic method. Serve
immediately with Mushroom Sauce.

## OPEN-FACE POTATO OMELET

Any diced or shredded cooked
meats or chopped cooked vegetables
can replace the Ham Loaf.

*Serves Three*
1/2 cup minced onion
2 tablespoons olive oil
2 cups diced cooked potatoes
3/4 cup crumbled Ham Loaf or
    Meatloaf
4 eggs, well beaten with
    1/2 teaspoon salt
Freshly ground black pepper

Sauté onion in olive oil until
browned. Add potatoes and meat
and heat through. Pour in eggs,
allowing mixture to completely
cover bottom of skillet. Brown
over medium heat until eggs are
set, about 4 to 5 minutes. Flip
over onto heated serving plate and
serve immediately with freshly
ground black pepper.

# ROLLED OMELETS

For each person you will need 2 eggs, 3 tablespoons filling and 1 to 2 tablespoons grated cheese. Have the filling ready before beginning to cook the omelets. The filling can be any warmed cooked meats or vegetables, but it should be of a fairly fine consistency so that the omelet can be easily rolled.

Beat the 2 eggs with 2 teaspoons water, 1/8 teaspoon salt and a dash of freshly ground white pepper. Melt about 1 teaspoon butter in a heavy 10-inch skillet until foamy. Pour in egg mixture and cook over medium heat, lightly stirring edges with a fork and then tipping the pan to allow the eggs to cover the entire bottom surface. Cook only until just set and lightly browned, about 1 to 2 minutes. Spread filling over surface of egg round, sprinkle with cheese and carefully roll up, folding in sides as you would for crêpes. Flip roll onto heated plate to serve and garnish as desired.

## OMELET FILLING SUGGESTIONS

All of these fillings should be warm when they are placed on the omelet. If topping the filling with cheese, add the cheese about one minute before the omelet is ready.

**HAM** Chopped cooked ham, minced onions and garlic sautéed in ham or bacon drippings with ground cumin, seeded and chopped jalapeño peppers, salt, freshly ground black pepper, Tabasco sauce; top filling with shredded Monterey Jack cheese. Garnish with halved black olives and coriander sprigs.

**TONGUE OR HAM** Diced cooked tongue or ham, thinly sliced fresh mushrooms and celery sautéed in butter and seasoned with Tabasco sauce, salt and freshly ground black pepper; top filling with grated Cheddar cheese.

**POT ROAST** Creole Sauce and shredded cooked pot roast. Sprinkle cooked omelet with freshly grated Parmesan cheese.

**CHICKEN** Diced cooked chicken, Grain Pilaf or cooked grain, chopped fresh chives, Bell's Seasoning or other poultry seasoning; top filling with shredded bel paese cheese.

**VEGETABLE** Diced cooked vegetables, such as carrots, turnips, potatoes, warmed in butter and a little stock, salt, freshly ground black pepper, chopped fresh tarragon or savory. Serve with plain yoghurt.

**CRAB** Chopped celery and sliced green onions and tops sautéed in butter, flaked crab meat or diced cooked prawns in Light Cream Sauce seasoned with dry mustard and Worcestershire sauce. Garnish with minced fresh chives and paprika.

**ARTICHOKE HEART OR BOTTOM** Thinly sliced onions sautéed in butter, sliced cooked artichoke hearts or bottoms; top filling with freshly grated Parmesan cheese. Garnish with minced fresh chervil or parsley.

**SORREL** Finely minced garlic, sorrel and fresh parsley sautéed briefly in butter. Garnish with minced fresh chives.

**ASPARAGUS** Cooked asparagus tips and Seasoned Croutons; top filling with shredded Monterey Jack cheese.

**BELL PEPPER AND TOMATO** Thinly sliced onions and bell peppers sautéed in butter and oil, salt, freshly ground black pepper, mashed garlic, sliced ripe tomatoes; top filling with grated sharp Cheddar cheese.

**CHIFFONADE** Chiffonade of lettuce, sorrel and spinach. Serve with sour cream.

## UNFILLED OMELET SUGGESTIONS

If you prefer an unfilled omelet, mix one of the following into the beaten eggs, pour into the skillet and cook, crease and fold as described in Basic Method for Omelets.

- Diced cooked potatoes lightly browned in butter, chopped fresh parsley and chives.
- Chopped pimientos and tomatoes, minced garlic, minced fresh parsley.
- Cooked peas and minced fresh herbs.
- Shredded cheese such as Monterey Jack, Cheddar, Tillamook, Samsoe.

## BASIC METHOD FOR FRITTATAS

The frittata is the Italian equivalent of the omelet, but is served open face rather than folded. For three or four persons, allow four eggs (adding additional yolks or whites you have on hand) and two cups diced or shredded filling, such as cooked vegetables, meats, seafoods, cheese, noodles or grains, alone or in combination. Beat the eggs until they are well blended but not frothy and stir in the filling. Season with salt, freshly ground black pepper and cayenne pepper, if desired.

Heat a heavy ten-inch skillet over medium heat, add one-half tablespoon each butter and olive or safflower oil (or as needed) and tilt pan to evenly coat the surface. Pour in the egg mixture and cook, uncovered, over medium heat; as egg starts to congeal, pull the edges away from the sides of the skillet with a spatula. When the bottom is golden brown and the eggs just set, cover the skillet with a flat plate or lid, invert the skillet so that the frittata rests on the plate, and slip the frittata back into the skillet, adding more butter and oil if needed to prevent sticking. Cook until the second side is golden brown, slide out onto a serving plate and cut into wedges.

You can place the frittata under a preheated broiler to brown the top rather than invert it in the skillet, but only if you are using an iron or other flameproof pan. Before placing under the broiler, sprinkle about one-third cup freshly grated Parmesan or Romano cheese on top if there is little or no cheese in the filling.

## RICE FRITTATA

*Serves Three or Four*

4 or 5 eggs, lightly beaten
1 cup cooked brown or white rice
2 tablespoons finely minced green onion and tops
2 tablespoons finely minced Italian parsley
1/2 cup finely chopped peeled ripe tomatoes
1/2 cup cooked peas or chopped cooked broccoli
1/4 cup freshly grated Parmesan or Romano cheese
1/2 teaspoon salt, or to taste
1/4 teaspoon freshly ground white pepper, or to taste
1/2 teaspoon crumbled dried basil or oregano
1 tablespoon olive oil
1/2 tablespoon butter, or as needed

Stir together eggs and all remaining ingredients, except oil and butter. In a heavy 10-inch skillet, heat oil and butter. Pour in egg mixture and cook as directed in Basic Method for Frittatas.

# RICOTTA FRITTATA

*Serves Two or Three*

4 eggs, lightly beaten
1 cup ricotta cheese or low-fat
   cottage cheese, at room
   temperature
1/2 cup finely minced cooked ham
1 teaspoon tomato paste
3 tablespoons freshly grated
   Parmesan or Romano cheese
3 tablespoons minced fresh Italian
   parsley
2 tablespoons finely minced green
   onions and tops
1 tablespoon minced pimiento
1 small garlic clove, very finely
   minced
1/4 teaspoon salt
1/4 teaspoon celery salt
1/8 teaspoon freshly ground white
   pepper
Pinch freshly grated nutmeg
1 tablespoon olive oil
1/2 tablespoon butter, or as needed

Stir together eggs and all remaining
ingredients, except oil and butter.
In a heavy 10-inch skillet, heat oil
and butter. Pour in egg mixture
and cook as directed in Basic
Method for Frittatas.

*Don't open a can of tomato paste
for a tablespoon or two. Substitute
catsup.*

# PASTA FRITTATA

*Serves Two*

2 eggs, lightly beaten
1 cup cooked small bowtie pasta
1/2 cup finely diced or shredded
   cooked lamb
1-1/2 tablespoons minced fresh
   parsley and/or chives
1/4 cup finely grated Gruyère
   cheese
1/2 tablespoon olive oil
1/2 tablespoon butter, or as
   needed
Paprika

Stir together eggs, pasta, lamb,
parsley and cheese. In a heavy 10-
inch skillet, heat oil and butter.
Pour in egg mixture and cook as
directed in Basic Method for
Frittatas. Sprinkle cooked frittata
with paprika.

# FRITTATA FILLING SUGGESTIONS

**POTATO** Shredded cooked potato,
minced ham, tongue or poultry,
freshly grated Gruyère cheese.

**ZUCCHINI** Cooked shredded or
sliced zucchini, sliced sautéed
mushrooms, sautéed minced onion
and garlic.

**TOMATO** Diced onion, diced bell
pepper, chopped ripe tomato,
minced fresh basil.

**ARTICHOKE HEART OR BOTTOM**
Sautéed onion slices, chopped
cooked artichoke hearts or bottoms,
toasted bread crumbs, freshly grated
Parmesan or Romano cheese,
minced fresh parsley.

**SPINACH** Chopped cooked spinach,
Swiss chard or other greens, minced
fresh chives, freshly grated Parmesan or Romano cheese.

**PILAF** Grain Pilaf or Grain Pilaf
Casserole.

**GREEN BEAN** Cut-up cooked green
beans, freshly grated Parmesan
cheese, minced fresh parsley and
thyme, fine dry bread crumbs.

# EGG FOO YUNG

The Chinese version of the omelet.
Use chopped cooked green beans
or cooked peas in place of the
water chestnuts and/or bamboo
shoots and minced cooked poultry
or seafood for the ham.

*Serves Two*

4 eggs, lightly beaten
3 tablespoons water
1/2 tablespoon soy sauce
1-1/2 tablespoons cornstarch
1/4 teaspoon Oriental sesame oil
2/3 cup crisped and well-drained
   bean sprouts

1/2 cup minced cooked ham
2 tablespoons minced green onions
  and tops
2 tablespoons minced water
  chestnuts
2 tablespoons minced bamboo
  shoots
2 teaspoons peanut oil, or as
  needed
1/2 cup chicken stock
Coriander sprigs

Beat together eggs, water, soy sauce, 1/2 tablespoon of the cornstarch and the sesame oil. With a fork, mix in bean sprouts, ham, onion, water chestnuts and bamboo shoots. In a heavy skillet, heat peanut oil. Ladle about 1/4 cup of the egg mixture into the skillet for each cake. When egg starts to set, push runny edges up and around each cake to make it a uniform 3 to 4 inches in diameter. Brown one side, turn and brown the second side. (Be sure to turn the cakes only once.) Repeat with remaining egg mixture. To make the gravy, dissolve remaining 1/2 tablespoon cornstarch in stock, place over medium heat and cook, stirring, until thickened. Pour gravy over cakes and garnish with coriander sprigs. Serve immediately.

*If using stiffly beaten egg whites, do not beat more than 5 minutes in advance of using, or they will "weep."*

## BASIC METHOD FOR SOUFFLES

For a soufflé, the yolks are combined with whatever ingredients you choose—cheese, puréed or minced cooked vegetables, ground or minced cooked meats or fish—and the whites are beaten until stiff and folded into the yolk base. The whole is baked in a preheated oven, and the light, fluffy result is served immediately to admiring diners.

The eggs should be at room temperature and the oven must be preheated. First prepare the soufflé dish, or any deep, straight-sided dish, so it will be ready to receive the soufflé mixture as soon as it is mixed. Butter the dish well (or use Lecithin Butter) and then lightly dust it with fine bread crumbs or a finely grated hard cheese, such as Parmesan. This coating will help the soufflé climb the sides of the dish.

The treatment of the egg whites is critical, for they give the soufflé its height. The whites must never be put in a plastic bowl, or one that has any oil residue or a speck of yolk. They must be beaten, usually with a little cream of tartar, until they are stiff but still moist and fluffy. For every two to three eggs called for in a soufflé recipe, add an extra white for a lighter result.

When combining the beaten whites and the yolk base, stir about one-fourth of the whites into the yolk base to lighten it, then pile the remaining whites on top and fold them in using a circular motion from the top to the bottom of the bowl. Do not overmix or the soufflé will not rise properly.

If you prefer a soft-topped soufflé, place the filled soufflé dish in a pan of hot water in the preheated oven. For a crusty top, omit the water pan. Never open the oven door as the soufflé cooks, or there is a danger that it will fall. A soufflé with a custardy center, like the true French type, will require slightly less cooking time than that suggested in the baking directions provided with each recipe. Serve the soufflé as soon as possible after removing it from the oven, for it will fall within just a few minutes.

## SWISS CHARD SOUFFLE

*Serves Two*

Finely grated Gruyère cheese
    for soufflé dish
2/3 cup Medium Cream Sauce
    made with well-seasoned
    chicken stock
2 eggs, separated
2/3 cup finely chopped and
    drained cooked Swiss chard
2 tablespoons grated Gruyère
    cheese
1/4 teaspoon salt
1/4 teaspoon freshly grated nutmeg
1/4 teaspoon freshly ground white
    pepper
1 egg white
1/8 teaspoon cream of tartar or
    baking soda

Preheat oven to 350°F. Prepare
soufflé dish as directed in Basic
Method for Soufflés, dusting with
Gruyère. Heat cream sauce, stirring
constantly, almost to boil. Remove
from heat and, one at a time, beat
in egg yolks. Blend in Swiss chard,
cheese and seasonings. Adjust
seasonings and set aside to cool.
Beat egg whites with cream of
tartar until stiff but not dry.
Following basic method, combine
whites and yolk base and transfer
to prepared dish. Bake in preheated
oven 25 to 35 minutes.

## SCALLOPED POTATO SOUFFLE

The success of this dish depends
on how you have prepared the
scalloped potatoes, which are best
if made with half milk and half
rich stock. (See potatoes in the
vegetable section.)

*Serves Two or Three*

Fine dry bread crumbs or finely
    grated Parmesan cheese for
    soufflé dish
2 cups mashed scalloped potatoes
3 tablespoons butter
2 teaspoons minced fresh parsley
    and/or chives
2 eggs, separated
1 egg white
Dash cream of tartar

Preheat oven to 350°F. Prepare a
6-inch soufflé dish as directed in
Basic Method for Soufflés, dusting
with Gruyère. Heat cream sauce,
stirring constantly, almost to boil.
Remove from heat and, one at a time,
beat in egg yolks. Blend in Swiss
chard, cheese and seasonings. Adjust
seasonings and set aside to cool.
Beat egg whites with cream of
tartar until stiff but not dry. Following
basic method, combine whites and
yolk base and transfer to prepared
dish. Bake in preheated oven 25 to
35 minutes.

## CHEESE GRITS SOUFFLE

Leftovers from your favorite cheese
grits recipe can be turned into this
rich soufflé. It will not reach the
height of most soufflés, but the
flavor more than makes up for the
absence of a puffy crown. Ham
Loaf or meatloaf are good substi-
tutes for the chili and bell peppers.

*Serves Two or Three*

Fine dry bread crumbs or finely
    grated Parmesan cheese for
    soufflé dish
1 cup cheese grits
1 cup shredded sharp Cheddar
    cheese
1/3 cup diced canned green chili
    peppers
3 tablespoons finely minced green
    bell pepper
1/4 teaspoon ground thyme
1/2 teaspoon finely minced garlic
Salt and freshly ground black
    pepper to taste
1 egg, separated
1 egg white
Pinch cream of tartar

Preheat oven to 350°F. Prepare a
6-inch soufflé dish as directed in
Basic Method for Soufflés, dusting
with bread crumbs. Combine cheese
grits, shredded Cheddar cheese,
chili pepper, bell pepper, thyme,

garlic, salt and pepper. Beat in egg yolk. Beat egg whites with cream of tartar until stiff but not dry. Following basic method, combine whites and yolk base and transfer to prepared dish. Bake in preheated oven 20 to 25 minutes.

## BASIC METHOD FOR TIMBALES

A cross between a soufflé and a custard, the timbale can be served as a vegetable accompaniment, or when more elaborately presented with a sauce, can star as an entrée. Whole eggs and egg yolks are mixed with puréed or finely chopped cooked vegetables and/or meat and seafood and then transferred to individual straight-sided molds for baking.

Combine the eggs and filling ingredients. Heavily butter the molds (or use Lecithin Butter) and then dust with fine dry bread crumbs or a finely grated hard cheese, such as Parmesan. Fill the molds about two-thirds full and place close together in a shallow baking pan. Add boiling water to the pan to come halfway up the sides of the molds. Bake in a preheated 325°F oven for the time indicated in each recipe. Insert a cake tester or thin bladed knife to test for doneness; no custard should adhere to the tester. Remove the molds from the oven and the water bath and let stand five minutes. To unmold, loosen edges with a thin knife blade and invert onto a heated serving platter or individual plates.

## ASPARAGUS TIMBALE

Spoon Mushroom Sauce, Cheese Sauce or Basic Hollandaise on these timbales for a luncheon entrée. Finely cut cooked broccoli, mushrooms, cauliflower, green beans, spinach, brussels sprouts and carrots or puréed peas and scraped corn kernels may be substituted for the asparagus, or reduce the vegetable measure by half and use equal amounts vegetable and minced cooked poultry, meat, fish or shellfish.

*Serves Six to Eight as Side Dish, Three or Four as Main Dish*
Fine dry bread crumbs for molds
1/2 cup finely minced green
   onions and tops
4 tablespoons butter
1/4 to 1/2 teaspoon salt
1/8 teaspoon freshly grated
   nutmeg, or 1/4 teaspoon celery
   salt
5 eggs, lightly beaten
1/2 cup finely grated Gruyère
   cheese
2/3 cup fine dry bread crumbs or
   cracker crumbs

1 cup milk, or 1/2 cup *each* half-and-half cream and stock
2-1/2 cups finely cut cooked
   asparagus
1/4 cup finely minced fresh parsley

Preheat oven to 325°F. Prepare six to eight 1-cup molds or three or four 1-1/2-cup molds as directed in Basic Method for Timbales, coating with bread crumbs. Cook onions in 1 tablespoon of the butter, covered, just until soft. Transfer to mixing bowl and add seasonings, eggs, cheese and bread crumbs. Scald milk with remaining butter, stirring to melt butter, and gradually beat into egg mixture. Stir in asparagus and parsley. Adjust seasonings. (At this point, the mixture may be refrigerated, covered, up to 3 days. Bring to room temperature before baking.) Pour asparagus mixture into prepared molds. Bake in preheated oven 25 to 35 minutes.

## SWEET POTATO TIMBALES

*Serves Six as Side Dish*
Fine dry bread crumbs for molds
6 pecan halves
2 eggs, lightly beaten
1 egg yolk
3/4 cup milk
1/3 cup chopped pecans
1/2 teaspoon salt
1/4 teaspoon freshly ground black
    pepper
1/4 teaspoon ground ginger
1/4 teaspoon freshly grated nutmeg
1 cup mashed cooked sweet
    potatoes or yams

Preheat oven to 325°F. Prepare
six 1-cup molds as directed in
Basic Method for Timbales, dusting
with bread crumbs. Place a pecan
half in center of bottom of each.
Beat together eggs, egg yolk and
milk. Stir in chopped pecans,
seasonings and sweet potatoes.
Carefully pour sweet potato mixture
into prepared molds. Bake in preheated oven 25 to 35 minutes.

## STUFFED EGG CASSEROLE

For a heartier dish, add three-
fourths cup cooked white or brown
rice to the Swiss chard and mix
well before putting into the ramekins.
Quick Tomato Sauce is a good
substitute for the Cheese Sauce.

*Serves Two*
1 cup coarsely chopped cooked
    Swiss chard
2/3 cup Cheese Sauce seasoned
    with sherry and nutmeg
1/2 cup chopped cooked ham,
    turkey or shrimp
1 tablespoon chopped pimientos
4 stuffed egg halves, or 3 hard-
    cooked eggs, halved
1/3 cup fresh bread crumbs
1 tablespoon butter, melted
3 tablespoons freshly grated
    Parmesan cheese
Paprika
Chopped fresh parsley and/or
    chives

Preheat oven to 350°F. Divide
Swiss chard between 2 ramekins.
Combine Cheese Sauce with ham
and pimientos. Pour over chard
and tuck 2 egg halves into sauce
in each dish. Combine bread crumbs,
butter and Parmesan cheese and
sprinkle over sauce, then dust with
paprika. Bake 15 to 20 minutes, or
until heated through and crumbs
are browned. Just before serving,
sprinkle with parsley.

## ORIENTAL STEAMED EGGS

This unusual dish, suitable for
breakfast, lunch or dinner, has a
smooth, delicate texture and a
refreshing taste. Small pieces of
any cooked meat, poultry or
vegetable may be used in place of
the ham and mushrooms.

*Serves Four*
4 to 6 eggs
3/4 cup hot water
1 teaspoon corn or peanut oil
3 or 4 drops Oriental sesame oil
1/4 teaspoon salt
2 tablespoons minced green onions
    with some green
1 or 2 dried shiitake mushrooms,
    softened in warm water and
    diced (optional)
1/2 cup diced cooked ham
Oyster sauce

Have steamer with simmering water
ready. Beat eggs until frothy and
gradually beat in hot water. Add
oils, salt, green onions, mushroom
and ham. Pour into shallow serving
dish and place in steamer. Wrap
steamer lid in kitchen towel, cover
and steam 15 to 20 minutes, or
until set. Do not allow water to
boil. Drizzle oyster sauce over and
serve immediately.

## STUFFED EGG FILLING SUGGESTIONS

Hard-cook eggs (they may be cooked a day ahead), peel and halve lengthwise. If halves do not stand straight, cut a thin slice off bottom. Remove yolks and push through medium sieve (1/8-inch mesh). Combine yolks with any of the following filling suggestions, using a fork so as not to mash to a paste. Add salt and freshly ground white or black pepper to taste. Mound yolk mixture into egg white halves and decorate as suggested or as desired. Sprinkle with paprika if color is needed. Refrigerate, covered with plastic wrap, until serving. Do not keep more than twenty-four hours.

The following suggestions can be used to fill twelve large or fourteen medium eggs.

**CHICKEN LIVER PATE** Combine yolks with 1/2 cup Chicken Liver Pâté, 1 tablespoon finely minced fresh mushrooms and 1 tablespoon minced fresh chives. Moisten with Sour Cream Dressing if needed. Decorate with a thin sliver of black olive.

*Sea salt adds marvelous texture to any dish, plus it's better for you than regular commercial salt.*

**BUTTER** Combine yolks with 2 tablespoons softened butter and 1/2 to 1 teaspoon dry mustard. Moisten with Herb or Green Mayonnaise. Decorate with a tiny cooked shrimp and a parsley leaf.

**CURRY** Combine yolks with 1 to 2 teaspoons curry powder, 1 teaspoon soy sauce and 1 to 2 teaspoons fresh lemon juice. Moisten with Basic Mayonnaise. Decorate with a fresh coriander leaf.

**CHILI SAUCE** Combine yolks with 1/4 cup Chili Sauce, 1 tablespoon minced fresh parsley, 3 tablespoons minced green onions and tops, 2 teaspoons finely minced celery and Dijon-style mustard to taste. Moisten with Basic Mayonnaise. Decorate with a tiny celery leaf.

**OLIVE** Combine yolks with 1/2 cup minced black olives and dry mustard to taste. Moisten with Basic Mayonnaise. Decorate with a thin crosswise slice of black olive.

**SOUR CREAM OR YOGHURT** Combine yolks with 1/4 cup sour cream or plain yoghurt, 2 tablespoons finely minced pimiento-stuffed olives, 1 tablespoon *each* minced fresh parsley, fresh chives and celery and Dijon-style mustard to taste. Decorate with a tiny sliver of green bell pepper.

**BEARNAISE** Combine yolks with 1/2 cup Béarnaise Sauce. Decorate with a tiny sliver of cherry tomato.

**CAVIAR** Combine yolks with 1/2 cup lumpfish caviar and dry mustard and Worcestershire sauce to taste. Moisten with Lemon Mayonnaise. Decorate with a tiny sliver of lemon rind.

**SORREL** Combine yolks with 1 cup finely minced sorrel and 3 tablespoons minced shallots sautéed in 4 tablespoons butter and cooled, and fresh lemon juice to taste. Decorate with a tiny watercress leaf.

**GRUYERE** Combine yolks with 1/2 cup finely shredded Gruyère cheese, 5 tablespoons softened butter or cream cheese and minced fresh dill or parsley and Tabasco sauce to taste. Decorate with a tiny sliver of Gruyère cheese.

**HAM** Combine yolks with 1 cup ground cooked ham, 2 tablespoons minced green bell pepper, and grated onion and garlic, Dijon-style mustard, minced fresh parsley and/or chives and Tabasco sauce to taste. Moisten with Basic Mayonnaise. Decorate with a drained caper.

# SAVORY PASTRIES

This chapter contains a number of pastry dough recipes, including one for a homemade puff pastry, and complete instructions on how to shape them into a variety of forms for encasing leftovers. There are also directions on how to create your own filled savory pastries—turnovers, quiches, deep-dish pies, patty shells—with what you have on hand.

For savory pastries, add any complementary ground herb to the dough recipes that follow. To use the same recipe for a dessert pastry, add one tablespoon granulated sugar, if desired.

Pastry dough should be part of your planned leftovers schedule. For example, when making the Egg Yolk Pastry recipe for a quiche, double it, line a second pie plate and freeze the shell. Your next quiche will go together in just minutes.

## GENERAL DIRECTIONS FOR PASTRY

**MAKING DOUGH IN A FOOD PRO-CESSOR** Whole-Wheat, Egg White, Egg Yolk and Sour Cream Pastry can be mixed in a food processor fitted with metal blade. (See the recipe for Puff Pastry for making that type of dough in a processor; the hand method for the pastries specified here is provided with each recipe. Do not attempt to make the Biscuit Pastries in a processor.)

Combine the dry ingredients in the bowl of the processor and pulse once or twice to mix. Strew the butter and/or lard evenly in bowl and, with on/off pulses, process until mixture is the con-sistency of coarse cornmeal. Rub the mixture between your fingertips to check for proper consistency. With processor motor running, add liquid and process *just* until dough *begins* to gather on one side of bowl. Do not overprocess; it is better to undermix than to overmix. Remove dough from the bowl, lightly form into a rough ball and then gently flatten into a disc about 1/2 inch thick. Do not handle too much; the disc need not be compact and too much handling will toughen the dough. Wrap in waxed paper, place in a plastic bag and refrigerate at least one hour before rolling out.

*Keep ruler handy for measuring pans, pastry rounds.*

**ROLLING THE DOUGH** Any dough mixed in a food processor or by hand, except the Biscuit Pastries, should be chilled at least one hour before rolling. Remove the disc of dough from the refrigerator and let stand three to four minutes at room temperature before proceeding. Place dough on a lightly floured board. Using a long, slender, lightly floured rolling pin, roll from the center of the disc outward, pressing gently rather than sliding across the dough. Always roll from the center of the disc outward and, as you roll, gradually radiate the strokes around the entire disc.

When the pastry round is about 8 inches in diameter, carefully slip a long, thin-bladed, flexible metal spatula under it, lift up, flip the round over onto your hand and forearm, lightly flour the board and then slip the dough back onto it so that the side of the round on which you were rolling is now facing the board. Continue rolling out the dough in the same manner, always remembering not to force it by applying too much pressure and to begin all of the strokes at the center. Loosen the round with a spatula and flip as many times as are necessary to prevent it from sticking. The final round should be about 1-1/2 inches greater in diameter than the pie plate to be lined and no more than 1/8 inch thick.

**LINING THE PIE PLATE** When the pastry round is the proper size, carefully fold it in half, gently lift and set down on one-half of the pie plate. Unfold the round and center it on the plate. Lifting the edges of the round as you work, gently press the dough to the sides of the plate. With kitchen shears, trim edges evenly to leave a 1/2-inch overhang. (Gather scraps into a rough ball, wrap in waxed paper, place in a plastic bag and refrigerate. See section on rolling scraps for how to work with them.) Gently but firmly press the edges of the dough to the rim, folding under the overhang and forming a nice flute around the rim with your fingertips. The plate edge must be completely covered and the rim of pastry must stand out from the plate to accommodate any shrinkage of the dough during baking. Chill at least twenty to thirty minutes before baking. If time allows, wrap the pastry-lined plate in plastic wrap and freeze several hours; defrost in the refrigerator fifteen minutes before baking. This freezing will result in a flakier crust.

**MAKING INDIVIDUAL TARTS, TARTLETS AND BARQUETTES** Use Egg White, Egg Yolk or Whole-Wheat Pastry for forming these shells. Sour Cream Pastry may be used, but it is necessary to weight the shell when baking it or the pastry will not hold its shape. To make individual tarts (usually in tins about 4 inches in diameter), roll out dough as just described and cut in rounds 3/4 to 1 inch greater in diameter than the tins to be used. Line the tins as you would line a pie plate. To make tartlets (tiny tarts about 1-1/2 inches in diameter), roll out dough and cut in 2-1/2-inch rounds. Carefully and gently press the rounds into muffin-tin wells 1-3/4 inches wide and 7/8 inch deep. For barquettes, you will need barquette tins, which are small, boat-shaped molds. Use a mold as a guide and cut out ovals about 1/2 inch greater in size, then gently press the pieces of dough into the tins. All three of these shells should be refrigerated fifteen to twenty minutes before baking, or may be wrapped and frozen for several hours as for a pie shell.

These shells are usually fully baked before filling. For best results, weight and bake the shells as explained in the section on fully baked pastry shells that follows, but reduce the baking time for the first step to five minutes and for

the second step to five to eight minutes. Alternately, do not weight the shells. Prick the bottoms well with the tines of a fork and bake in a preheated 350°F oven twelve to fifteen minutes, or until lightly golden. Cool on a wire rack before filling.

Puff Pastry may be used to make these shells in the same way. Once the molds are lined, prick the bottoms with the tines of a fork (do not fill with weights) and bake as directed. Remove from the oven and immediately loosen and lift off top layer of pastry with a sharp knife; this "top" can serve as a lid for the shell. Then, with a fork, carefully scrape out the uncooked dough in the center of the shell and discard.

**MAKING A TWO–CRUST PIE** Use Egg White, Egg Yolk, Whole-Wheat or Sour Cream Pastry. For the bottom crust, line the pie plate as described, rolling out the round only 3/4 inch greater in diameter than the plate and trimming the overhang to 1/4 inch. Chill thirty minutes and then fill the shell. Roll out the dough for the top crust as for the bottom, making the round 1 inch greater in diameter than the plate. Transfer the round to the filled shell in the same way as the bottom-crust round was handled, and center it on the plate. With kitchen shears, trim overhang to 1/2 inch. Turn overhang of top crust under and gently press it against edge of lower crust, building up the rim and making an attractive, high flute as you would for a single-crust pie. Make several slashes in top to allow steam to escape during baking and brush with Egg Wash. Bake ten minutes in a preheated 450°F oven, then reduce heat to 350°F and bake thirty-five minutes, or until nicely browned. Cool on a wire rack.

**ROLLING PASTRY SCRAPS** Flatten the ball of pastry scraps into a disc about 1/2 inch thick and, with a *very small* amount of water, mend any seams, cracks or other breaks in the surface of the disc. Rewrap dough in waxed paper and refrigerate at least twenty minutes. Now roll out the dough as you would any pastry dough.

If working with Puff Pastry scraps, gather, wrap and refrigerate as for other pastry dough. When ready to roll out, flatten the ball of dough into a thin disc, spread a 1/16-inch-thick layer of softened butter on top, fold the disc in half, seal the edges with a *very small* amount of water, wrap in waxed paper and refrigerate twenty minutes. When chilled, the dough can be rolled out in the same way as any dough. (These Puff Pastry scraps will not puff very high when baked because the dough has been handled a great deal.)

See Filling Suggestions for Hors d'oeuvre Pastries and Dessert Suggestions for Using Pastry and Puff Pastry Scraps for ideas on what to do with this "saved" pastry.

**PREBAKED PASTRY SHELL** Preheat oven to 400°F. Carefully line the pie shell with a sheet of lightweight aluminum foil large enough so that it can be easily lifted out. Fill the foil-lined shell with metal pie weights or with raw rice or legumes halfway up the sides of the shell. Bake in a preheated oven ten minutes. Remove from the oven, lift out the foil and weights, prick the entire bottom surface of the shell with the tines of a fork and return the shell to the oven. Bake an additional five minutes, then remove, transfer pie plate to a wire rack and let cool completely before filling.

**FULLY BAKED PASTRY SHELL** Proceed as directed for prebaked shell. After removing the weights and pricking the shell, lower oven heat to 350°F and bake shell fifteen to twenty minutes, or until golden. Cool on wire rack.

*Canning-jar rings are a good substitute for a cooling rack for cakes and pies.*

**STORING UNBAKED AND BAKED PASTRY DOUGH AND SHELLS** The disc formed once the dough has been mixed can be wrapped in waxed paper, placed in a plastic bag and refrigerated up to twenty-four hours before rolling out. Only in an emergency should the disc be frozen, in which case wrap it in aluminum foil and freeze no more than two weeks. Defrost the disc in the refrigerator and be patient when working with the dough, for it will be much more difficult to roll out than freshly made pastry dough.

If you have prebaked or fully baked a pie shell, it will keep at room temperature for six hours before filling. Unbaked, prebaked and fully baked pie shells may be wrapped in plastic wrap or aluminum foil and frozen up to three or four weeks. They will defrost quickly in or out of the refrigerator.

# BISCUIT PASTRY

For sweet or savory deep-dish pies. If doubling the recipe, do not double the baking powder measure.

*Makes One Eight- to Nine-inch Top Crust*
1 cup unbleached flour, or 1/2 cup *each* unbleached flour and whole-wheat pastry flour
2 teaspoons baking powder
1/2 teaspoon salt
1/4 teaspoon ground sage, marjoram or oregano*
1 egg, lightly beaten
2 tablespoons corn oil
2 tablespoons butter, softened
Ice water, if needed

Combine flour, baking powder, salt and sage in a large mixing bowl. Combine egg, oil and butter. With a fork, quickly stir egg mixture into flour mixture until just mois- tened, sprinkling with ice water as needed to form dough into a loose mass. With fingers, gently form into a rough ball, flatten into a disc about 1/2 inch thick and place on lightly floured board. Roll out as described in General Direc- tions for Pastry and top as described in Savory Deep-Dish Pies.

*If pastry is to be used for a fruit cobbler, omit sage and add 1 to 2 teaspoons granulated sugar (optional).

# BISCUIT PASTRY WITH CHEESE

For savory deep-dish pies. If doubling the recipe, do not double the baking powder measure.

*Makes One Eight- or Nine-inch Top Crust*
1-1/3 cups unbleached flour
1 tablespoon baking powder
1/2 teaspoon salt
1 teaspoon finely crumbled celery flakes
1/4 teaspoon dry mustard
Dash cayenne pepper
4 tablespoons butter, cut into bits and chilled
1/4 cup finely grated Cheddar cheese
Approximately 1/3 cup milk

Combine flour, baking powder, salt, celery flakes, mustard and pepper in a large mixing bowl. With fingertips, pastry blender or 2 knives, crumble butter into flour mixture until the consistency of coarse cornmeal. Toss in cheese. With a fork, stir in milk until just moistened and mixture forms a loose mass. With fingers, gently form into a rough ball, flatten into a disc about 1/2 inch thick and place on lightly floured board. Roll out as described in General Direc- tions for Pastry and top as described in Savory Deep-Dish Pies.

# WHOLE–WHEAT PASTRY

For quiches, deep-dish pies, turn- overs (six) and fruit pies.

*Makes Two Eight-inch Pastry Shells*
2/3 cup whole-wheat pastry flour
2/3 cup unbleached flour
1/2 teaspoon salt
1/4 pound butter, cut into bits and chilled
Approximately 3 tablespoons ice water

Combine flours and salt in a large mixing bowl. With fingertips, pastry blender or 2 knives, crumble butter into flour mixture until the con- sistency of coarse cornmeal. With a fork, quickly stir water into flour-butter mixture until just moistened. (Or mix dough in a food processor as explained in General Directions for Pastry.) With fingers, gently form into a rough ball, flatten into a disc about 1/2 inch thick, wrap in waxed paper, place in a plastic bag and refrigerate at least 1 hour. Let stand at room temperature 3 to 4 minutes before rolling out, then roll out as described in General Directions for Pastry.

---

*Have all ingredients and equipment ready before beginning to make any pastry dough.*

## SOUR CREAM PASTRY

For quiches, deep-dish pies, turnovers (six) and dessert pies. This pastry puffs considerably when baked unfilled. It will also shrink more than most pastries when baked, so the fluted edge must be high and generously cover the rim of the pie plate.

*Makes One Ten-inch Pastry Shell*
1 cup unbleached flour, or 1/2 cup *each* unbleached flour and whole-wheat pastry flour
1/8 to 1/4 teaspoon salt
1/4 pound butter, cut into bits and chilled
1/2 cup sour cream

Combine flour and salt in a large mixing bowl. With fingertips, pastry blender or 2 knives, crumble butter into flour mixture until the consistency of coarse cornmeal. With a fork, stir in sour cream until just moistened. (Or mix dough in a food processor as explained in General Directions for Pastry.) With fingers, gently form into a rough ball, flatten into a disc about 1/2 inch thick, wrap in waxed paper, place in a plastic bag and refrigerate at least 1 hour. Let stand at room temperature 3 to 4 minutes before rollling out, then roll out as described in General Directions for Pastry.

## EGG WHITE PASTRY

For quiches, turnovers (eight) and fruit or other dessert pies.

*Makes Two Nine-inch Pastry Shells*
2 cups unbleached flour
1/2 teaspoon salt
1/2 teaspoon ground thyme, savory or marjoram*
4 tablespoons butter, cut into bits and chilled
4 tablespoons lard, cut into bits and chilled
2 egg whites (unbeaten), chilled
Approximately 1/4 cup fresh lemon juice, chilled

Combine flour, salt and thyme in a large mixing bowl. With fingertips, pastry blender or 2 knives, crumble butter and lard into flour mixture until consistency of coarse cornmeal. Place egg whites in a measuring cup and add lemon juice to measure 1/2 cup. With a fork, quickly stir liquid into flour-butter mixture until just moistened. (Or mix dough in a food processor as explained in General Directions for Pastry.)

Divide dough in half. With fingers, gently form into rough balls, flatten each ball into a disc about 1/2 inch thick, wrap in waxed paper, place in a plastic bag and refrigerate at least 1 hour. Let stand at room temperature 3 to 4 minutes before rolling out, then roll out as described in General Directions for Pastry.

*If pastry is to be used for dessert, omit thyme and add 1 tablespoon granulated sugar (optional).

## EGG YOLK PASTRY

For quiches, turnovers (six) and dessert pies. When fully baked for filling with a mousse or with Lemon Cream, this pastry has an especially flaky texture.

*Makes One Ten-inch Pastry Shell*
1-1/3 cups unbleached flour
1/2 teaspoon salt
4 tablespoons butter, cut into bits and chilled
4 tablespoons lard or vegetable shortening, cut into bits and chilled
1 egg yolk
Approximately 3 tablespoons ice water

*A marble surface is best for rolling out pastry. It "keeps cool."*

Combine flour and salt in a large mixing bowl. With fingertips, pastry blender or 2 knives, crumble butter and lard into flour mixture until the consistency of coarse cornmeal. Place egg yolk in a measuring cup and add ice water to measure 1/4 cup. With a fork, quickly stir liquid into flour-butter mixture until just moistened. (Or mix dough in a food processor as explained in General Directions for Pastry.) With fingers, gently form into a rough ball, flatten into a disc about 1/2 inch thick, wrap in waxed paper, place in a plastic bag and refrigerate at least 1 hour. Let stand at room temperature 3 to 4 minutes before rolling out, then roll out as described in General Directions for Pastry.

## FILLING SUGGESTIONS FOR HORS D'OEUVRE PASTRIES

Egg White, Egg Yolk, Whole-Wheat, Sour Cream Pastry or Puff Pastry may be used to make these hors d'oeuvres. The pastry may be rolled and cut out up to three days ahead and frozen, well wrapped, until ready to use. You may also fill the pastries and freeze them up to two weeks. Defrost at room temperature about twenty minutes, brush with Egg Wash and then bake as described below.

Roll out pastry dough as explained in General Directions for Pastry. With a cookie cutter or a guide and a sharp knife, cut into 1-1/2-inch rounds. Place 1/2 teaspoon of filling in the center of a round, lightly moisten the edge of the round with water or Egg Wash, top with a second round and seal edges together with the tines of a fork. Place filled pastries on an ungreased baking sheet. Alternately, cut out 2-inch rounds, place 1/2 teaspoon filling on one-half, moisten edge of round lightly with water or Egg Wash, fold over to form a half-moon shape and seal with tines of a fork. Place the filled pastries flat side down on an ungreased baking sheet, or stand them on their seamless side so the seam points upward and press gently to flatten bottom slightly. Refrigerate pastries fifteen to twenty minutes before baking.

Remove the pastries from the refrigerator and brush with Egg Wash. Bake in a preheated 375°F oven ten to twenty minutes, or until golden. Serve at once.

You may also make simple unfilled hors d'oeuvre pastries. Roll and cut out as directed, but use a variety of variously shaped cutters, if desired. Spread the pastry cutouts with softened butter and then sprinkle with freshly grated Par-mesan cheese. Bake as directed for filled pastries, reducing cooking time slightly. To make a very simple filled pastry, wrap the dough rounds around the chosen filling—cubes of veal roast or cheese or small balls of leftover steak tartare—and bake in the same way.

**SPINACH** Finely minced onion and garlic sautéed in butter, well-drained finely chopped, cooked spinach, Swiss chard or other leafy green, freshly grated nutmeg, finely minced fresh parsley, dill and chives, crumbled feta cheese, egg yolk to bind.

**CHICKEN** Finely minced onion and mushrooms sautéed in butter, finely minced cooked chicken, cooked rice, chopped hard-cooked eggs, sour cream to bind, seasonings as desired.

**MEATLOAF** Crumbled cooked meat-loaf, hamburgers or lamb patties, grated sharp Cheddar cheese, minced canned mild green chili peppers, minced black olives, minced green onions and tops, seasonings as desired.

**VEAL** Finely minced cooked veal roast, softened cream cheese, crumbled feta cheese, minced fresh parsley and chives, seasonings as desired.

## BASIC METHOD FOR QUICHES

There are basically two kinds of fillings for quiche, one in which the ingredients are layered and one in which the ingredients are mixed together. Regardless of which type you make, you will need to fill the pie shell three-quarters full, which means 2-1/2 to 3 cups filling for an eight- or nine-inch quiche and 3-3/4 cups filling for a ten-inch quiche. A layered quiche can be made with chopped or sliced cooked firm vegetables, such as asparagus, zucchini, broccoli or mushrooms, while a quiche in which the filling ingredients are combined is best made with finely chopped cooked soft vegetables, such as spinach or Swiss chard, or with rice or finely cut meat such as cooked ham.

If making a quiche with a layered filling, use equal amounts of the vegetable and liquid; for a filling in which the ingredients are mixed together, use 1-1/2 parts vegetable to 1 part liquid. The liquid should be made of 2 parts milk or half-and-half cream and 1 part eggs. The filling can be seasoned as desired, and onion or shallot should be added for flavor.

Following General Directions for Pastry, roll out the Egg White, Egg Yolk, Whole-Wheat or Sour Cream Pastry, line a pie plate with it, prebake and cool on a wire rack. Brush cooled pie shell with Egg Wash, let dry, then strew two to three tablespoons grated Gruyère cheese over bottom of shell. Fill shell in one of two ways, depending on type of filling used: Combine finely chopped vegetable, which has been sautéed with onion or shallot and cooled, with egg-milk mixture and pour into shell; or layer sautéed onion or shallot on top of the cheese, then the chopped or sliced vegetable and finally pour over the egg-milk mixture. Strew two to three tablespoons cheese over the top and bake in a preheated 375°F oven twenty-five to thirty minutes for an eight- or nine-inch quiche, or thirty to forty minutes for a ten-inch one. The quiche is done when a thin knife inserted in the center comes out clean. Cool three to five minutes before cutting into wedges. Quiche may be eaten hot, at room temperature or cold. Reheating, even in a microwave oven, will make the pastry soggy.

The following quiche recipes illustrate these two styles of filling. Use this basic method and the recipes as guides to putting together your own quiche combinations. For example, try mushrooms and crab meat, asparagus and ham, or broccoli and anchovies.

## GREEN TOMATO QUICHE

For the green tomatoes that remain in the garden at the end of the season. Sliced Baked Zucchini may be used in place of the tomatoes.

*Makes One Eight- or Nine-inch Quiche*

1 prebaked 8- or 9-inch pie shell
Egg Wash or lightly beaten egg white
1/2 cup finely minced onion
1/2 teaspoon finely minced garlic
1 tablespoon butter
2/3 cup grated Gruyère cheese
3 or 4 green tomatoes, thinly sliced (about 2 cups)
1/2 teaspoon salt
1/4 teaspoon freshly ground black pepper
1/4 teaspoon ground oregano
1/4 teaspoon sugar
1/4 cup grated Cheddar cheese
3 tablespoons minced fresh parsley
2 eggs, lightly beaten
1 egg yolk (optional)
3/4 cup half-and-half cream
Paprika

Brush shell lightly with Egg Wash and set aside. Preheat oven to 375°F. Cook onion and garlic, covered, in butter until soft. Remove from heat and set aside. Sprinkle half

the Gruyère cheese on bottom of pie shell. Arrange a layer of tomato slices on top of cheese, sprinkle with half the onion/garlic mixture, half the seasonings, half the Cheddar cheese and half of the parsley. Repeat layers. Beat eggs, egg yolk and cream until blended and pour over. Sprinkle with remaining Gruyère cheese and paprika. Bake 25 to 30 minutes, or until a thin knife inserted in center comes out clean. Let stand 3 to 5 minutes before cutting into wedges.

## SWISS CHARD QUICHE

*Makes One Eight-inch Quiche*
1 prebaked 8-inch pie shell
Egg Wash or lightly beaten egg
    white
3 tablespoons minced shallots
1 garlic clove, minced
2 tablespoons butter
1 cup firmly packed finely chopped
    cooked Swiss chard, well
    drained
1/4 teaspoon salt
1/4 teaspoon freshly grated nutmeg
1/8 teaspoon freshly ground black
    pepper
2 eggs, lightly beaten
1 egg yolk (optional)
3/4 cup half-and-half cream
1/2 cup flaked cooked firm white
    fish or salmon
1/3 cup grated Gruyère cheese
Paprika

Brush pie shell with Egg Wash and set aside. Preheat oven to 375°F. Saute shallots and garlic in butter 3 minutes. Add chard and cook, stirring, 1 to 2 minutes. Remove from heat, add seasonings and cool slightly. Beat together eggs, egg yolk and cream to blend well. Stir into chard mixture and gently stir in fish. Sprinkle prepared shell with half of cheese. Pour chard mixture into shell and sprinkle with remaining cheese. Sprinkle with paprika and bake in preheated oven 25 to 30 minutes, or until a thin knife inserted in center comes out clean. Let stand 3 to 5 minutes before cutting.

---

*Always measure and cut up lard and/or butter first when making pastry. Lard will then have time to chill again before being added.*

---

## TURNOVERS

Egg White, Egg Yolk, Whole-Wheat or Sour Cream Pastry can be used to make turnovers. Fill with any gravied poultry or meat and/or vegetable in the proportion of about 2 tablespoons medium-thick gravy to 1/4 cup poultry or meat and/or vegetables. Use that small portion of turkey in gravy from last evening's dinner and combine it with the onions or peas that accompanied the bird; or fill with Corned Beef Hash or Fish Hash moistened with Chili Sauce, meatloaf and gravy, or Ham Loaf and Mustard Sauce.

Roll out the pastry dough as described in General Directions for Pastry. Using a sharp knife and the lid of a 2-pound coffee tin as a guide, cut out rounds about 5-1/2 inches in diameter. Place 1/4 cup filling on one-half of each round. Lightly moisten edges of round with water or Egg Wash and fold round over to form a half circle, pressing edges with tines of a fork or fluting with your fingertips to seal. Prick top of turnover with tines of fork and brush with Egg Wash. Bake in a preheated 400°F oven 10 minutes. Reduce heat to 350°F and bake 15 to 20 minutes, or until golden. Baking time will depend upon which pastry recipe is used. Serve hot or at room temperature.

# SAVORY DEEP–DISH PIES

Biscuit Pastry and Biscuit Pastry with Cheese are ideal for topping any savory deep-dish pie, but Whole-Wheat and Sour Cream Pastry can also be used. You will need a 9- or 10-inch straight-sided deep-dish pie plate or 10-ounce individual custard dishes. Fill the dish almost to the very top with any leftover gravied or sauced meat, poultry, seafood and/or vegetables that have a stewlike consistency and are at room temperature. Chicken fricassee, goulash, turkey divan, a blanquette of veal, beef Stroganoff, Hot Chicken or Turkey Salad, the filling for Corn-bread Pie, Chicken Livers, Hearts and Gizzards, Creamed Veal (sliver ham into veal and sauce and omit cornbread), or Creamed Vegetables would make a good filling. If necessary, a little stock may be added to the filling to create the proper consistency.

Roll out pastry as described in General Directions for Pastry, making the round about 1 to 1-1/2 inches greater in diameter than the dish to be topped. (Alternately, roll out the pastry in a large round and cut out rounds 1/2 inch greater in diameter than the custard dishes, if making individual pies.) Fold the round in half, carefully lift to the dish, place on one-half, unfold and center on filling. With kitchen shears, trim edges evenly to leave a 1/2-inch overhang. Gently but firmly press the edges of the dough to the rim, folding under the overhang and forming a nice, high flute around the rim with your fingertips. (The pastry flute should be high enough to allow for shrinkage during baking.) Brush the pastry with Egg Wash and, with a sharp knife, make a few slashes in a pattern in the top to allow steam to escape during baking. Bake in a preheated 400°F oven 10 minutes. Reduce heat to 350°F and bake 15 to 20 minutes, or until golden. Baking time will depend upon which pastry recipe is used. Let stand 5 minutes before serving.

## PORK PIE

This is just one example of a good filling for a two-crust savory pie. Substitute pears for the apples in this combination, or create your own combination using the proportion of solid to liquid ingredients given here.

*Serves Four to Six*
1 recipe Egg White Pastry
1 large apple, thinly sliced
1/2 teaspoon granulated sugar
1/2 teaspoon fresh lemon juice
1/2 to 2/3 cup pork gravy
2 cups shredded cooked pork roast
1 small sweet red or white onion, thinly sliced
1/2 teaspoon ground ginger
1/4 teaspoon ground thyme
1/4 teaspoon freshly ground black pepper
1/4 teaspoon salt
Egg Wash

Working with one-half of pastry and keeping other half refrigerated, roll out and line a 9- or 10-inch pie plate as explained in section on two-crust pies in General Directions for Pastry. Chill shell 30 minutes. Toss together apple slices, sugar and lemon juice and set aside. Preheat oven to 450°F. Combine pork and gravy and spoon into shell. Cover with onion slices and sprinkle with a little of the ginger, thyme, pepper and salt. Layer apple slices over and sprinkle with remaining ginger, thyme, pepper and salt. Roll out reserved pastry and top filled shell as described in general directions. Brush with Egg Wash, make several slashes in top and bake in preheated oven 10 minutes. Turn oven heat to 350°F and continue baking 35 minutes, or until nicely browned. Cool several minutes before cutting into wedges.

**PASTRY VARIATIONS** A double recipe of Sour Cream Pastry or Egg Yolk Pastry may be used to make this pie.

# PUFF PASTRY

This recipe makes about three pounds of pastry dough, or enough for one large (8-inch) patty shell (vol-au-vent), ten individual-entrée-size (3-1/2-inch) patty shells (bouchées), or twenty-four to thirty tiny (2-inch) shells (petites bouchées). Two methods are provided here, the traditional, labor-intensive one and a quick one in which the dough is mixed in a food processor and rolled out in three short steps. With both methods, it is important that the dough always remain chilled and that it not be worked any more than is necessary, for too much handling will toughen it and it will not "puff" properly in the oven. Directions on how to form the shells and suggestions for fillings follow the methods.

1 pound unsalted butter, chilled
3 cups unbleached flour
1 cup cake flour
1 teaspoon salt
1 tablespoon fresh lemon juice
About 1 cup ice water

**TRADITIONAL METHOD** Immerse butter in a large bowl of cold water and work it with your fingertips until it is malleable, smooth and has a waxy finish. Remove butter from bowl, wrap in a lightweight towel and press out any water with the palms of your hands.

Pinch off about 1/2 cup of the butter, cut it into bits, place on a plate and refrigerate. Form the remaining butter into a 1/2-inch-thick round, wrap in waxed paper and refrigerate. Sift together the flours and salt into a large mixing bowl. Remove the 1/2 cup butter from the refrigerator and, with a pastry blender, 2 knives or your fingertips, crumble the butter into the flour until the mixture is the consistency of coarse cornmeal. Sprinkle lemon juice over flour mixture and, stirring with a fork, *gradually* add ice water, using only as much as is needed for the dough to be lightly formed into a ball. The dough should be handled as little as possible at this point. Flatten the ball into a disc on a lightly floured board and gently roll into a rectangle about 1/4 inch thick. Remove butter round from refrigerator and place in center of rectangle. Bring narrow side of rectangle farthest from you over butter round to cover it, then fold narrow side closest to you over the top, forming an envelope shape. Press edges together, wrap in waxed paper and chill 25 to 30 minutes until firm.

Remove dough from refrigerator, unwrap and place on lightly floured board with one of the narrow sides facing you. Roll dough out to form a long, narrow rectangle, being careful not to split the surface of the dough and expose the butter. (Exposing the butter releases some of the air that gives the pastry its puffiness. Patching the dough is possible, but is not advisable for best results.) Fold the rectangle into an envelope shape as before, then rotate the dough a quarter turn so that a narrow side faces you. Roll as before into a long rectangle, fold again in an envelope shape, wrap in waxed paper and chill 25 to 30 minutes. Repeat this procedure—rolling out, folding, rotating, rolling out and folding—two more times, chilling 25 to 30 minutes between the two procedures. After the final folding, wrap "envelope" in waxed paper, place in a plastic bag and chill at least 3 hours or up to 24 hours before rolling out, then roll as described in General Directions for Pastry.

**FOOD PROCESSOR METHOD** Cut butter into 16 slices, then cut each slice into quarters. Place butter pieces on a plate and refrigerate 15 to 20 minutes. Put flour and salt in food processor bowl fitted with metal blade and pulse 2 or 3 times to mix. Strew pieces of butter evenly into processor bowl and, with on/off pulses and checking frequently, process *just* until the butter pieces are the size of large fresh peas. This should take only several seconds. With motor running, add lemon juice and water to processor and process *just* until dough *begins* to gather on one side of bowl. Do not overprocess; it is better to undermix than to overmix. Remove dough from the bowl, lightly form into a rough ball and then flatten into a disc. Wrap disc in waxed paper and refrigerate 20 minutes.

On a lightly floured board, roll the dough into a rectangle 3/8 to 1/2 inch thick. Fold the narrow side farthest from you over the center of the dough, then fold the side nearest you over the top, forming an envelope shape. Rotate the dough a quarter turn so that a narrow side faces you. Roll as before into a rectangle, fold again in an envelope shape and rotate another quarter turn. Repeat rolling and folding again, then wrap in waxed paper, put in a plastic bag and chill at least 3 hours or up to 24 hours before rolling out. Roll as described in General Directions for Pastry.

**MAKING A LARGE PATTY SHELL (VOL–AU–VENT)** Divide 1 recipe Puff Pastry in half, wrap and refrigerate one-half and place the other half on a lightly floured board. Following General Directions for Pastry, roll out into a round at least 9 inches in diameter and 1/2 inch thick. Using a guide (cut from cardboard or a pan lid or other top), cut out an 8-inch round with a sharp knife. Gather up the pastry scraps into a ball, wrap in waxed paper and refrigerate. Lightly brush a large baking sheet with water and flip round over onto one-half of it. Cover baking sheet with waxed paper and refrigerate.

Now remove second half of pastry dough from refrigerator and roll and cut out as you did the first one. Then, with a guide, cut out a 5-inch round from the center of the 8-inch one to form a ring 1-1/2 inches wide. Wrap the 5-inch round in waxed paper and refrigerate. Remove the baking sheet with the first 8-inch round from the refrigerator. Lightly and carefully brush water on the outer 1-1/2-inch edge of the round. Fold the ring in half and carefully lift the ring onto one-half of the round, trying not to stretch it. Unfold the ring and position it on the round so that the outside edges are aligned. Gently press the ring to the round; the water will act as a sealer. With the back of a knife, make shallow impressions along the top and down the sides where the two layers join. The impressions should be at 1-inch intervals along the entire circumference of the round. (If the pastry has begun to warm by this point, cover and refrigerate until well chilled.) With a sharp knife, make a checkerboard pattern on the surface of the shell inside the ring, cutting no deeper than one-third of the way through the dough, then run the knife around the inner edge of the ring to make a shallow impression. This final step will make it possible to lift the center portion out intact after the shell is baked and to use it as a lid. Brush the entire surface of the shell with wash made of 1 egg beaten with 2 teaspoons heavy cream, then cover with waxed paper and refrigerate.

The center of the shell can become the lid of the vol-au-vent as just described, or you can make a decorative top with the 5-inch round and the pastry scraps that remain. (If you choose not to make a top with these, use them to make tiny patty shells or see Filling Suggestions for Hors d'oeuvre Pastries and Dessert Suggestions for Using Pastry and Puff Pastry Scraps for ideas on how to use them.) Remove the 5-inch round from the refrigerator and place on a lightly floured board. Roll out large enough to cut out an 8-inch round, cut out the round and refrigerate any pastry scraps. With a round cookie cutter 1 inch in diameter, make light impressions around the edge of the round by pressing one-half of the cutter against the dough, forming half-moon shapes. Prick the surface of the round, except the patterned edge, with the tines of a fork and transfer to the baking sheet with the shell. Cover the baking sheet with waxed paper and place in the refrigerator.

Remove the ball of pastry scraps from the refrigerator and roll as described in section on pastry scraps in General Directions for Pastry. With cutters or freehand, cut out small shapes—stars, crescents, clovers, etc.—for decorating the lid. Remove the baking sheet from the refrigerator, brush the lid with some of the egg-cream wash and arrange the cutouts on the lid in a decorative pattern. Brush the cutouts with wash, recover and refrigerate for 25 to 30 minutes, or until well chilled.

Preheat oven to 375°F. Remove the baking sheet from the refrigerator, uncover and immediately place in the preheated oven. Bake 50 minutes, or until pastry is nicely browned and puffed. If it begins to brown too quickly, cover with a sheet of parchment paper or brown-bag paper that has been buttered with Lecithin Butter. When pastry is done, remove from the oven and turn oven heat off. With a sharp knife, loosen and then lift out the center of the shell, being careful not to break it, and place on the sheet. With a fork, lightly pull uncooked dough from center of shell and discard. (It is much

easier to do this when the shell is still hot than when it has cooled.) Return the baking sheet to the oven for about 15 minutes. With a large spatula, remove shell and lid to a wire rack and let cool.

The patty shell can be stored at room temperature in an open container or on the wire rack up to 6 hours, stored in an airtight container up to 48 hours, or frozen in an airtight container up to 2 weeks. Regardless of the way it has been stored, the patty shell should be recrisped before it is served. To do this, place on a baking sheet in a preheated 350°F oven 10 minutes. (The frozen shell may go directly from the freezer to the preheated oven.) Fill and serve the shell while it is still hot.

If you have made a decorative lid, the center of the shell that is removed once the shell is baked can be used as a base for any creamed foods for a simple family luncheon or dinner.

---

*Keep a set of measuring cups for dry ingredients with sifter in cupboard. They will not need to be washed after each use, saving minutes in the kitchen.*

---

## MAKING INDIVIDUAL–ENTREE–SIZE PATTY SHELLS (BOUCHEES)

Working with one-half recipe of Puff Pastry dough at a time and keeping the other half refrigerated, roll out dough on a lightly floured board into a round 1/2 inch thick. (See General Directions for Pastry for method.) Using a round cookie cutter 3-1/2 inches in diameter (or a guide and a sharp knife), cut out rounds. Lightly brush a large baking sheet with water and flip rounds over onto it about 2 inches apart. Cover baking sheet with waxed paper and refrigerate 30 minutes. Repeat with remaining dough, adding rounds to same baking sheet if there is room, or using a second sheet.

Remove baking sheet(s) from refrigerator and, with a 2-inch round cutter (or a guide and knife), cut an impression two-thirds of the way through dough in the center of each 3-1/2-inch round. This impression will rise during baking to form the lid of the shell. Brush rounds with a wash of 1 egg beaten with 2 teaspoons heavy cream. Cover sheet(s) with waxed paper and refrigerate 30 minutes.

Preheat oven to 375°F. Remove baking sheet(s) from refrigerator, uncover and immediately place in the preheated oven. Bake 25 minutes, or until pastry is nicely browned and puffed. If shells begin to brown too quickly, cover with a sheet of parchment paper or brown-bag paper that has been buttered with Lecithin Butter. When shells are done, remove from the oven and turn oven heat off. With a sharp knife, loosen and carefully lift off the center of each shell and place on sheet(s). With a fork, lightly pull uncooked dough from the center of each shell and discard. Return the baking sheet(s) to the oven for about 10 minutes. With a large spatula, remove shells and lids to a wire rack and let cool. Store and recrisp as for large patty shell.

**MAKING TINY PATTY SHELLS (PETITES BOUCHEES)** Proceed as directed for individual-entrée-size shells, but use a cutter 1-1/2 inches in diameter to form the round and a cutter 3/4 inch in diameter to make the impression that forms the lid. Reduce baking time to 15 minutes, or until nicely browned and puffed. Store and recrisp as for large patty shell.

## FILLING SUGGESTIONS FOR TINY PATTY SHELLS

Fill shells with hot filling just after baking or recrisping. Serve immediately or keep hot in a moderate oven up to ten minutes. The following filling suggestions are suitable for serving as hors d'oeuvres

and may be used to fill tartlets and barquettes as well. Tiny patty shells may also be filled with Cooked-Vegetable Purée or chopped cooked vegetables heated in Cream Sauce Enriched with Egg Yolk and served as a garnish for roast meats.

**CHICKEN** Ground cooked chicken and finely diced cooked asparagus heated in Enriched Cream Sauce made with chicken stock.

**CHICKEN LIVER** Chopped cooked chicken livers, chopped cooked mushrooms and minced fresh parsley heated in Medium Cream Sauce mixed with sour cream.

**TURKEY** Minced cooked turkey, minced cooked mushrooms and coarsely chopped blanched almonds heated in Egg Cream Sauce made with turkey or chicken stock.

**FISH** Flaked cooked firm white fish or chopped cooked shellfish and cooked peas heated in Enriched Cream Sauce made with fish stock.

**HAM** Ground cooked ham, sieved hard-cooked eggs, minced green bell pepper and freshly grated Parmesan cheese heated in Medium Cream Sauce.

*Don't try to make puff pastry on a hot day. It will "melt."*

## FILLING SUGGESTIONS FOR LARGE AND MEDIUM PATTY SHELLS

Fill shells with hot filling just after baking or recrisping. Garnish with parsley or watercress sprigs and serve immediately with a firm, colorful vegetable such as broccoli, green beans, carrots or asparagus.

**CHICKEN** Diced cooked chicken and artichoke bottoms heated in Shallot Cream Sauce.

**VEAL** Omit cornbread from Creamed Veal on Ham and Cornbread. Cut ham in julienne and heat in the creamed veal.

**SWEETBREADS** Cooked sweetbread pieces, diced cooked chicken or turkey and/or diced cooked ham heated in Enriched Cream Sauce seasoned with dry white wine or fresh lemon juice.

**FISH** Flaked cooked salmon or firm white fish and chopped cooked broccoli heated in Cheese Sauce.

**VEGETABLE** Any of the Creamed Vegetable suggestions.

**HARD-COOKED EGG** Coarsely chopped hard-cooked eggs, diced cooked ham and cooked peas heated in Curry Cream Sauce.

# TOP-OF-THE-STOVE DISHES

## WELSH RABBIT

A dish to use up that opened can of beer.

*Serves Two*
1/4 cup stale beer or ale
1 teaspoon Worcestershire sauce
1/4 teaspoon dry mustard
1/4 teaspoon paprika
2 to 3 drops Tabasco sauce
2 cups firmly packed finely
   shredded sharp Cheddar cheese
Salt and freshly ground black
   pepper to taste
Toast or toasted English muffins

Heat beer slowly in the top pan of a double boiler placed over simmering water or in a Teflon-type skillet. Combine Worcestershire sauce, mustard and paprika. Stir into beer, add Tabasco sauce and when beer is hot (not boiling), gradually stir in cheese. Cook over medium-low heat just until cheese is melted. Do not overcook or cheese will harden. Season with salt and pepper and serve immediately over toast.

## KEDGEREE

*Serves Two*
1/2 garlic clove, minced
2 tablespoons butter
1/2 teaspoon curry powder
3 tablespoons half-and-half cream
1 cup cooked brown rice
2 hard-cooked eggs, chopped
1/2 cup flaked cooked firm white
   fish
Salt, freshly ground black pepper
   and paprika to taste
Sliced pimiento-stuffed green
   olives
3 tablespoons minced fresh parsley

Sauté garlic in butter 2 minutes. Sprinkle with curry powder and cook, stirring, 2 minutes. Add cream and toss in brown rice. Mix well and with 2 forks gently toss in chopped eggs, fish and seasonings. Heat in the top pan of a double boiler placed over simmering water, or in a Teflon-type skillet over medium-low heat, 15 minutes, or until well heated. Garnish with sliced olives and minced parsley.

*Use kitchen tongs to turn a piece of meat, fish or poultry as it cooks; a fork will pierce the skin and release precious juices.*

## FISH CAKES

*Makes Eight Cakes*
2 slightly stale slices white or
   whole-wheat bread
1/2 cup milk
1 egg, lightly beaten
3 tablespoons chopped fresh parsley
2 tablespoons chopped green
   onions and tops
1/2 teaspoon salt
1/4 teaspoon freshly ground black
   pepper
1/4 teaspoon freshly grated nutmeg
2 cups flaked cooked firm white
   fish
Butter and safflower oil for
   browning
Lemon wedges

Soak bread in milk to soften. Mix in egg, parsley, onions and seasonings. With a fork, stir in fish; chill. Form mixture into 8 cakes. Heat equal amounts butter and oil in a heavy skillet over medium heat, add cakes and brown on both sides, turning only once. Garnish with lemon wedges.

## FISH HASH

*Serves Four*
2 eggs, lightly beaten
1/4 cup heavy cream
1/2 cup shredded fontina cheese
1/2 teaspoon salt
1/4 teaspoon freshly ground white
    pepper
1/4 teaspoon crumbled dried
    tarragon
1/4 teaspoon paprika
1/2 cup minced onion
3 tablespoons butter
1 egg white
Pinch cream of tartar
2 cups diced baked or boiled
    potatoes
1/2 teaspoon Seafood Seasoning
1/4 cup dry sherry
2 cups flaked cooked firm white
    fish
Minced fresh parsley and/or chives

Combine eggs, cream, fontina, salt,
pepper, tarragon and paprika.
Cook onion in butter, covered,
until soft. While onion is cooking,
beat egg white and cream of tartar
until stiff but not dry. Fold into
egg-cream mixture. Add potatoes
and Seafood Seasoning to pan with
onion and stir with fork to coat
well. Add sherry and cook several
minutes. Toss in fish and heat
gently. Pour egg mixture over,
cover and cook until egg is starting
to set. With a fork, stir gently until
egg is cooked. Adjust seasonings
and sprinkle with parsley.

## MASHED POTATO–FISH CAKES

*Makes Six Cakes*
1 egg, lightly beaten
1/2 teaspoon dry mustard
1/2 teaspoon crumbled dried dill
1/2 teaspoon salt
1/4 teaspoon freshly ground white
    pepper
3 tablespoons minced green
    onions and tops
1 cup mashed potatoes
1 cup flaked cooked firm fish
Butter for browning
Parsley sprigs
Halved cherry tomatoes

Combine egg, seasonings and green
onions and mix in potato. With a
fork, stir in fish; chill. Form mixture
into 6 cakes. Heat butter in a
heavy skillet over medium heat,
add cakes and brown on both
sides, turning only once. Garnish
with parsley sprigs and cherry
tomatoes.

**NOTE** These cakes may also be
coated with fine dry bread crumbs
before browning. Form the cakes,
dust them with the crumbs, then
refrigerate until well chilled before
cooking.

## CHICKEN LIVERS, HEARTS AND GIZZARDS

If you have been freezing the
gizzards, hearts and livers that
came with the whole chickens you
purchased, use them now to prepare
this satisfying dish. Serve over
steamed rice.

*Serves Four to Six*
8 chicken gizzards, very thinly
    sliced
1 tablespoon butter
1 tablespoon safflower oil
8 chicken livers, halved
8 chicken hearts, sliced
1 teaspoon minced garlic
8 cooked pork link sausages,
    cut into thirds
1/4 cup sliced water chestnuts
1/2 cup diagonally sliced celery
1 teaspoon minced ginger root
3/4 cup pork or chicken stock,
    or as needed
1 tablespoon soy sauce
1/4 teaspoon salt
1/8 teaspoon freshly ground
    black pepper
1/2 tablespoon cornstarch
2 tablespoons water
Minced fresh parsley

Cook gizzards in butter and oil, covered, 10 minutes. Raise heat slightly and add livers and hearts. Cook just until livers have stiffened and livers and hearts are lightly browned. Add garlic and cook, stirring, 2 minutes. Add sausage, water chestnuts, celery, ginger, stock, soy sauce, salt and pepper. Cover and cook over medium heat 10 minutes. Dissolve cornstarch in water, add to pan and cook, stirring, until thickened. Adjust seasonings and sprinkle with minced parsley.

## FRIED CHICKEN WINGS

*Serves Two to Four*
6 to 8 chicken wings
1 recipe Teriyaki Marinade
1/4 cup unbleached flour, or as
   needed
Peanut oil for frying
Shredded lettuce
Sweet and Sour Sauce
Toasted sesame seeds
Oriental pickled cucumber
   vegetable relish (optional)

Cut tips from wings and cut wings into 2 pieces at joints, removing any excess fat and loose skin. (Reserve tips, fat and skin for soup stock.) Place wing pieces in bowl and pour marinade over. Turning occasionally, marinate 3 to 4 hours or overnight. Sprinkle wing pieces with flour and toss to coat well, adding more flour if needed. Heat 1/2 inch of oil in a skillet or fryer and fry wings in a single layer, turning once, until golden. Drain on paper toweling and arrange on bed of shredded lettuce. Pour sauce over, sprinkle with sesame seeds and serve hot or cold with relish.

---

*Don't let pieces touch when browning stew meat. Contact will draw juices.*

---

*If you have oversalted your stew, cook a chunk of raw potato in it to absorb the excess salt.*

---

## BUSECCA

Serve this stewlike dish in shallow soup plates.

*Serves Three or Four*
1/4 cup minced onion
1/4 cup minced carrot
1/4 cup diagonally sliced celery
1 to 2 sage leaves, minced
1/4 teaspoon granulated sugar
1 tablespoon butter
1/2 tablespoon olive oil
2 cups chopped ripe tomatoes
   or Italian plum tomatoes
1 to 2 cups rich beef stock
2 cups julienned cooked tripe
1 cup cooked small white beans
1/4 cup minced fresh parsley
Salt and freshly ground black
   pepper to taste
Freshly grated Parmesan cheese

Sauté onion, carrot, celery, sage and sugar in butter and oil until lightly browned. Add tomatoes, stock, tripe, beans and parsley. Cook, uncovered, 15 minutes to blend flavors. Adjust seasonings with salt and pepper and sprinkle generously with cheese.

## BEEF ROLLS

Purchase thin slices of top round, each weighing 2 to 3 ounces, and pound until very thin. Sprinkle the slices with salt and pepper. On each slice place about 3 tablespoons of chopped cooked chicken livers and/or ham, seasoned grated boiled potatoes, sauteed mushrooms, cooked bread stuffing, or any minced meat and/or vegetable combination desired, and roll up tightly. Secure the ends of each roll with string. Dredge beef rolls in flour and brown on all sides in a heavy skillet in rendered beef fat. Add rich beef stock mixed with a little tomato paste to pan to a depth of about 1/2 inch, cover and cook over medium-low heat 1 hour, or until tender.

## CORNED BEEF HASH

Hash, long a favorite way to use up leftover corned beef, can be tailored to individual tastes. Some like the meat and potato mixture ground, while others prefer it chunky. You can alter the meat and potato proportions, use raw instead of cooked potatoes, substitute roast beef or cooked chicken or turkey for the corned beef, or add diced cooked vegetables. If you like hash with eggs, make two or three hollows in the mixture after turning it, break an egg into each hollow, cover the pan and cook the eggs until set to your liking.

The recipe that follows calls for grinding the ingredients; use the medium blade on your hand meat grinder. Chili Sauce is a good accompaniment.

4 parts diced cooked corned beef
2 parts diced boiled or baked potato
1 part diced onion
Salt, freshly ground black pepper and ground thyme to taste
Brown Sauce, gravy, stock or rendered beef fat as needed for moisture
Rendered beef fat for browning

Grind together corned beef, potato, onion and seasonings. Depending upon how much fat is in the meat, add Brown Sauce as needed to moisten. Heat rendered fat in a heavy skillet, add meat mixture and cook over medium heat, adding more sauce as needed, until browned. Carefully flip portions of mixture over to brown other side.

---

*Steak tartare leftover from a large party can be refrigerated no more than 24 hours. If not eating within that time, form into balls, sheet freeze and cook as you would meatballs.*

---

## CORNED BEEF PATTIES

*Makes Eight Patties*
1 egg, lightly beaten
1/4 cup mayonnaise*
1/2 teaspoon prepared horseradish
1/2 teaspoon Dijon-style mustard (optional)
3 tablespoons minced fresh parsley
2 tablespoons grated onion and juices
2 cups finely minced cooked corned beef or ham
1 cup finely minced boiled or baked pototoes
1/4 teaspoon crumbled dried thyme
Salt and freshly ground black pepper to taste
1/3 cup fine dry bread crumbs, or as needed
Butter for browning
Creole Sauce

Combine egg, mayonnaise, horseradish, mustard, parsley and onion. Toss in corned beef, potatoes and seasonings. With fork, stir in bread crumbs, mashing mixture lightly and adding more crumbs if needed to bind. Adjust seasonings and chill at least 1 hour. Form into 8 loose cakes approximately 3-1/2 inches in diameter. Heat butter in a skillet and brown cakes on both sides in butter, turning once. Serve with Creole Sauce.

*Commercial mayonnaise will work better than homemade.

## CREAMED VEAL ON HAM AND CORNBREAD

Use chicken or turkey for the veal. Any hearty biscuit, split and toasted, can replace the cornbread.

*Serves Two*
2 thin slices cooked ham
2 tablespoons butter
2 tablespoons minced shallots
1-1/2 cups cubed cooked veal roast
1/4 teaspoon salt
1/4 teaspoon crumbled dried sage
1/8 teaspoon freshly ground white pepper
3 tablespoons dry white wine or vermouth
2 egg yolks, lightly beaten
2/3 cup half-and-half cream
2 tablespoons minced fresh parsley and/or chives
2 thick slices cornbread, toasted
1/4 cup freshly grated Parmesan cheese

Preheat broiler. Gently cook ham slices in butter until warmed and slightly browned. Remove and keep warm. Add shallots and veal to skillet, sprinkle with seasonings and cook, stirring, 2 minutes. Add wine and cook, stirring, 4 minutes. Beat egg yolks with cream and gradually add to veal mixture. Stirring constantly, cook until thickened. Do not allow to boil. Stir in parsley and adjust seasonings. Place a slice of ham on each cornbread slice, top with veal mixture, sprinkle with cheese and broil briefly to brown cheese.

## ENCHILADAS

An enchilada is a corn tortilla that has been softened in hot oil, dipped into a sauce and removed, wrapped around a filling and then topped with more sauce. A batch of enchiladas is a good way to use up that half package of corn tortillas, plus any number of other leftovers for the filling.

You must have everything ready before you begin to soften the tortillas so that the enchiladas will go together quickly. Prepare Mexican Quick Tomato Sauce, the filling and any garnishes. The filling may be shredded cooked beef, chicken or pork, chopped hard-cooked egg with minced white onion, shredded Monterey Jack cheese, or chopped cooked Swiss chard or beet greens heated in a little peanut oil with garlic and onion. All of the fillings should be seasoned with salt and pepper. The list of garnishes may include shredded lettuce, thinly sliced radishes, green or black olives, diced or sliced avocado sprinkled with fresh lemon juice, shredded cheese and chopped fresh coriander. You should also have bowls of Tomatillo Sauce and Uncooked Tomato Sauce at table.

Heat about 1/4 inch corn or peanut oil in a skillet until very hot. Slip a tortilla into the oil and leave it just until it softens; do not let it brown. Lift the tortilla from the skillet and briefly drain it on paper toweling. Now immerse the tortilla in the hot Mexican Quick Tomato Sauce, remove it, place about 2 tablespoons filling on the tortilla, roll up and place seam side down on a platter. When all of the enchiladas are ready, spoon more of the hot sauce over the top. Garnish as desired and serve immediately, or keep warm in a low oven. It is best to avoid putting the enchiladas in the oven, however, as the tortillas will become soggy.

---

*Make homemade corn chips with your stale tortillas: cut into wedges and fry until crisp in peanut oil; drain on crumpled paper toweling and sprinkle with salt.*

---

## CREAMED VEGETABLES

Combine and heat gently equal parts any Cream Sauce (except Heavy Cream Sauce) and chopped cooked vegetables. If mixture seems too thick, stir in stock to thin to desired consistency. Season with any of the Additions to Finished Cream Sauce suggestions. Serve in patty shells or on cooked noodles, rice or toast.

### CREAMED VEGETABLE SUGGESTIONS

● Cooked small whole onions and peas or snow peas with Light or Medium Cream Sauce seasoned with ground cardamom.

● Diced cooked carrots and cooked peas with Light or Medium Cream Sauce seasoned with dry sherry or fresh lemon juice.

● Sliced cooked artichoke hearts or bottoms with Shallot Cream Sauce; garnish with freshly grated Parmesan cheese.

● Cut-up cooked green beans and cooked sliced mushrooms with Shallot Cream Sauce.

● Cooked asparagus spears cut in 2-inch lengths with Enriched Cream Sauce; garnish with slivered almonds browned in butter.

● Cooked broccoli flowerets with Curry Cream Sauce; garnish with chopped or sliced hard-cooked eggs.

● Cooked cauliflowerets and diced cooked carrots with Cream Sauce Enriched with Egg Yolk; garnish with minced fresh parsley.

● Cooked brussels sprouts with Cheese Sauce; garnish with minced fresh chives.

---

*To crush crackers with no mess, put in brown-paper bag and press with rolling pin.*

## CROQUETTES

Croquettes are mixtures of ground cooked vegetables, meats or fish and cream sauce that are coated with egg and bread crumbs and then deep fried. They can be served as an hors d'oeuvre or an entrée and are a good way to use up small amounts of leftover cooked foods.

Coarsely grind the vegetable, meat or fish and mix with well-seasoned Heavy Cream Sauce to form a rather firm mixture that will hold together easily after it has been chilled. Cover and chill at least 1 hour. Form the mixture into ovals or balls and roll in unbleached flour, carefully shaking off any excess flour. Dip balls in egg beaten with a little fresh lemon juice and then roll in fine dry bread crumbs, coating lightly and evenly. Let dry on a wire rack 1 hour, then roll a second time in fine dry bread crumbs. In a saucepan or deep fryer, heat peanut oil to a depth of at least 2-1/2 inches to 375°F. A few at a time, deep fry croquettes until golden. Drain on crumpled paper toweling and serve at once with Mushroom Sauce, Quick Mushroom Sauce, Tomato Sauce, or any Cream or Cheese Sauce.

# RICE AND RED BEANS

*Serves Two*
1/2 onion, chopped
2 garlic cloves, minced
2 tablespoons bacon drippings
1/4 teaspoon chili powder, or
   to taste
1/4 teaspoon crumbled dried
   oregano, or to taste
1/8 teaspoon ground cumin, or
   to taste
3/4 cup cooked white rice
3/4 cup cooked red beans
1/4 cup bean cooking liquid and/or
   stock, or as needed
Salt and freshly ground black
   pepper to taste

Sauté onion and garlic in bacon
drippings until soft. Sprinkle with
chili powder, oregano and cumin
and cook, stirring, 2 minutes. Stir
in rice, beans and bean cooking
liquid, cover and cook over medium-
low heat until rice and beans have
absorbed the liquid and flavor has
been incorporated. It may be
necessary to add more liquid and
cook a few minutes longer. Season
with salt and pepper.

---

*Just before covering pot of Steamed
White Rice, mix a little raw
ground beef, pork or lamb with
chopped green onions, minced
garlic and soy sauce and crumble
over surface of rice. Eat for
lunch.*

# CURRIED BROWN RICE

*Serves Two or Three*
1 cup sliced onions
1 tablespoon safflower oil
1/2 teaspoon curry powder, or
   to taste
1 small garlic clove, minced
1 to 2 slices ginger root, minced
1/4 cup pork stock, or as needed
1 cup diced cooked pork roast
1-1/2 cups cooked brown rice
Salt and freshly ground black
   pepper to taste
1 tablespoon olive oil
1/4 cup raisins, plumped in
   2 tablespoons hot water
1/3 cup slivered blanched almonds

In a large Teflon-type skillet, sauté
1/2 cup of the onions in safflower
oil until soft. Stir in curry powder,
garlic and ginger root. Cook, stirring,
2 minutes. Add stock, pork, rice
and salt and pepper. Heat gently,
adding more stock if needed for
moisture. Sauté remaining onions
in olive oil until transparent.
Remove with slotted spoon and
keep warm. Drain raisins and
sauté in same skillet 3 minutes.
Remove with slotted spoon and
keep warm. Then sauté almonds
in same skillet until lightly golden.
Turn rice mixture onto heated
platter and make a well in the
center. Fill with onions and surround
with raisins and almonds.

# PECAN RICE SAUTÉ

*Serves Four*
3/4 cup minced onion
1 to 2 garlic cloves, minced
1 cup chopped mushrooms
4 tablespoons butter and/or
   rendered chicken fat
2 tablespoons peanut oil
1/2 teaspoon crumbled dried
   oregano
1/2 teaspoon salt
1/4 teaspoon freshly ground black
   pepper
Dash cayenne pepper
3/4 cup chopped pecans
3 to 3-1/2 cups cooked white
   and/or brown rice
1/4 cup rich stock, or as needed
2 tablespoons dry vermouth
Minced fresh parsley

Sauté onion, garlic and mushrooms
in butter and oil, sprinkling with
seasonings as they cook, until
mushrooms start to brown. Push
vegetables aside and add pecans.
Cook, stirring, until lightly browned.
Toss in rice and mix in stock and
vermouth. Cook, covered, until
heated through, adding more stock
if needed for moisture. Sprinkle
with parsley.

---

*Cook brown and white rice to-
gether for a wild rice substitute.*

## FRIED RICE

This recipe can be based on what is available. Use slivered cooked pork, beef, chicken or crumbled sausage in place of the ham; add small amounts of vegetables—cooked peas, diced water chestnuts, bamboo shoots, raw carrots and celery—as desired.

*Serves Three or Four*
6 medium dried shiitake
　mushrooms
2 tablespoons peanut or corn oil
1-1/2 cups finely slivered cooked
　ham
1 teaspoon soy sauce
1/4 cup chicken stock
2-1/2 cups cooked white rice
1 tablespoon oyster sauce
1/4 cup chopped green onions and
　tops
2 to 3 tablespoons chopped fresh
　coriander
1 recipe Egg Garnish
Salt and freshly ground black
　pepper to taste

Soak mushrooms in warm water to cover until softened. Drain (reserve liquid for soups and sauces). Dice the mushrooms and sauté in oil 2 minutes. Add ham and sauté 1 minute. Add soy sauce and stock, cover and cook until moisture has almost evaporated. Add rice, oyster sauce, green onions and coriander and toss to coat rice well. Toss in all but 1/2 cup of the Egg Garnish. Season with salt and pepper, cover and heat gently. Garnish with reserved Egg Garnish.

**VARIATION** Prepare Fried Rice as directed, but do not garnish. Bake in preheated 350°F oven until heated through, adding a little of the mushroom soaking water for moisture. Top with Egg Garnish and serve with roast turkey or chicken.

## TOFU WITH BROWN BEAN SAUCE

Brown bean sauce in jars and cans can be found in Oriental markets and some supermarkets.

*Serves Two*
One-half 12-ounce package of firm
　tofu (bean curd)
2 teaspoons peanut oil
3 tablespoons brown bean sauce,
　combined with 1 tablespoon water
1 cup cubed cooked pork roast
2 to 3 tablespoons chopped green
　onions and tops
Coriander sprigs

Gently wash and dry tofu. In large skillet, heat oil and cut tofu into squares directly into skillet. Toss lightly and pour brown bean sauce mixture over. Gently toss in pork. Cover and cook over medium-low heat 3 to 5 minutes until heated through. Add green onions and mix well. Garnish with coriander sprigs.

## SOYBEANS AND NOODLES

Serve this dish with a tossed salad as a vegetarian meal.

*Serves Two*
1/2 cup minced onion
2 tablespoons butter
1/2 cup slivered blanched almonds
　or raw cashews, pine nuts
　and/or peanuts
2 tablespoons sesame seeds
1 cup cooked soybeans
1-1/2 cups cooked flat noodles
1/2 cup plain yoghurt
2 tablespoons freshly grated
　Parmesan cheese
1/2 teaspoon salt
1/4 teaspoon freshly ground white
　pepper
1/4 teaspoon freshly grated nutmeg

Sauté onion in butter until soft. Add almonds and sesame seeds and cook, stirring, until lightly browned. Add soybeans and noodles and heat through. Toss in remaining ingredients, adjust seasonings and serve immediately.

---

*A thin layer of superfine diato-maceous earth (purchased at organic nurseries) on the bottom of your grain or legume canisters will help deter bugs. Or poke bay leaves down into the canister's contents.*

---

When time permits, cook up a good-sized pot of lentils. At dinner time it will take only minutes to prepare one of the following three recipes.

## TAGLIARINI AND LENTILS

*Serves Two*
1-1/2 cups cooked tagliarini
　noodles
1 cup cooked lentils or garbanzo
　beans
1/2 cup shredded cooked lamb
　roast
5 to 6 black olives, slivered
1 cup Quick Tomato or Marinara
　Sauce
Salt and freshly ground black
　pepper to taste
Minced fresh parsley

In a large skillet, combine tagliarini, lentils, lamb, olives, tomato sauce and salt and pepper. Heat thoroughly and sprinkle with minced parsley.

## CURRIED LENTILS AND RICE

Don't be limited by the ingredients listed here. Substitute cooked split peas for half or all of the lentils and cooked bulghur for the rice. Firm tart apples are a good stand-in for the pears and cooked chicken can replace the pork. Serve with a dish of yoghurt on the side.

*Serves Two*
1 garlic clove, minced
1/4 cup chopped green onions and
　tops
2 tablespoons butter
1/2 to 1 teaspoon curry powder
3/4 cup diced cooked pork
1 cup coarsely chopped unpared
　firm pears
1-1/2 cups cooked lentils
1 cup cooked brown rice
Pork or chicken stock, if needed
Salt and freshly ground black
　pepper to taste
Paprika

Sauté garlic and onions in butter, covered, 3 minutes. Add curry powder, pork and pears. Stir to coat well with curry, cover and cook, stirring often, 3 minutes or until pears are just starting to soften. Add lentils and rice, stir well but gently, cover and cook until just heated through, adding stock if needed for moisture. Season with salt and pepper and sprinkle with paprika.

---

*Lentils complement many foods, from corn, meats and grains to pineapple.*

---

## LENTILS AND CORN

Spoon this vegetarian entrée over cooked bulghur, millet or white or brown rice and serve with plain yoghurt or Yoghurt Sauce.

*Serves Two or Three*
3/4 cup chopped onion
1 large garlic clove, minced
1/4 cup thinly sliced carrots
1 tablespoon safflower oil
1/2 teaspoon chili powder
1/4 teaspoon ground cumin
1/2 teaspoon crumbled dried
   oregano
1/2 teaspoon salt
1/4 teaspoon freshly ground black
   pepper
Dash cayenne pepper
1-1/4 cups chopped ripe tomatoes
1/4 cup slivered black olives
3/4 cup scraped cooked corn
   kernels
1 cup cooked lentils
1/2 cup grated sharp Cheddar
   cheese

Sauté onion, garlic and carrots in oil, covered, until starting to soften. Sprinkle with seasonings and cook, stirring, 2 to 3 minutes. Add remaining ingredients except cheese, mix well, cover and cook over low heat 15 minutes or until well heated and flavors are blended.

Stir in cheese and cook, covered, over medium-low heat just until cheese is melted. Serve on bulghur, white or brown rice, or other grain.

## REFRIED BEANS

Cooked red, kidney, pinto or pink beans can be used for making this staple of the Mexican table. By custom, the whole cooked beans are added to a hot skillet with lard and then mashed with the back of a spoon, adding cooking liquid as needed. An alternative is to mash them, either by hand or until coarsely blended in a food processor, before adding them to the hot skillet. This recipe uses this alternative method, but either one may be used.

*Makes One and One-half Cups*
1 tablespoon lard, bacon drippings
   or corn oil, or as needed
1-1/2 cups mashed cooked beans
1 tablespoon bean cooking liquid
   or stock
Shredded Monterey Jack cheese
   (optional)

In a heavy skillet, heat the lard until very hot. Add the beans and liquid and cook until the beans are dry and the lard has been absorbed. The beans will pull from the sides of the pan when they are done. If desired, strew with cheese, then serve immediately.

## VEGETABLE CURRY

Use any leftover cooked vegetables— cauliflowerets, broccoli flowerets, diced potatoes, okra, coarsely cut carrots, cut-up green beans, peas, coarsely cut eggplant—to prepare this flavorful main dish. Serve with plain steamed rice.

*Serves Two*
2 tablespoons butter or peanut oil
2 onions, thinly sliced
3 garlic cloves, minced
1 teaspoon finely minced ginger
   root
1 or 2 dried red chili peppers,
   seeded and minced
1 to 2 tablespoons curry powder
2 cups chicken stock, heated
4 cups cooked cut-up vegetables
1/2 small head Chinese cabbage
   or iceberg lettuce, shredded
1 ripe tomato, chopped
1 tablespoon fresh lemon juice

Melt butter in a saucepan and sauté onions, garlic, ginger and chili pepper until soft. Add curry powder and cook, stirring, 3 minutes. Pour in stock and stir in well. Add cooked vegetables and cabbage and cook over medium heat until cabbage is tender and vegetables are heated through. Remove from the heat and stir in tomato and lemon juice. Let stand, covered, 3 minutes to blend flavors.

## CURRY SAUCE FOR POULTRY OR SEAFOOD

*Serves Two*
1 or 2 fresh hot green chili
    peppers, seeded and cut up
4 black peppercorns
1/2 small onion, cut up
2 garlic cloves
1 teaspoon grated lemon rind
1/4 teaspoon ground turmeric
1/4 teaspoon salt
1/4 teaspoon ground coriander
1/4 teaspoon ground cumin
1/2 teaspoon chopped ginger root
2 tablespoons chopped fresh
    coriander
1 teaspoon peanut oil
1-1/2 cups coconut milk
1-1/2 cups cut-up cooked chicken,
    turkey or flaked firm white fish,
    or 1 cup cooked shelled prawns
1/2 teaspoon minced fresh hot
    green chili pepper
Salt to taste
Coriander sprigs

In a blender container, combine the cut-up chili peppers, peppercorns, onion, garlic, lemon rind, turmeric, 1/4 teaspoon salt, ground coriander, cumin, ginger root, 1 tablespoon of the chopped coriander and oil, and blend to a smooth paste. (It may be necessary to add a teaspoon of water or a few drops more oil to blend the ingredients thoroughly.) Combine the curry paste and about 1/2 cup of the coconut milk in a saucepan. Place over medium heat and cook, stirring constantly, 3 to 5 minutes, or until very fragrant. Add the remaining coconut milk and bring to simmer. Add poultry or seafood, minced chili pepper and remaining chopped coriander, stir gently with fork and cook until heated through, about 5 minutes. Season with salt to taste. Serve garnished with coriander sprigs.

## LAMB CURRY

*Serves Two*
2 tablespoons butter
1 medium onion, thinly sliced
2 garlic cloves, minced
1 teaspoon minced ginger root
1 fresh hot green chili pepper,
    seeded and minced
1/8 teaspoon ground cinnamon
1 tablespoon curry powder
2 ripe tomatoes, chopped
1-1/2 cups diced cooked lamb
    roast
1-1/2 tablespoons minced fresh
    mint
1 tablespoon fresh lemon juice
Mint sprigs for garnish

Melt butter in a skillet and sauté onion, garlic, ginger and chili pepper until soft. Stir in cinnamon and curry powder and cook, stirring, 3 minutes. Add tomatoes and blend well with onion mixture. Stir in lamb, minced mint and lemon juice and cook over medium heat until heated through and flavors are blended, about 10 minutes. (Add a tablespoon or two of water or stock if needed for moisture.) Serve garnished with mint sprigs.

## EGG CURRY

*Serves Four to Six*
2 tablespoons butter
2 medium onions, chopped
3 garlic cloves, minced
1/2 tablespoon finely minced
    ginger root
1 or 2 fresh hot green chili
    peppers, seeded and minced
1/2 teaspoon ground turmeric
1/4 teaspoon ground coriander
1/2 teaspoon salt
1-1/2 cups coconut milk
6 hard-cooked eggs, halved
1-1/2 tablespoons fresh lemon
    juice
1 tablespoon minced fresh
    coriander

Melt butter in a saucepan or deep skillet and sauté onions, garlic, ginger and chili peppers until soft; do not brown. Stir in turmeric, ground coriander and salt and cook 1 minute. Add coconut milk and simmer gently, uncovered, 10 minutes. Place eggs in pan and simmer 6 to 8 minutes. Remove from the heat and stir in lemon juice. Garnish with minced coriander.

## STIR FRY MEATS AND VEGETABLES

Small amounts of raw vegetables stir fried with meat, poultry or seafood are a complete meal with a bowl of steamed rice. Use your imagination to create interesting combinations with the leftover raw vegetables you have on hand. Suggested vegetables, meats, poultry and seafoods and directions for preparing them follow the basic recipe.

The addition of liquid depends upon the type of vegetable you are using. Leafy greens, such as cabbage, Swiss chard and lettuce, do not require the addition of liquid. Vegetables with little water content, such as carrots, green beans, broccoli and cauliflower, will require about three tablespoons of liquid. Cooking times will also vary: two to three minutes are sufficient for leafy vegetables, while three to five minutes are necessary for firm vegetables. It is important that you do not overcook the vegetables. They should be barely tender when served. If you wish to thicken the pan juices, add a cornstarch binder at the end of cooking and heat briefly until the pan juices are thickened.

The basic method outlined here can also be used when stir frying vegetables without meat. For three cups of prepared vegetables, omit the sherry and reduce the soy sauce to one-half tablespoon. Stir in the soy sauce, salt and sugar when the vegetables are almost tender.

*Serves Two*
1/2 pound meat, poultry or seafood
2 teaspoons soy sauce
2 teaspoons dry sherry
1/8 teaspoon sugar
1/8 teaspoon salt
2 tablespoons peanut oil
2 thin slices ginger root
2 garlic cloves, bruised
1 or 2 dried red chili peppers (optional)
1-1/2 cups prepared vegetables
Approximately 3 tablespoons stock or water, depending on type of vegetable
1/4 teaspoon Oriental sesame oil
Cornstarch binder of 2 teaspoons cornstarch dissolved in 3 to 4 tablespoons stock or water (optional)
Coriander sprigs and chopped green onions

Cut or slice the meat according to the directions that follow, and toss it with soy sauce, sherry, sugar and salt. (If possible, let the mixture stand for 20 minutes to blend flavors.) Heat 1 tablespoon peanut oil in a wok or heavy skillet, add the ginger, garlic and chili pepper and stir fry 30 seconds. Add the meat mixture and cook, stirring constantly, until just tender. Remove from the wok and set aside. Heat the remaining tablespoon oil in the wok, add the vegetables and stir fry briefly to coat well with oil. Add the stock if using firm vegetables, cover, and let steam rise to surface, or until vegetables are just tender. Return meat mixture to wok and add sesame oil. Reheat quickly and, if desired, stir in cornstarch binder to thicken pan juices. Garnish with coriander and green onions.

**SUGGESTED VEGETABLES AND THEIR PREPARATION** Asparagus, cut on diagonal; carrots, julienned or thinly sliced; turnips, julienned; green or red bell peppers, julienned or cut in small squares; celery, green or wax beans, cut on diagonal; whole snow peas or small whole green beans; shelled peas; crisped and well-drained bean sprouts; lettuce, cabbage, bok choy, Swiss chard, spinach, beet greens, mustard greens, coarsely cut; eggplant, cut in strips or cubes; cauliflower or broccoli flowerets; zucchini, bamboo shoots or water chestnuts, sliced.

**SUGGESTED MEATS, POULTRY AND SEAFOODS AND THEIR PREPARATION** Skirt or flank steak or pork butt, thinly sliced across the grain; poultry, ham or lamb, julienned; firm fish fillets, cubed; whole shrimp.

## MEATLOAF

With this one recipe, you can prepare four dinners in advance. Combine all of the ingredients for the basic mixture, then divide it into four portions. Wrap the portions individually and freeze them. When you are ready to cook a meatloaf, defrost one of the portions, combine it with one of the suggested ingredient combinations, sauté a small amount, taste and adjust seasonings. Form the mixture into a loaf and place in a shallow baking dish, or pat into a small bread pan or a muffin tin with large wells. Bake as directed and serve topped with one of the suggested sauces, if desired. Each portion will serve three or four. The recipe for the basic mixture can easily be halved.

### BASIC MEATLOAF MIXTURE
3 or 4 eggs, lightly beaten
1/3 cup milk
2 to 3 teaspoons Worcestershire sauce
2 teaspoons salt
1/3 cup Quick Tomato or Chili Sauce or Tomato Catsup

1/2 cup chopped Italian parsley, including tender stems
1/4 teaspoon freshly ground black pepper
1-1/3 cups broken stale bread
2 pounds ground beef
1 pound ground veal
1/2 pound ground pork
1/2 to 2/3 cup minced onion
2 to 3 teaspoons minced garlic

Suggested ingredient combinations (following)
Sauce suggestions (following)

In a large bowl, combine eggs, milk, Worcestershire sauce, salt, tomato sauce, parsley and pepper. Toss in bread and let stand until bread has absorbed the liquid and is soft. Mix in meats, onion and garlic. Divide into 4 equal portions. Add one of the suggested ingredient combinations to a portion and mix well. (Freeze remaining portions for future meals.) Preheat oven to 350°F. Put the meat mixture into one of the suggested baking pans and bake in preheated oven 1 hour if using a shallow baking dish or bread tin and about 40 minutes if using a muffin tin. Serve with a sauce, if desired.

### SUGGESTED INGREDIENT COMBINATIONS

● One cup cooked barley and 1/2 cup chopped ripe tomato.
● One cup grated baked or boiled potato, 1/3 cup ricotta cheese, and 1/3 cup minced green bell pepper.
● One-half cup puréed cooked broccoli with almonds (Cooked-Vegetable Purées) and 2 tablespoons ricotta cheese.
● One cup chopped fresh sorrel and/or raw or cooked New Zealand spinach, 2/3 cup cooked garbanzo beans, mashed, and 1/2 cup chopped ripe tomato.

**SAUCE SUGGESTIONS** Tomato Sauce, Quick Tomato Sauce, Mexican Quick Tomato Sauce, Creamy Quick Tomato Sauce, Creole Sauce, Mushroom Sauce, Quick Mushroom Sauce, Leek Sauce, Wine Sauce.

---

*Toss grated raw carrot into pot of freshly steamed rice or into mixture for meatloaf.*

## CHEESE AND BREAD SOUFFLE

There is no end to the variations this rich dish makes possible. Use white, whole-wheat, whole-grain, French or Italian bread, buttered if desired, in either slices or cubes. Tillamook, Wisconsin Cheddar, Samsoe, Gruyère or Monterey Jack cheese may be used. For the ham, substitute minced cooked turkey, chicken or tongue. Or transform this dish into a heartier meal by topping the ham with a second slice of bread to make "souffléed sandwiches."

*Serves Three or Four*
6 slices 2-day-old bread
3/4 cup minced cooked ham
1 to 1-1/2 cups loosely packed
   grated cheese
2 eggs, lightly beaten
1 cup milk
1/4 cup dry white wine or milk
1 tablespoon grated onion and
   juices
1/4 teaspoon salt
1/4 teaspoon paprika
1/2 teaspoon dry mustard
Dash cayenne pepper

In a buttered shallow baking dish, layer bread, ham and cheese. Combine eggs, milk, wine, onion and seasonings. Pour over layers, cover and refrigerate 4 hours or overnight. Two hours before baking, remove to room temperature. Preheat oven to 350°F and bake, uncovered, 50 minutes or until puffy and browned.

## ASPARAGUS WRAPPED IN HAM

*Serves Three*
18 cooked asparagus spears
6 thin slices cooked ham
2 cups cooked brown or white
   rice
1-1/2 cups Light Cream Sauce
   made with asparagus steaming
   water and heavy cream
1/8 teaspoon freshly grated nutmeg
1/8 teaspoon freshly ground white
   pepper
1/4 teaspoon salt
1/2 cup freshly grated Parmesan
   cheese
Paprika

Preheat oven to 400°F. Wrap 3 asparagus spears in each slice of ham. Cover the bottom of a buttered shallow baking dish with the rice. Arrange ham bundles, seam side down, on rice. Season cream sauce with nutmeg, pepper and salt and pour sauce over rice and ham bundles. Sprinkle evenly with cheese and paprika. Bake in preheated oven 15 minutes, or until heated through.

## HAM LOAF

*Serves Six*
2 eggs, lightly beaten
1 egg white
1/2 cup milk
1/2 cup dry coarse bread crumbs
2 tablespoons Chili Sauce
1 teaspoon dry mustard
1 tablespoon Worcestershire sauce
2 tablespoons grated onion and
   juices
1/4 cup minced fresh parsley or
   celery leaves
1/4 teaspoon celery salt
1/4 teaspoon freshly ground black
   pepper
3 cups coarsely ground cooked ham
1 cup cooked white or brown rice
1 cup shredded mozzarella cheese
Salt, if needed
Mustard Sauce (optional)

Combine eggs, egg white, milk and bread crumbs. Let stand until crumbs have softened. Preheat oven to 350°F. Add remaining ingredients to egg mixture and mix well. Sauté a small amount, taste and adjust seasonings. Form into a loaf shape and place in a shallow baking pan. Bake in preheated oven 40 to 50 minutes, or until lightly browned. Cool several minutes before slicing. Serve plain or with Mustard Sauce.

# HAM ROLLS

*Serves Three*

1 cup cooked barley
1/4 cup finely chopped unsalted
   peanuts
1/4 cup finely minced cooked
   chicken or turkey
2 teaspoons minced fresh parsley
1 teaspoon minced fresh chives
Freshly ground black pepper, salt
   and Bell's Seasoning or other
   poultry seasoning to taste
6 large very thin slices of cooked
   ham
1-1/2 cups Mushroom, Quick
   Mushroom or Cheese Sauce

Preheat oven to 325°F. Toss together the barley, peanuts, chicken, herbs and seasonings. Moisten with 1/4 cup of the Mushroom Sauce. Divide mixture between ham slices. Roll up tightly and arrange close together, seam side down, in a buttered shallow baking dish. Pour remaining sauce over the top and bake in preheated oven 20 minutes, or until heated through and lightly browned.

## VARIATIONS

● Substitute for the barley, cooked brown, white or wild rice or bulghur.

● Omit Mushroom Sauce. Moisten filling with a little milk or half-and-half cream. Cover baking dish tightly and heat in a 350°F oven 15 minutes.
● Sprinkle with freshly grated Parmesan cheese and return to oven for 10 minutes.

# HAM AND ENDIVE ROLLS

If your budget does not permit Belgian endive, use a heart of Romaine lettuce, cut into quarters.

*Serves Four*

2 cups water
1 tablespoon sugar
4 medium Belgian endive,
   trimmed and washed
8 thin slices baked ham
1/2 cup chicken stock
3 tablespoons butter
1/4 cup dry bread crumbs
1 cup grated Gouda cheese

Preheat oven to 350°F. Bring water and sugar to boil, dip endive in for 2 minutes and drain thoroughly. Wrap 2 slices of ham around each endive and arrange in a single layer in a buttered shallow baking dish. Pour stock over the top and dot with butter. Sprinkle with crumbs and cheese. Bake in preheated oven 30 minutes, or until heated through and cheese is melted.

# RICE AND SALMON LOAF

*Serves Four to Six*

2 eggs, lightly beaten
1/3 cup milk
2 teaspoons fresh lemon juice
1/4 cup dry bread crumbs
1/4 cup chopped green onions
   and tops
2 tablespoons minced fresh parsley
1/2 cup chopped cooked broccoli
2 hard-cooked eggs, chopped
1-1/2 cups flaked cooked salmon
Salt and freshly ground black
   pepper to taste
1/2 cup freshly grated Parmesan
   cheese
Paprika

Preheat oven to 350°F. Combine beaten eggs, milk, lemon juice, bread crumbs, onions, parsley, and broccoli. With a fork, toss in hard-cooked eggs, salmon, and salt and pepper. Transfer to a well-buttered standard loaf pan (or use Lecithin Butter) and sprinkle evenly with Parmesan cheese and paprika. Place in a shallow baking dish and pour in boiling water to reach 1/2 inch up sides of pan. Bake in preheated oven 35 to 40 minutes, or until set. Remove from water and let stand 5 minutes. Turn out onto serving plate and slice to serve.

# TONGUE TORTILLAS WITH REFRIED BEANS

*Serves Two*
1/4 cup minced onion
2 garlic cloves, minced
2 teaspoons corn oil
1/2 to 3/4 cup diced boiled tongue
1/2 cup Mexican Quick Tomato
   Sauce
Salt and freshly ground black
   pepper to taste
Corn oil for heating tortillas
4 corn tortillas
1-1/2 cups Refried Beans, heated
1/2 cup shredded Monterey Jack
   cheese
Sour cream
Coriander sprigs
Tomatillo Sauce or Uncooked
   Tomato Sauce

Preheat oven to 375°F. Sauté
onion and garlic in 2 teaspoons
corn oil until just beginning to
soften. Add tongue and tomato
sauce and heat thoroughly, then
season with salt and pepper. Heat
1/4 inch corn oil in a skillet until
very hot. Slip a tortilla into the oil,
and when it softens, remove and
drain briefly on paper toweling.
Spoon one-fourth of the tongue-

tomato mixture onto the tortilla,
fold it in half and place in a
shallow oiled baking dish. Repeat
with remaining tortillas and filling,
arranging close together in the
dish. Spread the refried beans
over the filled tortillas and sprinkle
with cheese. Bake in preheated
oven 10 to 15 minutes, or until
cheese is melted and casserole is
heated through. Garnish with sour
cream and coriander sprigs and
serve with Tomatillo Sauce at table.

# CORNBREAD PIE

*Serves Six*
1/3 cup minced onion
1 to 2 garlic cloves, minced
1/2 tablespoon corn oil
2 cups shredded cooked pot roast
1 cup cooked white or brown rice
1/2 cup cooked corn kernels or
   scraped corn
1/4 cup chopped pimiento-stuffed
   olives
1/3 cup canned green chili peppers
1/2 cup shredded Cheddar or
   Monterey Jack cheese
1/2 teaspoon salt
1/2 teaspoon ground cumin
1/4 teaspoon freshly ground black
   pepper
3 tablespoons chopped fresh
   coriander
2 ripe tomatoes, chopped
1 cup Marinara Sauce
1 recipe Cornbread Topping
   (following)

Sauté onion and garlic in oil until
soft. Add all remaining ingredients
except Cornbread Topping and
cook, stirring occasionally, until
rice and meat have absorbed the
tomatoes and the sauce. Mixture
should be moist but not runny.
Transfer mixture to shallow 10-
1/2- by 6-1/2-inch baking dish.
Preheat oven to 425°F. Prepare
Cornbread Topping and spoon
evenly on top of rice mixture.
Bake in preheated oven 15 minutes
or until cornbread has pulled slightly
away from sides of dish and cake
tester inserted in center comes out
clean.

**CORNBREAD TOPPING** Sift together
1/2 cup whole-wheat pastry flour
or unbleached flour, 2 teaspoons
baking powder, 1/4 teaspoon baking
soda and 1/3 teaspoon salt. Combine
flour mixture with 1/2 cup nondegerminated yellow cornmeal.
Beat together 1 egg, 1/2 cup
buttermilk, 2 tablespoons melted
and cooled lard or bacon drippings
and 1-1/2 tablespoons honey or
molasses until well blended. Stir
dry ingredients into wet ingredients
just until moistened.

---

*Line your bread basket with
aluminum foil, then with the
napkin to wrap around the hot
bread. The foil will help retain
heat.*

## CORNED BEEF– POTATO CASSEROLE

*Serves Four*
1 recipe Corned Beef Patties
8 slices Monterey Jack cheese

Preheat oven to 350°F. Prepare mixture for Corned Beef Patties. Transfer mixture to shallow baking dish and cover with slices of cheese. Bake in preheated oven 20 minutes, or until heated through and cheese is melted.

## CHICKEN OR TURKEY ROLLS

Pound boned half chicken breasts or fillets of turkey breast until very thin. Fill and roll as for Beef Rolls, but do not dredge in flour. Place rolls close together in a buttered shallow baking dish, dot tops with butter, cover and bake in a preheated 350°F oven 35 minutes. Remove cover and bake 10 to 15 minutes longer, or until browned.

## HOT CHICKEN OR TURKEY SALAD

*Serves Two or Three*
1/2 cup mayonnaise*
1/4 cup minced celery
2 tablespoons minced green bell pepper
2 tablespoons minced green onions
2 tablespoons minced green onion tops
2 tablespoons minced fresh parsley
1/2 cup Parmesan Croutons
2 tablespoons fresh lemon juice
2 tablespoons sliced pimiento-stuffed olives
1 cup cubed cooked chicken or turkey
Salt and freshly ground white pepper to taste
1/3 cup sliced almonds
Paprika

Preheat oven to 400°F. Lightly beat mayonnaise with a fork and stir in celery, bell pepper, green onions and tops and parsley. Toss in croutons, lemon juice, olives and chicken. Season and transfer to a small shallow baking dish. Cover evenly with almonds and sprinkle with paprika. Bake 10 to 15 minutes until well heated and lightly browned.

*This recipe works best if commercial rather than homemade mayonnaise is used.

## BAKED CHICKEN WINGS

These crisp and succulent chicken wings make an excellent hors d'oeuvre for four, or an entrée for two. Serve them on a bed of shredded lettuce with a bowl of Sweet and Sour Sauce on the side.

*Serves Two to Four*
6 to 8 chicken wings
1 recipe Teriyaki Marinade
1 egg, lightly beaten
1/2 cup Sesame Bread Crumb Coating, or as needed
2 tablespoons butter, melted

Cut tips from wings and cut wings into 2 pieces at joints, removing any excess fat and loose skin. (Reserve tips, fat and skin for soup stock.) Place wing pieces in a shallow dish and pour marinade over. Turning occasionally, marinate 3 to 4 hours or overnight. Drain wing pieces and pat dry. Dip wing pieces, one at a time, into beaten egg and then coat well with crumb coating. Place on wire rack set over a plate, not touching, and let stand 1 hour, or refrigerate up to 5 hours. Preheat oven to 375°F. Place wing pieces, not touching, on a baking sheet with sides. Drizzle butter over and bake in preheated oven 30 to 45 minutes, turning several times.

## CHICKEN AND CORN CASSEROLE

*Serves Four to Six*

1 cup minced onion
1/2 cup raisins
2 tablespoons safflower oil
1 to 1-1/2 teaspoons chili powder
1 to 1-1/2 cups diced cooked chicken
3 hard-cooked eggs, sliced
12 to 14 pitted black olives, halved
1 cup milk
2 eggs, separated
2 tablespoons unbleached flour
2 tablespoons butter, melted and slightly cooled
1 teaspoon granulated sugar
1/2 teaspoon salt
1/4 teaspoon freshly ground black pepper
2 cups scraped cooked corn, well drained
1/8 teaspoon cream of tartar

Cook onion and raisins in oil, covered, sprinkling with chili powder and stirring often, 5 minutes. Remove from heat and add chicken, stirring to coat chicken. Transfer to a shallow 6-1/2- by 10-1/2-inch baking dish. Preheat oven to 350°F. Arrange egg slices and olive halves on chicken mixture. Beat together milk, egg yolks, flour, butter, sugar, salt, pepper and corn. Beat egg whites with cream of tartar until stiff but not dry. Fold about 1/2 cup of corn mixture into whites and then fold into remaining corn mixture. Pour over chicken mixture in casserole and bake in preheated oven 40 minutes, or until cake tester inserted in center comes out clean. Let stand 3 minutes before cutting into squares to serve.

## CHICKEN LIVER–RICE CASSEROLE

*Serves Two or Three*

2 dried shiitake mushrooms
2 tablespoons unbleached flour
1/8 teaspoon ground thyme
1/8 teaspoon paprika
1/4 teaspoon salt
1/8 teaspoon freshly ground black pepper
Several dashes ground turmeric
2 teaspoons butter, or as needed
2 teaspoons safflower oil, or as needed
6 chicken livers, halved
2 tablespoons minced onion
1 garlic clove, finely minced
3/4 cup chicken stock
2 tablespoons dry white wine
1 tablespoon minced fresh parsley
1-1/2 cups cooked white or brown rice
1/4 cup freshly grated Parmesan cheese
Paprika

Soak mushrooms in warm water to cover until soft. Drain, reserving liquid. Mince the mushrooms and set aside. Combine 1 tablespoon of the flour with the seasonings. Pat livers dry and dust with flour mixture. Heat butter and oil in a skillet and brown livers over medium-high heat until they stiffen and are just cooked through. Do not overcook. Remove from skillet and set aside. Preheat oven to 350°F. Adding more butter and/or oil to pan if needed, sauté onion, garlic and reserved mushrooms 3 minutes. Sprinkle with remaining 1 tablespoon flour and cook, stirring, 2 minutes, then gradually add stock, reserved soaking liquid and wine. Cook, stirring, until lightly thickened. Stir in parsley and adjust seasonings. Spread rice evenly in a well-buttered shallow baking dish. Tuck chicken livers into rice and pour mushroom sauce over. Sprinkle with Parmesan cheese and paprika. Bake in preheated oven 15 to 20 minutes until heated through and lightly browned.

## TURKEY WITH HEARTS OF PALM AND SORREL

*Serves Six*
6 large slices cooked white meat
   of turkey, cut in julienne
3 hard-cooked eggs, sliced
4 to 5 hearts of palm, sliced
4 tablespoons butter
3 firmly packed cups chopped
   sorrel
1/4 cup unbleached flour
1 cup rich turkey or chicken stock
1 cup half-and-half cream
2 teaspoons fresh lemon juice
1 tablespoon minced fresh chives
Salt, freshly ground white pepper
   and paprika to taste
One-half 2-ounce jar pimientos,
   drained and cut in julienne
1/2 cup coarse dry bread crumbs
Butter

Preheat oven to 350°F. Arrange turkey and egg slices in a shallow baking dish. Arrange slices of hearts of palm between turkey and eggs. Melt 4 tablespoons butter until bubbly, add sorrel and cook, stirring, 2 minutes. Sprinkle with flour and cook, stirring, 2 minutes. Gradually add stock and cream and cook, stirring, until thickened. Add seasonings and continue cooking 5 minutes, stirring often. Pour over turkey and arrange pimientos on top. Sprinkle with crumbs and dot with butter. Bake in preheated oven 15 to 20 minutes, or until heated through.

## TURKEY MOUSSE

The major components of this elegant luncheon or supper dish—the turkey mixture and the sauce—may be prepared ahead, then combined and cooked just before serving. (Reheat the sauce in a heavy Teflon-type pan, double boiler or microwave oven.) Asparagus make a good accompaniment.

*Serves Four to Six*
2 cups diced cooked turkey
2/3 cup cooked spinach, well
   drained
1/3 cup chopped fresh or cooked
   mushrooms
3 tablespoons chopped fresh parsley
1-1/2 cups Enriched Cream Sauce
   made with chicken stock
1-1/2 tablespoons dry sherry or
   fresh lemon juice
2 eggs, separated
Salt and freshly ground white
   pepper to taste
1 egg white
1/8 teaspoon cream of tartar
2/3 cup heavy cream, whipped

Using the fine blade of a meat grinder or a food processor fitted with a metal blade, grind the turkey and then grind the spinach. Put turkey, spinach, mushrooms and parsley through grinder again. (The turkey mixture may be covered and refrigerated up to 2 days at this point. Bring to room temperature or reheat partially before proceeding with recipe.) Preheat oven to 325°F. Combine 1/4 cup of the sauce, the sherry, egg yolks, turkey mixture and salt and pepper. Adjust seasonings. Whip egg whites and cream of tartar until stiff but not dry. Fold beaten egg whites into yolk mixture alternately with whipped cream. Mixture will be quite stiff. Mound into 4 well-buttered 8-ounce custard cups or six 4-ounce custard cups. Arrange close together in a shallow baking dish. Pour boiling water into dish halfway up sides of cups. Bake in preheated oven 40 minutes or until set and cake tester inserted in center comes out clean. Mixture will not rise as much as a soufflé does. Remove cups from water and let stand 3 or 4 minutes. Invert onto serving plates and serve with remaining cream sauce poured over the top.

*When unmolding baked dishes—from mousses to timbales—loosen edges with a thin-bladed knife before inverting dish.*

# TURKEY PIE WITH STUFFING CRUST

*Serves Three or Four*

1-1/2 cups well-seasoned cooked bread stuffing
1 cup shredded cooked turkey
1/3 to 1/2 cup shredded fontina or Monterey Jack cheese
2 eggs, lightly beaten
1 cup half-and-half cream, or 1/2 cup *each* milk and turkey gravy or stock
2 tablespoons finely minced fresh parsley
1 tablespoon finely minced fresh chives
1/4 teaspoon salt
1/8 teaspoon freshly ground white pepper
1/4 teaspoon crumbled dried thyme
Paprika

Preheat oven to 350°F. Blend stuffing in blender or food processor until smooth, or mash well with fork. Press into a well-buttered 7- to 8-inch pie plate and bake in preheated oven 15 minutes, or until starting to brown. Cool on wire rack. Strew turkey over shell and top with cheese. Beat eggs with cream, parsley, chives, salt, pepper and thyme. Pour over turkey and cheese and sprinkle with paprika. Bake in preheated oven 35 to 40 minutes, or until puffy and golden and cake tester inserted in center comes out clean.

# TURKEY NOODLE PIE

*Serves Two*

1-1/2 cups cooked flat noodles
1/3 cup ricotta cheese
3 to 4 tablespoons stock
Salt and freshly ground black pepper to taste
2/3 cup turkey gravy
1 cup diced cooked turkey
1/4 cup sliced pimiento-stuffed olives (optional)
1/3 cup finely shredded fontina cheese
Paprika

Preheat oven to 350°F. Mix together well the noodles, ricotta cheese, stock, salt and pepper. Press into a well-buttered 7- to 8-inch pie plate and bake in preheated oven 10 minutes. Combine turkey gravy and turkey and spread on top of noodle crust. Sprinkle evenly with olives and fontina cheese and dust with paprika. Bake in preheated oven 15 to 20 minutes, or until heated through and cheese is melted.

---

*When dehydrating small quantities of herbs, wash, pat dry, place in single layer on paper plate and put in microwave oven on Hi 4 minutes. Crumble, jar, cover tightly and store in cool, dark place.*

---

# TURKEY TETRAZZINI

*Serves Two*

2 tablespoons butter
1 tablespoon unbleached flour
1/2 cup evaporated milk
1/2 cup stock
1 tablespoon dry sherry or dry white wine
1/8 teaspoon freshly grated nutmeg
1/8 teaspoon freshly ground white pepper
1/4 teaspoon salt
1/3 cup sliced fresh mushrooms
1-1/4 cups cooked spaghetti or tagliarini noodles
3/4 cup diced cooked turkey
1/4 cup freshly grated Parmesan cheese
3 tablespoons fresh or dry coarse whole-grain bread crumbs
Paprika
Butter

Melt 1 tablespoon of the butter until foamy. Stir in flour and cook, stirring, 2 minutes. Gradually add milk and stock; cook and stir until smooth and thickened. Add sherry and seasonings; adjust to taste. In separate skillet, melt remaining 1 tablespoon butter and sauté mushrooms until they start to brown. Preheat oven to 350°F. Combine mushrooms with half the sauce and the spaghetti. Transfer to a buttered shallow baking dish and make a hollow in center of mixture. Combine remaining sauce with turkey and mound in hollow. Mix together the cheese and crumbs and sprinkle evenly over entire mixture. Dust with paprika and dot with butter. Bake 15 to 20 minutes, or until bubbly and lightly browned.

## PENNE WITH EGGPLANT

Other "shaped" pastas, such as fusilli, shells, rigatoni, bowties and cockscombs, would also be good prepared this way. If pecorino is unavailable, use Romano or Parmesan.

*Serves Four*
1-1/2 cups Quick Tomato or Tomato Sauce
1/2 cup ricotta cheese
2 tablespoons freshly grated pecorino cheese
8 large pitted black olives, slivered
2 cups cooked penne (tubular pasta)
1-1/4 cups coarsely chopped cooked eggplant
Salt and freshly ground black pepper
1/2 cup shredded mozzarella cheese
Paprika

Preheat oven to 325°F. In a large bowl, combine Tomato Sauce, ricotta cheese, pecorino cheese and olives. Toss in penne and eggplant, season to taste and transfer to 4 ramekins or a shallow baking dish. Sprinkle with mozzarella cheese and paprika. Bake in preheated oven 20 minutes, or until heated through and bubbly.

## FUSILLI AND PORK CASSEROLE

*Serves Three or Four*
1 cup fresh bread crumbs
2 tablespoons butter, melted
1/2 teaspoon paprika
1 cup Light Cream Sauce
1/4 cup pork or chicken stock, or as needed
1/2 teaspoon ground sage
1/2 to 1 tablespoon Dijon-style mustard
3/4 cup shredded white Cheddar, Monterey Jack or fontina cheese
1-1/2 cups cooked fusilli pasta
1 cup diced cooked pork roast or chops
3/4 cup chopped unpared apple
1/4 cup minced fresh Italian parsley and tender stems
1 tablespoon minced fresh chives
Salt and freshly ground black pepper to taste

Toss bread crumbs in butter until evenly coated; mix in paprika and set aside. Preheat oven to 350°F. If cream sauce has been made ahead, reheat gently and blend in stock, sage and mustard. Add 1/4 cup of the cheese and stir until melted. Remove from heat and toss with remaining ingredients, adding additional stock if mixture seems too stiff. The pasta and pork should be well coated with sauce but not runny. Transfer to a shallow baking dish, sprinkle with remaining cheese and cover with foil. (At this point, the casserole may be refrigerated up to 2 days or frozen up to 1 week. Defrost overnight in the refrigerator and bring to room temperature before baking.) Bake in preheated oven 30 minutes. Remove foil, sprinkle evenly with bread crumb mixture and bake an additional 10 minutes, or until casserole is bubbly and crumbs have browned.

# THREE NOODLE CASSEROLES

These three recipes are guides. Use the proportions given here to create your own casseroles with the leftovers you have on hand. You may need to change the seasonings to complement whatever you have selected to substitute for the turkey, pork and ham suggested here. Each recipe serves four.

If you end up with leftover noodle casserole, make a frittata using two eggs for each cup of casserole.

2 eggs, lightly beaten
1 cup low-fat cottage cheese
1 cup sour cream or plain yoghurt
1 tablespoon grated onion and
   juices
2 teaspoons minced fresh chives
1/4 cup minced fresh parsley
3/4 cup ground cooked turkey
3 cups cooked flat noodles
1/2 teaspoon Bell's Seasoning or
   other poultry seasoning
Worcestershire sauce and Tabasco
   sauce to taste
Salt and freshly ground black
   pepper to taste
1/2 cup Buttered Bread Crumbs
Paprika

Preheat oven to 350°F. Beat together eggs, cottage cheese, sour cream and onion. Toss in chives, parsley, turkey, noodles and seasonings. Transfer to a well-buttered shallow baking dish and sprinkle evenly with crumbs and paprika. Bake in preheated oven 25 to 30 minutes, or until bubbly and crumbs are browned.

3 ounces cream cheese, at room
   temperature
1/2 cup low-fat cottage cheese
1/2 cup milk
1/2 to 1 cup shredded cooked
   pork roast
1 tablespoon grated onion and
   juices
1 tablespoon minced fresh parsley
1 tablespoon minced green onion
   tops
3 cups cooked noodles
1/2 teaspoon crumbled dried sage
Salt and freshly ground black
   pepper to taste
1/2 cup whole-grain bread crumbs
1/4 cup freshly grated Parmesan
   cheese
Butter
Paprika

Preheat oven to 350°F. Mash cream cheese and blend in cottage cheese until smooth. Add milk, pork, onion, parsley, green onion tops, noodles, sage and salt and pepper. Transfer to a buttered shallow baking dish and sprinkle evenly with crumbs and Parmesan cheese. Dot with butter and sprinkle with paprika. Bake in preheated oven 20 to 25 minutes, or until bubbly and top is browned.

1/2 cup chopped onion
2 tablespoons butter
1-1/4 cups minced cooked ham
1/4 cup minced green onion tops
1 egg, lightly beaten
3/4 cup buttermilk
3/4 cup shredded bel paese cheese

Preheat oven to 350°F. Sauté onion in butter until soft. Combine with all remaining ingredients except cheese. Transfer to a buttered shallow baking dish and sprinkle evenly with cheese. Bake in preheated oven 25 to 30 minutes, or until bubbly and cheese is melted.

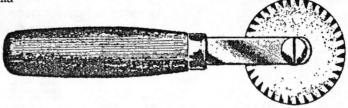

# MACARONI CASSEROLE

Diced cooked turkey, lamb or goat can be substituted for the ham.

*Serves Four to Six*
2 cups cooked elbow macaroni
1 cup diced cooked ham
1-1/2 cups Light Cream Sauce
　seasoned with dry mustard
3 tablespoons chopped fresh chives
　and/or parsley
1 cup coarsely shredded fontina or
　bel paese cheese
1/4 cup chopped pimientos
1/2 cup coarsely shredded
　mozzarella cheese
1/2 cup Buttered Bread Crumbs
Paprika

Preheat oven to 350°F. Combine macaroni, ham, cream sauce, chives, fontina and pimientos. Spread half of mixture in a lightly buttered shallow baking dish. Sprinkle mozzarella over and top with remaining macaroni mixture. Cover tightly with foil. (At this point, the casserole may be refrigerated up to 24 hours or frozen up to 2 weeks. Defrost overnight in the refrigerator and bring to room temperature before baking.) Bake in preheated oven 20 to 25 minutes. Remove foil, sprinkle evenly with bread crumbs and paprika and bake 5 to 10 minutes, or until bubbly and crumbs are browned.

# GRAIN PILAF

A grain pilaf is an excellent way to use small amounts of fresh vegetables. The accompanying chart gives the correct measure, amount of cooking liquid, oven temperature, cooking time, and approximate yield for each grain. Suggestions for vegetables and fruits and cooking liquids follow the basic recipe. Select the cooking liquid according to what you are serving with the pilaf. For example, pilaf to be served with a fish entrée should be made with fish stock, or with chicken stock if served with chicken. If you wish to add diced cooked meat or poultry to freshly made pilaf, toss it with the pilaf and return to the oven for five to ten minutes. Fluff with a fork just before serving.

Make enough pilaf so there are leftovers for another meal. To reheat, place the pilaf in a double boiler over simmering water, or in a Teflon-type skillet, adding a little stock if necessary. Add chopped cooked meats, poultry, fish or vegetables, if desired, and heat gently. Or reheat the pilaf by wrapping it in foil and placing it in a moderate oven for ten to fifteen minutes.

To add breaded meats or seafood, such as chicken breasts, veal or pork steaks, or calimari steaks, to leftover grain pilaf, the pilaf and breaded food must be reheated separately. To reheat the breaded food, warm a small amount of butter and/or oil in a skillet over medium heat and add chopped tomatoes. When the tomatoes just begin to soften, dice the breaded

## GUIDELINES FOR COOKING GRAIN PILAFS

| GRAIN | AMOUNT | LIQUID | OVEN TEMP. | COOKING TIME | APPROX. YIELD |
|---|---|---|---|---|---|
| Barley | 1 cup | 3 cups | 375°F | 45–50 min. | 3 cups |
| Bulghur | 1 cup | 2 cups | 350°F | 30 min. | 2 cups |
| Brown rice | 1 cup | 2 cups + 2 T. | 350°F | 40–45 min. | 3 cups |
| Millet | ½ cup | 1 cup + 2 T. | 350°F | 30 min. | 4 cups |
| Rice and broken, very thin coil vermicelli | ½ cup each | 1¾ cups | 350°F | 20–25 min. | 2 cups |
| Steel-cut oats | 1 cup | 2 cups | 350°F | 30 min. | 2 cups |
| White rice | 1 cup | 2 cups | 350°F | 30 min. | 3 cups |
| Wild rice* | 1 cup | 3 cups | 375°F | 45–60 min. | 4 cups |

*Wash, soak in water to cover 1 hour and drain thoroughly.*

food and add to the skillet. Raise the heat and cook until just heated through. Too much cooking will toughen the meat. Toss the tomato-meat mixture with reheated pilaf just before serving.

Leftover grain pilafs can also be made into soups with cooked vegetables you have on hand. Heat the pilaf with any rich stock, add the vegetable, heat thoroughly and season as desired. Some complementary pilaf and vegetable combinations are: steel-cut oats and julienned cooked beets, bulghur and shredded beet greens, brown rice and cauliflowerets (purée and then reheat), and millet with corn kernels and green beans or peas.

These versatile pilafs can also be combined with cheese, ham and herbs to make Grain Pilaf Casserole, added to beaten eggs to make a frittata, cooked with diced raw root vegetables in stock to make Grain and Root Vegetable Soup, and used as a filling for stuffed vegetables.

1/4 to 1/3 cup minced raw vegetables
1 to 2 garlic cloves, minced
2 tablespoons butter and/or rendered chicken fat or peanut oil
Grain
Cooking liquid
2 to 3 tablespoons chopped fresh herbs

Preheat oven. Sauté vegetables and garlic in butter 3 minutes, stirring often. Add grain and cook, stirring, 5 to 10 minutes to brown lightly. Bring cooking liquid to boil. Pat grain evenly into pan and pour boiling liquid over grain. Cover tightly, transfer pan to preheated oven and bake until moisture is absorbed. Fluff with a fork and toss in herbs.

**SUGGESTED COOKING LIQUIDS**
Well-seasoned stock, stock and dry white wine, stock and tomato or V-8 juice, tomato juice, fish stock (if serving with seafood).

**SUGGESTED RAW VEGETABLES AND FRUITS** Onion, bell pepper, carrot, celery, mushrooms, apples, pears.

**SUGGESTED ADDITIONS JUST BEFORE SERVING** Toasted walnuts, pine nuts, slivered almonds; sliced olives; chopped sautéed chicken livers; plumped raisins or currants; grated Parmesan or Romano cheese; shredded Monterey Jack, Gruyère, or fontina cheese; cooked lentils, peas, or green beans; grated lemon rind.

---

*Lightly toasted unsalted hulled sunflower seeds are a passable substitute for pine nuts.*

# GRAIN PILAF CASSEROLE

You can mix and match any Grain Pilaf with almost any meat or poultry—duck, chicken, turkey, veal, pork, game, beef or lamb tongue—using this basic recipe as a guide. One-third cup cooked vegetables—peas, cut-up green beans, chopped broccoli—or chopped raisins and/or water chestnuts can also be added.

*Serves Three or Four*
3/4 cup freshly grated Parmesan cheese
3 cups cooked any Grain Pilaf
1/2 cup minced cooked ham
3/4 cup sour cream
1/2 cup milk
1/4 cup chopped fresh parsley
1/2 cup minced green onions and some tops
1 teaspoon crumbled dried basil
1/2 teaspoon paprika
1/4 teaspoon salt
1/4 teaspoon freshly ground black pepper

Preheat oven to 350°F. Reserving 1/4 cup of the Parmesan cheese, combine all ingredients. Transfer to a buttered shallow baking dish, sprinkle with reserved cheese, cover with foil and bake in preheated oven 25 to 30 minutes or until heated through.

## WHEAT BERRY AND LAMB CASSEROLE

*Serves Two or Three*
1/2 cup minced onion
3 large garlic cloves, minced
2 tablespoons butter
2 teaspoons dry mustard
1 cup shredded cooked lamb
1-1/2 cups cooked wheat berries
1 large ripe tomato, chopped
1/4 cup chopped fresh parsley
1/4 cup chopped green onion tops
1/2 cup coarsely shredded fontina
   or Gruyère cheese
Salt and freshly ground black
   pepper to taste
Paprika

Preheat oven to 350°F. Sauté onion
and garlic in butter, covered, until
soft. Sprinkle with mustard and
cook, stirring, 2 minutes. Add
lamb and cook, stirring, 2 minutes.
Add wheat berries, tomato, parsley,
onion tops, cheese and salt and
pepper. Blend well and transfer to
a shallow baking dish. Sprinkle
with paprika and bake in preheated
oven 15 to 20 minutes, or until
heated through.

## SOYBEAN–MILLET CASSEROLE

Serve this healthful combination
with a green salad. Add flaked
cooked firm white fish or shellfish
marinated in fresh lemon juice for
a heartier meal.

*Serves Two*
1/2 cup minced onion
1/4 cup minced celery
1 teaspoon minced garlic
1/4 cup sliced mushrooms
3 tablespoons butter
3/4 cup cooked soybeans
1/2 cup cooked millet
1/2 cup chopped tomato
1/3 cup grated Cheddar cheese
1/2 teaspoon salt
1/4 teaspoon freshly ground black
   pepper
1/4 teaspoon ground thyme
1/4 teaspoon ground oregano
1 egg, lightly beaten
1 tablespoon dry bread crumbs

Preheat oven to 350°F. Sauté
onion, celery, garlic and mushrooms
in 2 tablespoons of the butter
until onion starts to soften. Combine
with soybeans, millet, tomato, 3
tablespoons of the cheese, seasonings and egg. Transfer to a buttered
shallow baking dish and sprinkle
with bread crumbs and remaining
cheese. Dot with remaining butter
and bake in preheated oven 25 to
30 minutes until top is golden.

## ZUCCHINI AND RICE CASSEROLE

*Serves Two*
2/3 cup shredded fontina or
   Monterey Jack cheese
1 egg, lightly beaten
1/4 cup milk
3 tablespoons sour cream
1 tablespoon grated onion and
   juices
1/2 cup cooked shredded
   zucchini or frozen peas
   (unthawed)
1 cup cooked white or brown rice
1/2 teaspoon salt
1/4 teaspoon freshly ground black
   pepper
2 tablespoons minced fresh parsley
3 tablespoons minced green onion
   tops
2 teaspoons melted butter or
   safflower oil
1 teaspoon fresh lemon juice
Paprika

Preheat oven to 350°F. Combine
1/3 cup of the cheese with all
remaining ingredients except paprika.
Transfer to a buttered shallow
baking dish. Sprinkle remaining
cheese evenly over top and sprinkle
with paprika. Bake in preheated
oven 20 to 25 minutes, or until set
and lightly browned.

*Reserve legume cooking water to
use as part of the liquid in
whole-grain bread dough.*

## MASHED POTATO CASSEROLE

*Serves Four to Six*

1/3 cup grated sharp Cheddar
   cheese
2 cups mashed potatoes
1 cup finely diced cooked veal
1/4 cup freshly grated Parmesan
   cheese
2 ounces cream cheese, cut into
   bits
2 tablespoons minced green bell
   pepper
2 tablespoons minced green onion
   and some tops
2 tablespoons minced pimiento
1 egg yolk

Preheat oven to 350°F. Reserve 2
tablespoons of the grated Cheddar
cheese. With a fork, combine all
remaining ingredients thoroughly
and transfer to a well-buttered
shallow baking dish. Sprinkle with
reserved Cheddar cheese and bake
in preheated oven 15 to 20 minutes,
or until puffed and browned. (This
dish may be made a day ahead
and kept refrigerated, or it may be
frozen up to 2 weeks. Defrost in
refrigerator overnight and bake an
additional 10 minutes when going
directly from refrigerator to oven.)

---

*Mash cooked potatoes or yams
and add to yeast bread doughs.*

---

## MASHED POTATO CRUST

Fill this lightly crisp, rich crust
with hot Mushroom Sauce, Creamed
Vegetables, plain steamed vegetables
or sautéed mushrooms.

*Enough for One Nine-
or Ten-inch Crust*

2 cups seasoned mashed potatoes
2 eggs, lightly beaten
1 cup coarsely ground cooked
   meat or vegetable
Seasonings and herbs to taste
Butter

Preheat oven to 350°F. Combine
all ingredients, except butter, and
press lightly and evenly into a
well-buttered 9- or 10-inch pie
plate. Dot with butter and bake 20
minutes or until bubbly.

### VARIATIONS

● Sprinkle grated Cheddar,
Monterey Jack or Gruyère cheese
over filled crust and broil to melt
cheese.
● Add sautéed minced onions
and garlic to potato mixture.
● Omit filling; sprinkle with grated
Cheddar, Monterey Jack or Gruyère
cheese and broil to melt cheese.

● Fold grated Cheddar, Monterey
Jack or Gruyère cheese into potato
mixture. Omit filling, pour a little
heavy cream over crust and bake
in 375°F oven until heated through.

## SHEPHERD'S PIE

Though traditionally prepared with
lamb, this well-known English dish
can be adapted to any leftover
stew, gravied meat, or creamed
poultry or vegetables.

*Serves Two*

1-1/2 cups prepared meat and/or
   vegetable mixture
1 egg, lightly beaten
1 cup mashed or riced potatoes
2 tablespoons freshly grated
   Parmesan cheese
Salt, freshly ground black pepper
   and chopped fresh herbs to
   taste

Preheat oven to 350°F. Divide
meat mixture between two 6-inch
ramekins and place in preheated
oven to heat through. Combine egg,
potatoes, cheese and seasonings
and mix until well blended. Mound
potato mixture on top of meat
mixture, covering entire surface.
Immediately return to oven and
bake 15 to 20 minutes, or until
bubbly and golden.

## SPANISH RICE CASSEROLE

Almost any cooked vegetable, such as peas, cut-up green beans, diced asparagus, is a good substitute for the corn. Diced cooked chicken or turkey can replace the ham.

*Serves Two or Three*
2 cups cooked white and/or brown rice or Rice Pilaf
1/2 cup cooked corn kernels
1/2 cup diced cooked ham or tongue
1-1/2 cups Creole Sauce
1/4 cup grated sharp Cheddar cheese

Preheat oven to 350°F. Layer half the rice in a well-buttered shallow baking dish. Strew corn and ham over and cover with remaining rice. Pour sauce over and sprinkle with cheese. Bake in preheated oven 30 minutes, or until heated through and cheese is melted.

---

*Wild rice is not a true rice. It is a difficult-to-harvest water grain.*

---

## WILD RICE CASSEROLE

*Serves Two*
2 cups cooked wild rice
3 tablespoons slivered blanched almonds, browned in 1 table-spoon butter
4 to 5 black olives, slivered
1/2 cup shredded fontina or bel paese cheese
1/2 teaspoon crumbled dried basil
Salt and freshly ground black pepper to taste
1/4 cup stock, or as needed for moisture

Preheat oven to 350°F. Combine all ingredients and transfer to a buttered shallow baking dish. Bake in preheated oven 20 minutes, or until heated through and bubbly.

## WILD RICE STUFFING

For duck, goose, chicken or Cornish game hens.

*Makes Approximately Two and One-half Cups*
1/2 cup dried currants
2 tablespoons sweet vermouth
1 cup minced onion
1/2 cup minced celery and leaves
2 tablespoons rendered chicken fat or butter
2 cups cooked wild rice (cooked in stock)
Salt and freshly ground black pepper to taste

Combine currants and vermouth. Stirring occasionally, let stand until currants are soft. Sauté onion and celery in rendered fat until onion is soft. Add currants and any remaining liquid, rice and salt and pepper. Cook, stirring often, until rice has absorbed any liquid. Let cool and spoon into bird just before roasting.

## BULGHUR STUFFING

For chicken or Cornish game hens.

*Makes Approximately Two and One-half Cups*
2 cups cooked bulghur
6 tablespoons chopped raisins
6 tablespoons chopped blanched almonds
1/4 teaspoon ground turmeric
1/4 teaspoon ground cinnamon
1/8 teaspoon ground ginger
1/8 teaspoon ground cloves
2 to 3 tablespoons honey
Salt and freshly ground white pepper to taste

Combine all ingredients and toss together until well mixed. Spoon into bird just before roasting.

---

*When roasting wild duck, place chopped celery and apple in cavity to reduce gamey taste; bake stuffing in a casserole.*

---

# BASIC BREAD STUFFING

This bread stuffing recipe can be adapted to individual taste and to what you have on hand. Allow approximately one-half cup stuffing for each pound of bird.

*Makes Approximately Six Cups*
1 cup chopped onion
1 cup chopped celery and leaves
1 to 2 garlic cloves, minced
1/3 cup butter and/or rendered
   chicken fat
1/2 cup chopped fresh parsley
1 to 2 eggs, lightly beaten
   (optional)
6 cups 1- to 2-day-old bread cubes
Stock or milk to moisten, as desired
1 teaspoon salt
1/2 teaspoon freshly ground black
   pepper
1/2 teaspoon Bell's Seasoning or
   other poultry seasoning
1/4 teaspoon ground sage

Sauté onion, celery and garlic in butter until onion is soft. Transfer to a large mixing bowl, add all remaining ingredients and toss well; adjust seasonings.

## SUGGESTED ADDITIONS TO BREAD STUFFING

● One to 2 cups minced cooked ham and/or chicken.
● One to 2 cups cooked crumbled sausage or beef.
● One pint oysters, frizzled in butter and coarsely chopped; use the juices for part of the liquid.
● Chopped cooked giblets and livers.
● Chopped cooked sliced or diced mushrooms.
● Madeira, dry sherry or brandy for part of the liquid.
● Chopped unpared tart apples, raisins, cranberries; use fresh orange juice for part of the liquid.
● Chopped cooked chestnuts.
● Cornbread for part of the bread.
● Chopped fresh spinach, Swiss chard or sorrel.
● Chopped raw sunchokes.

## TIPS ON PREPARING AND COOKING BREAD STUFFINGS

● Mix ingredients together by tossing with 2 forks.
● To test for seasoning, sauté a small amount of stuffing in a little butter.
● Stuffing may be made ahead and refrigerated up to 24 hours.
● Never fill a bird until just before roasting.
● Put extra stuffing into buttered muffin tins and bake with the bird. Serve as a garnish to roasted bird.

## LEFTOVER STUFFING SUGGESTIONS

● Form into balls and brown on all sides in butter.
● Form into patties, brown on both sides in butter and top with poached eggs.

# BREAD STUFFING FOR FISH

*Makes Approximately One and One-fourth Cups*
1/4 cup minced onion
1/4 cup minced celery
3 tablespoons butter
3 tablespoons minced shallots
1/3 cup minced fresh mushrooms
1 cup finely chopped spinach
1 cup finely chopped sorrel
1/2 tablespoon fresh lemon juice
1/2 teaspoon salt
1/2 teaspoon paprika
1/4 teaspoon freshly ground white
   pepper
2 tablespoons heavy cream
1 to 2 cups coarse dry bread
   crumbs

Sauté onion and celery in butter 3 minutes. Add shallots and mushrooms and cook, stirring, 3 minutes. Add spinach and sorrel and cook until just wilted. Remove from heat and add lemon juice and seasonings. Stir in cream and toss in enough bread crumbs to make a mixture that will hold loosely together. Adjust seasonings and just before cooking fish, stuff cavity.

## BASIC METHOD FOR CREPES

Crêpes are a good addition to any menu: a batch can be filled and refrigerated or frozen for a future meal; they are easy to prepare and make an elegant presentation; they are money savers, especially when you have used leftovers to make the filling; and you can add an extra egg yolk or white to the crêpe batter. If you haven't enough filling for all of the crêpes, dust the unfilled ones with powdered sugar and serve for breakfast or lunch with jam or a fruit sauce.

Information on filling and baking pasta rolls and shells is also included in this section. The suggestions for filling crêpes can be used for stuffed pastas as well.

### BASIC CREPE BATTER

*Makes Twenty-four Crêpes*
1-1/3 cups milk
4 eggs
1 cup unbleached flour
1/2 teaspoon salt
1 tablespoon safflower oil or
    melted butter
Butter for cooking crêpes

Place all ingredients in a blender, mix well, cover and refrigerate for at least 2 hours or up to 3 days.

Heat a 6-inch crêpe pan or heavy skillet over medium heat. To test for proper temperature, flick a few drops of water on the surface of the pan. If the drops dance about on the surface, the pan is ready. Butter the pan lightly. When the butter bubbles, lower heat slightly, stir batter, and pour about 3 tablespoons of it into the pan. Quickly tilt the pan from side to side to coat the bottom. Cook until just golden on the underside. Turn, using your fingers to help, and cook the second side 1 minute, or until just starting to color. Remove crêpe to a cooling rack and repeat with remaining batter. It is important that you stir the batter each time before adding more to the pan. If the batter thickens, stir in extra milk to re-create original consistency. Stack the crêpes as they are cooked. When cool, fill or wrap well and refrigerate or freeze according to the directions that follow.

### FILLING AND BAKING CREPES

You may choose to make free-roll crêpes, where the crêpes are rolled around the filling and ends are left free, or tucked-roll crêpes, where the ends are folded in as the crêpe is rolled, forming a more compact cylinder. To prepare 8 free-roll crêpes or 12 tucked-roll crêpes, you will need 1-1/2 cups filling, 1 to 1-1/2 cups sauce and 2/3 cup grated Gruyère cheese. Use 2 tablespoons filling on crêpe for tucked-roll style and 3 tablespoons for free-roll style and form as described. Spread 1/2 cup of the sauce on the bottom of a shallow 6-1/2- by 10-1/2-inch baking dish. Arrange crêpes close together, seam side down, on sauce, free-rolls crosswise in dish, tucked rolls in 4 rows lengthwise. Spread 1/2 to 1 cup sauce over crêpes and sprinkle with the 2/3 cup grated cheese. Bake in preheated 350°F oven 15 to 20 minutes, or until heated through and bubbly and cheese is melted.

If you prefer to serve the free-roll crêpes on individual plates rather than sauced in a baking dish, arrange them in a buttered shallow baking dish and bake in a preheated 350°F oven 8 to 10 minutes, or until heated through. Arrange the crêpes on warm serving plates, spoon hot sauce over the top and garnish.

Crêpes filled with soft mixtures, such as Cooked-Vegetable Purées, are usually best if not sauced. Prepare and bake them in the same manner as for serving crêpes on individual plates, but butter the baking dish heavily and drizzle about 1-1/2 tablespoons melted butter over the crêpes before placing them in the oven. Transfer to warm serving plates, pour butter from baking dish over and garnish.

## FILLING AND BAKING PASTA ROLLS AND SHELLS

Cook manicotti in boiling salted water, to which 1/2 teaspoon of oil has been added, for 6 minutes. Drain well, then immerse in ice water to stop the cooking. (The manicotti can be stored, immersed in water, up to 3 days in the refrigerator.) Carefully remove from the water and place on a wire rack to drain well. An 8-ounce package of manicotti contains 14 rolls; you will need 3-1/2 to 4 cups of filling and 2 cups of sauce for this amount. Line a shallow baking dish with 1 cup Tomato Sauce, place filled rolls in one layer close together on sauce and top with an additional cup of sauce. Cover dish with foil and bake in a preheated 350°F oven 15 minutes. Remove foil, sprinkle with 1/2 cup freshly grated Parmesan or Romano cheese and return to the oven for 10 to 15 minutes, or until sauce bubbles and cheese is browned.

Cannelloni squares are cooked and drained in the same way as manicotti shells, but reduce the cooking time to about 1 to 2 minutes for fresh pasta. Fill each wrapper (usually about 4 inches square) with approximately 3 tablespoons filling and roll as for free-roll crêpes. Sauce and bake as directed for manicotti. Or bake as

for unsauced crêpes, transfer 2 rolls to each warm serving plate and sauce one with a cream sauce and one with a tomato sauce.

Jumbo shells are also cooked and drained in the same way as manicotti, but require about 9 minutes of cooking time. Each shell will take about 2 tablespoons of filling. Line the baking dish with sauce as directed for manicotti and place the filled shells on top with the openings facing upward. Blanket with sauce and bake as for manicotti.

## FREEZING CREPES, FILLED CREPES AND FILLED PASTA

Unfilled crêpes may be stacked, wrapped well in aluminum foil and frozen up to 2 months, then defrosted in the refrigerator. Filled crêpes and pasta in which cream sauce has been used to bind the filling may be frozen on a baking sheet (sheet frozen), then wrapped well and kept up to 1 month. Line the baking dish with sauce as described in the section on Filling and Baking Crêpes, place frozen filled crêpes or pasta in the dish and defrost in the refrigerator. Blanket with sauce and bake as directed. Crêpes and pasta that are arranged in a baking dish and sauced before freezing should be covered tightly with aluminum foil and frozen no longer than 2 weeks.

Defrost completely in the refrigerator before baking. Filled crêpes and pasta in which an egg yolk has been used to bind the filling or those which have a puréed filling, such as squash, should never be frozen. If you are using these types of fillings, freeze the unfilled crêpes and fill shortly before baking.

## CREPE-BATTER VARIATIONS

● Substitute whole-wheat pastry flour for all or part of the unbleached flour. Crêpes will be less delicate.
● Substitute skim milk, half-and-half cream, heavy cream, rich stock, club soda or soft tofu (bean curd) for 1/3 cup of the milk.
● Substitute nondegerminated cornmeal or potato or garbanzo flour for 1/3 cup of the flour.
● Season batter with ground thyme, oregano or marjoram; minced fresh chives and/or parsley; freshly grated nutmeg; or freshly ground white pepper.

## SAUCE SUGGESTIONS

The following sauces may be used to line and blanket the baking dish or may be spooned over crêpes that have been baked unsauced. (You may need to thin the sauces if they have thickened from standing, especially the cream sauces.)

- Tomato Sauce, Quick Tomato Sauce, Creole Sauce, Marinara Sauce.
- Curry Cream Sauce, Medium Cream Sauce seasoned with dry mustard, Cheese Sauce, Creamy Quick Tomato Sauce, Tomato Cheese Sauce.
- Mushroom Sauce or Quick Mushroom Sauce.

## CREPE AND PASTA FILLING SUGGESTIONS

All of these filling suggestions are suitable for crêpes, manicotti or jumbo shells. Only the smooth cream-sauce-based fillings should be used to fill cannelloni. To prepare a coarsely ground or finely minced cooked meat, poultry or fish filling, use equal parts ground meat, or part puréed or finely minced cooked vegetable, and Medium Cream Sauce, and season as desired. Lamb, beef, chicken, turkey, calves' liver, veal, ham, firm white fish and shellfish are all good prepared in this way.

Remember, these are only suggestions. Vary the choice of sauce given with each filling to your own taste.

**BROCCOLI** Finely chopped cooked broccoli, grated onion, very finely minced garlic, grated Cheddar cheese, ground marjoram, salt and freshly ground black pepper, Medium Cream Sauce to bind, if desired. Mushroom Sauce or Quick Mushroom Sauce for lining and blanketing; grated Cheddar cheese for topping.

**CORN** Cooked corn kernels or scraped cooked corn, ground beef frizzled with minced onion and garlic, chopped ripe tomato, ground oregano, salt and freshly ground black pepper, Cheddar Cheese or Tomato Cheese Sauce to bind. Cheddar Cheese or Tomato Cheese Sauce for lining and blanketing; shredded Monterey Jack, fontina or Cheddar cheese for topping.

**SPINACH** Chopped cooked spinach, cottage or ricotta cheese, minced fresh chives and/or parsley, salt and freshly ground white pepper, freshly grated nutmeg, paprika, egg yolk to bind. Medium Cream Sauce seasoned with dry mustard for lining and blanketing; grated Gruyère cheese for topping.

**SWISS CHARD** Chopped Swiss chard, chopped onion and minced garlic cooked until soft in butter, cream cheese, chopped walnuts, freshly grated nutmeg, salt and freshly ground white pepper. Tomato Cheese Sauce for lining and blanketing.

**HAM** Coarsely ground or finely minced cooked ham and mushrooms, cottage cheese, minced fresh chives and/or green onion tops, salt and freshly ground black pepper, egg yolk to bind. Cheese Sauce for lining and blanketing; shredded Monterey Jack cheese for topping.

**TURKEY** Coarsely ground cooked turkey, finely minced cooked asparagus, finely minced hard-cooked eggs, minced fresh chives and/or parsley, Cheddar Cheese Sauce made with half stock and half milk, ground marjoram or thyme, salt and freshly ground white pepper. Creamy Quick Tomato Sauce for lining and blanketing; grated Cheddar cheese for topping.

**CHEESE** Ricotta cheese, shredded bel paese cheese, freshly grated Parmesan cheese, chopped fresh parsley and chives, freshly grated nutmeg, salt and freshly ground white pepper, egg to bind. Quick Tomato Sauce for lining and blanketing.

**CHEESE** Ricotta cheese, shredded mozzarella cheese, freshly grated Romano cheese, chopped fresh parsley, toasted pine nuts, freshly grated nutmeg, salt and freshly ground white pepper. Marinara Sauce for lining and blanketing; freshly grated Romano cheese for topping.

**POT ROAST** Shredded cooked pot roast, minced onion and garlic lightly sautéed in butter, coarse dry bread crumbs, shredded fontina cheese, minced fresh oregano, salt and freshly ground black pepper, stock to moisten. Creole Sauce for lining and blanketing; freshly grated Parmesan cheese for topping.

**LAMB** Coarsely ground lamb roast, finely minced cooked spinach or Swiss chard, finely minced garlic, freshly grated Parmesan cheese, crumbled dried rosemary, salt and freshly ground black pepper. Quick Tomato Sauce for lining and blanketing; shredded fontina cheese for topping.

**FISH** Minced flaked cooked firm white fish or salmon, freshly grated Parmesan cheese, finely chopped fresh parsley, finely chopped pimiento, Medium Cream Sauce made with equal parts fish stock and half-and-half cream, Seafood Seasoning, salt and freshly ground white pepper. Medium Cream Sauce (as above) for lining and blanketing; medium-fine dry bread crumbs and paprika for topping.

## PUMPKIN CREPES

Use cooked winter squash or yams for these rich crêpes. Extra grated Parmesan cheese may be sprinkled on the crêpes before baking.

*Makes Fourteen or Sixteen Filled Crêpes*
1 cup ricotta cheese
1 cup pumpkin purée
1 teaspoon grated onion
1/2 cup freshly grated Parmesan cheese
3 tablespoons minced fresh parsley
1 tablespoon minced fresh chives
1/2 cup finely chopped pecans
1 tablespoon dry sherry
Freshly grated nutmeg, ground cloves, salt and freshly ground white pepper to taste
14 or 16 crêpes
3 to 4 tablespoons butter, melted
Freshly grated Parmesan cheese

Preheat oven to 350°F. Beat ricotta cheese lightly and blend in pumpkin purée, onion, 1/2 cup Parmesan cheese, parsley, chives, pecans, sherry and seasonings. Following Basic Method for Crêpes, fill crêpes with a scant 2 tablespoons pumpkin mixture, leaving ends untucked. Arrange just touching in a heavily buttered shallow baking dish and drizzle melted butter over the top. Bake in preheated oven 8 to 10 minutes until heated through and lightly golden; do not allow to dry out. Transfer to heated plates or platter and pour any butter left in dish over crêpes.

## CHICKEN LIVER AND SWEETBREAD CREPES

*Makes Eight or Twelve Filled Crêpes*
4 cooked chicken livers
2/3 cup diced cooked chicken
1/2 cup finely diced cooked sweetbreads
1/4 cup freshly grated Parmesan cheese (optional)
1 ounce cream cheese, softened
1 cup Medium Cream Sauce made with half stock and half milk or half-and-half cream
Crumbled dried basil, salt and freshly ground white pepper to taste
8 or 12 crêpes
1-1/2 cups Light Cream Sauce flavored with dry sherry
2/3 cup grated Gruyère cheese

On medium blade of meat grinder, grind together chicken livers, chicken and sweetbreads. Place in a bowl and toss with Parmesan cheese; set aside. Add cream cheese to Medium Cream Sauce and heat until cheese is incorporated into the sauce. Remove from the heat and cool slightly. Stir in liver mixture and seasonings. Following Basic Method for Crêpes, fill crêpes, sauce with Light Cream Sauce, top with Gruyère cheese and bake.

*A 3- to 3-1/2-pound chicken will yield 2-1/2 to 3 cups chicken meat.*

# DESSERTS

## WHITE CAKE

*Makes One Eight-inch*
*One-layer Cake*
1/4 pound butter, softened
1 cup granulated sugar
1/2 cup cornstarch
1 cup cake flour
2-1/2 tablespoons baking powder
1/2 teaspoon salt
1/2 cup milk
1 teaspoon pure vanilla extract
3 egg whites
1/8 teaspoon cream of tartar

Butter an 8-inch square cake pan
with Lecithin Butter. Preheat oven
to 350°F. Cream together butter
and sugar. Sift together cornstarch,
flour, baking powder and salt.
Combine milk and vanilla. Add
liquid to butter mixture alternately
with flour mixture, blending well.
Beat egg whites with cream of
tartar until stiff but not dry.
Gently fold whites into batter and
spoon into prepared pan. Bake in
preheated oven 35 minutes, or
until cake tests done. Cool on wire
rack.

*Cake is done when it pulls away*
*from pan sides and tester inserted*
*in center comes out clean.*

## YELLOW CAKE

*Makes One Eight-inch*
*Two-layer Cake*
1/4 pound butter, softened
1 cup granulated sugar
3 egg yolks
1-3/4 cups cake flour
2 teaspoons baking powder
1/2 cup milk
1/2 teaspoon almond extract

Butter two 8-inch round cake pans
with Lecithin Butter. Preheat oven
to 350°F. Cream together butter
and sugar, add yolks and blend
well. Sift together flour and baking
powder and add to butter mixture
alternately with milk. Divide equally
between prepared pans. Bake 20
to 25 minutes, or until cake tests
done. Cool on wire rack.

## CHOCOLATE CAKE

*Makes One Eight-inch*
*Two-layer Cake*
1/2 pound butter, softened
1 cup granulated sugar
1 egg yolk
1 teaspoon baking soda, dissolved
   in 1/2 tablespoon hot water
1 cup milk
1-1/2 cups unbleached flour
2 ounces unsweetened baking
   chocolate, melted and cooled
   slightly
1 teaspoon pure vanilla extract

Butter two 8-inch round cake pans
with Lecithin Butter. Preheat oven
to 350°F. Cream together butter
and sugar, add egg yolk and blend
well. Add baking soda and water,
1/2 cup of the milk and 1 cup of
the flour, beating while adding.
Stir in chocolate and add vanilla,
remaining 1/2 cup milk and remaining 1/2 cup flour. Blend well and
spoon equally into prepared pans.
Bake in preheated oven 25 minutes,
or until cake tests done. Cool on
wire rack.

*You need 1-1/2 cups icing to*
*frost the top and sides of an*
*8-inch cake.*

## COCOA ANGEL REFRIGERATOR CAKE

*Makes One Eight-inch*
*One-layer Cake*
3/4 cup egg whites (7), at
    room temperature
1/4 teaspoon salt
1/2 tablespoon cream of tartar
2/3 cup granulated sugar
1/2 teaspoon pure vanilla extract
2/3 cup unbleached flour
2-1/2 tablespoons unsweetened
    cocoa powder
1 cup Pastry Cream (any flavor)
1 recipe Butter Cream (any flavor)

Preheat oven to 400°F. Beat together egg whites and salt until light and frothy. Add cream of tartar and continue beating until stiff peaks form. Two tablespoons at a time, beat in 1/3 cup of the sugar until mixture is smooth, glossy and holds firm peaks. Stir in vanilla. Sift together 3 times the

> *Add powdered sugar or gelatin (softened in cold water, then dissolved over hot water and cooled) in a thin stream to heavy cream being whipped for use as a cake filling. The cream will stay stiff longer.*

> *When freezing frosted cakes, wrap with plastic wrap that has been rubbed with unsalted butter. The wrap won't stick. Or prop the plastic wrapping away from the cake with toothpicks.*

remaining sugar, the flour and cocoa powder. Sprinkle about 2 tablespoons over egg white mixture and gently fold in, being careful not to overmix. Repeat with remaining flour mixture until all is incorporated. Spoon into an ungreased 8-inch angel food cake pan. Bake in preheated oven 25 minutes, or until cake shrinks away from sides of pan. If cake appears to be browning too fast, cover with a piece of aluminum foil the last 10 minutes. Remove pan from oven and invert onto a glass to cool completely. Remove cake from pan and slice in 3 layers. Place a layer on a serving plate and spread with half of the Pastry Cream. Top with a second layer and spread with remaining Pastry Cream. Set last layer on top and ice top and sides of cake with Butter Cream. Cover and refrigerate overnight before serving.

## TRIFLE

Use stale white, yellow, sponge or pound cake sliced three-fourths inch thick or halved ladyfingers for this English holiday favorite.

*Serves Four to Six*
2 cups fresh raspberries
3 tablespoons sifted powdered
    sugar
6 to 8 pieces stale cake
1/3 cup rum or dry sherry
1-1/2 cups Pastry Cream
1/2 cup heavy cream
Lightly toasted sliced almonds

Set about 30 berries aside. Toss remaining berries with powdered sugar and set aside. Cut cake pieces into 1-inch strips and drizzle evenly with rum. Let stand 20 minutes. Arrange half the cake strips in a 6-inch soufflé dish or straight-sided crystal bowl. Cover with half the sugared raspberries and pour half the Pastry Cream over. Repeat layers. Cover and chill no more than 30 minutes. Whip cream until stiff peaks form and spread over layers. Ring whipped cream layer with reserved raspberries and sprinkle center with almonds. Serve immediately.

# ALMOND BISCUIT COOKIES

*Makes Approximately Thirty-two*
1/2 cup lard, softened
1/3 cup granulated sugar
2 egg yolks
1/4 teaspoon anise extract
1 teaspoon freshly grated lemon
   rind
1 cup ground almonds, or
   as needed
1/2 cup sifted unbleached flour
1/8 teaspoon salt
1/4 cup dry sherry

Prepare a baking sheet with Lecithin Oil or Lecithin Butter. Preheat oven to 400°F. Cream together lard and sugar until well blended. One at a time, beat in egg yolks. Blend in anise extract, lemon rind and 1/2 cup of the almonds. Sift flour with salt and stir into almond mixture alternately with sherry, mixing well. Spread remaining ground almonds on a sheet of waxed paper. Drop dough onto almonds in rough balls the size of a large marble. With your fingertips, gently roll dough into smooth balls, coating on all sides with the ground almonds and adding more almonds if needed. Place balls 1 inch apart on prepared baking sheet. With 2 fingers, gently flatten balls to 1/2-inch thickness. Bake in preheated oven 10 minutes, or until golden. Remove immediately to wire rack, cool and store in airtight container up to 3 days, or freeze up to 2 months.

# ALMOND MACAROONS

*Makes Four to Five Dozen*
1 cup almonds
3 egg whites
1/8 teaspoon cream of tartar
1/8 teaspoon salt
1-1/3 cups firmly packed brown
   sugar, sieved
1/4 teaspoon ground allspice
1 teaspoon pure vanilla extract, or
   1/2 teaspoon almond extract

Oil a baking sheet with Lecithin Oil. Grind almonds in a nut grinder (a blender or food processor will release too much oil) to measure approximately 2-1/3 cups very loosely packed. Set aside. Preheat oven to 325°F. Beat together egg whites, cream of tartar and salt until stiff peaks form. Combine sugar and allspice. Two tablespoons at a time, beat sugar mixture into egg white mixture until smooth, glossy and holds firm peaks. Beat in vanilla. Sprinkle about 2 tablespoons ground almonds over egg white mixture and gently fold in, being careful not to overmix. Repeat with remaining almonds until all are incorporated. Drop by heaping half-tablespoonfuls onto prepared baking sheet about 1 inch apart, swirling top to form a cookie about 3/4 inch thick. Bake in preheated oven 12 minutes, or until lightly golden. Remove immediately to wire rack, cool and store in airtight container up to 2 days, or freeze up to 3 weeks.

**PECAN MACAROONS** Use 1 cup pecan halves in place of the almonds. (When ground, there will be only about 1-2/3 cups loosely packed.) If desired, substitute 1/2 teaspoon ground cinnamon for the allspice.

**CHOCOLATE PECAN MACAROONS** Mix with ground pecans in Pecan Macaroons before folding into egg white mixture 1/2 cup finely grated semisweet baking chocolate.

---

*Check expiration date on baking powder can. To test, stir 1 teaspoon into 1/3 cup hot water. If mixture really bubbles, baking powder can still be used.*

---

*If you've ground too many nuts for a recipe, store the extra in the freezer. They keep well and can be used without defrosting first.*

## LINZER COOKIES

*Makes Approximately
Three and One-half Dozen*
1/4 pound butter, softened
1/2 cup firmly packed brown
   sugar, sieved
1 egg yolk
1/2 teaspoon firmly packed freshly
   grated lemon rind
3/4 cup sifted unbleached flour
1/2 teaspoon ground cinnamon
1/4 teaspoon ground cloves
3/4 cup ground almonds
Cherry, plum, apricot, peach or
   other jam

Cream together butter and sugar
until well blended. Beat in yolk
and lemon rind. Sift together flour,
cinnamon and cloves. Toss with
almonds and mix into butter mixture. Form into a ball, wrap in
waxed paper, place in a plastic
bag and refrigerate at least 1 hour
or overnight. It is best to divide
the dough into workable-size portions and to keep remaining portions
refrigerated until you are ready to
roll them. Let each portion stand
at room temperature 5 minutes
before rolling. Roll dough as thinly
as possible (1/8 inch thick) between
sheets of waxed paper. Cut into 2-

*Store brown sugar in the freezer
to prevent lumping. Let stand 20
minutes at room temperature before
using.*

inch rounds and place 2 inches
apart on an ungreased baking
sheet. Top each round with about
3/4 teaspoon jam. Cut thin strips
from rolled-out dough and make a
crisscross pattern on top of each
round, using 6 strips. Refrigerate
20 minutes. Preheat oven to 375°F.
Bake cookies 10 to 12 minutes, or
until just starting to brown. Remove
immediately to wire rack. Cool
and store in airtight container up
to 5 days, or freeze up to 2
months. Try eating them straight
from the freezer.

## SPRITZ COOKIES

Bake a double batch of these
buttery cookies and store one in
the freezer to serve during the
Christmas holidays. Best eaten
right out of the freezer.

*Makes Approximately Four Dozen*
1/4 pound butter, softened
1/4 cup granulated sugar
1 egg yolk
1/2 teaspoon pure vanilla extract
1/2 teaspoon freshly grated lemon
   rind
1 cup unbleached flour, or
   as needed
1/8 teaspoon salt
1/8 teaspoon baking powder
Colored sugar

Cream together butter and granulated sugar and blend in egg yolk,

*Butter will cream faster if you
warm the bowl and beaters first.*

vanilla and lemon rind. Sift together
flour, salt and baking powder.
Beat flour mixture into butter
mixture to make a soft dough,
similar to the consistency of pastry
dough, adding more flour as needed.
Form into a rough ball, wrap in
waxed paper, place in a plastic
bag and refrigerate at least 1 hour
or overnight. To form cookies, let
dough stand at room temperature
5 minutes. Following directions for
your particular cookie press, form
long, fluted strings of dough on
work surface. Pinch off pieces
about 2-1/2 inches long and form
each into a small wreath. Dip top
of wreath in colored sugar and
place on an ungreased baking
sheet about 1 inch apart. Refrigerate
20 minutes. Preheat oven to 350°F.
Bake cookies in preheated oven 8
to 10 minutes, or until lightly
golden. Remove immediately to
wire rack. Cool and store in airtight
container up to 1 week, or freeze
up to 3 months.

## CHOCOLATE CHIP–COCONUT KISSES

*Makes Approximately Two Dozen*
2 egg whites
1/8 teaspoon cream of tartar
Dash salt
1/2 cup granulated sugar
1/4 cup unsweetened grated
    coconut
1 teaspoon pure vanilla extract
2/3 cup semisweet chocolate bits

Oil a baking sheet with Lecithin Oil. Preheat oven to 300°F. Beat together egg whites, cream of tartar and salt until stiff peaks form. Two tablespoons at a time, beat sugar into mixture until smooth, glossy and holds firm peaks. Sprinkle coconut over and beat just until well mixed. Fold in vanilla and chocolate bits. Drop by tablespoonfuls onto prepared baking sheet about 2 inches apart. Bake in preheated oven 20 minutes, or until just golden. Remove immediately to wire rack, cool and store in airtight container up to 2 days, or freeze up to 3 weeks.

---

*Keep your Lecithin Oil in a plastic squeeze bottle for easy application. Also, keep one brush just for the oil; it need never be washed.*

## FRESH FRUIT TART

Use plums, peaches, nectarines, apples, halved cherries or whole blueberries for this unusual tart. Serve with Crème Fraîche or lightly sweetened whipped cream.

*Makes One Nine-inch Tart*

### CRUST
12 tablespoons (3/4 cup) butter,
    softened
1/4 cup granulated sugar
1 egg yolk
2 cups unbleached flour
1 tablespoon brandy

### FILLING
4 to 5 cups sliced fresh fruit
2 eggs
2 egg yolks
1 cup granulated sugar
1 cup half-and-half cream, scalded
1/8 teaspoon salt
1/4 teaspoon pure vanilla extract

First make the crust. Butter a 2-1/2-inch-deep, 9-inch-square springform cake pan with Lecithin Butter. Preheat oven to 350°F. Cream together butter and sugar and beat in egg yolk. Blend in flour and brandy until well mixed. Press into bottom and sides of prepared cake pan. Bake in preheated oven 20 minutes or until puffed and firm but not browned. Cool on wire rack. (At this point, the crust may be left in the pan, covered with plastic wrap, and frozen up to 2 weeks; defrost at room temperature 30 minutes before filling).

To make the filling, preheat oven to 350°F. Arrange fruit on cooled crust and bake in preheated oven 10 minutes or until fruit is just tender. (Omit this step of precooking the fruit if using blueberries.) Remove to wire rack. Reduce oven heat to 325°F. Beat eggs and egg yolks with sugar 5 minutes until very thick, creamy and lemon colored. In a steady stream, slowly beat cream into egg mixture until well blended. Cook, stirring with a wooden spoon, over medium heat until just starting to thicken and mixture lightly coats spoon. Remove from heat and stir in salt and vanilla. Pour over fruit and bake in preheated oven 40 minutes, or until custard is set. To test, shake gently. If custard moves, continue to bake until set. Remove from oven and cool on wire rack until barely warm. With a sharp knife, loosen pastry edges from pan sides. Place your hand on bottom of pan and carefully push tart through top opening. Place tart with cake pan bottom on a serving plate and cut into squares to serve.

## LEMON CREAM TARTLETS

The tangy custardlike filling for these miniature pastry cups can also be served as a dessert in individual glass dishes. It will cleanse the palate after a rich entrée, providing a refreshing finish to the meal. It is equally delicious spread between the layers of a cake or piled in meringue nests. For a richer filling or dessert, fold in 1 cup heavy cream, whipped until stiff.

The tartlets are equally versatile. Fill them with Mocha Mousse, Rum Bavarian Cream or any Pastry Cream.

This recipe makes approximately 1-3/4 cups of the Lemon Cream (with whipped cream folded in, 2-1/4 cups) and two dozen of the tartlets.

*Makes Two Dozen Filled Tartlets*

### TARTLETS
1/4 pound butter, softened
1/4 cup powdered sugar
1 egg yolk
1 teaspoon pure vanilla extract
1 cup unbleached flour

---

*When beating egg whites or heavy cream with hand beaters, place bowl on a dampened dish cloth to prevent bowl from spinning.*

---

### FILLING
3 eggs
2 egg yolks
1/2 cup granulated sugar
1/2 cup fresh lemon juice
1 tablespoon freshly grated lemon rind
4 tablespoons butter, cut into bits, at room temperature

First make the tartlets. Cream together butter and sugar. Beat in egg yolk and vanilla and blend well. Gradually beat in flour until well mixed. With fingers, form into a rough ball, flatten into a disc about 1/2 inch thick, wrap in waxed paper, place in a plastic bag and refrigerate at least 1 hour. Let stand at room temperature 3 to 4 minutes, then roll and cut out as directed in section on making tartlets in General Directions for Pastry. The dough will be delicate, yet workable. Once you have cut out as many rounds as possible, gather up the pastry remaining on the board and reroll and cut until all the pastry is used. (If the dough starts to stick when rolling the second time, refrigerate briefly to harden a bit.) Line muffin-tin wells and chill as directed, then preheat oven to 375°F. (This dough recipe works best with a slightly higher oven temperature than is normally used for tartlets.) Bake tartlets 10 minutes, or until lightly

golden. Remove to wire rack and cool before filling.

To make the filling, beat together eggs, egg yolks and sugar with electric beaters in the top pan of a double boiler 5 minutes until very thick, creamy and lemon colored. Place top pan over lower pan of simmering water and, with a wooden spoon, stir in lemon juice and lemon rind. Stirring almost constantly, cook until mixture heavily coats the spoon. Remove from heat and, bit by bit, stir in butter, whisking until well blended. Let cool, stirring occasionally to prevent a skin from forming. Fill tartlets with cooled cream just before serving. (Or store cream in a covered container in the refrigerator up to 5 days.)

## RUM BAVARIAN CREAM PIE

This chocolate-wafer crust may also be filled with ice cream and frozen until firm. Or interchange the crusts for this pie and the Frozen Brandy Pie that follows.

*Makes One Nine-inch Pie*

### CRUST
1-1/2 cups crushed chocolate wafers (about 24 wafers)
6 tablespoons butter, melted
2 tablespoons granulated sugar

## FILLING

6 egg yolks
3/4 cup superfine granulated sugar
1 tablespoon unflavored gelatin
1/2 cup cold water
2 cups heavy cream
1/2 cup dark rum
Powdered sugar to taste
Grated unsweetened baking
   chocolate

First make the crust. Butter a 9-inch pie plate with Lecithin Butter. Toss together all ingredients until well mixed. Press crumb mixture into bottom and sides of prepared plate. Cover and refrigerate until ready to fill.

To make the filling, beat together egg yolks and sugar with electric beaters or a wire whisk until very thick, creamy and lemon colored. Soften gelatin in water and transfer to saucepan. Bring to a full boil and quickly pour into egg mixture, beating well with a wooden spoon. Let cool, stirring occasionally. Whip cream until stiff peaks form. Remove about 2/3 cup and set aside; fold remaining cream into egg mixture.

Gently fold in rum, cover and refrigerate until just starting to set. Stir gently several times, then pour into prepared crust and refrigerate until well chilled. Gently beat powdered sugar into reserved whipped cream, cover and refrigerate. Just before serving, decorate pie with sweetened cream and sprinkle with grated chocolate.

## FROZEN BRANDY PIE

*Makes One Nine-inch Pie*

### GRAHAM CRACKER CRUST

1-1/2 cups crushed graham crackers
   (about 22 squares)
1/3 cup powdered sugar, sifted
1/2 teaspoon ground cinnamon
   (optional)
5 tablespoons butter, melted
1 teaspoon pure vanilla extract,
   or 1/2 teaspoon almond extract

### FILLING

4 egg yolks
1/2 cup sifted powdered sugar
1/4 cup brandy
2 tablespoons crème de cacao
1/2 teaspoon almond extract
1 cup heavy cream
Grated semisweet or unsweetened
   baking chocolate

First prepare crust. Preheat oven to 375°F. Butter a 9-inch-round spring-form pan or pie plate with Lecithin Butter. Mix together graham cracker crumbs, sugar and cinnamon. Toss in butter to coat mixture well. Add vanilla and mix thoroughly. Reserve 1/2 cup of crumb mixture and press remaining portion into bottom of prepared pan. Bake in preheated oven 5 to 7 minutes. Cool completely on a wire rack before filling.

To make filling, beat together egg yolks and sugar with electric beaters or a wire whisk until very thick, creamy and lemon colored. With a spoon, mix in brandy, crème de cacao and almond extract. Whip cream until stiff peaks form and gradually fold into yolk mixture. Pour into prepared shell and sprinkle with reserved crumb mixture. Freeze until firm. To serve, let stand at room temperature 5 minutes, then cut into wedges. To store, wrap frozen pie airtight and freeze up to 2 months.

---

*Save overwhipped cream by mixing in 1 to 2 tablespoons cold milk.*

## SHOO-FLY PIE

*Makes One Eight-inch Pie*
1 unbaked 8-inch Sour Cream,
   Egg White, Egg Yolk or
   Whole-Wheat Pastry shell
3/4 cup sifted unbleached flour
1/2 teaspoon salt
1/2 teaspoon ground cinnamon
1/8 teaspoon ground cloves
1/8 teaspoon freshly grated nutmeg
1/2 cup firmly packed brown
   sugar, sieved
2 tablespoons lard or vegetable
   shortening, chilled
1/3 cup light molasses
1 egg yolk, lightly beaten
1/2 tablespoon baking soda,
   dissolved in 2/3 cup boiling
   water and cooled

Prepare pastry shell and refrigerate.
Preheat oven to 400°F. Sift together
flour, salt and spices, then toss in
sugar to mix well. With fingertips,
2 knives or a pastry blender,
crumble in lard until mixture is the
consistency of coarse cornmeal.
Blend molasses and egg yolk into

---

*When measuring honey (or mo-
lasses), oil the measuring cup
first. The honey will not cling to
the cup.*

---

cooled soda and water mixture.
Layer one-third of flour mixture in
pastry shell. Top with half the molasses mixture and then half of the
remaining flour mixture. Cover
with remaining molasses mixture
and sprinkle remaining flour mixture
on top. Bake in preheated oven 10
minutes, reduce heat to 350°F and
bake 15 minutes longer, or until
mixture is set. Cool on wire rack
and serve at room temperature.

## PEACH BAVARIAN CHARLOTTE

Substitute nectarines or cherries
for the peaches. Stale yellow or
white cake, cut in strips, can
replace the ladyfingers.

*Serves Twelve*
1 dozen 2- or 3-day-old ladyfingers,
   halved
1/4 cup kirsch
1 tablespoon unflavored gelatin
1/4 cup cold water
3 egg yolks
6 tablespoons granulated sugar
1 cup milk, scalded
1 teaspoon pure vanilla extract
Dash salt
1/2 teaspoon freshly grated lemon
   rind
2 cups diced ripe peaches
1 cup heavy cream
1/2 cup lightly toasted sliced
   almonds

Place ladyfinger halves on a tray
or cookie sheet and sprinkle with
3 tablespoons of the kirsch. Sprinkle
gelatin over water and set aside to
soften. Beat together egg yolks
and sugar until thick and lemon
colored. In a steady stream, slowly
beat milk into egg mixture until
well blended. Place over medium
heat and, stirring constantly, cook
until mixture just starts to thicken.
Remove from heat and stir in
gelatin until dissolved. Add vanilla,
salt and lemon rind. Cover and
refrigerate, stirring occasionally,
until mixture begins to thicken.
With a fork, mash peaches with
remaining 1 tablespoon kirsch.
Fold into egg mixture and chill
until almost set. Cover bottom of
an 8-inch soufflé dish with ladyfinger halves. Stand remaining
halves upright along sides of dish.
Whip cream until stiff and gently
fold into thickened peach mixture.
Carefully pour into prepared soufflé
dish, cover and refrigerate 4 to 6
hours until set. Just before serving,
sprinkle with almonds.

---

*When whipping cream, sugar
may be added at any time, but
flavorings (vanilla extract, liqueurs,
etc.) should only be added after
cream starts to thicken.*

---

## PEACH SHERBET

This refreshing dessert is best when served within three to four hours of the final freezing. Use strawberries, persimmons, pineapple or raspberries in place of the peaches. Adjust the sugar measure according to taste and to the sugar content of the fruit. If desired, substitute kirsch for half of the water measure.

*Makes Two Pints*
1 cup granulated sugar
1 cup water
2 cups puréed peaches
3 tablespoons fresh lemon juice
1 to 2 teaspoons freshly grated
   lemon rind
2 egg whites

In a heavy saucepan, combine sugar and water. Stirring to dissolve sugar, bring to boil. Boil 5 minutes, remove from heat and stir in peaches, lemon juice and lemon rind. Chill well. Beat egg whites until stiff peaks form. Fold into peach mixture until well blended and all whites have been incorporated. Pour into a shallow dish or ice tray and freeze until slushy. With a fork, stir well (the peach mixture will have sunk to the bottom). Return to freezer and repeat process. Pack into freezer container and freeze solid.

## ICE CREAMS

Making ice cream is a particularly delicious way to use up extra egg yolks. For soft and creamy ice cream, store no more than a few hours before serving. If the ice cream is frozen very solid, ice crystals will sometimes develop. When this happens, let the ice cream soften slightly and beat it a little before serving. Freeze ice cream no more than two weeks, or the flavor and texture will be diminished.

The following recipes give the method for making ice cream in a freezer compartment. If you have an ice cream maker, simply put the mixture into it and freeze according to the manufacturer's instructions. If you use an ice cream maker, the yields for the following recipes will be slightly larger.

## STRAWBERRY CUSTARD ICE CREAM

You can make a frozen strawberry charlotte by whipping the heavy cream, folding it into the chilled strawberry mixture and then spooning the light and fluffy result into a crystal dish lined with stale ladyfingers or fingers of stale cake that have been soaked in sherry or fruit liqueur. Or change the flavor of this easy-to-make ice cream by using whole raspberries or diced peaches in place of the strawberries.

*Makes Approximately*
*One and One-half Pints*
3 egg yolks
1/2 cup granulated sugar
1/2 cup milk, scalded
1-1/2 cups strawberries, puréed
1/2 teaspoon pure vanilla extract
2 teaspoons fresh lemon juice
Dash salt
1 cup heavy cream

Beat together yolks and sugar with electric beaters 5 minutes until thick, creamy and lemon colored. In a steady stream, pour in milk, stirring with a wooden spoon until well mixed. Transfer mixture to a heavy saucepan and place over medium-low heat. Stirring constantly and vigorously with a wooden spoon and scraping bottom and sides of saucepan, cook 7 to 10 minutes, or until mixture heavily coats the spoon. Remove from the heat and stir in strawberries, vanilla, lemon juice and salt. Chill well. Stir in cream and pour into a shallow dish or ice tray. Freeze until the 1 inch of the mixture that borders the edge of the tray is solid. Stir with a fork and return to freezer. Freeze until almost firm, stir once more and pack into a freezer container. Freeze until firm.

## CHOCOLATE CUSTARD ICE CREAM

This rich, yet simple ice cream is especially good with the addition of crumbled macaroons or meringue crusts or chopped pecans; fold in just before the final freezing. For a more intense chocolate flavor, add two or three additional tablespoons cocoa powder.

*Makes Approximately
One and One-half Pints*
3 egg yolks
1/2 cup granulated sugar
1/4 cup unsweetened cocoa powder
1/2 cup milk, scalded
Kahlúa or pure vanilla extract
   to taste
1 cup heavy cream
Mint sprigs

---

*To make superfine sugar, blend granulated sugar in small amounts in blender or food processor, using on and off pulses.*

---

Beat together yolks and sugar with electric beaters 5 minutes until thick, creamy and lemon colored. Beat in cocoa until well blended. In a steady stream, pour in milk, stirring with a wooden spoon until well mixed. Transfer mixture to a heavy saucepan and place over medium-low heat. Stirring constantly and vigorously with a wooden spoon and scraping bottom and sides of saucepan, cook 7 to 10 minutes, or until mixture heavily coats the spoon. Remove from the heat and stir in Kahlúa. Chill well. Stir in cream* and pour into a shallow dish or ice tray. Freeze until the 1 inch of the mixture that borders the edge of the tray is solid. Stir with a fork and return to freezer. Freeze until almost firm, stir once more and pack into a freezer container. Freeze until firm. Serve with a garnish of mint sprigs.

*For a lighter ice cream, whip the cream until thick but not stiff and fold into cooled chocolate mixture.

**MOCHA CUSTARD ICE CREAM** Add with cocoa powder 1 to 2 teaspoons espresso-type coffee powder (not granules).

## TORTONI

Transform those whole persimmons (the large variety) tucked away in the freezer from last fall's bumper crop and that lone egg white into this elegant dessert. Make ahead and bring out from the freezer for an unplanned-company meal. For a large party, line tiny muffin-tin wells with candy paper-cup liners, fill with Tortoni mixture and serve as a walk-around dessert. (This will make about five dozen candy-size desserts.)

Use your imagination: Substitute puréed peaches or nectarines for the persimmons. In place of the chocolate melt a half pound of caramel candies with a half cup of hot water or milk. Crumbled macaroons can replace the almonds.

*Makes Ten to Twelve*
1 egg white
Pinch cream of tartar
1/4 cup sifted powdered sugar
1 cup heavy cream
1 teaspoon pure vanilla extract
2 large ripe persimmons, puréed
   (1-1/4 to 1-1/2 cups)
3/4 cup semisweet chocolate bits
1 tablespoon butter
1/2 cup finely chopped toasted
   sliced almonds

Beat together egg white and cream of tartar until soft peaks form. Sprinkle with 2 tablespoons of the sugar and beat until stiff peaks form. With clean beaters, whip cream until almost stiff, sprinkle with remaining sugar, add vanilla and whip until stiff. Stir about one-third of the egg white into the cream to lighten it, then gently fold in remaining egg white. Transfer mixture to ice trays or a shallow dish. Freeze until the 1/2 inch of the mixture that borders the edges of the trays is frozen solid. While mixture is freezing, line 10 to 12 muffin-tin wells with 2-ounce paper-cup liners and set aside. Break up mixture with a fork and gradually stir in puréed persimmon. Return trays to freezer and freeze until solid. Melt chocolate bits with butter over hot water. Place a large mixing bowl in a nest of ice, transfer persimmon mixture to bowl and stir *just* until smooth. Work quickly. Gradually drizzle in melted chocolate mixture, stirring so the chocolate hardens into small bits or ribbons. Quickly fold in almonds and spoon into prepared cups. Return to freezer until solid, then serve. Or wrap airtight and freeze up to 3 months.

---

*Use a 1/8-inch-mesh sieve to sift brown or powdered sugar—much easier than using a sifter.*

---

## ZABAGLIONE

*Serves Two*
4 egg yolks
1/4 cup granulated sugar
5 to 6 tablespoons Marsala
1/2 teaspoon pure vanilla extract
   (optional)
1/4 teaspoon freshly grated orange
   or lemon rind

In the top pan of a double boiler set over simmering water (not touching), beat together egg yolks and sugar 5 minutes until thick, creamy and lemon colored. Gradually beat in Marsala, vanilla and orange rind and continue beating until very thick and fluffy. Pour into parfait glasses or crystal bowls and serve immediately or lightly chilled.

## CAROB MOUSSE

*Serves Four to Six*
4 tablespoons butter
2 tablespoons unbleached flour
6 tablespoons finely sieved
   carob powder
1/4 cup mild honey
1 cup milk or evaporated milk
2 egg yolks
1 teaspoon pure vanilla extract
1 cup heavy cream
Powdered sugar
Additional pure vanilla extract
   (optional)
Carob bits

In a deep skillet or large saucepan, melt butter until foamy. Combine flour and carob powder and sprinkle over butter. Cook over medium to medium-low heat, stirring, 1 to 2 minutes. Blend in honey and, a little bit at a time and blending well after each addition, add milk. Cook, stirring, until smooth and thickened, beating with a fork or whisk to prevent lumping. Beat egg yolks lightly and beat in a little hot carob mixture. Whisk into remaining carob mixture and, stirring almost constantly, cook until mixture just starts to boil (when a few large bubbles appear at edges of pan). Remove from heat and, stirring often, let cool. Whip cream until stiff peaks form. Fold about two-thirds of the cream into the carob mixture and spoon into 4 to 6 crystal serving bowls. Whip powdered sugar and vanilla to taste into remaining whipped cream and spread evenly over the mousse. Garnish with carob bits, cover and chill 8 hours or overnight before serving. Store in the refrigerator up to 3 days.

## MOCHA MOUSSE

*Serves Six to Eight*

1 cup (6 ounces) semisweet
    chocolate bits
2 tablespoons water
3 egg whites
1/4 cup powdered sugar
2 teaspoons instant espresso-type
    coffee powder (not granules)
1 cup heavy cream
1 tablespoon coffee liqueur
1 teaspoon pure vanilla extract
1/4 cup toasted slivered blanched
    almonds
Fresh mint sprigs

In top of double boiler or in a
heavy saucepan, melt chocolate
with water. Cool slightly. Whip egg
whites until soft peaks form, then
very gradually whip in sugar and
instant coffee powder until stiff
and glossy. Stir one-fourth of egg
whites into chocolate mixture, then
gently fold in remaining whites.
Whip the cream until stiff and fold
in liqueur and vanilla. Fold cream
into egg white mixture and then
carefully fold in almonds. Spoon
into 6 or 8 individual crystal
serving dishes and chill. Just before
serving, garnish with mint.

---

*For best results, bring egg whites
to room temperature before beating.*

---

## CITRUS ANGEL MOUSSE

This dessert is light and refreshing.
Use white, yellow, sponge or pound
cake in place of the angel food
cake.

*Serves Eight to Ten*

1 tablespoon unflavored gelatin
1/4 cup cold water
1/2 cup boiling water
1/2 cup granulated sugar
1/2 cup fresh orange juice
1/4 cup fresh lemon juice
1 tablespoon freshly grated orange
    rind, or to taste
1-1/2 cups heavy cream
4 cups cubed (1-inch) stale angel
    food cake
2 tablespoons powdered sugar
Whole strawberries or raspberries
Toasted coconut flakes

Sprinkle gelatin over cold water to
soften. In a large bowl, combine
softened gelatin with boiling water
and granulated sugar, stirring to
dissolve gelatin and sugar. Stir in
orange juice, lemon juice and
orange rind. Nest bowl in a bowl
of ice and, stirring often, let stand
until mixture starts to thicken.
Whip cream until stiff peaks form
and fold two-thirds of the whipped
cream into the orange juice mixture.
Fold in cake and transfer to a
crystal serving dish. Cover with
plastic wrap and refrigerate 4
hours or, preferably, overnight.

Sprinkle powdered sugar over
remaining whipped cream and
carefully beat in. Cover and refrigerate. Just before serving, spread
sweetened whipped cream over
the top of the mousse, arrange
strawberries around rim and sprinkle
center with coconut flakes.

## CREME BRULEE

*Serves Six*

6 egg yolks
6 tablespoons superfine granulated
    sugar
3 cups heavy cream, scalded
1 teaspoon pure vanilla extract
Brown sugar

Preheat oven to 350°F. Beat together
egg yolks and sugar 5 minutes,
until very thick, creamy and lemon
colored. Gradually stir in cream in
a steady stream and place over
medium-low heat. Stirring constantly
with a wooden spoon, cook until
mixture thickens slightly and coats
the spoon. Pour into a 7-inch
soufflé dish. Place dish in a pan of
hot water to come 1 inch up sides
of dish and bake in preheated
oven 45 minutes, or until thin knife
inserted in center comes out clean.
Remove from hot water, cool,
cover and refrigerate. When custard
is cold, preheat broiler. Cover top

of custard with a layer of brown sugar 1/4 inch thick. Protect rim of soufflé dish with aluminum foil and nest dish in a pan of ice. Watching *very* carefully, broil just until sugar is melted; do not let the sugar burn. Remove, cover and refrigerate until well chilled before serving.

## RICE PUDDING BRULEE

*Serves Six to Eight*

1-1/2 cups cooked white or brown rice
1-1/2 cups milk
3 tablespoons granulated sugar
1/2 teaspoon ground allspice
1/8 teaspoon salt
3 ounces cream cheese, cut into bits, at room temperature
1 teaspoon pure vanilla extract
1 teaspoon freshly grated lemon rind
1 cup heavy cream
1-1/2 cups sliced strawberries
Brown sugar
Whole strawberries

In a heavy saucepan, combine rice, milk, granulated sugar, allspice and salt. Bring slowly to a gentle boil, stirring to dissolve sugar. Cook over medium heat, stirring often, 40 to 50 minutes, or until thick and creamy and rice kernels are very soft. Remove from heat

and, bit by bit, stir in cheese until melted. Stir in vanilla and lemon rind. Cool, cover and chill. Whip cream until it just begins to hold its shape and fold into rice mixture. Chill thoroughly. Preheat broiler. Place sliced strawberries on the bottom of a 7-inch soufflé dish. Spoon rice mixture over strawberries and cover evenly with a layer of brown sugar 1/4 inch thick. Protect rim of soufflé dish with aluminum foil and nest dish in a pan of ice. Watching *very* carefully, broil just until sugar is melted; do not let the sugar burn. Serve at once garnished with whole strawberries, or chill 30 minutes and garnish just before serving.

## BREAD PUDDING WITH DATES

*Serves Eight to Ten*

2/3 cup chopped dates (about 4 ounces)
1 cup fresh orange juice
3 cups cubed stale white or whole-wheat bread
2 cups milk
1/4 teaspoon salt
3 eggs
1/3 cup granulated sugar
1 tablespoon fresh lemon juice
1 tablespoon freshly grated orange rind
1/4 to 1/2 teaspoon ground cardamom
Crème Fraîche or Custard Sauce

*Crème fraîche, unlike heavy cream, won't curdle when boiled.*

Soak dates in orange juice 30 minutes. Combine dates and juice with bread, milk and salt. Let stand at room temperature 20 minutes. Butter a 6-1/2- by 10-1/2-inch shallow baking dish. In a large mixing bowl, lightly beat 1 of the eggs. Separate remaining 2 eggs, adding yolks to bowl with beaten egg and setting whites aside in another bowl. Beat the egg and yolks with the sugar until thick and lemon colored. Add lemon juice, orange rind and cardamom. Stir in bread-milk mixture. Preheat oven to 350°F. Beat egg whites until stiff but not dry and fold into bread-egg mixture. Pour into prepared dish and bake in preheated oven 45 minutes, or until a thin knife inserted in center comes out clean. If browning too fast after 30 minutes, cover loosely with aluminum foil. Serve warm or at room temperature with Crème Fraîche.

## BREAD PUDDING WITH DRIED APPLES

*Serves Eight to Ten*
1 cup dried apples, coarsely cut
1/3 cup hot water
1/2 cup golden raisins
3 tablespoons kirsch
5 tablespoons butter, softened
1 teaspoon ground cinnamon
1/4 teaspoon freshly grated nutmeg
8 to 10 large slices (1/2 inch thick)
　　stale French or Italian bread
1/2 cup firmly packed brown sugar
2 eggs, lightly beaten
1 egg yolk, lightly beaten
2-1/2 cups milk or half-and-half
　　cream
1 teaspoon pure vanilla extract
Crème Fraîche or heavy cream

Soak apples in water until softened. Soak raisins in kirsch 30 minutes. Mix butter with cinnamon and nutmeg and spread on bread slices. Drain apples. Layer half the bread on the bottom of a buttered 6-1/2-

by 10-1/2-inch shallow baking dish. Cover with half the apples, half the raisins (undrained) and half the sugar. Repeat layers. Beat eggs and yolk with milk and vanilla and pour over layers. Let stand at room temperature about 30 minutes. Preheat oven to 350°F and bake pudding 45 minutes, or until a thin knife inserted in center comes out clean. Serve warm or at room temperature with Crème Fraîche.

## BROWN BETTY

Serve this old-fashioned favorite with Crème Fraîche, heavy cream or with heavy cream whipped with a little powdered sugar and seasoned with pure vanilla extract. Use peaches or pears in place of the apples.

*Serves Eight*
1/3 cup raisins
1/3 cup dry sherry
1-1/2 cups medium-coarse dry
　　bread crumbs
4 tablespoons butter, melted
2-1/2 to 3 cups sliced apples
3/4 cup firmly packed brown sugar
1 teaspoon ground cinnamon
1/2 teaspoon ground allspice
1/4 teaspoon freshly grated nutmeg
2 teaspoons freshly grated lemon
　　rind
1/4 cup fresh lemon juice
2 tablespoons butter, cut into bits

Soak raisins in sherry 30 minutes. Toss bread crumbs in melted butter to coat evenly and strew one-third of the crumbs over the bottom of an 8-inch-square shallow baking dish. Preheat oven to 350°F. Drain raisins, reserving sherry. Arrange half of the apples and half of the raisins over the crumbs. Combine brown sugar, spices and lemon rind. Strew half of this mixture over the apples. Combine reserved sherry and lemon juice with enough water to measure 1 cup. Pour half of the mixture over the apples. Sprinkle with half the remaining bread crumbs, arrange remaining apples and raisins over, sprinkle with remaining sugar mixture and pour remaining liquid over. Top with remaining bread crumbs and bake in preheated oven 30 minutes. If Brown Betty appears to be drying out before apples are tender, sprinkle with equal parts fresh lemon juice and water. Remove from oven, dot with butter, return to oven and bake 10 to 15 minutes longer. Serve warm or at room temperature.

---

*Freeze cake and cookie crumbs in a plastic container. Use in place of streusel topping or mix with bread crumbs for Brown Betty.*

# VANILLA BUTTER CREAM

*Makes Approximately*
*One and One-half Cups*
3 egg yolks
1/2 cup sifted powdered sugar
3/4 cup milk, scalded
1/2 pound unsalted butter, cut up,
   at room temperature
1 teaspoon pure vanilla extract

In the top pan of a double boiler, beat together egg yolks and sugar 5 minutes until thick, creamy and lemon colored. Bring water in bottom of double boiler just to a simmer and maintain heat; set top pan in bottom pan. Gradually whisk milk into yolk mixture. Stirring constantly with a wooden spoon, cook 10 to 15 minutes, or until mixture coats spoon with a heavy, creamy coating. Mixture should register about 160°F on a candy thermometer. Remove from heat and cool to lukewarm. With electric beaters, beat in butter, bit by bit, until all is incorporated. Stir in vanilla. If not using immediately, refrigerate in a covered jar up to 4 days. Bring to room temperature before using. Once refrigerated, mixture may need to be beaten with a wooden spoon to its original creamy, smooth consistency.

**COFFEE BUTTER CREAM** Substitute 2 tablespoons coffee liqueur for the vanilla extract.

**MOCHA BUTTER CREAM** Mix with the milk while scalding 1/2 tablespoon *each* instant espresso-type coffee powder (not granules) and unsweetened cocoa powder.

**CHOCOLATE BUTTER CREAM** Mix with the milk while scalding 1 tablespoon unsweetened cocoa powder.

---

*It's easier to split a cake layer if you refrigerate the cake until very cold before cutting.*

---

# WHITE ICING

*Makes Approximately One Cup*
1 egg white
Pinch salt
Pinch cream of tartar
1-1/2 cups powdered sugar, sieved
1 teaspoon pure vanilla extract

Beat together egg white, salt and cream of tartar until stiff peaks form. Two tablespoons at a time, beat in sugar until mixture is smooth, glossy and holds firm peaks. The longer the beating, the better the icing. Beat in vanilla. If not using immediately, refrigerate in a covered jar up to 5 days, or freeze up to 1 month. Bring to room temperature and beat lightly with a wooden spoon before icing cake.

**BUTTERSCOTCH ICING** Substitute sieved brown sugar for the powdered sugar.

**LEMON ICING** Omit vanilla extract and add 1 teaspoon fresh lemon juice and 2 teaspoons freshly grated lemon rind.

**ORANGE ICING** Omit vanilla extract and add 1 teaspoon fresh orange juice and 1 tablespoon freshly grated orange rind.

# CHOCOLATE ICING

*Makes Approximately*
*One and One-half Cups*
3 tablespoons butter, softened
1-1/3 cups powdered sugar
3 egg yolks
3 tablespoons half-and-half cream
1 teaspoon pure vanilla extract
1/4 teaspoon ground cinnamon
1/4 teaspoon freshly grated nutmeg
3 ounces semisweet chocolate,
   melted and slightly cooled

Cream together butter and sugar, beat in yolks and blend well. Beat in cream, vanilla, cinnamon and nutmeg. Stir in chocolate until well blended. If not using immediately, refrigerate in a covered jar up to 4 days. Bring to room temperature and beat lightly with a wooden spoon before icing cake.

# PASTRY CREAM

This smooth, rich mixture of egg yolks and milk can be the filling or icing for a cake, the filling for patty shells or cream puffs, the base for a fresh fruit tart, or a simple dessert served in individual glass bowls. To serve as a dessert or to use as a filling for patty shells, fold 1 cup heavy cream, whipped until stiff with 3 to 6 tablespoons sifted powdered sugar and 1/2 teaspoon almond extract, into cooled Pastry Cream. To use as a filling for cream puffs or as an icing for cakes, stir two egg whites, beaten until stiff but not dry, into Pastry Cream while it is still hot.

It is difficult to make the perfectly thickened pastry cream, so do not be discouraged. If the mixture thickens too much upon cooling, beat in a little heavy cream, lemon juice or liqueur to thin it to the proper consistency. If the mixture is not thick enough, use it as a delicious custard sauce spooned over cakes and puddings.

*Makes Approximately Two Cups*
4 egg yolks
1/2 cup granulated sugar
1-1/2 cups milk, scalded
3 tablespoons unbleached flour
2 tablespoons cornstarch
3 tablespoons butter, cut into bits, at room temperature
2 tablespoons brandy or liqueur, or 2 teaspoons pure vanilla extract
1 teaspoon fresh lemon juice

Beat together yolks and sugar with electric beaters until very thick, creamy and lemon colored. To test, lift beaters from bowl; if mixture falls from them in thick, broad ribbons and "melts" into the portion that remains in the bowl you have beaten it enough. This should take about 4 to 5 minutes. Add flour and cornstarch to yolk-sugar mixture and beat in just until blended. With a wooden spoon, gradually beat in scalded milk, mixing thoroughly. Transfer mixture to a heavy saucepan and place over medium-low heat. Stirring constantly and vigorously with a wooden spoon and scraping sides and bottom of pan well to prevent sticking, heat until mixture is very thick and pulls away from the surfaces of the pan. At this point, the cream will heavily coat the spoon. Remove from heat and, with the wooden spoon, beat in

butter, bit by bit, until well blended. Stir in brandy and lemon juice and let cool at room temperature, stirring occasionally to prevent skin from forming. Cover and refrigerate up to 3 days, or freeze up to 3 to 4 months.

**CHOCOLATE PASTRY CREAM** Melt 2 ounces semisweet baking chocolate in milk as you scald it.

**COFFEE PASTRY CREAM** Add 2 teaspoons instant espresso-type coffee powder (not granules) with flour and cornstarch.

**MOCHA PASTRY CREAM** Add 2 teaspoons instant espresso-type coffee powder (not granules) and 1 tablespoon unsweetened cocoa powder with flour and cornstarch.

**BANANA PASTRY CREAM** Increase flour measure to 1/4 cup. When cream has cooled, mix in 1/2 cup mashed ripe banana.

**PASTRY CREAM SUGGESTIONS**

● Fill graham cracker crust (see Frozen Brandy Pie) or chocolate-wafer crust (see Rum Bavarian Cream Pie) with Pastry Cream.

● Bake any cake in 3 layers. Spread layers with Pastry Cream; sprinkle top with powdered sugar and ground almonds.

# CUSTARD SAUCE

Spoon on fresh fruit, bread puddings and uniced cakes. For extra body and flavor, stir crushed macaroons or meringues into the sauce.

*Makes Approximately*
*One and Three-fourths Cup*
4 egg yolks
1/2 cup superfine granulated sugar
   or sifted powdered sugar
1-1/2 cups milk, scalded
1 teaspoon pure vanilla extract,
   or 1/2 teaspoon almond extract

In the top pan of a double boiler, beat together egg yolks and sugar 5 minutes until thick, creamy and lemon colored. Bring water in bottom of double boiler just to a simmer and maintain heat; set top pan in bottom pan. Gradually whisk milk into yolk mixture. Stirring constantly with a wooden spoon, cook 10 to 15 minutes, or until mixture coats spoon with a heavy, creamy coating. Mixture should register about 160°F on a candy thermometer. Remove from heat and stir in vanilla. Transfer to a bowl and let cool at room temperature, stirring occasionally to prevent skin from forming. Serve warm or chilled. Refrigerate in a covered jar up to 3 days.

# MERINGUES

The secret to making a finely textured meringue is to beat the egg whites, cream of tartar and salt together until the whites form soft peaks, and then to add the sugar very, very gradually, continuing to beat until stiff peaks form. Unless you are certain that your electric mixer will fill the whites with lots of air, use an electric hand beater or beat by hand with a wire whisk. If the mixture loses its airy quality, it is still edible, but will not be very attractive when baked.

To avoid the common problem of the cooked meringue sticking to the baking surface, generously brush the sheet or pie plate in which you will be forming the meringues with Lecithin Oil. If you haven't any Lecithin Oil on hand, heavily butter and flour the sheet or pie plate and then shake out the excess flour.

The following recipe will make one 8-inch shell or six individual nests. You may also double the recipe, and bake three layers that can be stacked to make a meringue cake. To form the shell, pile the beaten whites in the prepared pie plate, then with a rubber spatula swirl the whites to the edge of the plate to form a rim. The meringue should be no more than 3/8 to 1/2 inch thick and the rim must stand fairly high to compensate for the shrinkage that will occur when the shell is baked. To form the individual nests, divide the beaten whites into six equal-size mounds on a prepared baking sheet, then swirl each mound into a nest shape with a spatula, building up the sides to form a rim as with the shell. For layers, simply form the beaten whites into rounds about 1/2 inch thick on a prepared baking sheet. Those experienced with a pastry bag may, of course, pipe the beaten whites onto the baking sheet.

Other kinds of ground nuts may be substituted for the almonds suggested here, or use an equal amount of quick rolled oats. Fill the shell or nests with Mocha Mousse, Carob Bavarian Cream, the filling for Peach Bavarian Charlotte or Lemon Cream Tartlets (with whipped cream), Rum Bavarian Cream, ice cream, or fresh fruit topped with sweetened whipped cream. If making a layered meringue cake, spread the layers with any of the Pastry Creams and ice with

---

*If you overbeat your meringue or add the sugar too fast and the meringue mixture falls, bake it anyway. The flavor is still good and you can crumble it onto cakes, or mix it into ice creams or puddings.*

any of the Butter Creams, or spread them with ice cream and top with fresh fruit. Garnish your meringue desserts with whipped cream, chocolate curls, grated chocolate, whole fresh berries or fresh mint sprigs.

Unless you are an experienced hand at meringues, you will find it necessary to trim the meringue layers before building the cake so that they will be even. Save the trimmings, fold them into whipped cream with some fresh fruit and chill for any easy, refreshing dessert. You can also mix the trimmings into slightly softened ice cream, refreeze and serve garnished with fresh fruit.

*Makes One Eight-inch Shell*
  *or Six Individual Nests*
2 egg whites, at room temperature
1/8 teaspoon salt
1/8 teaspoon cream of tartar
1/2 cup granulated sugar
1/2 cup ground almonds
1 tablespoon cornstarch
1/2 teaspoon pure vanilla extract

---

*If your whipped cream begins to "droop" after a few hours, save its "looks" by rewhipping it in a chilled bowl.*

---

Prepare baking sheet or pie plate as described above. Preheat oven to 275°F. Beat together egg whites, salt and cream of tartar until soft peaks form. Two tablespoons at a time, beat sugar into egg white mixture until smooth, glossy and holds firm peaks. Combine almonds and cornstarch. Sprinkle about 2 tablespoons over egg white mixture and gently fold in, being careful not to overmix. Repeat with remaining almond mixture until all is incorporated. Beat in vanilla. Transfer to prepared baking sheet or pie plate and form as described above in nests, layers or a shell. Bake in preheated oven 50 minutes for shell and 40 minutes for layers and nests, or until just lightly golden. If you prefer meringue with a slightly sticky texture, transfer to a wire rack and let cool. If you prefer a drier meringue, or if the weather is very humid, turn off the oven and let the meringue remain there 30 minutes, then transfer to a wire rack to cool completely. Once cool, the meringue may be filled and served. If not using within several hours or if the weather is humid, place in an airtight container and freeze up to 3 weeks. Remove from freezer and fill; the meringue will defrost quickly.

## DESSERT FILLING SUGGESTIONS FOR TINY PATTY SHELLS

Fill tiny patty shells (petites bouchées) with any of the following suggestions. The shells must be freshly baked or recrisped, barely cooled, filled and served at once.

● Zabaglione. Top with fresh strawberries.

● Lemon Cream with or without whipped cream. Garnish with fresh mint sprigs.

● Mocha Mousse with or without whipped cream. Top with toasted sliced almonds.

● Carob Bavarian Cream. Decorate with carob bits.

● Filling for Peach Bavarian Charlotte. Garnish with baking-chocolate curls.

## DESSERT SUGGESTIONS FOR USING PASTRY OR PUFF PASTRY SCRAPS

Pastry scraps to be used for desserts may be rerolled in granulated sugar instead of flour and should be no more than 1/8 inch thick, preferably thinner. (See General Directions for Pastry for rolling method.) Cut rolled dough into rectangles, squares, rounds or other decorative shapes and prepare with one of the following suggestions, sealing edges with a little water if the pastry is topped with a second piece of pastry. Place prepared scraps on an ungreased baking sheet and chill fifteen to twenty minutes. (Prepared scraps may also be frozen, well wrapped, up to one week. Defrost fifteen to twenty minutes before baking.) If making topped pastries, brush the tops with Egg Wash or with a mixture of one egg beaten with two teaspoons heavy cream. Bake in a preheated 375°F oven ten to fifteen minutes, or until golden. Remove to wire rack to cool. If not serving immediately, store in an airtight container several hours, or freeze up to one month. Pastry scraps filled with apple or other fruit do not freeze well baked or unbaked, so eat them within a few hours of making.

● Spread any pastry with softened butter and sprinkle with ground cinnamon and granulated sugar.

● Spread any pastry with softened butter, sprinkle with brown sugar, top with a thin slice of apple and sprinkle with ground cinnamon. Top with second pastry and seal edges.

● Cut any pastry into 4-inch squares. Mix softened butter with chopped raisins, brown sugar and ground cinnamon. Place a teaspoonful of mixture on each square. Fold over and seal edges.

● Cut any pastry into rounds and use as a topping for fruit cobbler.

*For easy return of any extra to flour bin or sugar box, sift flour or sugar onto a piece of waxed paper.*

● Place any pastry cutouts on baking sheet and brush with any leftover cream and egg wash or Egg Wash. Sprinkle with chopped slivered almonds and ground cinnamon.

● Cut Puff Pastry into rectangles, bake and cool. Spread half of the rectangles with Pastry Cream. Spread the other half of the rectangles with Butter Cream. Place the second half on top of the first and drizzle over the Butter Cream a little semisweet baking chocolate melted with a little lard.

● Cut Puff Pastry into rectangles. Cover half of the rectangles with dried currants and sprinkle with granulated sugar. Top with another rectangle and seal edges.

● Cut Puff Pastry into squares. Place 1/2 teaspoon jam in center, fold over and seal edges.

● Cut Puff Pastry into squares. Sprinkle with granulated sugar and roll like a jelly roll. Cut roll into 1/4-inch-thick slices and make a cut halfway into center of each slice. Place on baking sheet and pull cut edges apart slightly. Turn slices over halfway through baking.